Karl —

Life Changes when
Your goal fits your
Soul!

Ride Safe,

Debi 2021

RIDING Soul-O

Debi Tolbert Duggar

Cover photo by Mike Potthast, Potthast Studios in Winter Haven, Florida 33880

ISBN: 978-1-54397-897-1 (print)
ISBN: 978-1-54397-898-8 (ebook)

Printed in the United States of America

Edited by Writing Your Life
P.O. Box 541527
Orlando, Florida 32854
WritingYourLife.org

First Edition: October 2019

10 9 8 7 6 5 4 3 2

This book is dedicated
to my beautiful daughters—one near, one far—
both forever in my heart,
and
to my Daisy Ann, (1935-2018), who believed in this
project long before I did.

CONTENTS

Photo Credits

Chapter	Caption	Credit
I'm Getting My Own	Grand Canyon Summer '07	None
Most Likely to Wear Leather	Bessie One	Self Portrait - Author
The Sun Also Rises Over Manhattan	Bessie One	Tim Wilder, Wilder Photo Art
Riding Deliberately	Bessie One	Self Portrait - Author
A Tattoo to Mask the Pain	Bessie One	Tim Wilder, Wilder Photo Art
Riding Soul-O	Bessie One Blue Ridge Parkway	Author
Indiana Wants Me	Bessie One Indiana	Brent Silveus
Dicks I've Known	Bessie One Somewhere Along the Southeast Coast of Florida	Self Portrait - Author
C. Dick Run	Bessie One Kelly Island, Lake Erie Ohio	Author
Spirit Animal	Aguasabon Falls and Gorge Terrace Bay, Ontario, Canada	Photo taken by an unknown fellow traveler
Tears In The Wind	Bessie One Lake Michigan	Photo taken by an unknown fellow traveler
Old Woman Bay	Lake Superior Northern Ontario, Canada	Photo taken by an unknown fellow traveler
Sequins Are Not Adequate Protection	The day after arriving home from the hospital	Photo by My Daughter who named me her Trauma Mama
Knocked Off Course	Me photographing my trusty steed: Bessie One	Tim Wilder, Wilder Photo Art

Chapter	Caption	Credit
Solitary	Bessie Two Florida Backroad	Tim Wilder, Wilder Photo Art
All is Right With My Universe	Me, triumphantly holding the 'Sold' sign for Bessie Two. Notice I changed the tag to read 'Road Queen!'	The nice man at Tampa Harley Davidson
Like A Lover – Only Better	Leesburg Bike Fest	Shaman Don
Mental Masturbation		Author Selfie
Loose Gravel	Somewhere on a backroad in the Carolinas	Author
Dragon Slayer	The Tail of the Dragon – U.S. 129 On the border of Tennessee and North Carolina	129 Photos
Salvation in the Heartland	James Dean's Gravesite Fairmount, Indiana	Author
It's Not About Potato Salad	Rain on the Windshield Skyline Drive, Virginia	Author
Surrender		Author
36.0726N, 79.7903W	The first day I met my Wingman North Carolina	Photo taken by an unknown fellow traveler
Charleston	Sullivan Island, North Carolina	Photo taken by an unknown fellow traveler
Letting Go	NO PHOTO	
My Wingman	Paul Seward Peninsula, Alaska	Author
Boudin Balls And Hot Sauce	Cadillac Ranch, Route 66 Amarillo, Texas	Photo taken by an unknown fellow traveler

Chapter	Caption	Credit
Apple Pie, Cadillacs, and Barbeque	The Apple Store Medina, Texas	Paul
Curves Give Me Clarity	Atop Pike's Peak Colorado	Photo taken by an unknown fellow traveler
Father's Day	My Dad, John and Me at my Niece Kiley's Wedding in 2010	My daughter
Homeward Bound – Part One	Paul and I Red Rocks Amphitheater Colorado Springs, Colorado	My daughter
Homeward Bound – Part Two	Somewhere on the road during that hellish ride to Indiana	Author Selfie
The Gathering Part One and Two will NOT have any photos	NO PHOTO	
Final Thoughts Carry Me Home	Somewhere along the road in Kentucky. We have weathered the storm and we are still smiling.	Author Selfie
Aftermath: Stuck in Neutral	Arriving home from my Dad's funeral, I discovered our photo had fallen off the wall causing a tiny crack down the middle of the glass.	Author
Somewhere I've Never Been	Bessie and Me Ybor City, Tampa, Florida	Tim Wilder, Wilder Photo Art
Aloha to You Too	Paul and I Diamond Head, Oahu, Hawaii	Author Selfie

Chapter	Caption	Credit
Never Hesitate to Run the Breakdown Lane	Virginia	Author Selfie
Extreme Geography	West Quoddy Head Lighthouse Quoddy Point, Maine	Author Selfie
Cabot Trail – Part One	Finally made it to the Cabot Trail! Nova Scotia, Canada	Author Selfie
Cabot Trail – Part Two	Southwestern portion of the Cabot Trail Nova Scotia, Canada	Author Selfie
Nova Scotia Tioraidh!	Bessie waiting to board the ferry that will take us from Halifax, Nova Scotia to Portland, Maine	Author
Non-Negotiable	Me and My Wingman Daytona Bike Week Daytona, Florida	Author Selfie
Chasing a Dream	Main Street Daytona, Florida	Paul
Straining at the Harness	Ride Strong!	Paul
Cross Country: The South	B. B. King's Tombstone at the B. B. King Museum and Delta Interpretive Center Indianola, Mississippi	Author
Cross Country: Arkansas and the Midwest	Me, waiting not-so-patiently for a tow. Outside of Bentonville, Arkansas	Author Selfie
Cross Country: The Great Plains	Bessie Two The Black Hills and Badlands, South Dakota	Author

Chapter	Caption	Credit
Cross Country: The Pacific Northwest	Meltdown on the edge of Wildhorse Canyon, Washington	Author Selfie
Alaska	Me and My Wingman on rental bikes. Turnagin Arm, Seward Peninsula, Alaska	Photo taken by an unknown fellow traveler
Journey's End	Me and Bessie Two	Tim Wilder, Wilder Photo Art
Author Bio Photo		Mike Potthast, Potthast Studios

ACKNOWLEDGEMENTS

My journey is not complete without acknowledging several loving, caring, and supportive people who nurtured, cheered, and encouraged me to this end. My First Born: thank you for being the voice of reason, the sunshine to my day, the epitome of all the good things about your dad and I, and delivering my first grandchild (and the best son-in-law any mom could ask for) in this process. I love you more than life itself.

My Goddesses; Ann (may you rest in peace), Mickie, Charmian, Virginia, Jan, Lin, Arlene, Julie, and Trish. My tribe of nurturers and warriors, my coven lush with intellect. Thank you for encouraging this project and lifting me up when I faltered.

My friend Steve; your presence in mine and my daughter's lives has been the ballast in an often times turbulent sea. I value your input in all matters of sanity.

My friend Julie; keeper of the Fur-Babies when I'm on the road, energetic assistant in all efforts related to this project, and the one person who keeps me laughing no matter what. Thank you for always helping me recognize my truth and being the first person to read this story…and like it.

My friend Brenda F., who reminded me on several occasions I was too close to the edge and when I ignored her advice, was there to help me pick up the pieces. Your support and friendship along this journey have been invaluable.

The many family and friends who I don't see often but have encouraged me through social media, phone calls, and the occasional face-to-face: my brother David and his wife Jacquie, my nieces Kiley and Kasey, Amanda Lubin, Kelly Ireland, Donna Crenshaw, Brian Flynn (who looks a lot like my first boyfriend), Rick and Robyn Fox, Lisa Gotschall Barney, Tracy Cox, Michael Lykins, Marta DePoy, Maryanna Zito, Joanne Homenick, Joyce Arbuckle, Jan Steusloff, Delores Patterson Brown, Edward McIlwain, Randy Poulson, and all the people too numerous to mention here, who have been kind enough to 'Like' my book page and read the excerpts. Your support and comments are appreciated.

To the 'Dicks' in my life who helped me recognize my strengths and weaknesses; you may not appreciate my portrayal of our time together, but rest assured your presence was instrumental in my spiritual growth.

My Editor Patricia Charpentier; Thank you for taking a wanna be writer and nudging me into the area of published author.

My feline co-authors, Blondie and Gemma who kept vigil near or on my desk for every writing session.

And because I saved the best for the last my Wingman Paul. I am forever grateful you clicked on my picture! I never could have brought this project to completion without your love, support, and unwavering belief in my capabilities. You make it easy to be me and for that I love you infinitely.

I'M GETTIN' MY OWN

(Prologue)

IN THE SUMMER OF 2007, AFTER A FRANTIC, ASS-NUMBING, nine-day, 6,800-mile-cross-country ride as a passenger astride Butch's Harley-Davidson Classic, I climbed off the bike, looked him squarely in the eye and said, "I'm gettin' my own." It didn't occur to me then that I was making a decision that would affect me so profoundly, one that I would eventually claim "saved my life."

My epiphany came during our hellish ride as we flew past the south rim of the Grand Canyon. We first experienced scorching heat, followed by freezing rain and a smattering of hail blown in by honest-to-God dust devils that appeared out of nowhere along the horizon. This drastic change surrounded us so quickly; it caught us completely off guard, like so many life-altering events.

After traveling like this for the better part of two years, I knew in that one galvanizing moment on a dangerously slick piece of Arizona asphalt that my desire was not to outrun life but to slow down and experience it fully. To do so, I needed to get my own bike.

MOST LIKELY TO WEAR LEATHER

Unfulfilled desires are dangerous forces.

– Sarah Tarleton Colvin, American nurse and suffragist

THE INSTRUCTOR FOR THE NEW RIDER COURSE AT THE Harley-Davidson Riding Academy put his hands on his knees and peered down at my crumpled form on the pavement and then inquired as to whether I was okay.

Lying still and mentally checking for damage to my body, I assured him that the only thing harmed was my pride. The instructor was not one to miss a teachable moment, so he asked, "What did you learn about the bike?"

My right shoulder throbbed as I lay prone on the asphalt; the 492cc Buell Blast, one of Harley-Davidson's lightest and most versatile bikes, rested on its side a few feet away. I needed this course to earn a motorcycle endorsement on my driver's license, and only on day two, I was already sprawled out on the pavement, my humiliation mingling with the dirt and grit. I thought about what I did just before going head-first over the handlebars.

"Never squeeze the brake while the front wheel is turned?" I offered in my quietest voice.

"Yep," he replied knowingly, as he offered a hand to help me up off the pavement.

Then he looked at me and jerked his thumb in the direction of the bike, indicating I should pick it up and get back on it. And for the next forty-eight hours, I maneuvered that Buell Blast all over the designated course with a vengeance. I accelerated through the gears, practiced a slow stop (controlled), then a fast stop (not so controlled), threaded my way through the orange plastic cones, rode boldly over two-by-four-inch boards to simulate a realistic road hazard, mastered left and right turns, as well as learned the rules of the road. I felt fearless in that empty parking lot.

By Sunday afternoon, I passed every test required and earned my motorcycle endorsement as required by the Motorcycle Safety Association. I possessed my license to ride, the legal documentation I needed to *get my own* bike.

———

Technically, I learned to ride a motorcycle long before I arrived to take the New Riders course; my friend Butch taught me on his Harley-Davidson Ultra Classic, one of the touring class of motorcycles. After several thousand miles as a passenger, I had at least a thousand questions about the operation of the bike, such as:

Which is the clutch?

So, the other is the brake?

What's that thing you click with your foot? No, the other foot?

How many gears does it have?

Where is the carburetor?

Does it have a choke?

Why are there foot and hand brakes?

Where does the oil go?

What's the difference between synthetic oil and the other?

How many gallons of gas does it hold?

Is there a reserve? (I found out the hard way that the answer is *no* on a desolate stretch of asphalt in West Texas.)

How heavy is the bike?

What if the tire goes flat?

What if the motor gets too hot?

Watching and listening from my perch on the back of the bike, I heard when it was time to shift gears, and I could tell by the sound if we were in second or third. I knew not to lean into the curves but to relax my body and go with the direction of the bike. I felt when the asphalt was slick and the difference between hot, slick asphalt, with or without rain. I learned what the bike sounded like normally and when something was awry mechanically. I discovered that a giant wad of bubble gum would hold a busted shifter rod in place long enough to ride to the nearest dealer. (I couldn't determine if the mechanics were astounded that the gum held the shifter rod in place or that the girl passenger thought of it). I learned to ride by being an observant passenger, always the passenger. I started hopping on the back of a boy's motorcycle when I was sixteen years old and not much changed as I grew older. The bad boy persona of a biker, the thrill of riding, the need for speed still attracted me.

That is, until one day, shortly after our ass-numbing, cross-country trip and my declaring that "I'm gettin' my own." Butch and I were on a short ride around town when he pulled into the parking lot of a local community college and directed me to hop off the back. He shut off the motor, put the kickstand down, climbed off himself, and then looked at me and said, "Here, get on and learn to ride."

Hot damn! I didn't realize it then, but his offer to teach me to ride on his $20,000 Ultra Classic was a gesture of love, pure and simple. He had absolute faith in me that I would not hurt myself or, more importantly, his bike.

Fortunately, when I was sixteen years old, I learned to drive in a Volkswagen Beetle, so I had the whole clutch-shift-brake thing down. Once a person learns to operate a vehicle with a manual transmission, it becomes second nature, regardless of the vehicle or the transmission. I swung my leg over the bike and into the saddle on Butch's Ultra Classic in the vast, empty parking lot. With the kickstand still down, and the bike leaning to the left, I looked at Butch for direction. He had stepped well away from the bike, folded his arms across his chest, and stood there looking at me and the bike.

"OK, now what?"

Butch remained immobile, but in his deep, melodic baritone, he calmly told me, "First get a feel for the bike's weight. Keep the kickstand down but set the bike upright."

I planted both feet firmly on the asphalt and righted the bike. *Whoa! This is heavy!*

"Now just sit there and find your balance with the weight of the bike," he commanded.

I decided the bike looked a lot bigger from the saddle. I glanced at Butch; he apparently would offer no further assistance than verbal directions.

"When you're ready, put the kickstand up," he said, as he turned and strolled further away from the bike and me.

My left foot groped for the kickstand and finally connected; I pulled it back, and with the familiar click, it snapped into place beneath the bike.

Learning to ride a huge hunk of steel with one hundred-plus horsepower was a fine balancing act at best and would serve as the metaphor I needed to find balance in my life.

"Turn on the ignition and make sure the bike is in neutral, then flip the starter switch," Butch directed from what seemed like a long distance away from me and help if I needed it.

And as I had seen Butch do a thousand times, I instinctively reached for the ignition, turned it, listened to the soft whir of the mechanics engaging, and clicked the bike into neutral with the heel of my boot. Without waiting for Butch to issue the command, I hit the starter switch with my right thumb, and the bike roared to life between my legs.

I was hooked. On that very spot that day, I became a devotee, a disciple of that *thump, thump, thump* of the Harley-Davidson V-twin engine throbbing between my legs and the vibration in the handlebars coursing energy up through my arms and into my chest. I loved everything associated with the motorcycle—the look, the feel, the sound, the clothes, the camaraderie among riders, the wind in my face, and most of all, those two wheels as a mode of travel. I knew in that split second between turning on the ignition and hitting the starter switch that I would kneel at the altar of Harley-Davidson as its most fervent of disciples and stop at nothing *to get my own*.

I glanced at Butch. He hadn't moved; he just grinned his toothy, megawatt smile, and gave me the *thumbs-up* sign, which I interpreted as *you go, girl.* I popped the bike into first gear with the toe of my boot and gently squeezed the throttle while slowly releasing the clutch. I moved forward across the parking lot on two wheels.

Life would never be the same for me from that point forward. Two wheels moved me into a new life, leaving Butch and the detrimental relationship we shared for two years behind. The love of the motorcycle that first brought Butch and me together would be, in the end, what finally separated us.

Butch strolled into my life with a cocky self-assuredness that caught me completely off guard. My life as a single mom rocked along fairly well. My girls did fine in middle school, I had finished a national certification that increased my teaching salary dramatically, and we managed to spend most of our summer breaks traveling. From the outside looking in, our life appeared nearly perfect, but my inside looking out was in turmoil. I felt as though my life was softly imploding from the center and becoming raggedy around the edges.

My love life was bankrupt, almost by design. I didn't have time for the complicated ins and outs of a relationship. Because I devoted full time to my daughters and my career, I didn't have much left over at the end of the day for anyone else, myself included. I yearned for companionship, physical touch, and a shared experience with the opposite sex but was too exhausted to pursue it genuinely.

And then, Butch sat down beside me at a school function. The attraction was instantaneous for both of us. Butch was the epitome of "tall, dark, and handsome." When he walked into a gathering, every woman in the room, regardless of her age, stopped what she was doing to stare at his lithe frame and striking features. I was no exception.

I was seated alone with an empty chair on either side of me. I looked up as the small crowd at the front of the room parted to allow him passage; his eyes locked on mine. Brandishing a dazzling smile, he made a beeline for one of the empty seats next to me. I offered a slight smile, which was all the encouragement a guy like Butch needed as he stopped near the empty chair and inquired, "Is this seat taken?" in his deep, melodious voice. His voice was like velvet, and it alone could seduce a woman into doing things she only fantasized about. Feeling the heat of this brief exchange and his penetrating gaze, I answered rather coquettishly, 'I've been waiting for someone to take it."

Butch unbuttoned the single button on his navy suit coat—a suit that fit him like a fine leather driving glove—and folded his lanky frame into the hard metal chair. He crossed one long leg over the other with the air of an aristocrat and then turned his attention fully in my direction.

In hindsight, I learned Butch loved women—old, young, short, fat, beautiful, not-so-beautiful, white, or black. Butch was a serial Don Juan, who romanced virtually every woman he met to some degree. He especially loved women he couldn't have because he saw them as a conquest, a challenge, a sport. And my lonely heart played right into his hands.

I knew Butch had a wife and children; they lived in my neighborhood, and his children went to school with mine. The relationship began solely as a flirtation on my part. For years, my self-confidence and sexual desire had been beaten down by my poor choices in men over a lifetime of bad decisions. Little by slowly, each poor choice siphoned off the essence of my soul until I was empty inside.

Butch's attention felt like cool, clear water for a thirsty soul. I responded to his texts, I answered the clandestine phone calls, and finally, I accepted an invitation to ride with him to Bike Week in Daytona

Beach on a Saturday afternoon. As I look back on all those poor choices that derailed my life, this one also started with the self-deceptive idea that "it seems like a good idea."

I learned a long time ago that when I am reluctant to share my plans with my closest confidants, they are probably not good plans. A niggling feeling in the pit of my stomach says, "This is probably wrong, but I won't tell anyone out of fear they will stop me because I intend to do it anyway." It is the bondage of *self* I had yet to find relief from.

Butch roared into my driveway on the weekend my girls spent with their dad, and I hopped willingly on the back of his motorcycle.

The second I straddled the bike and wrapped my legs around Butch's taut body from the passenger's seat, felt the rumble of the bike beneath us, and the exhilarating rush of the wind, I was hooked. There was no going back from the excitement this man had brought to my doorstep.

Our ride to Daytona brought back many memories of previous boys on motorcycles who roared into my parent's driveway. My teenage self would grab a jacket, shout *see ya* to my parents, and dash out the back door before they could raise too many objections.

The cacophony of sounds made by the several thousand motorcycles that surrounded us as we cruised into Daytona overwhelmed me. My head swiveled back and forth as I tried to take it all in from the back of the bike. Butch headed for Main Street where even more bikers packed the road, creating more thunderous noise. Main Street Daytona during a bike event is akin to the Roman Bacchanalia—a festival of freedom, intoxication, ecstasy, and music.

Butch parked the bike, and I hopped off, eager to join the boisterous crowd. I pulled off my jacket since it had warmed up considerably and grabbed the sunscreen out of the saddlebag. I turned around to ask Butch if he wanted any, and I stopped mid-sentence, the tube of sunscreen suspended in the space between us. Butch had stripped off his sweatshirt and long-sleeved T-shirt, exposing a six pack of abs and a chest that would make Adonis feel inferior. My knees went weak. In that split second, I stood perched at the top of a high slope, plummeting down at lightning speed until that *swoosh* feeling hit the pit of my stomach. I wanted to be defiled, right there on the pavement with that chiseled tanned chest heaving on top of me. All I could manage was, "Do you want any sunscreen?"

Butch flashed his infectious smile—a smile that beckoned like a homing device and pulled you in with the promise of something pleasurable—said *sure*, and grabbed the tube. I tried not to watch as he slathered it down his long, muscular arms. The heat of the asphalt rose between us. He turned his back to me, handed me the tube, and asked, "Can you get my back?"

A second *swoosh* hit my groin. I smeared sunblock ever so slowly across his broad back. Time stood still, the connection made, skin-to-skin. I never looked back or let up on the throttle for more than two years.

After that first trip to Daytona, Butch picked away at the threadbare fabric of my moral fiber until he found a loose strand. He tugged and pulled gently enough and began to unravel the slender threads that connected right from wrong. I fell in lust with what I couldn't have. His deep baritone voice across the wireless connection melted my resistance to the point I couldn't say no. His suggestive texts awakened a long-dormant desire. I was Edna Pontellier from Kate Chopin's feminist novel, *The Awakening*, who "was becoming herself and daily casting aside that fictitious self which we assume like a garment with which to appear before the world."

Butch awakened something raw and primal deep within me. The bike beneath us set free the wild thing that was my spirit. No boundaries could keep us in; there were no rules we could not break. Our desire for each other took precedent over common decency. I felt transfixed by the sight of my pale skin next to his tanned torso. Smooth, sun-bronzed skin stretched tight over well-developed muscles. Butch had the body of a professional athlete; we turned heads wherever we went. Our boldness was shocking. Together, we showed up at school events, social gatherings, and family functions.

Denial was my constant companion in my two-year affair with Butch. As my soul grew sicker and my spiritual self withered, I told myself, and others, every conceivable lie I could muster to justify the liaison:

His wife doesn't know. (She did.)

His wife is okay with our relationship. (She certainly was not.)

His wife doesn't like the motorcycle. (Probably, the only truth to my lies.)

We are just friends (with benefits).

I'm the only other *woman.* (I wasn't. Butch had many.)

He loves me. (Butch loved every woman.)

My girls love him. (They did but not with their mom.)

We are good together. (Only in bed.)

The fact he is married is convenient for me. (It wasn't.)

The incorrectness of the affair notwithstanding, our affair ignited an ardor that still burns hot today. Butch stoked in me a passion for riding and provided the encouragement to *get my own*. My affair with him was that of an artist and her muse. When I examine my photography and writing from that period, it is some of the best work I have ever produced; rife with creative tension, fervidness, and angst.

On that sweltering day back in July 2007, I didn't realize it, but my declaration of "I'm gettin' my own," as I climbed off the back of Butch's motorcycle would be a metaphor for life as well. My soul craved nurturing. My desire to ride my own bike was a siren call to live my own life, to resurrect that which was lost, to acknowledge the "me" that yearned to be unleashed. I would get my own motorcycle, and, in the process, excavate my own life from the dismal heap of circumstances surrounding me.

———————

On Sunday afternoon at the end of the three-day, Rider's Edge course, fourteen out of the original fifteen who survived stood together in triumphant solidarity on the asphalt as the instructor proclaimed us *riders*.

Only one woman in our group did not make the cut. Unfortunately, on our first day with the bikes, she could not ascertain the brake from the clutch nor the fact that you had to let go of the throttle to stop. After a few hair-raising attempts and an unfortunate encounter with a light pole, she was asked to leave the group "for further one-on-one instruction."

Many times, I wondered about this unfortunate soul. On the eve of our first instructional session in a classroom, the instructor asked each of us to explain why we wanted to ride. She explained that her husband bought her a Sportster (one of Harley Davidson's smallest, lightweight bikes) and wanted her to learn to ride. She never mentioned what *she* wanted, so perhaps her inability to differentiate between clutch and brake grew out of a subconscious attempt to sabotage her efforts while trying to please her husband.

The lesson for me after watching her near catastrophe on two wheels: Don't learn to ride for someone else. The desire to ride must be intrinsic and stem from a deep passion.

The course culminated with all of us—except Sportster girl—receiving our endorsement certificates to be applied to our driver's licenses. The instructor also awarded his *own* certificates, based on his sense of humor and his perception of our unique personalities. He awarded me "Most Likely to Wear Leather." An accurate prophecy.

THE SUN ALSO RISES OVER MANHATTAN

Excitement is found along the road, not at the end, and likewise, peace is
not a fixed point—except perhaps in the unwanted 'rest in peace' sense.
Peace [emphasis added] is the breathing space between destinations,
between excitements, an occasional part of the journey, if you're lucky.
Peace is a space you move through very rarely, and very briefly—but
you're not allowed to stay there. You have to keep moving and go do
what you do. Because you can…

– Neil Peart, *Far and Away: A Prize Every Time*

AFTER TAKING DELIVERY OF BESSIE IN JANUARY OF 2008, I
slowly started to ride in the opposite direction of the people and choices
in my life causing me harm, grief, and discontent. My self-confidence

was in direct proportion to my increased confidence in handling my bike.

After purchasing Bessie, I spent the first six months becoming familiar with the bike and gaining experience as a new rider. The first few weeks, I never got out of third gear, making repeated right turns, which I found easier than left turns—for some odd reason—around my neighborhood. I practiced my starts and stops until they were smooth. Next, I ventured out onto the secondary roads, testing my skills in actual traffic. I started riding to local Bike Nights held weekly at various restaurant and bars that catered to the biker crowd and meeting like-minded people. The bike opened a whole new existence for me, and I liked it. I couldn't wait to arrive home from work, shed my teacher clothes, don my biker outfit, and cruise the back roads in the late afternoon. I fell in love with the Central Florida back roads, where moss-draped oaks shaded the roadway or fragrant groves of orange trees lined the roadways as I practiced my riding skills. I was eager for a road trip on my own bike.

My relationship with Butch was on the decline, and we saw less and less of each other after I bought Bessie. I refused to ride with the club he was in. I refused to ride anywhere at ninety miles per hour, which his group was committed to doing. The club riders seemed more focused on "how fast can we arrive" and "how many miles can we log" toward a destination as opposed to enjoying the journey. I was not then and am not now attracted to the biker mentality of *how fast and how far can I go.* I've met many bikers over the years who ride at warp speed on interstates to click off the miles as fast as possible so they can arrive *somewhere.* It seems a badge of honor for those bikers to claim victory in traveling from Key West, Florida, to Anchorage, Alaska, in six days or some such absurd amount of time.

After reading every book Neil Peart, intrepid biker and drummer for the rock band Rush, penned, I too admit, I'm a *shunpiker,* the kind of biker who shuns the interstates and turnpikes in favor of roads "less traveled." Shunpikers embrace the journey and welcome the destination. In March of 2008, I started to plan my first trip on the bike; I spent long nights gazing over the atlas, reading details of Peart's journeys, and longing to escape on two wheels.

By April, Butch heard I was planning a summer road trip up the East Coast to Canada to ride the Cabot Trail in Nova Scotia as well as make several stops along the way. I still had not learned to totally trust my gut in matters of the heart. While all the voices in my head screamed *no* in unison to Butch's suggestion he go with me, my mouth said *okay*. I suppose I still feared the ride alone, and Butch was always good company. I duped myself into thinking if we were not part of the group, the pace would be leisurely rather than frantic. Right?

I spent several weeks planning the route; I slept with an atlas beside my bed, and visions of back roads danced in my head. I marked every place up the East Coast on the map that caught my attention: Savannah, Charleston, Ocean City in Maryland, Chesapeake Bay Bridge-Tunnel, Ocean Drive in Newport, the White Mountains of New Hampshire and Vermont, Acadia National Park in Maine, and, of course, the ferry from Bar Harbor, Maine, to Yarmouth, Nova Scotia. The return trip would include the Blue Ridge Parkway and a couple of Civil War sites. I spent hours packing and re-packing Bessie, eliminating gear I didn't think I would use and contemplating gear I might need. I realized somewhere in the frozen forest of coastal Maine a few months later that I didn't have adequate clothing for cold or rain.

I made plans to leave the day after my two daughters went to visit their dad for a portion of the summer. I had at least three weeks to make the trip at a leisurely pace before they returned home. Butch and I communicated off and on about our adventure; he made no preparations—that's just how he rolled. I knew that at the last minute, a half hour before he decided to leave, he would toss a change of clothes in his saddlebag and head out. Butch wasn't much on gear either. In hindsight, I had learned a lot of bad habits from him. I gave him the date and hour of departure and advised him that if he weren't there on time, I'd leave without him. He didn't believe me.

The night before Bessie and I rolled out my driveway, I was filled with anticipation, excitement, and foreboding—all mixed together. I didn't sleep well—still a pattern today, many years later, just before a road trip.

Butch called the night before to say he wanted to delay the trip a day, something about family obligations. My mind screamed, "What about *me*?" for the thousandth time. I said he could delay it all he wanted, but I intended to leave at 5:00 a.m. tomorrow. He chuckled softly and said good-bye. He didn't believe me.

The alarm sounded at 4:00 a.m., but I was already wide awake, waiting on the buzzer to signal it was time for my feet to hit the floor. I sipped my coffee, read my meditation, and silently gave thanks for the opportunity that lay ahead of Bessie and me.

A half hour later, in the dark driveway, I secured my pack to the bike, did a last-minute check of the saddlebags, and returned to my coffee. As I sat in my quiet house, I waited to hear Butch's bike approach the block and turn into the driveway. I thought, *How many times before today have I allowed him to disappoint me, humiliate me, and leave me sitting alone?* But not today; today was the day for me to take charge and get in gear.

I glanced at the clock—4:55 a.m., exactly ten minutes past the time I told Butch to be in my driveway. I deliberately rinsed out my coffee cup, made a final check of the house, grabbed my waist pack, and locked the door behind me. Without hesitating, I straddled Bessie, situated myself in the seat, asked my Higher Power to help me arrive safely at my destination, fired the engine, and roared out of my driveway in the pre-dawn morning.

The air was refreshingly cool for July, and I loved the feel of it on my face. At the first stoplight, I realized I was on this trip alone. A smile crept across my face, that *swoosh* feeling of exhilaration hit the pit of my stomach, and I throttled forward when the light turned green.

I rode steadily for a couple of hundred miles until Bessie needed gas, and I needed more coffee. When I looked at my cell phone, I saw several missed calls from Butch, which I ignored. I stopped just off Interstate 95 and walked into the McDonald's attached to the gas station and ordered coffee. The young girl behind the counter exclaimed, "Oh, I love your hat and waist pack! You have so much cool Harley-Davidson stuff!"

I replied, "Thank you! And I have the ultimate accessory."

"Oh, which one?" she squealed as she handed me my coffee.

"The bike," I quipped as I gestured toward Bessie in the parking lot and sashayed out.

As I sipped my coffee, I rechecked the pack on the bike making sure the straps attaching it to the backrest were secure and then consulted the atlas. I already had decided to meander a little and head off I-95 as I crossed the Georgia state line. Savannah looked like a viable destination for the day. I hopped off the interstate at Yulee, Florida, and cruised over to US 301 North.

Seventeen million tourists visit Florida each year, but, unfortunately, not many of them see the *real* Florida. Miles and miles of secondary asphalt wind through orange groves, strawberry fields, swampland, towering oaks festooned with Spanish moss, inland lakes, and ranchlands.

US 301 North skirted the Okefenokee Swamp, the largest "blackwater" (water darkly stained by decomposing vegetation) swamp in North America. Mom-and-pop hotels dotted the highway, once busy with tourists, now overlooked for fancier lodging along I-95. I enjoyed a leisurely ride up to Savannah; not once did I regret leaving without Butch.

I hit the outskirts of Savannah by late afternoon and stopped at the Comfort Inn, a short ride from the downtown historic district. The day was hot, the ride long, and I couldn't wait to get in the shower. I felt victorious as I unpacked Bessie and settled into the room. My phone indicated several more calls from Butch, all of which I ignored. I didn't want to hear the same tired excuses: "I was delayed at work;" "my daughter needed my car;" "my wife looked at my texts;" or "I'll catch up with you later."

After a shower, I walked down the street in search of a place to eat dinner. Hankering for a burger (I'm neither a vegan or a dedicated carnivore and only occasionally crave a good, lean burger) I stumbled onto a Five Guys. So began my love affair with one of the few fast food restaurants I enjoy; their juicy, lean burgers are served with a generous side of fries in a friendly atmosphere. When I returned to the Comfort Inn, I decided to answer the last call from Butch. His message sounded frantic, and he just wanted to know if I was okay. Fair enough. I told him not only was I all right, but I planned to continue without him, and I wasn't interested in his sorry explanations. I said I intended to stay in Savannah two nights to enjoy the sights. Big mistake.

Butch caught up with me in Savannah the next night; he didn't receive a warm reception. For the life of me, I still don't know how he found the exact hotel where I stayed. The next morning, I laid out an itinerary—something I hate doing to this day, but I felt a schedule of stops for sightseeing would slow Butch down. If he agreed to a planned route, he might not be inclined to travel ninety miles per hour and bypass where I wanted to go. Twisted thinking for a twisted relationship. He looked over my plans and agreed, although he scoffed at "the time it would take to get there and back." I reminded him I was in no hurry.

We left Savannah before 9:00 a.m. and continued the ride on the secondary roads. By the first stop for gas, Butch was already bitching that we had gone "too slow" on the back roads. Ugh. It was the California trip all over again. The chorus of voices in my head that sings in unison when they want to be heard started humming, "I told you so." As I filled my gas tank, I glanced over at Butch and reminded him he could take the same road south that he took to get this far.

By early afternoon, I insisted we stop for lunch. Butch can subsist on Necco wafers and Grape Nehi; I cannot. I requested two checks when the waitress took our order, refusing to give Butch any slack; he was notorious for allowing me to pick up the check. Reluctantly, I agreed to head over to the interstate after lunch, leaving the back roads, and ride north. I decided the best defense was a compromise: a little interstate and a little back road.

Back on Interstate 95, Butch set a punishing pace, twisting the throttle to not quite ninety miles per hour, and with each mile, my resentment grew stronger. Physically, I was keeping up, but emotionally, the distance between the two of us increased. As was his practice, we stopped only for gas over the next 500 miles between Savannah, Georgia, and just south of the Chesapeake Bay Bridge-Tunnel, completely bypassing Charleston, Myrtle Beach, and Cape Fear, all places on my list. So much for a schedule. The only scenery I saw was the antiseptic kind found along I-95—endless four-lane road, intermittent clusters of commerce sprouting around an exit, and nerve-racking traffic.

I insisted we stop for the night near Norfolk, Virginia, so we could ride across the Chesapeake Bay Bridge in the late morning. Of course, stopping for the night was always another war of wills between Butch and me. His cheapness when it came to paying for a decent hotel was epic. We stopped at half a dozen hotels, none of which he wanted to pay for once he inquired about the rates.

By now, the sky was pitch dark, and it well past the dinner hour; I became fed up with the process, pulled into a Holiday Inn, and paid for the room myself. If Butch had his way, we would ride till our eyelids drooped from lack of sleep, pull into a rest area, and sleep on top of a picnic table for a few hours just to save a buck. He felt the same about restaurants. I loved to seek out local places off the beaten path and experience the pleasure of regional fare. He preferred a hot dog at the 7-Eleven where we stopped for gas.

Despite the brutal ride the day before, I awoke excited about crossing the Chesapeake Bay. Butch, who wasn't a coffee drinker, went to the lobby to fetch me a cup and see what *free* breakfast he could scavenge. I used the time to consult the atlas and planned our route—the back way to the bridge. We loaded the bikes—Butch's shaving kit, the only baggage he brought—and I reminded him, "You can follow me today."

The cool air was fragrant, a mixture of saltwater and the fecund smell of freshly tilled earth. Later, I learned that part of Virginia and Maryland was a cornucopia of vegetable farming as well as being an area known for bay scallops, clams, and other fresh seafood.

One of the many aspects of motorcycle travel I love is its olfactory sensation. The experience isn't just a whiff of something in passing; it is an entire physical sensation as the smells envelop me, permeating my exposed skin, seeping into my pores. I know the fragrance of orange blossoms while riding through a grove in spring or of ripe strawberries resting in fields as I crisscross the back roads outside Plant City, Florida. I have ridden through pistachio farms in West Texas with the nutty, sweet smell of blossoms filling the air. Traveling through the pine forests of Maine, Ontario, and Colorado is like riding through Christmas. The pureness of scents envelopes my very being. I call it *flavored oxygen*.

My routes have taken me along oceans on both coasts—A1A and US 1 in Maine. I looped the island of Nova Scotia, tooled along the Pacific Coast Highway, cruised every portion of the Florida coastline, and enjoyed the ride on BC-101 from British Columbia to the redwoods of California. Each strip of ocean smells different in various parts of the country: salty, pure, kissed with sunshine or darkened by clouds.

I have even learned to embrace the foul smells—the fresh road-kill on sizzling hot asphalt, the pig farm in northern Indiana, and the carnage left by a semitruck hitting a moose on the north shore of Lake Superior. I smelled it a half mile away and had to concentrate on avoiding the slippery mess as I dodged chunks of moose meat and other vehicles. *Aah*, the smells of the road.

In 1964, the Chesapeake Bay Bridge-Tunnel was named one of the Seven Engineering Wonders of the Modern World, according to their website, along with the Panama Canal, Empire State Building, CNN Tower, and Golden Gate Bridge. The bridge-tunnel spans 17.6 miles of the Chesapeake Bay and cuts ninety-five miles off the journey between Virginia Beach to points north—a positive selling point I used on Butch: "It's faster." Aerial views of the structure show the bridge portion dropping in a stomach-lurching dive into two patches of water where the mile-long tunnels are located.

The sun was already hot as we waited in the line of traffic to pay the toll to cross. As our bikes idled in the heat, I knew, in his head, Butch weighed the cost of the toll versus the ninety-five-mile trip around Baltimore and tried to decide if *faster* was better than *cheaper*. I didn't give him an opening to air his opinions.

As I cruised onto the causeway, the expanse of the Chesapeake Bay opened around me; sun glinted off the water, and the salt air cleared my head. Large freighters and naval ships dotted the water on two sides; they would cross directly over us once we entered the tunnel. I ran Bessie at a nice moderate pace of forty miles per hour for sightseeing while staying in the right-hand lane, and Butch remained hot on my rear wheel—his way of saying, "Go faster, dammit." I didn't. In fact, I did what Butch hated most.

Three and a half miles into the ride across the bay, I pulled into the parking lot of a restaurant, gift shop, fishing pier, and scenic overlook and parked my bike.

As I started to get off, Butch pulled up beside me and asked, "What's wrong?"

"Nothing."

"Then why are we stopping?"

"Because I want to take pictures." I cast the words over my shoulder as I pulled my camera from the saddlebag.

Butch grudgingly turned off his ignition and got off the bike. Hands on hips, he quickly surveyed the startling beauty that surrounded us for about two minutes and then sat back in the saddle. I continued to snap photos and even sauntered into the rest area, leaving Butch to bake in the sun. Before leaving the scenic overlook, I asked him to snap a picture of Bessie and me.

A few weeks later when I downloaded all my photos, I saw the look of frustration and unhappiness on my face in several scenes from that trip. And, I wondered for the hundredth time why I waited so long to disengage myself from such a toxic relationship.

We entered the first tunnel where the highway dips under the water into an eerily lit, tiled tube. After a few minutes in the tunnel, I started experiencing a weird kind of vertigo. My wheels moved under me, but I felt like I was on an asphalt treadmill in someone's green-tiled, tubular bathroom cloaked in a freakish yellow light. Only when another vehicle traveling in the opposite direction passed me did I feel grounded to the earth.

Then some dumb-ass on a motorcycle approaching me from the opposite direction honked his horn. The sound, reverberating off the tiled walls of the tunnel, startled me, sending me into the stratosphere. My mind was helter-skelter, looking for the light at the end of this tunnel, and then *boom!* The asphalt began an incline out of the tube and into the bright sunlight again. Safe!

After a short reprieve from the yellowish gloom, Butch and I dipped into the second tunnel. As vertigo hit again, I gave into it, hypnotized by the motion. I realized I was riding through my own kind of dizzy, hypnotic tunnel on this trip with Butch, but the relationship was going nowhere fast. Something had to give. Thankfully, I felt the incline, signaling an end to the tunnel. I burst into the light, accelerated beyond the speed limit for the first time all day, and rode Bessie like I had stolen her to the north end of the bridge.

I pulled off the highway at the first opportunity and into Kiptopeke State Park, located on the Delmarva (Delaware, Maryland, and Virginia) Peninsula, overlooking the Eastern Shore National Wildlife Refuge at the north end of the Bay Bridge. A patient person can sit atop the rise at the north end of the bridge with its spectacular view of the Atlantic Ocean and spot a plethora of wildlife such as whales, dolphins, and seals. I wasn't traveling with a patient person. I grabbed my camera and walked a few feet from the bikes—amid Butch's protestations that we had stopped yet again—to snap the view of the bridge and collect my thoughts. The ride through the tunnel had freaked me out; I would never go through a tunnel again and feel comfortable. It was a precursor of the bumpy ride with Butch yet to come.

By early afternoon, Butch and I approached the megalopolis that is Baltimore, Philadelphia, and New York City. I planned the trip to ride through this area early on a Sunday morning, avoiding the worst traffic. In later years, as I logged more time on Bessie, I stayed clear of the East Coast altogether because of its vehicle density.

We hit the New Jersey Turnpike—eight lanes of wretched pavement, crowded rest areas, and rude people. (My apologies to anyone I know and love from Jersey; you are not all rude). I targeted a hotel off the turnpike late that afternoon and called it a day. Butch wasn't happy about stopping so early, but I experienced an epiphany in that green-tiled tunnel, and I was beyond caring what made him happy. This was my trip, my choices, my pleasure, my experiences.

After a shower and an easily forgettable dinner, I calculated the mileage to New York City. If we left at 4:00 a.m. from where we were in Jersey, we should hit the Big Apple about 6:00 a.m., just as the sun was coming up. Just like Butch could exist on a diet of Necco Wafers and Grape Nehi, he never slept more than four hours. He never complained about the early hours I chose to travel.

I've always loved to watch the sun come up while in the saddle; the sun shining on chrome is the best alarm clock. Leaving New Jersey was not a problem for me. (I've returned only once since that trip, and it was the same unpleasantness.) Butch was in the lead this time, which meant we traveled at warp speed north on I-95 toward New York. Traffic was minimal, as I had hoped. The air was cool but tainted with that big-city-smog smell. The horizon in the east was tinted pink, signaling the beginning of a new day.

As we got closer to Staten Island and the tip of Manhattan, the sun hung behind the dense wall of skyscrapers that defines the Manhattan skyline. Within minutes, the sun was a gigantic orangish-pink orb suspended over Gotham. I couldn't take my eyes off the scene, but there was nowhere to stop the bike for a photo. It was one of those moments seared into my consciousness for all eternity. The realization that I was riding out of the darkness and into the light of a new day ran through my head as I kept my eyes on that glorious sunrise.

All too quickly, I-95 veered east and crossed the Hudson River on the George Washington Bridge, affording me a glimpse south to the tip of Manhattan where the sun still hovered over the island. I looked at it as a positive omen for my exasperating situation; the sun also rises over Manhattan.

East of the Bronx, we headed north on I-95 through Connecticut. Initially, I had intended to stop and see my stepson, but alas, it was just too difficult to negotiate such a visit with Butch.

I'm sure Connecticut is lovely, but I saw only a blur of its beauty as we sped through on our way to Rhode Island. I signaled to Butch to take the next exit. Once we stopped, I showed him the map and explained we were taking the exit for Route 138 East to the Claiborne Pell Newport Toll Bridge. Butch, still sitting on his idling bike, dropped his chin to his chest, put his hands on his hips, and then looked up at me, holding his arms out wide as if to say, "What can I do?" He was not happy, but he was willing to humor me. I felt relieved to get off the interstate and head out to the Newport area. I learned to associate back roads with safety on that trip and still do today after a few hundred thousand road miles.

The three-and-a-half mile Newport Cliff Walk and its gilded mansions sat near the top of my list of places to see. In hindsight, Newport, Rhode Island, was not exactly *biker friendly*. Most people on the street turned to gaze down their noses as we passed. I navigated the dense traffic, negotiating space in the narrow streets alongside the BMWs, Mercedes, Jaguars, and Range Rovers. My boots, jeans, and leather were out of place with the madras plaid shorts, Sperry Dock Boat shoes, and L.L. Bean couture. I found the parking area at the south end of the Cliff Walk and switched off my ignition, waiting for Butch to pull up next to me. He climbed off his bike, made no effort to take off his helmet or gloves, as I stowed my gear in my saddlebags.

"How long will this take," Butch whined.

"I have no idea. Maybe as long as it takes to walk from one end to the other, I guess," I said over my shoulder as I took my camera out of the saddlebag.

"What does it cost?"

"It's free—your kind of place."

"Are we going in those big houses?

"No, we won't go into one of the big houses. God forbid you should actually participate in a tourist activity." At this comment, he smiled, pulled off his helmet and followed reluctantly as I made my way to the start of the Cliff Walk. For all his faults, Butch possessed an endearing sense of humor.

I walked the precarious cliff in my motorcycle boots while ignoring his rant. Butch seemed incapable of enjoying himself on this kind of trip. He always seemed preoccupied with whatever came next, totaling missing out on the present moment.

I snapped pictures of the magnificent homes that overlooked the Atlantic Ocean from atop the cliff, remains of a bygone, gilded era. I sat on one of the stone benches along the walk, closed my eyes, and imagined myself a character in Edith Wharton's novel *Age of Innocence*: The dashing character Newland Archer twirling me around the grand ballroom, my crimson skirts voluminous, my heavily bejeweled cleavage the envy of every other girl in the room.

"Are we finished here yet?"

Butch's impatient query burst through my reverie, shattering the illusion and jolting me back to my reality.

"Sure, why don't you snap a photo of me, and then we can walk back to the bikes." I handed him my camera and posed along the stone wall overlooking the water.

Just like before, these pictures tell a story. When I reviewed the photos a few weeks later, I looked puffy, tired, and worn out after only four days into the trip.

The next day, Butch and I made the treacherous trip around Boston where every interstate in the area was under construction. Keep in mind, I was still a novice rider: (Note: You *ride* a motorcycle; you don't *drive* a motorcycle. Conversely, the *passenger* is just that, a *passenger*, not a *rider*.) I had only taken possession of my bike just five months before embarking on this journey. Negotiating eight lanes of traffic in a major metropolitan area on an interstate that is under construction takes every ounce of concentration on four wheels, let alone two.

As if road construction was not hazardous enough, it started to rain, and rain makes hot asphalt as slick as ice. I had some experience riding in wet weather, although never on a crowded interstate with road construction. The rain-plus-construction combination was potentially fatal, and I gripped the handlebars with white knuckles.

Butch never stopped for inclement weather, applying his philosophy, "Ride faster, and ride out of the rain." We made it around Boston only by the grace of God, and I insisted we hop over to US 1, which hugs the coastline of Maine. We would still have rain, but far less traffic, or so I thought.

The first few coastal towns we rode through looked postcard perfect. The picturesque Nubble Lighthouse with its bright, red light tower situated atop a craggy rock was a stark contrast to the gray misty day. We enjoyed lobster rolls for lunch near York Beach, the rain still dampening the ride considerably. Although US 1 in Maine is the scenic byway, the nooks and crannies of coastal Maine make it a slow ride.

Butch seethed with the thirty-mile-per-hour speed zones and frequent traffic lights—the Maine Tourist Division wants to make sure people see every inch of the coastline—and sometimes bumper-to-bumper traffic. Just south of Kennebunkport, Maine, traffic came to a standstill. With the steady drizzle and wearing only a cheap, rain-resistant jacket over my leather and no rain gear for my bottom half, I was soaked, cold, and tired of the tedious pace.

I pulled into a mom-and-pop hotel and inquired about a room in the midafternoon. Butch sat in the parking lot and silently fumed, his bike idling, his arms crossed angrily across his chest. The rate was an astronomical $236 per night, but I didn't care. Another hour in that traffic mess in the rain would have chilled me to the bone and tempted me to commit an egregious act of road rage.

I mentioned to the hotel owner as he checked me in and ran my credit card that I had not anticipated this kind of traffic on the coastal road.

"It's always hoppin'," he replied in a thick Maine accent, "when the First Family is in residence."

Great! Rain, traffic, a disagreeable travel partner, *and* the Republicans. The George W. Bush family was in residence in Kennebunkport.

I left the small lobby and motioned to Butch to pull his bike up under the portico, out of the rain.

He shouted over the noise of his bike idling, "Why are we stopping so early?"

I walked over to where he sat, looked him in the eye and said, "I'm wet, cold, tired of jockeying this bike in traffic, and I'm hungry. You are welcome to return to the interstate and go on. I'm stopping for the night." I turned, pulled my bag from the saddlebag, and walked the short distance to the door marked with my room number. I unlocked the door, stepped inside and pulled the door shut behind me. I heard Butch's bike idle for several more minutes and then heard him pull under the portico and switch off the engine.

The next morning, I decided to traverse back to I-95 to make better time to Bar Harbor, banking on the hope all the Republicans and Bush sightseers would stay near Kennebunkport and off the interstate. By this point in the trip, I stopped asking Butch what he preferred; it just didn't matter. I was quite amazed he was still with me, given my surly indifference towards him.

The ferry to Yarmouth, Nova Scotia, left out of Bar Harbor twice a week, and we had one day to travel the two hundred miles.

The steady drizzle we had endured for days became a downpour, and the temperature dropped considerably. Neither one of us owned the appropriate clothing to be anywhere near comfortable in this weather.

My light leather jacket was soaked through as were my leather chaps and the jeans underneath. My hands were frozen to the handgrips, and rain pelted my face despite the windshield, making the already low visibility even worse. I was miserable.

The heavy rain and poor visibility were so bad that semitrucks pulled off the interstate, their emergency lights flashing caution. Not us! We trucked right along, zero visibility, zero rain protection, and zero scruples. My life was in jeopardy in those conditions, but all I could think about was someplace warm and dry.

I stayed in the right-hand lane, moving about forty miles per hour with my emergency lights flashing. When I spotted the exit for Augusta, Maine, I headed off the interstate, not really checking or caring whether Butch saw me leave the highway. I spied a billboard advertising a Harley-Davidson dealership a few miles down the road—my destination.

I pulled into the parking lot of the dealership, which was nestled in a woodsy location. Butch was indeed behind me with his customary, "Why are we stopping?" I ignored him, unclenched my frozen fingers from the handgrips, switched off the ignition, and peeled off my wet jacket. My rain-soaked boots squished as I made my way toward the entrance, legs unsteady, body numb with cold.

I followed the directional sign to the ladies' room, oblivious to the stares of the employees who didn't expect many customers on such a foul riding day. My hands were too cold to manage the zipper on my jeans, so I had to wait until my frozen fingers thawed before I could relieve my bladder. I turned on the tap and waited for the water to heat up.

I was horrified by the reflection that stared back at me from the bathroom mirror. I barely recognized myself: hair plastered to my head, complexion a ghastly white, eyes bloodshot, lips with a bluish tint, shirt soaked. Shivering from the cold and fearing hypothermia had started to set in, I held my hands under the warm water until the numbness began to dissipate, my fingers stinging painfully as their feeling returned. I washed my face, ran my fingers through my hair, and the warmth helped me gather my thoughts.

I strolled out to the showroom and headed for the clothing department; a saleswoman followed me over and asked if she could help. I wanted to say I needed far more help than she was prepared to give, but I refrained, thanked her, and indicated I needed some warm gear. I chose dry jeans, a sweatshirt, a long-sleeved shirt, a rain-resistant jacket, warm gloves, a face-neck warmer, and a new pair of riding boots. What may have started out as the saleswoman's worst commission day turned into one of her best. I dropped several hundred dollars in the Augusta Harley-Davidson dealership on that dreary and miserable day.

The clerk gave me a dry towel, and I returned to the restroom, peeled off my wet clothes, rubbed my skin back to life with the towel, and donned all the warm clothes I had purchased. I dropped all my wet clothes in the plastic bag and returned to the lobby. Butch was by the door, wet and shivering, ready to leave, having decided the purchase of any warm gear for him was "unnecessary." Translation: "I would rather freeze or die from hypothermia than spend money on warm gear."

I packed my saddlebag with the damp clothes, pulled on my gloves, adjusted my helmet, and headed out of the parking lot without saying a word.

The rain had not let up, but this time, I was better dressed and more confident with the right gear on to ride in inclement weather. We were near the exit for Alternate Route US 1, which would take us east to Bar Harbor; the ferry to Yarmouth left the next day.

On US 1 once again, we were in the thick of L.L. Bean country, but the ride from Bangor to Bar Harbor was beautiful. We skirted the northern portion of Acadia National Park, situated on Maine's Mount Desert Island. The area offers spectacular views of the Pine Tree state's rocky coastline and is dominated by Cadillac Mountain, where one can see the first sunrise in the United States during part of the year. Roadside lobster shacks, selling all varieties of the tasty crustacean, lined the route. I stopped for another lobster roll while Butch fussed about the price. After paying for mine, I took a seat at the soggy picnic table and proceeded to enjoy the local delicacy. On the way into town, we passed the terminal for the ferry, and I made a mental note of the turnoff.

Bar Harbor is everything I dislike about a tourist town—crowded, overpriced, and clogged with L.L. Bean-wearing tourists. I stopped at the first hotel I came to, walked into the lobby, inquired about a room, and didn't even flinch when the girl behind the desk told me the price. I had previously concluded that Maine was expensive. Half expecting me to refuse, the clerk tilted back her head and lowered her eyes to inventory my biker attire. I met her gaze head-on as she plucked the credit card from my outstretched hand, stiffly turned to her register, and ran my card. I signed the receipt as she flashed a cold smile over my shoulder in Butch's direction. He melted her resolve to dislike us with his mega-watt smile, said "good evening" to her, and held the door open for me as I exited the lobby. He was still smiling at the clerk as he backed out the door.

Blissfully, the rain had stopped and given way to a damp coolness, void of any sunshine. I carried my gear into the expensive Ethan Allen furnished room complete with mint green damask curtains and plopped my gritty bag onto the floral down comforter. I turned the shower on, stripped off my clothes, and selfishly stood in the hot shower until the water ran tepid. Butch would have to wait for his hot water until it heated up again.

After I warmed up and checked in with my daughters, Butch and I strolled down the congested main street looking for what, I'm not sure. Neither one of us talked, and the abundance of gift shops selling every imaginable item involving a lobster, crab, or lighthouse held no interest for me.

I stopped at a restaurant with covered patio dining and tall, propane heaters blowing warm air over the outside diners. It looked cozy and inviting. The tall, stylishly dressed brunette standing behind the podium marked "Please Wait To Be Seated" looked startled when I asked for a table outside. She raised one eyebrow, looked over at Butch, back at me and said, "For two?"

"Yes, for two."

She snatched two menus from the stack under her podium, said, "Follow me," and walked primly toward the patio, back stiff, head high. She plunked the menus down on the table, and before we even sat down, she announced our server would be with us momentarily, then pivoted and left.

Our young server was friendlier, eager to please, and efficient. I ordered a bowl of clam chowder, and Butch said, "I'm not hungry," which meant he didn't want to pay for dinner. Once again, I ignored him as I enjoyed the creamy warmth of the chowder and watched the clogs of tourists stroll by, clutching expensively bagged items from the surrounding shops.

By 6:00 a.m. the next morning, I was up and packed, ready to head to the ferry terminal. The drizzle had not stopped, and another gray, wet day loomed ahead—a reflection of my mood. While Butch packed his bike, I walked to the lobby and checked out.

I negotiated the slick road back to the terminal and parked Bessie. Butch followed me in, and we stood, looking at the informational signs posted near the ticket counter. I decided against purchasing our tickets in advance.

The terminal rented small lockers where I planned to leave my .45 automatic—a constant companion for Bessie and me—until Butch and I returned. Canadians are not as fond of firearms as we Americans are.

As I rearranged my gear, Butch looked at me, and asked, "We need passports to go to Nova Scotia?"

My spine stiffened, my neck rigid, I slowly said, "Yes. I told you before we left that you needed your passport to make this trip," enunciating each word slowly as if I were speaking to a two-year-old.

He looked at me with that stupid I-don't-know-what-you're-talking-about look and revealed he didn't have his passport.

I froze.

My .45 sat within easy reach, and in one split second, I contemplated whether this man was worth going to prison for. He wasn't. I grabbed my waist-pack and stomped into the terminal lobby to escape the drizzle. Butch was close on my heels.

"What do you mean you don't have your passport?" I growled, as I turned on him before he was barely in the door.

"I didn't know where it was and didn't have time to look for it," he replied sheepishly, his hands open, palms up, his gaze drifting from mine as he tried to slide further inside the terminal to avoid me.

"And you are just now telling me this as we are standing in this terminal?" And that was it. That was all it took. I exploded and made the kind of public scene Butch detested.

I stomped away from the door of the terminal and marched across the lobby in utter frustration. A knot of tourists scanning the pricing board above the ticket counter, turned to see what the commotion was about.

"Let me get this straight Butch," I bellowed, as I stood front and center in the lobby. "We have traveled all week toward this destination, only to arrive and you now tell me you don't have your passport!"

"Shhhhh! Keep your voice down," he pleaded, glancing warily at the tourists.

"Why? Why should I keep my voice down?" I fussed even louder, turning away from Butch to glare at the knot of tourists who were now more interested in the drama unfolding than buying tickets.

"Are. You. Fucking kidding me?" I spat, as I threw my helmet across the terminal lobby. The round headgear slid menacingly across the polished concrete floor, clattering to a stop against the opposite wall.

"You bastard. You fucking bastard," I screamed at Butch, who stood steadfast, not flinching at my wrath, but glancing wryly at the gawking tourists. I stomped back and forth in front of him, calling him everything but the proud man he was until I had no more insults to hurl.

I crossed the lobby, gathered up the helmet and backpack, stormed out of the terminal, leaving the clutch of tourists inside slack-jawed, and returned to our bikes. I was so angry my body shook. I had endured a blistering travel pace, passed up several stops on my list of things to see, jeopardized my safety in the rain, navigated endless road construction on detested interstates, only to arrive at this terminal today, and Butch tells me he doesn't have a passport? Butch followed me outside and tried to ameliorate the situation.

"Look, I'm sorry. I didn't think we would make it this far," he pleaded.

"What did you think we were doing?" I screeched. "Just out for an afternoon ride for Chrissakes?"

"Maybe they will take my driver's license as identification," he said.

"This is post-9/11, Butch. Passports are required to enter Canada," I scoffed.

"But maybe--" he replied, trying feebly to soften the situation.

"Stop, Butch. I've had enough." As I secured my backpack to my bike, hot, angry tears and sobs choked their way up my throat. I whipped around, looked him in the eye, and said in an even tone, "Our ride ends here. I need you to leave, and I need you to leave now."

Butch sat down dejectedly on his bike as if my words had knocked him off his feet and stared at me. "Oh, you want me to leave," he repeated. Then he stood up, all 6'3", puffed up his chest, and leaned in close.

I leaned into his bulk, undeterred. "Yes, Butch, that's exactly what I want you to do." My rigid stance and angry demeanor suggested there would be no further negotiation.

Without a word, fuss, whine, or even a hint of bargaining, Butch climbed onto his bike, started the engine, and peeled out of the parking lot, spewing gravel that ricocheted off the side of the building.

I stood alone for a few minutes, breathing deeply and collecting my thoughts until the full impact of what I had done hit me. I looked back at the terminal where everyone inside was peering out, watching the scene that had unfolded between Butch and me.

In the parking lot of the ferry terminal in Maine that day, I gathered up all the pieces of myself that I'd given away in that relationship. I tucked them securely inside the saddlebag, glanced at the atlas, and then headed in my own direction at my own pace. I decided against taking the ferry that day, and it would be six years before I made the trip to Nova Scotia.

I was 1,600.7 miles from home and alone on my motorcycle. I felt a freedom on Bessie I had not felt before. I had shed 185 pounds of dead weight, and I was finally riding *soul-o*. I was at peace.

Butch and I had no contact for the next year and a half. He literally rode into the gray mist that day and didn't look back, nor did I ride after him. When we ran into each other again, I had let go of the resentment, and, thankfully, we remained friends.

Tragically, Butch's life was cut short in a motorcycle accident a few years after the East Coast trip. His penchant for running hard, running fast, and never stopping to enjoy the journey cost him his life. Rest in peace, Butch.

RIDING DELIBERATELY

We have not even to risk the adventure alone,
for the heroes of all time have gone before us;
the labyrinth is thoroughly known;
we have only to follow the thread of the hero-path.
And where we had thought to find an abomination,
we shall find a God.
And where we had thought to slay another,

we shall slay ourselves;
where we had thought to travel outward,
we shall come to the center of our own existence;
where we had thought to be alone,
we shall be with all the world.

– Joseph Campbell, *The Hero with a Thousand Faces*

"WHAT DO YOU MEAN, HE JUST LEFT YOU?" SHRIEKED MY
friend Brenda when I called that night after telling Butch to leave.
"It's okay, B. I told him to go," I reassured her.

"I don't care if you told him to go. You are 1,600 miles from home, a novice rider, and he just left you," she barked into the receiver. "Men don't do that to women they care about." The line went silent between us.

Before she could retract her painful comment and rephrase, I picked up the conversation again and reinforced her feelings. "I know B., I know. That's why it is okay. I will be just fine. I have money. I have a map, and I've got time."

We talked for a long while, reassuring each other that all would be okay. I promised to call each evening and let her know my status. I will always be grateful for the angels who guide me on my journeys. Brenda is one of them.

Next, I called my daughters. I refrained from telling them I was now alone. Both of my girls had slowly been pulling away from me over the last few years. Independence? Teenage angst? I hoped. Deep in my heart, I knew the relationship between Butch and me caused them distress and embarrassment. The emotional distance from my daughters was killing me. For seventeen years, it was just us, the three Duggar Girls—all for one, one for all—with their dad a mere shadow of support. My choice to stay with Butch, regardless of my daughters' feelings would become my only regret as a parent.

With false conviction, I assured my girls I was okay and having a wonderful time. They both sounded subdued, unconcerned. Our children bring us the greatest joy in life while simultaneously wielding power to plunge us to the depths of heartache and sorrow. I remained positive in my conversation despite the anguish I felt over my daughters' indifference. I inquired about their activities, then listened to their half-hearted retelling of their day's events. I said I loved them and would see them soon.

After leaving the ferry terminal in Bar Harbor, the rain finally stopped, and I embraced a leisurely pace. I felt light. I felt emancipated. I felt invincible. I arrived at a crossroads near Ellsworth. I could go left and head back to Florida, or I could go right and take US 1 to Canada. I chose right. For the better part of my first day solo, I hugged the coast of Maine, deeply breathing the salt air, savoring the spectacular ocean views, and praying that Butch would arrive safely at his destination, wherever that might be.

US 1 is the longest north to south road in the United States; it starts in Fort Kent, Maine, and ends in Key West, Florida. I stopped just north of Perry, Maine, to gaze out on the Bay of Fundy. I had become obsessed with visiting Nova Scotia and the Bay of Fundy after reading Ami McKay's haunting novel *The Birth House* several years ago. The book recounts an unforgettable tale of a midwife in rural Nova Scotia. It is a story of the struggles women have faced to have control of their own bodies and keep the best parts of tradition alive in the world of modern medicine. The rich detail of the book's setting, the pure isolation of the region, and my fondness for rocks lured me to the edge of Maine for a closer look.

The Bay of Fundy was dark, dreary, and foreboding, exactly as I had pictured it. I perched on a large boulder, trying to will the sun into action. The strong, cold wind and salt air worked its magic on my toxic soul; it would have helped to have the sun warming my skin.

I thought about all the heartache my relationship with Butch had caused my daughters, my friends, his family, and, myself, but it was over; now the reconstruction could begin. I asked for forgiveness that day. I prayed for redemption and safe passage home.

I cruised up to Fort Kent and spent the night. Fort Kent sits on the Canadian border on the US side of the Saint John River. The town was small with only a scattering of mom-and-pop hotels; the clerk at the one I chose handed me an actual room key, not a plastic card. Each room faced the tiny parking lot, so I positioned Bessie in front of the room number assigned to me. I hefted the pack off my bike, lugged it to the door of my room, turned the key in the lock, and pushed the door forward.

Few things strike me as forlorn as a tiny hotel room for one. The room smelled musty; an amalgamation of hundreds of other bodies over the years, occupying the same tiny space on their stopover to wherever.

I showered, changed into clean clothes, and walked a few blocks to a small restaurant overlooking the river to Canada beyond. Here was as close to Canada as I would come on this trip.

The temperature had dropped considerably since I left Bar Harbor, dipping into the thirties. The waitress steered me through the nearly empty restaurant to a table overlooking the river. The cold air clung to the window as if it desired to come inside as well; its damp draft slipped down my neck. A quick glance at the Daily Specials board on the wall told me I should order something with lobster or prepare myself for disappointment.

I requested a bowl of the lobster bisque and then glanced out over the river to the Canadian side. Dusk, mixed with the cold river fog, had descended. It was the perfect dreary backdrop if someone wanted to be maudlin or suicidal. I almost felt an obligation to feel remorseful over Butch's departure, but the feeling wouldn't surface. Instead, I sat in smug satisfaction, anticipating the lobster bisque and my next day's journey solo.

The waitress set the steaming bowl of bisque in front of me along with a basket of warm, crusty bread and real butter. The creamy bisque was chocked full of rich, meaty lobster. I tucked into the bread and butter as if cholesterol and calories had no bearing on my health at that moment. The hot meal was exactly what I needed to warm my core. I didn't hesitate when the waitress returned to whisk away my empty bowl and asked if I wanted dessert; Maine is the blueberry capital of the United States, and I spied blueberry pie on the menu. "Yes, please. With a scoop of vanilla ice cream." The pie was warm, gooey, and tart, ample evidence why some dishes are referred to as *comfort food*.

I associate so many fond memories with food. On that damp evening, alone in a tiny restaurant smelling of mildew and lobster, I was 1,600 miles from everyone I knew and loved. After one bite of the pie, I closed my eyes, and the taste transported me back to the warm, familiar comfort of my grandmother's kitchen. She always had a pie sitting on the kitchen counter, ready to serve, and a fresh pot of coffee brewing.

My grandma Dorothy was strong, resourceful, loving, and the gutsiest woman I knew. Had I been sitting at her kitchen table instead of this dreary restaurant, lamenting my story of the past few days, she would have told me, "Pull yourself up, dust yourself off, and get on with your life!" Then she would have gathered me up in her arms and drawn me close to her soft body for a fierce hug and a kiss on the cheek, leaving the scent of White Shoulders lingering on my skin. I finished the pie while reminiscing about my grandma who taught me every practical thing I know.

By the time I paid for my meal and walked back to the hotel, it had started to rain again. I turned the little window heater on in the room to take the chill out before climbing into bed. I slept like the dead that night and enjoyed the most restful sleep I had had in a few years.

My back roads' research for this trip included SR 9, the Airline Road, in Maine, which runs 290 miles from Calais, Maine, to Berwick, New Hampshire. It is a rugged strip of asphalt through majestic Maine woods, stomping grounds of Thoreau, who wrote, "I went to the woods because I wished to live deliberately, to front only the essential facts of life, and see if I could not learn what it had to teach, and not, when I came to die, discover that I had not lived." I sought a deeper walk; I yearned for a deeper meaning to my life, a deliberate existence.

The morning was frosty cold; I layered on all the warm clothes I had, checked out of the hotel, and gulped a hot cup of coffee. I planned to stop later down the road for breakfast. When the air temperature is forty-six degrees, and one is traveling sixty miles per hour on a motorcycle, the wind chill factor sits way below the comfort level. Fortunately, I had a windshield that deflected a good deal of the cold wind, plus the heat of a 1450cc V-Twin engine to warm my lower body.

I fell in love with the crisp, frosty smell of woodsy air on that trip in 2008. As a self-professed *hodophile*, a lover of roads, I would forever seek Robert Frost's "road less traveled," especially if it were a two-lane strip of blacktop winding its way through dense forest. For the first time in over a week, the front end of my bike technically pointed south, but I had no intention of heading home just yet.

I passed a road sign warning of "Moose Crossing" for the next sixteen miles. The last thing I wanted to encounter on my Heritage Softail was a moose. A few hours into the ride, thankfully, no moose, and I saw a sign for the Airline Snack Bar just outside of Beddington, Maine; food and coffee was exactly the things I needed.

With a parking lot full of pickup trucks—always a good endorsement for a restaurant or honky-tonk—I eased Bessie forward in the loose gravel and parked. I peeled off the outer layer of leather and walked inside the fifties-style diner. All conversation stopped; every pair of eyes turned toward the door and stared me directly in the eye. I waved a pleasant *good morning* and took the only empty seat at the horseshoe-shaped counter. The patrons went back to their breakfast; I guess I didn't pose a threat.

I wedged myself in between two local men, both of whom were extremely friendly. "I guess you're not from around here," the guy to my left said. When I told him I was from Florida, he looked at me, looked out the window at my bike, then back at me, and asked, "You rode that thing all the way from Florida?"

"Yes, yes, I did." Over the next few years and several thousands of miles, I heard that question a lot, followed by, "All by yourself?"

The waitress headed my way with a steaming pot of coffee, poured it without asking, rightly assuming I needed the hot liquid. One glance at the menu showed everything involved a blueberry—blueberry pancakes, blueberry muffins, blueberry syrup, blueberry pie, blueberry waffles, blueberry tea, blueberry jam, French toast topped with blueberries, and the list went on. I had no idea a blueberry could be part of so many other foods. I ordered the blueberry pancakes and slugged back my first cup of coffee. Being the pro she was, the waitress was right there for the refill.

I chatted with my counter mates and found out virtually everyone in the place was a local. The topic which had everyone buzzing that morning was a story about the local game warden who shot a large male black bear, weighing nearly 400 pounds, that had wandered into town last night, apparently looking for food.

The atmosphere felt warm, welcoming, and the food was delicious, just like what was in my grandma's kitchen. I lingered long after I finished eating, sipping another cup of coffee, and plotting the day's route. I asked the waitress to put two blueberry muffins in a to-go bag for me before she totaled my check. Later, I enjoy the baked goods with my mid-morning coffee. I bid farewell to my counter mates, thanked them for the enjoyable conversation, and left a generous tip. I carefully tucked the muffins into my saddlebag, pulled on the heavy leather again, and rolled cautiously out of the gravel parking lot.

Somewhere outside Bethel, Maine, I lost SR 9 and found myself on US 2 West. No worries—I was still on a back road, still heading west. I crossed into New Hampshire where the scenery rolling by looked postcard perfect with white birch forests, rustic cabins perched on pristine lakes, and the northern tip of the White Mountains coming into view. The elevation changed as I wound my way up to Mount Washington, the highest peak in the Northeastern United States. The air smelled sparkling clean, pine fresh, and the asphalt flowed curvy and smooth.

Best of all, virtually no other vehicles impeded my enjoyment of this unspoiled place. Quickly, I realized I had crossed into Vermont as the elevation continued to climb.

When US 2 intersected with Interstate 91, I decided to ride the highway and find a hotel for the night. The weather remained cool, and dark clouds formed on the horizon as I considered my destination in Vermont—the Green Mountain National Forest. I planned to pick up SR 9 again and head west across the southern tip of Vermont.

The next morning dawned cold, wet, and dreary as I pulled onto SR 9, also known as the Molly Stark Byway. Molly was the wife of General John Stark who rallied the local farmer-soldiers for the Battle of Bennington during the Revolutionary War in 1777. She was a nurse and the mother of General Stark's eleven children. The forty-eight-mile byway winds through historic villages, covered bridges, and various monuments to legendary Vermont natives.

The weather deteriorated as I made my way along the highway. As I climbed in elevation, a dense fog enveloped me, making it impossible to see five feet in front of me. The day went from overcast to dusk, despite the late morning hour. Road conditions on a narrow, mountain road with sheer drop-offs are treacherous at best. Once again, I was soaked, cold, and fearful of my riding skills in wet, slick conditions.

The pullout for the Hogback Mountain scenic overlook in southern Vermont appeared out of the gloom, and I pulled over and got off the bike. Supposedly, a person can see one hundred miles and three states from this vantage point, but the fog was so thick, I couldn't even see the gift shop, which was closed and only one hundred feet from where I parked.

I was tense, frustrated, and weary, so I decided to head back the way I had come since sightseeing was impossible that day. I stood in the chilly murkiness and felt a wave of homesickness wash over me. I was bewildered by the feeling. I will admit, at that moment I wished I was Dorothy in the Land of Oz, and all I had to do was click my heels and repeat "There's no place like home" to be transported safely back down the mountain toward home.

The rain now came down in sheets and soaked me. I trembled from the cold. At Brattleboro, Vermont, I stopped at a convenience store to warm up. I felt miserable—wet, cold, fearful, lonesome for my daughters, and angry at Butch. I wanted a hot shower and some dry clothes, but it was only 1:30 p.m., too early to check into a hotel. I hit I-91 South in a torrential downpour, flipped on my emergency flashers, and rode in the right-hand lane, praying. I couldn't see one car length in front of me. The deluge of rain seemed to assault me from every angle. Spray flew up from the road and soaked my legs; the windshield seemed useless. Never one to wear a full-face helmet, I felt the water running down my face, blowing up underneath my glasses, stinging my eyes. I rode on for nearly three hours with no relief from the misery.

Somewhere in northern Massachusetts, I pulled off the interstate and into a hotel parking lot. Hypothermia had set in. I shook so violently that I could barely keep the bike on an even keel. The desk clerk took one look at me, asked if I needed a room, and checked me in while I stood at the counter dripping and shaking.

For the second time on this sojourn, my hands felt numb, my fingertips had turned white, and my lips were blue. I dragged the pack off the bike, dropped it by the door, and started running water in the bathtub as I peeled off my wet clothes. I sat in that tub for more than an hour, periodically adding hot water until the chills subsided.

As my body thawed, I had an epiphany in that cheesy hotel bathroom. I realized this trip was *the trial*. According to mythologist Joseph Campbell, trials and subsequent failures are a part of a hero's journey from the ordinary world to the extraordinary world. This was me; I had heeded the call to adventure by heading into the unknown. I had met—and subsequently ditched—my mentor. Now, I was crossing the threshold, being challenged to pass the test. On this pilgrimage, I had experienced growth and acquired new skills for the transformation that lay ahead. Heady thoughts as one is thawing in a hotel bathroom.

I spent the rest of the afternoon in that dreary hotel room, watching the weather report on TV. Hurricane Dolly battered the Gulf Coast of Texas; tornadoes ripped through New Hampshire in the very region I rode through earlier that morning. Tropical storm warnings permeated the South with torrential rain and wind. It was as if the weather gods were throwing everything in their power directly at Bessie and me.

I spent a restless night, listening to the thunder and rain. I prayed for safe passage to clear weather.

Leaving early the next morning in a steady downpour, I embraced the maelstrom as my baptism, baptism by fire and rain. I rode most of the day in the rain, stopping to warm up only when Bessie needed gas. I traveled south until I found a break in the weather, somewhere north of the Appalachian Mountains in Virginia.

I shook off the cold, dried out, and spent the next few days enjoying the ride. Bessie and I traveled the Skyline Drive through Virginia, stopping to photograph a momma bear and her two cubs eating berries on the side of the road. I arrived at the Shenandoah National Park early on a weekday morning and enjoyed long stretches of twisty, turning road, where I was the only traveler.

I was alone except for the abundant wildlife that munched on tasty berries along the road—deer with their fawns, a fat red fox, and wild turkeys. Several shades of hazy blue hung over the landscape like a heavy tapestry, giving the Blue Ridge Mountains its name. I stopped at one of the scenic overlooks, switched off my bike, and sat in the absolute stillness of the mountains. Their silence was a soothing balm for my soul. The maternal rhythm of nature is a tonic that heals emotionally. I just wanted to sit still, breathe deeply, and match my heartbeat to that rhythm. Closing my eyes, I lifted my face to the warmth of the sun and said a prayer of gratitude for my safe journey thus far.

Nature and meditation can draw us to our deeper selves. After what seemed like hours—but was probably thirty minutes—of restorative meditation, I gradually pulled my thoughts back to the present. In an unhurried, deliberate manner, I zipped up my leather coat, pulled on my gloves, and fastened my helmet. I was reluctant to leave the sanctuary of the park, but I had worked up a powerful appetite. Bessie and I made our way out of the park, seeking hot coffee with scrambled eggs and grits.

I cruised into a nearby Cracker Barrel Old Country Store, parked the bike near the front, and pulled off the heavy leather. A woman sitting in a rocking chair on the front porch commented, "You look so awesome riding up here!" She noticed the Florida plates and asked me where I had been on my trip. *Oh Lord, if you only had an hour or so.* I related the highlights and left out the low points of my travels.

The woman then confided that she "used to ride," but she dropped her bike in loose gravel and never got back on it. I offered some words of encouragement, thanked her for the chat, and walked inside to be seated.

A few minutes later, I noticed the same woman with a friend seated across the dining room. I scarfed my eggs and grits as if I hadn't eaten in a few days, drank several cups of coffee, and waited for the check. When the waitress returned to clear my plate, she indicated that the two women across the room had paid for my breakfast.

Somewhat astonished at the woman's gesture, I finished my coffee, walked over to the women's table, thanked them, and mildly protested that the gesture wasn't necessary. The one I spoke with earlier replied, "You are my hero. You are an inspiration to me, and it is my pleasure to buy your breakfast!" I felt stunned, humbled, and grateful.

I rode the Blue Ridge Parkway for several miles, hugging the tight curves, feeling a rhythm with the road. I thought about the woman at Cracker Barrel and how she gave up riding her motorcycle. I'd met too many women, myself included, who set aside their dreams and aspirations for a variety of reasons—kids, jobs, divorce, death, financial struggles, the wrong man; the list is endless. I made the following entry in my journal that night, July 25, 2008:

Years from now, if my girls are reading this journal, I want you to know how important it is to:

1. *Have a dream.*

2. *Pursue that dream.*

3. *Don't let anyone or anything stand in the way of the realization of that dream.*

4. *Live the dream.*

We only have one *shot in this life—go for it. Find happiness and satisfaction from within yourself. Don't give someone else the power over you.*

I spent most of the next day traversing the Blue Ridge Parkway and began to tire of the endless curves and slow pace. I missed my daughters and my snug little bungalow in Central Florida. My heart felt heavy and called me home.

Somewhere along the winding road, I saw a sign indicating *information*. I stopped at a beautiful pristine white cottage with cobalt blue shutters perched on a bluff overlooking the mountains. An elderly couple, who appeared to be the caretakers of this little slice of heaven, were its only inhabitants. She tended the explosion of flowers—every shade of purple, red, and yellow imaginable—surrounding the cottage; he sat comfortably in an Adirondack chair in the shade, reading.

I felt guilty for roaring into their little gravel parking area and shattering the quiet, but they greeted me like a long-lost child. The woman stopped tending her flowers; the man put down his book and approached me with a warm greeting.

As Joseph Campbell said, "One has only to know and trust, and the ageless guardians will appear."

Even before I asked the question, the woman inquired, "Are you looking for the interstate, dear?"

"Yes, why yes, I am," I replied incredulously, my arms frozen in mid-air as I reached to pull the sunglasses off my face. I stood in the gravel lot next to Bessie, the heat of the bike settling around my legs, and the air so still I could hear the bees buzzing in the flowerbeds nearby.

She walked back to the cottage, returned with a map, and showed me where to pick up I-77 South. She then turned her weathered face toward mine, and softly asserted, "You look tired, dear. Perhaps it's time to go home."

Without a word, I nodded my helmeted head in agreement, climbed on Bessie, and headed in the direction of the interstate. I glanced in my review mirror and saw the elderly couple standing arm in arm, waving goodbye as I rode away.

It took Bessie and me two more days of hard riding to reach Florida. As I pulled into my driveway, I felt bone tired and ready to see my daughters but content in that this hero had arrived home safely— only to encounter a different kind of storm brewing.

A TATTOO TO MASK THE PAIN

Her tattoos told the story of her heartaches and of her glory.

–Daniel Saint, poet

AS I LAY FACE DOWN ON THE TATTOO PARLOR TABLE, I heard the shrill whir of the electric needle as the tattoo artist bent over me. The needle pierced the tender flesh on my lower back, igniting a fire wherever it touched. Within a few minutes, I deemed the experience worse than childbirth, as the artist painstakingly etched the indelible ink into the design on my back in the summer of 2009.

I embraced the moment as the needle seared its way across my skin, enduring the nausea, the sweats, and the light-headedness. I didn't fight the agony while the tattooist colored in the three red hearts entwined with barbed wire. I welcomed the scalding pain and prayed it would somehow mask the anguish I felt when my daughter Mallory made the decision to live with her Dad. As of this writing, I have not seen her in a decade. She virtually erased her mother from her life, giving herself a blank slate on which to write her life story.

I have never made sense of the reasons Mallory left home, let alone depict my heartache in words. How do I describe the insidious episodes, which, little by little, skulked their way into our existence? Losing her was not the result of a tangible tragedy, like a terminal illness or a car accident. It was an *intangible* tragedy.

It is true that children internalize what they see when their parents are at their worst, leaving many infected with an erroneous perception of their parents. I, too, perceived my mother as evil for having kept my biological father a secret from me for so many years. My righteous indignation and angst fed my alcoholism for a couple of tumultuous decades. Once sober and working a twelve-step program, I had no emotional room for such baggage. I discarded my mistaken perceptions for acceptance. My parents did the best they could with the love and awareness they had at the time, as I have done with my daughters.

Over the years, I have kept every homemade card and preschool craft with Mallory's name childishly printed on the back and words of adoration for her momma contained within. I have hoarded every scrap of her handwriting and artwork as if these childhood treasures are my direct connection to my daughter. They are the *something* I need to remind me that behind her angry exterior is the soul of a child who still loves her momma. They lie buried, like valuable gems, in the bottom drawer of my nightstand.

Occasionally, I take out an item, turn it over in my hands, and recall the day Mallory proudly gave it to me. She was triumphant in her accomplishment and told me she loved me. I remember her little girl smell of fresh shampoo and clean skin, her slender arms wrapped tightly around my neck, the silky feel of her thick blond hair, the sprinkle of freckles across her nose, and her luminous hazel eyes.

When the pain becomes too much, I gently return the treasure to the bottom of the drawer, laying it softly in among other tearstained memories as new tears fall. I say the same prayer every day:

Dear Lord, please watch over my children. Keep them safe and help them to make good choices. Circle your arms around my Mallory; let her know her momma loves her, and please help us connect again. Please help me practice acceptance of where she is today on her life's journey.

In the ten years since Mallory left, so far, God has answered only part of my prayer. I do know that she is safe and apparently happy. Though her hatred of me has not wavered, I have made it clear to her sister and others who love her that so long as I have breath in my body, I will take every opportunity to tell her I love her, and I will always be here for her.

Every year on her birthday, I climb astride Bessie for a ride. I offer my usual prayer for my children and add a special request that this birthday brings Mallory and me closer to reconciliation. Then, I continue my journey where the wind takes the tears, and the miles soften the memories.

I ride with my tattoo of three red hearts, intertwined with barbed wire, emblazoned across my lower back, two birthdates delicately etched above each heart. The dates remind me of the day my life changed for the better with each child's birth. The larger heart anchors the two smaller ones, albeit with barbed wire, but anchors them securely to each other—a reminder that a mother's relationship with her daughters is sometimes thorny and sometimes smooth. Regardless of the heartache, she stands securely in between as the anchor, her daughters' her most treasured glory.

RIDING SOUL-O

Home is the place where, when you have to go there,
they have to take you in.

– Robert Frost, "The Death of the Hired Man"

IN JULY OF 2009, BESSIE AND I TURNED THE CORNER ON 22ND
Street and rolled down my driveway for the first time in three weeks;
the odometer turned over 5,835 miles. I switched the bike off, sat still
for a few minutes to listen to the soft tick, tick, tick, of the engine cooling, and thanked God for a safe journey. I realized it wasn't just another
road trip: it was a psychological salvation and a spiritual renewal. It was
a simple but arduous trip that saved my life that summer.

I had endured the past year with my younger daughter's ugly accusations, punishing behavior, caustic communication, and her agonizing departure from home. I spent months defending myself to her
father with his barrage of threats, legal posturing, and belligerent attitude. My sister's interference with my parenting decisions where my
younger daughter was concerned created a deeper divide between us;

her incessant compulsion to intrude in my life left our tenuous relationship permanently disfigured.

My daughter's antics at school—I taught at the same school she attended—and home had prompted me to leave the school district where I lived and worked and seek employment in an adjacent school district to escape the web of lies my daughter spun around me. Financial calamity continued, although the hemorrhaging had stopped for the time being. My younger daughter was gone, and my older daughter would leave for college in the fall. My role as mom would be significantly diminished. Furthermore, my soul was sick, and my heart shattered, seemingly beyond repair. I needed consolation.

I sought redemption in the wind. I knew that on Bessie I could navigate around the soul sickness, find solace in the journey, and steer in the opposite direction of all the hefty feelings bearing down on me. The only direction I could afford to go that summer was north, back home to Indiana.

I called Dad to let him know the date I planned to head north on Bessie. He was my biggest fan until the day he died, especially giving a thumbs-up to my desire to ride my own motorcycle. He also knew it had been a tumultuous year for me, and, as always, he would be glad to see me: *Love you, ride safe! I'll see ya when ya get here!*

I gave him a *guesstimation* as to when I would arrive, promising to call when I settled for the night on the road to let him know I was all right. I'm not sure how he knew I was okay the hundreds of other nights when I traveled. Perhaps, like other dads, he thought, *If I don't hear from you, I know you're okay.* It was the unspoken sentiment between us. And as a parent, I get it. No matter the age of our grown children, all we want to hear from them is that they are happy and doing fine.

My older daughter, Caroline, graduated from the performing arts high school that spring and was looking forward to starting college in the fall. She had enrolled in a summer class at our local community college before leaving for the university in late August, so I agreed not to go on my trip until she finished her course.

We decided her dad would help move her clothes and belongings to her dorm; the last thing I wanted after a year of turmoil was animosity creeping in between her parents to mar the beginning of her college experience. I would be home from my trip in time to help Caroline unpack and settle into dorm life.

While my daughter was going to school and working, I spent six weeks tutoring students in reading to earn gas money for the trip. My loss of income was crippling, especially in trying to help my daughter prepare for college.

I put Bessie in the shop for service, prepared the house for my absence, and assembled my gear. I felt restless. I needed to ride, to get away.

I knew Caroline planned to spend time with her dad after finishing her class, so I kissed her goodbye, told her I was proud of her, loved her to pieces, and started the process of packing the bike.

I didn't sleep that night; the house was way too empty, eerily quiet, void of children. As I lay in my bed, waiting for the alarm to sound, I realized what my new reality would be. For all practical purposes, my children were gone. I was alone. From this point forward, I needed to redefine my life and decide how I would navigate my next passage. I knew only one direction—and that was forward. Bessie would be the vehicle moving me toward my new goals, shaping my reality without my children.

I left under cover of darkness, about 4:30 a.m., which would become a pattern for me whenever I embarked on a road trip. Anticipation, mixed with anxiety, made it impossible to sleep. There is a Swedish word, *resfeber*, which travelers know, for this affliction. It is the restless race of one's heart before a journey begins when anxiety and anticipation intertwine; it's a travel fever that can manifest as illness.

I calmed my *resfeber* with an ample amount of coffee as I mentally contemplated the route. No sense consulting an atlas—I didn't have much latitude financially to meander. It would be a straight shot north. I only had to decide where to spend the night, preferably somewhere near Asheville in the Appalachian Mountains.

I finished my morning meditation and asked my Higher Power for protection on this journey.

I always had a good feeling when it was time to swing my leg over the saddle, turn the ignition, and feel the bike come to life. My whole perspective toward my empty nest changed, and my scattered emotions fell into formation as it takes full concentration to operate the machine. Before I reached the corner of my block, however, tears were streaming down my cheeks.

Every journey is simultaneously a beginning and an ending: I was leaving my old life behind and starting on a road trip to find a new me.

Bessie is the perfect traveling partner; she never complains about the mileage, and she doesn't mind cold, heat, or rain. She sleeps anywhere we stop for the night and never fusses about the accommodations. She runs like a champion if I keep her service up-to-date. She doesn't mind if I frequently stop—like coming to a screeching halt without notice on a remote back road to take pictures and admire the view. Bessie patiently waits while I explore a roadside oddity, informational sign, or museum without asking, "Why are we stopping here?" I realize Bessie is only a machine, but in my heart and soul, deep within that adventuresome place, she is a kindred spirit.

Bessie, like me, is a child of the open road, a genuine entity that responds to my demands and encouragements. She is the fearless piece of me, the intrepid slice of my soul, and a possession I have vowed never to do without, regardless of how financially tough it might get to keep her. My motorcycle is much cheaper than therapy or medication, and as many posters proclaim, *you never see a motorcycle parked outside a psychiatrist's office.*

My motorcycle became known as Bessie shortly after my epic ride up the East Coast in 2008. After completing the Harley-Davidson Riders Edge course in 2007, I began researching the various models of Harley-Davidson motorcycles to see which one I'd like to purchase. Along with the technical information, I read stories about women motorcycling pioneers. The early days of motorcycling in the 1920s had its share of women who blazed the trail for those of us who ride today.

In an era of women's suffrage and few paved roads, bold women such as Della Crewe, along with her dog Trouble, sisters Augusta and Adeline Van Buren, mother-daughter duo Avis and Effie Hotchkiss, as well as Vivian Bales, and Bessie Stringfield made cross-country treks on their Harley-Davidsons. Bessie Stringfield's story inspired me to strike out cross-country solo, fearless in my pursuit of the open road.

Bessie Stringfield, essentially an orphan of Jamaican descent, had been removed from her parents' alcoholic and abusive home, and a white couple from Boston adopted her in or around 1916, as factual accounts and documentation of Stringfield's life vary. For her sixteenth birthday, Bessie asked for a motorcycle. According to several sources, Bessie's mother initially told her daughter, "Good girls don't ride motorcycles."

Bessie persisted, and, eventually, her parents gave her a powder-blue, 1928 Indian Scout. Three years later, Bessie purchased her first Harley-Davidson, also powder-blue, and at the age of nineteen, embarked upon one of several cross- country trips.

As the story goes, Bessie would close her eyes, toss a penny over a map of the United States, and wherever it landed, that became her next destination. I have used Bessie's method numerous times, kicking off on my own brand of penny tours. Her tours took her through the Jim Crow South where she was denied lodging because of her color. Not one to be deterred by racism, Bessie pulled into a gas station parking lot for the night, rolled her jacket into a pillow, placed it on the handlebars, and stretched out on her motorcycle to sleep.

During World War II, Bessie became the first woman of color to serve in the United States Army civilian motorcycle dispatch corps, transporting classified documents between bases on her 1961 Harley-Davidson. It, too, was powder blue. After the war, Bessie, a trained nurse, rode in circus stunt shows and dressed as a man to compete in fast-track motorcycle racing.

Bessie moved to Miami in the 1950s where she encountered more racism. Once stopped by a white Miami police officer, she was told, "Nigger women don't ride motorcycles."

Bessie's friend, Captain Robert Jackson of the Dade County Sheriff's Department, encouraged her to start her own motorcycle club as a way of bringing honor and respectability to riding. The Iron Horse Motorcycle Club of Miami was born; Bessie was subsequently crowned the Motorcycle Queen of Miami.

In between Bessie's eight solo cross-country tours, she managed to marry six times, each husband a good decade or two younger than she was. In one interview, Bessie admitted that her bikes had to be "new and blue; the only things used are my husbands!" It was her third husband, Arthur Stringfield, who implored Bessie to keep his last name, because, as he said, "I know in my heart, one day, you will make my name famous."

Bessie rode her motorcycle—she owned twenty-seven Harley-Davidsons in her lifetime—for more than sixty years and in 1993, at the age of eighty-three, she succumbed to complications from an enlarged heart. Several years before she died, her doctor had told her to stop riding because it contributed to her illness. She exclaimed, "Doc, if I don't ride, I will die!"

In 2002, the American Motorcyclist Association inducted Bessie into its Hall of Fame as well as honored her with a permanent exhibit at the Harley-Davidson Museum in Milwaukee, Wisconsin. Bessie Stringfield paved the way for women like me to do what I do from the saddle of my Harley-Davidson. Despite prejudice, racism, and life's disappointments, her courageous spirit guided her to achieve a place in motorcycle history.

I identify with Bessie's story; it is in her spirit that I ride.

The trip north the summer of 2009 was blessedly uneventful; I had good weather and no mechanical malfunctions. My mind cleared somewhere north of the Mason-Dixon line, and I looked forward to seeing my family. I stopped just north of Asheville for the night to call Dad to tell him my location and that barring any unforeseen circumstances, I'd be home late the next afternoon. I knew he would start pacing his driveway around three o'clock, listening for the sound of the bike to round the corner. I took comfort in that vision and fell into a sound sleep.

The next morning was bright and cold in the mountains; I dug the heavy leather jacket and chaps out of my bag, fortified myself with hot coffee, and departed for the short day's ride, the last leg of the journey. By ten o'clock, it had warmed up considerably, so I stopped at a rest area to stow the leather jacket. As I stuffed it into my saddlebag, a woman approached and started commenting on Bessie. She is a beautiful thing to behold and a surefire conversation starter!

This woman looked to be about my age, fiftyish, or possibly a little older. She asked me, "How long have you been riding? Is your husband with you?"

"I've been riding for two years, and no, I don't have a husband."

"Aren't you afraid to ride by yourself?"

I replied calmly that no, I was not afraid to ride by myself.

"I'm sixty-five years old, and I've always wanted to ride a motorcycle. Do you think I'm too old?"

I removed my sunglasses to look her in the eye, and exclaimed, "Hell, no, you are not too old! Too old is someone who drives a slate gray Hyundai. Too old is sitting in the nursing home *wishing* you had bought a motorcycle when you were sixty-five. Too old is when you give up and think you *are* too old."

She chuckled, backed away a step or two, wished me Godspeed, and as she started to walk away, she whispered, "My husband would never let me anyway."

That encounter marked one of many turning points in my life. The woman at the rest stop helped me be grateful for my life as it was at that moment. *Too old* will always be just out of reach for me. At a time when many women my age bought those silly red hats and purple boas, I bought a Harley-Davidson.

With the many challenges and changes in my life during 2009, Bessie became my salvation. She was the glue that has held the broken pieces of my life together. She served as the therapist's couch, Dr. Phil, Oprah, Ellen, an entire library of self-help books, the antidepressant, and the social conduit. I hope I never limit myself with the question, *Do you think you are too old?*

Late that afternoon, I rounded the corner into Dad's neighborhood, and, as predicted, I saw him in the driveway, ostensibly cleaning his car's windshield. I noticed that his dirty-blond hair had turned a grayish blond. My dad was tall and slender with broad shoulders and an old man's paunch. His shoulders were more stooped than I remembered; perhaps this past year had taken its toll on him as well. Dad always pulled his car out of the garage to make room for my bike when I visited. He waved me into the driveway as if he were the ground handler at O'Hare and the concrete driveway a landing strip. I switched off the bike, stiffly climbed off, and returned my dad's hug.

Dad was never a big hugger, so I always pulled him a little closer than he was willing to initiate. After the customary pleasantries—How was the weather? Did you have any trouble? How was your hotel last night? —I retrieved my gear from the saddlebags and headed inside the house for a shower.

Home had not changed in the past year: the family pictures were the same, the curio cabinet still stood in the corner, its light shedding a soft glow on my mom's dusty collectibles, and the arrangement of the living room furniture was no different since Mom and Dad purchased the house more than a decade ago. It was not the house I grew up in, but one my parents bought when Dad retired and moved closer to my brother. For that reason, this house has always felt a little foreign to me. I guess that if we have living parents, "home" is where they reside.

By the time I returned, feeling refreshed, Dad had washed the bike down and was wiping off the excess water. A vehicle never stayed dirty in our household. Virtually every Saturday morning, except when it rained or the temperature was below zero, Dad would be in the driveway, washing vehicles. If you owned a car in the Tolbert household, you were expected to keep it clean, which is probably why I take great pride in polishing chrome today.

On this trip home, I connected with friends and family on a level I had not taken the time to do before. I spent long, slow afternoons with people I loved, and that was my salvation that summer. Since Mom died, Dad and I had had the opportunity to develop a closer relationship, free of the constraints she placed on everyone in her orbit. For most of my life, I recall a mother who was self-centered, judgmental, and needy. During the last ten years she lived, my mother was ill, which made her even needier. My dad was devoted to her for which I am grateful as he endured the demands of her illness and took care of her until the end.

My dad led a quiet, well-ordered life in his retirement. His routine was exactly what I needed to calm my soul. I fell into his patterns.

We took a long walk in the mornings after coffee and then completed household chores, followed by plans for where to eat lunch. A long nap was next—a couple of hours of reading for me; I could never get into the afternoon nap thing—then a few hours of sitting in the sunroom, watching squirrels antagonize the birds at the numerous feeders Dad had in the backyard.

In the afternoon, Dad played old-school country and western tunes. I grew up listening to Johnny Cash, George Jones, Hank Williams, and Conway Twitty. He and Mom used to slow dance in the living room to Patsy Cline's "Crazy" and Elvis' "Love Me Tender." The songs were sad, maudlin even, but I took comfort in their familiarity. Little did I know that the maudlin atmosphere Dad cherished was a harbinger of events, which would shatter our world a few years later.

My dad had not cooked much since Mom died. He had created a schedule of area restaurants he frequented for dinner, where all the waitresses knew him by name and which day of the week he would be seated for the early-bird special, served promptly at 4:30 p.m. I gave in to the routine and relished the wholesome, home-style restaurant fare, not giving two flips about my waistline. Good food was like a liniment for a festering soul: it felt soothing, comforting, and healing.

I tucked into the chicken and dumplings with gusto, ordered breaded pork tenderloin sandwiches (BPTs) at least three times a week, the go-to sandwich where I grew up, with fries. I shared Dad's fondness for ham and soup beans with a generous side of cornbread. Thursday was Italian night, featuring a huge plate of spaghetti with meat sauce.

In between the food, we talked. Momentarily, I could forget the sorrow of my absent daughter by being the daughter who was present. My dad felt heartsick over his granddaughter's behavior, but true to form, he did not take a side. He remained neutral where his adult children and grandchildren were concerned. He offered me his love and support, just as he did to his granddaughter, but he would be no ally for one side or the other.

During this trip, I got to know my dad on a level previously denied, and he got to know me. He was intrigued by my relationship with my motorcycle, although after fifty-four years of parenting a wild child, nothing I wanted to do surprised him. He asked questions about the bike itself, the gear I wore, the gas mileage, the cost of maintenance—practical questions only a dad would ask. He loved hearing stories and seeing photos of my travels. Dad didn't participate in the digital age, so the only time he saw the photos was when one of my nieces showed him my social media page, or I printed a picture and sent it to him via snail mail.

After dinner one night, I asked Dad to stop by Best Buy so I could pick up an extra memory card for my camera. He has been a supporter of my photography habit since grade school. Grandmother gave me my first camera, a funky Polaroid, which focused by squeezing the shutter release, for Christmas the year I was eight. Once the black and white photo was ejected from the camera, I pulled the squeegee from the tube containing chemicals and smeared it all over the paper, enthralled with the process of watching the image develop. Dad gave me my first 35mm camera when I was in high school, which fostered a lifelong obsession with photography. And in high school, where we had a full-scale darkroom, I learned to develop and print the negatives. Dad converted the spare closet in my bedroom into a darkroom and set up chemical trays and a printer. He ardently encouraged his children in whatever interest they had.

I picked up the extra memory card and looked around for Dad who had wandered over to a display of GoPro video cameras. He was fascinated with their diminutive size and the video, which looped on the display monitor. He was aware I tried to take videos with a small, handheld camera while on the bike and, right there in the store, he deemed the GoPro much safer to use since it could be attached to the bike or my helmet. He called the sales tech over to load us up with all the essentials, and we walked out of Best Buy with a new toy.

Evenings with Dad involved a lot of TV, which was not something I usually watched in my home, but this was Dad's domain, and I was happy to take part. During this trip home, Dad turned me on to the History Channel series, *Counting Cars* with Danny, "The Count" Koker. Danny is a "car guy," who buys, restores, and sells classic cars. It was common ground. Dad loved cars; I loved cars; Danny had cars *and* motorcycles, so we were both happy. We watched several episodes over those two weeks I spent at home, and now that Dad is gone, I still sit down at least once a week to catch up on *Counting Cars* episodes, fondly remembering my summer with Dad.

I was not in a hurry for those weeks I spent at home to pass. I embraced the miles and lavished the time it took to go slow. Bessie and I traversed the endless miles of Indiana back roads I knew so well. Asphalt strips laid out in perfect squares across Delaware and Grant counties created a patchwork of soybean, corn, and tomato fields. They were the same roads I followed as a teen, bored with small town life and seeking adventure, thrills, and a secluded place to engage in illicit activities with those Indiana boys on an Indiana night!

The only traffic on those roads was the gigantic farm equipment, tractors with the air-conditioned cabins moving from barn to field and back again. I affixed my new GoPro camera to the crash bar of the bike, switched it on, and raced over those roads, dodging potholes, and squishing tar bubbles that had sprung up in the summer heat. In the evening, Dad and I reviewed the video; he watched it with such rapt attention you would have thought it was a video of the second moon landing.

I spent time with my brother and his family, not an easy accomplishment for a man whose every waking minute is scheduled. My brother has done very well for himself, and as his big sister, I'm proud of him, but our lives couldn't be more different. Although we have moved through adulthood on entirely different paths, I guess the basic beliefs, attitudes, and values we grew up with are still the same.

My brother and I go for long periods of time without communicating, but there has never been any animosity between us; we catch up with each other's lives when we can. He has offered his ample resources to help me whenever I've needed it; my pride has enabled me to decline that assistance most of the time, although it is comforting to know he is willing.

Much to my chagrin, my brother and sister-in-law had severed ties with our sister over the trouble I experienced with my younger daughter. They stood with me in a twisted, sibling solidarity to send a message loud and clear to my sister that it was not okay to meddle in the parenting of each other's children. My heart ached; my brother and sister had always been closer to each other than I ever was to either of them. It wasn't right. I appreciated their sentiment, but I was powerless to fix the familial, generational discord running rampant in my family. I had pledged to cease fighting anything or anyone; only time and unrelenting prayer would ease the burden of the dissonance.

Bessie and I visited the plethora of aunts I feel privileged to call my own. The aunts are scattered in and around Gas City, Fairmount, and Sweetser. My *bio-dad* had several sisters who were prohibited from knowing me for the better part of four decades. The dad I love and know adopted me the year he married my mother; I was three years old. He always has, and always will be my dad. He may not have been the man who biologically fathered me, but he is the man who cared for me, loved me unconditionally, supported me, guided me, and never once treated me any differently than his biological children.

My biological father died in 1976; I never knew him, nor did my mother mention him. Mom excommunicated *bio-dad* shortly after I was born, thus barring any of his kin, *my kin*, to become acquainted with me. She was a pro at perpetuating the family disease of dysfunction.

I was thirty-six years old before I learned I had several aunts, numerous cousins, and three half-brothers from my biological father. It seems Mom, who had begun to experience more dire health issues, decided to purge her conscience and convey all this information in an oh-by-the-way moment after fetching my infant daughter and me from the airport one day in 1991.

Mom delivered the news as we sped around I-465 looping Indianapolis: "Your brother said to make sure you call him when we get in. Sue, from next door, says to make sure you bring the baby over, and, oh, by the way, you have six aunts, several cousins, and three half-brothers who are eager to meet you. Are you hungry? Did you eat on the plane?"

Being a veteran of my mother's wrath, I understood how her epic ire could keep several dozen blood relatives at a distance for nearly forty decades. I was impressed.

Once I got over the initial shock of Mom's bombshell disclosure and connected with those aunts, I found loving, kind, generous women who welcomed me with open arms. We have stayed connected over the past several years since reuniting. No bitterness, no resentment, just unconditional love for their niece. I could have wallowed in resentment for Mom's lack of honesty, but I didn't. Over time, I learned her reasons and accepted that both my parents did the best they could with the awareness they had at the time.

With the utmost love as our motivation, we sometimes think we are doing what is best for our children by protecting them from unpleasantness or cruelty. All we are really doing is shielding ourselves from owning up to misfortune or bad judgment. I couldn't afford the luxury of resentment and self-pity, so I chose to celebrate in the circle of love my aunts cast around me once the decades of distance disintegrated.

I needed their love, attention, and acceptance more than ever that summer of 2009.

I try to link up with a few friends from high school when I'm home. Some have motorcycles and enjoy the biker lifestyle as much as I do. It doesn't seem to matter how many years have passed; if I want to find certain people in my old hometown, all I do is walk into Folkie's Tavern, which has been around since 1941, or the Mill Restaurant. I gave up drinking years ago; however, I remain drawn to a familiar bar where the smoke hangs in the dim light, the jukebox music mingles with laughter, and everyone knows your name.

The pool table at Folkie's, a tiny, much-renovated building that sits adjacent to the jail on one side and the river on the other, was still in one corner near the back door; the shuffleboard table with its sandy surface occupied the other corner. In between sat the jukebox and the dartboard on the wall. I think a few people at the bar had been there since 1970, but that was okay too; all was as it should be.

It was soothing to sit with life-long friends, the cacophony of bar sounds around us while we caught up on our lives and talked about the glory days of high school at Marion High School. My life since then had been on an accelerated trajectory, not always aimed in the best direction. I acquired a sense of well-being from those friends who married their high school sweethearts, set up housekeeping a stone's throw from where they grew up, and kept the heartbeat of small-town living beating rhythmically.

Alas, two weeks after I had arrived, it was time to point Bessie south and head home. My daughter was expecting me to help her unpack her things and settle into her dorm. With bittersweet anticipation, I looked forward to the journey. My dad stood in the driveway that morning, not quite sunup, the overhead light from the garage door opener casting an eerie, yellowish glow, and solemnly watched me pack my saddlebags. He wanted to help but understood that loading the small saddlebags was a precise effort done by me alone. Instead, he handed me the items, and kept asking, "Do you have enough cash?" It didn't matter how old I was or how long I had been self-supporting, my dad always asked, "Do you have enough cash?"

When there was nothing left to do, but say goodbye, I hugged my dad, thanked him for the hospitality, and we both agreed it had been a good visit. Tears welled up in his eyes, and I realized at that moment, it doesn't matter how old our children or parents are, it doesn't get any easier to say goodbye. I had lost my younger daughter; my oldest will have moved out by the time I return home, and Dad was saying goodbye to his oldest daughter. The circle of life connected us. How many times over the last forty-plus years had my dad reluctantly, with tears in his eyes, said goodbye to me? It made my own situation with my daughters more poignant.

I fastened my helmet, pulled on my gloves, and as Dad kept a careful eye, I backed out of the driveway, fired up the engine, and gave a final wave. When I glanced in my rearview mirror, Dad was still waving. I turned the corner and disappeared as the tears snaked their way down my cheeks, fogging my glasses.

I connected with so many people during this simple but heartwarming journey. I wasn't a stranger on this trip. I was a seeker, I was a daughter, a friend, a sister, an aunt, a niece, but most of all, I was true to myself. I honored a part of me that was weary, that had been bruised, challenged, broken, and used up. I asked God to renew my spirit and help me be grateful for the blessings in my life, and He did.

This *soul-o* trip on Bessie was a spiritual renewal, a healing, a time to realize that no matter what life throws in my direction, I can cope, endure, and reach the other side of any situation a stronger woman. Friedrich Nietzsche wrote, "That which does not kill us makes us stronger."

After traveling 5,800 miles, almost every joint on my body ached, but it was the kind of pain that lets you know you are *alive*. The kind of ache that says, "Yeah, we're bad; we kicked ass. Now let's rest a little." The only other time I have felt that painfully exhilarated was after completing my first marathon.

Resting is not something I do well, but I'm learning it's necessary to rejuvenate for my next adventure. I keep an atlas next to my bed along with all my other reading materials. When I'm too tired to concentrate on a novel, a professional journal, or magazine article, I *read* the atlas. I review all the places I've been and the people I've met along the way. I wonder what it would be like to be from a place like Coon Rapids, Iowa, or Lazbuddie, Texas. I look at back roads, mountain ranges, and coastlines, imagining what it would be like to cruise along with Bessie to the next destination, and most of all, while Bessie rests in the driveway, I dream and plan our next odyssey.

The United States is a vast and beautiful country, which I have had the privilege of exploring from north to south and east to west on the number of occasions I've journeyed by train, car, bus, plane—and by hitchhiking. (Shhh! It's not something I want my daughters to try.) Without a doubt, the most satisfyingly unique mode so far is by motorcycle. I am grateful to have crossed this diverse country from the seat of my Harley-Davidson.

This was my first legitimate solo road trip with Bessie. I wish I had a dollar for every person who commented, "You rode that bike all the way from *Florida...by yourself*?" I could have easily funded my next adventure. I'm not real sure why that was such a point of interest, but come to think of it, in all those miles, I never saw one other woman on a motorcycle—riding alone.

INDIANA WANTS ME

> You look at where you're going and where you are and it never makes sense, but then you look back at where you've been and a pattern seems to emerge. And if you project forward from that pattern, then sometimes you can come up with something.
>
> – Robert M. Pirsig, *Zen and the Art of Motorcycle Maintenance.*

"MOM, ARE YOU GAY?"

My daughter, Mallory, flung this question at me as she and her sister came hurtling out of the back door as if someone was chasing them several years ago, just before I bought my first motorcycle. You know your love life is in dire straits if your pre-pubescent daughters think you are gay.

"What?" I exclaimed, having just pulled into the driveway, home from work.

"Yeah, are you?" chimed in her older sister Caroline who always had the younger one's back. She stood with her hands on her hips, feet planted on the concrete, poised for my confirmation or denial.

"Girls, what on earth has prompted this?" I deferred as I gathered my teacher bags and headed for the door. Unfortunately, my two petulant and inquisitive daughters stood between the door and me. This conversation was going to take place right there in our driveway.

"We found pictures you took—of *women*," Mallory said. Always the drama queen, she delivered the evidence—several photos printed randomly on computer paper—with a look that radiated superiority and a dismissive sigh that signaled her disgust as she thrust the papers towards me.

"As a photographer, I take pictures of men *and* women; my choice of a subject doesn't determine my sexual preferences," I explained. "And what photos are you talking about? Have you been on my computer?" Now, I spoke with righteous indignation and an accusatory tone.

Caroline, sensing their intrusive efforts into my computer just might result in trouble, relinquished her authoritative stance, and allowed me to pass. My youngest, however, became more tenacious. She followed me into the house, trailed behind me through the kitchen, and stood steadfast as I dropped my bags on the dining room table.

"*These,*" Mallory said with a flourish as she brought the computer screen to life, exposing the photos I had taken last week at Bike Week in Daytona Beach. I glanced at the screen on my desk to assess the situation and caught a glimpse of the incriminating evidence the two of them had dug up on my computer, evidence that apparently convinced them Mom was a lesbian. Not that I haven't considered the option, as women just seem kinder and easier to get along with. Alas, my tendencies are definitely heterosexual.

A smile made its way across my face, and I had to restrain myself from laughing out loud. My daughters were dead serious about this situation, and I didn't want to offend them by taking their concerns lightly.

"So, are you?" persisted the younger, her seventy-something pounds pulled up to full height as she stood a mere arm's length from me, invading my space, and looking menacingly at me. My sexual preference was a huge issue for her; she had instigated this whole lets-confront-mom-with-being-gay business.

If you have never been to a bike event, specifically Daytona Bike Week, then you might not understand that lots of women at these occasions are, well, scantily clad, showing lots of cleavages, lots of skin. If you happen to be at one of the bars that feature dancing and wet T-shirt contests, then you see even more. I snapped photos of women in bikinis on motorcycles, women dancing at Froggy's, and women wearing nothing but body paint. The mantra is "What happens in Daytona, stays in Daytona," unless you have two inquisitive preteens.

My computer screen showed multiple pictures of women, some minimally dressed with lots of cleavage in plain view. In my defense, I started to explain I had just as many pictures of modestly dressed women riders participating in the fun and debauchery of Daytona's Bike Week as well as men. I also told them again, in an overly defensive tone, that I had lots of pictures of men and men with women enjoying the event.

Then, I switched tactics and chastised them for being on my computer. I had it password protected, but that never stopped Mallory. Some form of punishment for violating Mom's privacy loomed in her future.

Yet, Mallory didn't back down; she stood her ground and asked one more time, "Mom, are you *gay*?" I heard her emphasis on *gay* as she crossed her arms over her chest, cocked one leg to the side, and pierced me with her steel-gray eyes.

"Yeah," Caroline echoed from the other side of me, not quite as aggressive, but supporting her sister just the same.

"No, girls, I am *not* gay," I replied in my most convincing mom voice.

Caroline sighed with relief and exclaimed, "Oh, thank God!"

Mallory kept me locked on her radar screen, not yet convinced Mom was telling the truth. I felt ready to end this inquisition into Mom's sexual preferences, so I logged off the computer, making a mental note to change the password, again. I diverted the conversation to my daughters' lack of respect for their mom's privacy and the more important issue of homework.

After this exchange with my daughters a few years ago, I felt humbled, horrified, and indignant, all at once. *I'm fifty-something-years-old for Chrissakes; I don't have to explain myself to my children!* Then I realized their concern for Mom's love life was an act of love itself. They both understood that, as a single mom, I had made sacrifices to provide a home for them, finish my education, and create opportunities for their schooling and participation in multiple extracurricular activities. I simply had no time for dating, or so they thought.

While they were young, I had become adept at covert dating practices, occasionally seeing men only when the girls spent time at their dad's house, and I certainly did not bring anyone home for introductions. I understood their assumption; they just didn't know about my clandestine dating practices, which was how I wanted it.

I purchased my motorcycle, Bessie, in January of 2008, a few years after my daughters confronted me, at a time when they were completely clueless of the wealth of possibilities the bike offered my stagnate love life. If anything, a woman on a well-appointed Harley-Davidson is a man-magnet. The girls were also—initially—unaware of my affair with Butch. Our ride to Bike Week was the opportunity and source of the incriminating photos.

I have been exceptionally good at making bad decisions all my life. Fortunately, bad decisions make great stories. Unfortunately, most of my poor judgments have involved a man. It seems a shameful twist of irony that a woman's history is usually all about men.

My foray into social media was a blessing and a curse at times. I created a Facebook page the latter part of 2009 and enjoyed sharing photos with family and reconnecting with friends from high school. But, keeping up with the dating websites seemed like a part-time job; sifting through emails, separating the wheat from the chafe, acknowledging those who expressed genuine interest, and making "scratch-and-sniff" dates with those who looked promising took too much time.

During the evening of January 23, 2010, I lay in bed with my laptop propped up in front of me, checking emails for new prospects, and scrolling through my Facebook page. Then, I noticed I had a new friend request. I clicked on the request, saw his name, and instantly recognized the boyishly handsome face. My heart skipped a beat, and memories came rushing back.

In the fall of 1974, Bart (not his real name) and I were standing in my parents' driveway in our hometown of Marion, Indiana. I had not seen him since then. Barely nineteen, we had started dating shortly after high school graduation that spring. Most of our friends had gone off to college or married, but we both faltered with career plans and adult commitments, which was our common denominator.

After recognizing Bart's face, my first thought was, *Damn you, you broke my heart all those years ago, and now you want to be friends?*

I hesitated, ever so slightly, before clicking *confirm*, and writing a personal message: "You are the last person I expected to hear from after all these years, and how the hell are you? I haven't seen you since you backed out of my parents' driveway in 1974, driving out of my life and breaking my heart."

Bart's return message claimed he had no idea he had broken my heart and professed to have looked for me for several years. He asked for my phone number, and if he could call. Of course, I gave him my number but remained skeptical. He still lived in the same town my parents did (both still alive at the time he said he looked for me), and a phone call to them would have gone a long way in his finding me.

Two nights later, I answered the phone call, which took Bart thirty-five years to make. I immediately recognized the voice, his boyish charm, and casual, "How you doin', Sis?", all of which brought back memories of the tall, lanky, long-haired boy with over-the-top good looks I fell in love with so long ago.

"I remember you had long hair, big eyes, and I always thought you were beautiful—a long-haired, hippy chick with a free spirit and a camera," he confessed as we talked. Then, as if he had waited way too long to tell the story, Bart rushed headlong into a tale of a photograph I had taken long ago.

I had snapped a picture of a young Bart and his dog, Jake, on a windy, fall day in 1974 at Hanging Rock, an elevated piece of granite overlooking the Wabash River in rural Indiana. I remembered the day and the photo. I printed the black and white portrait myself, framed it, and gave it to him for his birthday. (Our birthdays are only a few days apart in May.) He gave me a painting he did of a tree with our initials carved within a heart in the trunk of the tree. On the same day we celebrated our birthdays, he pulled out of my parents' driveway and never looked back.

"No matter where I lived, after that day I hung the photo of Jake and me on my wall," he explained. "It reminded me of the good times we had and the girl whose spirit I loved. I thought of you often over the years with a melancholy I could never shake. And I had the photo to remind me of us."

After going our separate ways in 1974, Bart eventually married, as I did, had two children, as I did, and subsequently divorced, as I did. When Bart's daughter left for college, she asked him for the photograph to take with her. She had heard the story of the long-haired, hippy chick who had snapped the picture of her nineteen-year-old dad. It became her favorite photo of him.

By this point in our initial phone conversation, I sat speechless and in tears. I hung on every word as Bart continued his stories. In December of 2008, while Bart was at work, a fire destroyed his home, nestled in the woods of rural Indiana, and virtually every possession he had. One of the few belongings to survive the fire was the photograph at Hanging Rock, which was safe in his daughter's care.

"Once again, I remembered the girl who had snapped the photo and wondered if you still cared, if you ever thought about me and the way we were, once upon a time," he said. "After the fire, it became even more important to try and reconnect with you."

Bart described how he had painstakingly rebuilt his life after the fire. He was virtually homeless for many months, relying on family and friends for a roof over his head. Once the house was rebuilt, he retrieved the photo from his daughter and hung it in a place of honor. Also, about this time, Bart, too, waded into the social media surf, creating a Facebook page and connecting with friends.

I was stunned by Bart's story. Every romantic novel I had ever read came to life for me that night across the wireless connection. We talked for a few hours, our conversation peppered with hearty laughs, intense questions, and frequent exclamations of "I can't believe it!" We agreed to talk again soon and said goodbye.

A few minutes after disconnecting, his text message to me said, "Thank you for coming back into my life."

In the darkness, I whispered, "In my heart, I never left."

Over the next several weeks, Bart and I exchanged photos via Facebook and left comments on each other's timelines. Friends and family started to notice the sparks flying between us. Each night, he called, and we talked about common interests, the many parallels and coincidences in our lives, which were beyond our wildest dreams. In between the evening phone calls, we texted messages that bridged the distance between us—electronic intimacies that gave each of us a deeper understanding of the man and the woman we had become.

Bart sent me love poetry; I sent him song lyrics, which echoed that love. I shared photos with Bart that I had taken over the years, giving him an indication of who the long-haired, hippy chick with the camera had become. Each of us had become comfortable in our aloneness over the years, yet we yearned for a special partner who could unlock our hearts. Neither one of us had any idea it might be each other, nor whether the fire that started over three decades ago would be re-ignited electronically.

"I need a flesh and blood connection to see if this is real," I told Bart during one of our many phone conversations a few weeks after our initial contact.

"I need to see it in your eyes," he replied, indicating he would be at the airport with open arms on the date I specified.

The three weeks between the phone call and my flight to Indiana seemed interminable; the fears and anxieties of reconnecting with an old lover after so many years, mingled with the excitement of seeing each other again, drove both of us beyond distraction. (I kept thinking, *Thank God, I've taken care of myself. I'm not old, fat, and dumpy!*) We counted down the days together via text messages, emails, and sometimes, thrice daily phone calls.

I boarded the Delta flight in Orlando to Indianapolis on a February evening, a jumble of nerves and anxiety. I alternated between trying to concentrate on reading and listening to music, all to no avail; my thoughts kept slipping back to Bart and this reunion.

As the plane started its descent into Indianapolis, my heart pounded so loudly I was barely aware of the noise of the jet engines reversing, slowing our descent. The minute the silver tube came to a halt at the terminal, I grabbed my bag and bolted out the door of the plane the second it opened.

It was late in the evening, and the lounge at the gate looked nearly empty. I ran, ignoring the moving sidewalk, to the main terminal. I rounded the last corner and stopped in my tracks, breathless.

He stood, looking up at the schedule of arrivals and departures. Even with his back to me, I recognized the tall, dark-haired boy who had become the over-the-top, good-looking man. Bart turned, saw me standing at the end of the security area, and his face lit up with recognition. His arms opened wide, and I raced into his embrace, and just like in the movies when the hero and the heroine are united, time stopped. All motion slowed as he lifted me off the ground, exclaiming, "You are so beautiful!" I was nearly speechless and mumbled something to the effect that he hadn't changed a bit.

Bart and I embraced, kissed, and smiled at each other till it hurt. I can't say how long we stood in the main terminal, oblivious to anyone around us, and we literally floated to the parking garage.

Our four days together at Bart's house in the woods of rural Indiana passed much too quickly. We experienced no awkward moments between us, just an inherent comfortableness in our existence together. We spent the days laughing, riding the rural back roads of Indiana, just like we did when we were teenagers. We tromped through the snowy woods and hiked up to Hanging Rock to recreate the photograph that had endured time and brought us together again.

Bart and I talked about a future together and what that would look like. He wanted me to return in March, and I said I would. We said a tearful goodbye in the same terminal where only four days before, it had been a joyful reunion.

You are never quite ready for the moments that change your life. I rushed head first into planning a life with Bart, oblivious to the red flags tossed up all around me. How would I explain this man to my daughters? How could I uproot their lives to return to my hometown that I couldn't wait to leave?

Our constant phone calls and texts continued. Bart gave me every indication that he, too, was planning a life that included me in close proximity. After talking with our children and families about our love for each other, we planned to get together with them on my return trip in March.

If the reunion trip to Indiana in February was the honeymoon phase, then my second trip to Indiana in March proved the honeymoon was over. I sensed the disharmony from Bart shortly after I arrived and met his children. Although his children were polite, their coolness toward me was palpable in the small confines of Bart's two-bedroom cottage. The flame had cooled to barely a flicker.

On my previous visit, Bart had taken days off work to spend time with me. Not so on this visit. I was stuck in the middle of nowhere rural Indiana with no means of transportation while Bart worked ten or twelve-hour days. I took long, cold walks with my camera in hand, capturing the stark beauty of springtime in Indiana. The endless hours alone forced me to ponder the possibilities. In the very center of my gut, I had no desire to return to Indiana. Given the frosty reception by Bart's children, I felt no obligation to "fit into" an obvious tight-knit family unit. I felt as though I was deceiving or somehow cheating my girls if I forced them into a blended family. By the end of my week in Indiana, every instinct I had said, "Run!"

One evening, Bart and I met mutual friends at a bar, but I quickly discovered I was no longer interested in sitting for hours in a smoky bar, knocking back beer after beer, and talking about the glory days. We met my brother, my sister-in-law, and my dad for dinner one evening at a restaurant in Marion. The dinner went well enough, but my brother and I were both put off by the fact Bart didn't even try to pick up the check or insist on paying half. The few outings we had together, outside of a smoky bar, involved trudging through muddy cornfields, looking for arrowheads or fishing for crappie. I was determined to find joy in sharing his hobbies. Desperate women do desperate things. Alas, I could muster no joy in a muddy Indiana cornfield in late spring or pulling slimy fish off the hook and peeing in the woods.

The morning before I returned to Florida, we sat out on the stoop at Bart's house and talked. It was general banter, and I tried to steer the conversation to our relationship. Bart was evasive when I suggested it was his turn to visit me in Florida. Frankly, he couldn't get me to the airport fast enough that afternoon. Rather than answer my questions or commit to any further plans, Bart busied himself in his garage among the hundreds of fishing poles, ignoring me and answering in curt, one-word answers. The hour-long drive to the airport in Indianapolis was filled with loud music blasting from the dashboard, silencing any attempt at conversation. I guess I should have been grateful that he stopped the car at the terminal while I collected my things, rather than slow down and push me out.

Alas, the fire that had been re-ignited on the Hanging-Rock-Reunion tour was not meant to last. Bart was my rebound from Butch, from the financial woes plaguing me, and my fear of the empty nest I faced. The hopeless romantic in me latched onto the nostalgic reunion like a drowning person clutches a life preserver. More than one problem hampered my trying to rekindle the relationship:

- Bart didn't ride a motorcycle. Was I willing to sacrifice my new passion for riding and motorcycles for this recycled lover? NO.

- Bart didn't want to live five minutes away from his children. Was I willing to leave my daughters to relocate, especially back to my old hometown, which I consider the scene of the crime? NO.

- After spending time with Bart, I realized he was stuck emotionally at nineteen-years-old; he still liked to drink and hang out in bars. Was I willing to be in a relationship with a man who lacked maturity? NO.

- Bart apparently had a lover in his life he failed to mention to me. He eventually married this person, claiming it was for business purposes only (and subsequently divorced her as well). Was I willing to overlook dishonesty? NO.

- Quite simply, I could never be happy living in the woods, stomping around in the mud, fishing for crappie, and raising chickens.

Fortunately, Bart also realized several things about me he wasn't willing to accept—he will have to tell that story; this one is mine—and he ended it for us. Bart ended our relationship with a shoddy email, void of the romantic twaddle he spouted several months before. Like a jilted teenager, once again I tried to find a small slice of regret in his words, a tiny piece of salvation to clutch on my way down. Alas, Bart left no soft place for my heart to land.

The lesson is never let an old flame burn you twice. Although the fire still smoldered between the long-haired, hippy chick and the tall, lanky, good- looking boy, it was not meant to be a modern-day love story. The passion we shared at nineteen was not there at age fifty-something. The free-spirited girl he fell in love with so many years ago had grown into a free-spirited woman whom he could not contain or appreciate.

It had taken me a long time to realize I did not need a man to define me; I was not about to relinquish that truth. I did not require a soul mate for my life to have meaning.

I was learning to map my own course and determine my own destination now that my children were no longer at home. A fire burned within my soul, igniting possibilities I previously only dreamed for myself. I was choosing to feather my empty nest with leather and chrome, not a second-hand lover.

DICKS I'VE KNOWN

I want to make the world more interesting than
my problems. Therefore, I have to make my problems social.

– Chris Kraus, *I Love Dick*

AFTER MY EXPERIENCE WITH BART, I DECIDED TO GO DIGI-
tal to improve my love life. I dipped my toe into the online dating pool
with more than a little reservation. The reality was, I did not go to bars,
I had not met eligible men at the gym or local bike events, and desirable
partners were certainly not knocking down my door. Online dating
made practical sense to me; I could look at pictures, read profiles, and
chat with potential prospects while sitting on my sofa in pajamas.

I chose an attractive lure (photo of myself), painstakingly wrote
my profile, which was an honest, soul-baring discourse—unlike most
of what I read online—and cast my line into the murky internet waters.

Keeping up with dating websites began to feel like a part-time job: I sifted through emails, separated the wheat from the chaff, acknowledged those who expressed genuine interest, and made scratch-and-sniff dates with those who looked promising. I soon discovered that not all men were as earnest or as honest as I was in presenting themselves as eligible.

It didn't take long to understand how a smooth-talking; cyber Casanova could take advantage of lonely and desperate women. Digital courtship has its dangers, and I quickly figured out the game, whom to avoid, and which websites were more reputable than others. Some men wanted only a virtual relationship with ample winking, sexting, and email conversation. I let them know right away I wasn't interested.

If a profile looked promising, I sent an email and requested a *current* photo. Beware: Many men appear twenty years older than their profile picture when you meet them in person. If I received no response, then I deleted that profile and swiped left on my iPad with my finger to the next prospect. If I received a current photo, I sent that man my phone number. If he didn't call, I deleted his profile and swiped left again.

I established a protocol that led to some interesting first meetings or scratch-and-sniffs, as I called them. Our encounters reminded me of two dogs circling each other as their noses sniff the air for the other one's scent; with rigid tails and paws scratching at the patch of dirt or grass, they seek to determine if they have encountered friend or foe. It was the same with a prospective date.

I chose public coffee shops or restaurants in broad daylight for the first encounter, and I never revealed where I lived or worked. Potential hazards exist for women who are not cautious or sensible with their information or their intentions. Although I met some genuine weirdos during my foray into online dating, I never felt threatened or had my safety compromised in any way. It may have been because of my personality and demeanor. The giant "fuck you" I had emblazoned on my forehead, visible only to the wannabes and posers, helped.

In three years of purposeful dating, I started to refer to the men I met by the generic name of "Dick," with a letter of the alphabet assigned in the order in which they appeared in my life: A. Dick, B. Dick, C. Dick, D. Dick, E. Dick. I was so popular on the over-fifty online dating sites that I damn near ran out of alphabet letters to assign to Dicks. (Most of them didn't stick around long enough for me to get attached, so why try and remember all the names?) It became a favorite topic of discussion at my Thursday night dinners with women friends.

"How did your ride go on Sunday with the new prospect?"

"You mean with Dick? I'm afraid there will not be a second date," I replied. "Next…!" I reenacted my hand swiping left.

I chose men who claimed they liked to ride motorcycles and even posted pictures of themselves posing with their bikes. But their idea and my idea of riding were often miles apart. Most men were intimidated by the miles I put on my bike, *solo*.

I met one attractive, eligible, and basically honest guy whom I designated *A. Dick*. We lived about an hour and a half apart from each other. I wanted a certain geographical distance with my men, which was part of my design, for I was not interested in being joined at the hip— then or now. A. Dick was dedicated in his pursuit, honest with his profile and his intentions, but he didn't have the follow-through. We enjoyed a few months of lunch-date rides in which he talked incessantly about his son, who also had a bike, and even more incessantly about his son's girlfriend. When I suggested all of us meet and go somewhere together, A. Dick put the brakes on.

I didn't hear from A. Dick for several weeks. Then, I received a phone call in which he told me he rode "all the way to Tennessee" with his son. I congratulated him—with a hint of sarcasm in my voice on his long-distance trip. I mentioned that Daytona Bike Week was coming up and asked him if he would like to go. He then disclosed his plans to return to his native Ohio, where I discovered he was taking care of his ex-wife who had multiple sclerosis. The long lapses between our lunch-date rides and his phone calls had been due to his frequent trips to Ohio to care for her. I was torn between anger and admiration for the guy. I wished A. Dick much happiness and swiped left. Next.

I agreed to meet one prospect who did not have a motorcycle but seemed like a nice man. I rode my bike to the coffee shop, where we agreed to meet on a Saturday morning. B. Dick was gregarious, attractive, attentive—a little overly so—and gentlemanly. He seemed to have a good job and a nice home, but the fact he didn't have a bike was a sticking point for me. He was no stranger to the sport, as he had owned bikes in his youth and claimed he planned to be back on the road again. We talked for a few hours, and I gently extricated myself from the encounter, claiming I had a previous commitment with my daughter. I always made sure my daughter or one of my women friends knew who I was meeting and where. They were instructed to text me thirty minutes into the scratch-and-sniff, so I would always have an out. Frankly, I had no intention of seeing this man again. I thanked him for the time and said goodbye.

That evening, B. Dick called to tell me that he had left our coffee date, driven to a nearby Harley-Davidson dealership and bought a motorcycle. In the same breath, he described his new bike and asked, "So now, we can date, right?"

I was not surprised as B. Dick had been exceedingly eager to please while we drank coffee. I wondered, *If I say no, can he return the bike?* I felt sorry for him, which is no reason to date someone, but I replied, "Yes, let's get together for a ride."

I enjoyed riding dates, as I had my own bike, a guy had his, and there was not much opportunity to make small talk. Of course, at some point, bikers stop for food and drink and then you are both burdened with the responsibility for small talk.

B. Dick was no stranger to small talk; the man could carry the weight of a conversation. As I listened to him chatter, I felt no affection for or attraction to him at all. We took a few more trips after the initial date in which B. Dick always wanted more than I was willing to give. I've often wondered if he kept the bike after I told him I wasn't interested in pursuing a relationship.

I encountered many more Dicks in that purposeful dating period. Most didn't make it past the first scratch-and-sniff encounter. I tried to let each one down gently if I wasn't interested. But, I will admit to being downright rude to one.

The most pleasurable man was the Boy Toy—not a Dick by any means—who made a brief but satisfying appearance for a few months. Alas, our twenty-year age difference and his four children proved problematic.

I reeled in my first legitimate catch after six months or so of trolling a biker dating site. In hindsight, I should have thrown this one back. I was encouraged by his fondness for riding, though, so I stayed with him long after the relationship had proved fruitless and unsatisfying. I found my way out after an ill-fated camping trip to North Florida.

C. DICK, RUN

C. Dick ride into Jane's life.
C. Dick make every mistake a Dick can make in one year.
C. Dick look clueless when Jane says, "I've had enough."
C. Dick get left behind when Jane rides into the glorious sunset, Soul-O.

OF THE SEVERAL DICKS I DISCOVERED IN THE CYBERSPACE dating pool, C. Dick, an interesting catch, is worthy to be included in my story by the sheer fact that he stuck around for nearly a year. I wasn't in love with him, but we had several good times going places on our bikes; it was our common denominator. C. Dick helped me discover that I was no longer interested in redefining myself just to please a man, and I found out I could end a relationship simply because it wasn't meeting my needs.

C. Dick and I enjoyed an adventure on the roads virtually every weekend. He lived an hour and a half away from me, which made him geographically desirable, and I preferred traveling to visit him, rather than the other way around.

On our first outing, we took a Florida sunrise-sunset tour that started with the first peek of the sun on the east coast near Melbourne beach, followed by a ride through the central interior of the state and ended with the sunset on the west coast at the Don CeSar Hotel on St. Pete Beach. The ability to see the sunrise on the east coast and sunset on the west coast in the same day is unique to a select few places; Florida is one of those places. The interior of Central Florida is vast ranchland and is rich in wildlife and wide-open spaces. It's a Florida most tourists don't experience.

One of my favorite trips with C. Dick was biking down to Everglades City, the gateway to Ten Thousand Islands, through the Florida Panther National Wildlife Refuge. We also visited Clyde Butcher's photography studio in the middle of the Big Cypress National Preserve swamp; Butcher is known for his black and white fine-art photography. We were fortunate that day as Clyde himself was in residence and took the time to chat with me about his photos.

Chain hotels are non-existent in Everglades City. Several mom-and-pop hotels cater to the kayaking and fishing crowd. C. Dick rented one of the many private condos in Everglades City for our stay. I lugged my tour pack up the flight of stairs and stepped across the threshold into a dank, dark, musty living area. The only light came through two dirty windows—one in the living area, the other in the adjacent bedroom. The kitchen was a black hole at the back of the condo, which was fine as I didn't plan to cook.

C. Dick, with an artificial cheerfulness, claimed, "Isn't this great!?" as he moved through the living area to the bedroom. I followed with my tour pack, skeptical of what I would find in the bedroom. As he dropped his bag onto the one of the twin beds, he announced grandly, "There are two beds. I'll take the one by the air conditioner." C. Dick made it clear very early on in our relationship that sex was not a priority for him.

The new year started well enough with a trip to one of my favorite destinations in Florida, the Conch Republic, where C. Dick and I celebrated the arrival of 2011 on Duval Street, Key West style. In the three-plus decades I've lived in the Sunshine State, I have made it a priority to spend time in the Keys during December or January every year. It's worth the trip alone to ride across the Seven Mile Bridge, surrounded by the glittering azure waters of Moser Channel, the deepest passage between Florida Bay and the Gulf of Mexico. It connects the Middle Keys with the Lower Keys.

Key West's genuine Bohemian flavor has changed dramatically since cruise ships starting belching thousands of tourists into ports adjacent to Mallory Square a few decades ago. The polyester and Bermuda shorts crowds we saw mingled awkwardly with the Birkenstock, dreadlocked, ganja-smoking street people who are the rightful inhabitants of Mallory Square. Shiny-faced moms and dads hurried their prepubescent offspring quickly past gay bars, where leather daddies in jock straps tried to hustle tourists inside. If you're seeking a non-judgmental arena to let your freak flag fly, Key West is the place to be, especially on New Year's Eve.

Toward the stroke of midnight, on their own accord, the revelers on Duval Street segregated themselves between Sloppy Joe's Bar on the south end and the Bourbon Street Pub to the north. Straight-laced, albeit inebriated, tourists mingled around the south end. I was torn between watching the giant conch shell atop Sloppy Joe's drop or doing the Duval Crawl north to the Bourbon Street Pub to see the drag queen, sitting in a giant, red glittery shoe, drop from the balcony to the street below at the stroke of midnight.

Not wanting to miss the spectacle of the red glittery shoe dropping from the balcony of the Bourbon Street Pub, I grabbed C. Dick's hand, and we jostled our way toward the north end of Duvall Street and celebrated the arrival of 2011. I had no preconceived notions that the new year would be any different than 2010 where C. Dick and I were concerned. I only knew I enjoyed his companionship.

C. Dick planned a Valentine's Day weekend ride to the west coast to visit Fort Meyers and Captiva Island. Silly me. Once again, I had projected a hopeful, lovers' slant to an otherwise routine ride. After several months of "dating," C. Dick and I felt more like first cousins who shared a love of motorcycles than an amorous couple. He was an amiable enough guy to spend time with—sweet, well-mannered, funny, but so was my cousin Ron. I kept trying to imbue affectionate energy where there was no desire to have energy; it was like what I imagined it would be like to give mouth-to-mouth resuscitation to an already dead person. After the less-than-romantic Valentine weekend ride, I vowed to take the lead in the future and add a little energy and variety to our relationship.

I planned a trip for us during my spring break in March of 2011 to visit St. Joseph Island, Apalachicola, and Panama City in North Florida. I told C. Dick this would be a precursor, a dry run of my trip in July to see family and friends. I had scheduled a thirty-day ride north with the focal point being a circle tour of Lake Michigan and Lake Superior and had already invited C. Dick—who was mildly excited about it—to accompany me. He agreed that the North Florida Coast excursion in March was a good idea.

I got it in my head that a camping-motorcycle tour was just the sort of adventure I needed. It would also help us decide how to load the bikes with the essentials for camping. I had no idea it would be a death sentence for the quasi-relationship.

C. Dick had biked and camped before, so he did what he did best: tell me what to assemble, how to assemble it, and why I needed to assemble it. The man wasn't content unless he was telling me what I needed to do.

I bought a one-person sleeping bag—there was no need for a two-person sleeping bag—and several other pieces of gear that would make sleeping on the wet, hard ground comfortable. C. Dick had a small, two-person tent—I was shocked he didn't request two, one-person tents—a cooler, and two foldable chairs. He also told me I needed a new rear tire—which I didn't.

This type of directive was C. Dick's way of passively-aggressively expressing his hostility and discontent: If you don't do this, I won't do this. To keep the peace, I took Bessie to Jerry, my mechanic, a few weeks before it was time to depart. He looked at the rear tire and deemed it "more than safe." I rationalized the purchase of a new tire by asking Jerry to rotate the almost-new front tire to the back and put a brand-new tire on the front. That way, I could leave in a few months on my summer trip with very little mileage on the rubber. It made sense to Jerry, it pleased C. Dick, but it left a hard knot in the pit of my stomach.

Bessie, with her new tire, was loaded snugly with my camping gear for the trek to Florida's north coast. C. Dick's bike carried his gear plus some with no problem. We embarked on a cool, foggy morning from Central Florida, wearing heavy leather to ward off the chill.

US 19 North is one of my favorite roads in Florida. Before Interstate 75 cut a swath through pine forest and swamp, Route 19 was a major thoroughfare for travelers heading north and south. As interstates tend to do, I-75 sucked the life out of many mom-and-pop hotels dotting Route 19, leaving ramshackle pay-by-the-hour lodgings, or worse, abandoned dwellings. A few have had the tenacity to hang on, the soft glow of their ancient neon signs acting as a beacon to welcome travelers who shun the interstate. The tiny towns of Otter Creek, Chiefland, and Cross City are no more than wide spots in the road, simple places to buy gas or bait, or go to a feed store and a few local, down-home, southern-cooking type restaurants.

The two-lane highway was smooth and virtually free of traffic, and the sun had warmed up the air considerably, making our ride north pleasurable.

Just outside of Perry, Florida, C. Dick and I picked up US 98 West, another forgotten piece of highway once Interstate 10 provided a faster, more direct east-west route over the swamps of North Florida. US 98 hugs the irregular coastline along the Gulf of Mexico with spectacular views of Apalachee Bay from a surprising higher elevation for an otherwise flat state.

Just past St. Marks, I saw billboards advertising the Worm Gruntin' Festival taking place in April in Sopchoppy, a funky little town of 500 or so residents, nestled in the southeast corner of the Apalachicola National Forest. It claims the title of the Worm Gruntin' Capital of the World.

My curiosity got the better of me, so when we stopped for gas, I googled the words: *Worm Gruntin' Festival.* According to the blog, *Florida Backroads Travel*:

> Worm grunting is a technique to make earthworms come to the ground surface so they can be collected and used for fish bait. When that activity gets boring, folks turn it into a competitive sport. In Sopchoppy, they call it "worm gruntin'" and they've had an annual festival to showcase their skills since 2000. Worm gruntin' involves vibrating the soil. This makes the worms crawl up to the surface because they think the sound is made by moles digging in the soil to have a worm snack.

I was fascinated with the YouTube video that showed the process of worm gruntin' and was genuinely sorry we wouldn't be around for the festivities, especially the Worm Gruntin' Ball where one lucky woman would be crowned Worm Gruntin' Queen.

Our destination that day was Indian Pass Campground with its primitive tent sites, overlooking Apalachicola Bay and the Gulf of Mexico near Port St. Joe. The north coast of Florida, or Big Bend area as it's called, is home to several barrier islands such as St. George, St. Joseph, St. Vincent and several more; some are inhabited, most are not.

C. Dick and I pulled up to the general store and office to claim our piece of shoreline for three days of unrefined outdoor pleasure. I was no stranger to camping. My grandparents had taken me on their RV camping excursions when I was very small. My daughters and I tent-camped all over the United States during summer vacations. I had an intrepid spirit and considered myself an experienced camper and lover of all things woodsy.

After registering the bikes and paying the fee, C. Dick and I slipped and slid our way back to the camp spot on a mucky, gravel lane. I looked at our surroundings and lost a bit of my intrepidness. We were literally a stone's throw away from the water, where crabs lurched sideways along the sand at low tide. There were no pink-tinged, white sand beaches like what was at Fort Walton Beach. Here was a sticky-looking sludge, ringed with foam. Several foul-smelling fishing boats, anchored with bright orange buoys, bobbed in the water. To the left of our camp spot, bordering the poor-excuse-for-a-road we had just navigated, was a swamp, although the term used in the Indian Pass Campground brochure was "forested wetland." It doesn't matter how you spin it—a swamp is a swamp.

Bessie and I followed C. Dick into the numbered slot of swamp that was designated "ours" for the next three days. When I planted my feet on either side of Bessie, I heard a wet, squishing noise, which was the ground underneath me. Once I put the kickstand down, I prayed Bessie wouldn't slip and disappear into the primordial ooze. I wasn't a tourist; I knew all too well what crawled out of swamps in Florida, and

I was confident I didn't bring a tarp strong enough to ward off a slithering invasion of reptiles or act as protection against the sodden ground.

I put my game face on despite our dismal surroundings. I was eager to set up camp before the darkness unleashed the naked, muddy people whose faces were scarred with rage from the nearby swamp as in Dante's *Inferno: The Fifth Circle of Hell.* Pulling gear off the bikes, I put it carefully on the adjacent picnic table, fearful of anything dry touching the soggy surroundings.

C. Dick was in full, camp-director mode, telling me where to put this and where to put that, creating our home-away-from-home among the palmettos.

While C. Dick set up the tent, I plodded my way back along the road, making a mess of my riding boots in the wet sand, to where I had seen the restrooms and showers. Although the accommodations were clean and free of anything reptilian, they were a good two blocks from our tent. That meant squatting near the tent for middle-of-the-night nature calls in swampy darkness with my rear end exposed to whatever Dante's hell could imagine. I slept with the flashlight close-by.

C. Dick and I survived the primordial ooze and damp, chilly nights and enjoyed our tour of Apalachicola, Pensacola, and the barrier islands of the North Shore.

As we ate the large platter of fresh, steamed oysters at Boss Oyster in Apalachicola on our last night, I raised the subject of embarking on the Lake Superior trip with me in July. C. Dick was non-committal and commenced telling me things I would need to do before I could "safely" leave in the summer. As I listened to him make excuses, I became fully aware he would never accept a woman who rode her own motorcycle or made her own decisions.

The trip to North Florida ended with a lukewarm see-you-later between us when we arrived at my exit off the interstate.

When C. Dick and I talked a few weeks later, I caught him in a lie regarding another woman. I gently explained that it really made no difference to me as I just wasn't interested in continuing the charade. I wished him well and thanked him for the fun times. I sent him a text on the July morning I left for Lake Superior: *Headed north, soul-o.*

I ran into C. Dick a few years later at a biker hangout that I had introduced him to. He was with the woman he had been seeing all along in the spring of 2011 on the alternate weekends he was not with me. Turns out "Mandy" preferred to ride on the back of C. Dick's bike, not on her own. He asked about my Lake Superior trip. I told him it was spectacular. I had made it all the way into Canada and back without any of the gear he insisted I needed—and without him. Before he could respond, I said, "It was really good to see you again and meet Mandy."

Then I pivoted, turned, climbed astride Bessie and rode off into the sunset, *soul-o.*

SPIRIT ANIMAL

There is a time in life when you expect the world to be always full of new
things. And then comes a day when you realize, that is not how it will
be at all. You see that life will become a thing made of holes. Absences.
Losses. Things that were there and are no longer. And you realize, too,
that you have to grow around and between the gaps; though you can put
your hand out to where things were and feel that tense, shining dullness
of the space where the memories are.

–Helen Macdonald, *H is for Hawk*

MY CELL PHONE LIT UP WITH A NUMBER I DIDN'T RECOG-
nize. Reluctantly, I touched *accept*. "Deb, it's Cynthia. Where are you?"

Cynthia was an acquaintance, hardly a friend, so why was she
tracking me down when all who *were* friends knew I was traveling
on Bessie?

"Hey, Cynthia. I'm with my brother at his lake house in southern Indiana. What's up?" I asked suspiciously.

It was the Fourth of July weekend, 2011. Sweetwater Lake in Brown County, Indiana, was abuzz with summer parties, filled with holiday sounds: speedboats cutting across the lake, water slapping against the boathouse as the waves rolled into the cove, laughter ringing out in every direction, mixed with a steady backbeat of music. Meaty aromas from dozens of outdoor grills flavored the air. Bessie and I had arrived a few days earlier to enjoy the curvy, hilly back roads of Brown County and visit with my brother and his family.

"I called to tell you how sorry I am," Cynthia offered.

"Sorry? Sorry for what?" I asked. My words tinged with agitation.

"Oh, God, you don't know? You haven't heard…." Her voice trailed off, and my guts did a flip flop as my heart raced.

"Cynthia, what the hell are you talking about?" I half-screeched into my phone.

"Butch. Butch went down on his bike outside of Atlanta on I-75. He died instantly." And the rest of her words were an echo, drowned out by the sounds of summer floating off Sweetwater Lake.

I was sitting in a comfortable Adirondack chair on the deck, over-looking the cove, watching the family dogs scamper in and out of the water. My brother David tended the grill, and my sister-in-law Jacquie sat near me. My field of vision became a pinpoint of light as I tried to hang onto my phone and grapple with the words Cynthia kept spewing into my ear.

"I'm sorry. I thought someone would have called you by now," she prattled. "Are you alone? Is there someone with you?"

Dear God, why is she still talking?

"Stop, Cynthia, stop! How do you know this?" I queried.

"His son posted a call for prayers on his Facebook page with some of the details," she whimpered.

Now I remembered how she was connected to Butch. Cynthia went to school with Butch's son. Cynthia, who was one of those people who wallowed in the macabre, was enjoying the attention she was getting by delivering this gruesome news to me. I needed to disengage quickly and gather my thoughts.

"I've got to go, Cynthia. I need to make some phone calls." And I tapped *end* before she could sputter any further second-hand information.

My heart felt heavy. I glanced over at Jacquie and related the news.

My family never knew Butch, never met him. All they knew was that for a few years, I had this person called Butch in my life and that he was the motivation for me getting my bike.

Jacquie offered her concern while I quickly excused myself to find some quiet inside the house to gather my thoughts. I had severed ties with Butch a few years back, but we remained friends, occasionally taking a ride together or sharing a laugh via text messages about our experiences while riding. I knew he was traveling with a friend this summer. He had called a few weeks ago to ask if he could borrow my spare helmet for the trip.

Butch had sent me a few text messages over the last few weeks as he reported on his travels. He texted two days ago that he was in the Black Hills of South Dakota, and by that night, he sent a note to say he and his friend were in New Mexico. I calculated the distance in my head—more than eight hundred miles! Typical Butch mode of travel. I responded with my own text, "Are you crazy?! You are going too far too fast, as usual. Why don't you stop and take in the sights you seem to be flying by at ninety miles an hour?"

After I had texted Butch that he should slow down, he had written, "I love you. I will wait for however long it takes."

Wait for what? I wondered. *However long it took for me to realize I made a mistake walking away from a detrimental relationship? That* was Butch—ego running rampant. Most women didn't walk away from Butch's spell; they stayed locked in his web of deception. Butch lusted after what he could not have. Little did I know his words to me would be the last text message he ever sent.

My daughter Caroline texted me when she heard the news of Butch's accident, and I called to assure her I was okay and to calm her fears. Although she has always supported my decision to ride a motorcycle, I know Caroline fears the worst, much like I do whenever she gets in her car and backs out of the driveway.

While we talked, Caroline asked me to abandon my plans to circle Lake Superior and come home instead. I gently told her I would consider her suggestion, but the likelihood of something happening to me on the way home was just as real as my continuing on this trip.

For those of us with a rogue spirit, the choice to ride a motorcycle is a logical one; no explanation is necessary. For those who don't ride, no explanation is possible. An anonymous quotation we riders take to heart is this: "Four wheels move the body; two wheels move the soul."

My beloved Bessie came along at a critical time of transition in my life, and she has saved me many times over. If I should die on two wheels, please know that I will die chasing my passion and pursuing what feeds my soul. Butch perished doing what he loved. How many of us will be as lucky to leave this mortal earth in that fashion? To share the same spirit with others who feel the same is a rare gift indeed.

I had planned this summer's trip for several months, first with C. Dick, then solo. I had no intention of abandoning my plans because of an unfortunate accident. Butch wouldn't have wanted that. I decided to honor his shortened journey and take his spirit with me.

My immediate plans were to enjoy the Fourth of July weekend with my family, traverse the back roads of Brown County, Indiana, and then head north to visit my dad. I wanted to spend time with him both before and after my Lake Superior trip.

I said goodbye to David and his family two days later, which was the following Monday. Unlike most of the state, portions of southern Indiana are hilly and offer some incredible roads for riding. The Hoosier National Forest and its 266 miles of trails spreads south from Bloomington, all the way to the Kentucky River. The yellow, orange, and red foliage in the fall is spectacular.

I headed out toward the Monroe Reservoir, the largest lake in the state besides Lake Michigan, to enjoy a ride on a typically humid, sultry Indiana summer day. I embraced the curvy asphalt and allowed my thoughts to drift toward memories of Butch.

Every unique memory of Butch involved our time together on two wheels. He and I rode the Natchez Trace Parkway, a two-lane, 444-mile highway from Nashville, Tennessee, to Natchez, Mississippi. We said a prayer for the fallen Civil War soldiers on Prospect Hill at Fredericksburg Battlefield National Park.

Butch and I traveled north on US 61, called Blues Alley, and stood at the Devil's Crossroads in Clarksdale, Mississippi, where Robert Johnson, according to blues legend, sold his soul to the devil in exchange for talent to play the guitar. He wrote and recorded "Cross Road Blues," but the song doesn't refer to the myth about Johnson.

It was a gift to ride with Butch to the far reaches of West Texas with its blistering heat and the sweet smell of the pecan groves.

We rode the tattered remnants of historic Route 66 through Oklahoma, the Texas Panhandle, and New Mexico, and then journeyed on to the Grand Canyon. We witnessed the lights of Las Vegas illuminate the desert sky and later crossed the Mojave Desert as the July heat seared our lungs. North of Malibu, Butch and I navigated the Pacific Coast Highway, marveling at the spectacular Pacific Ocean as we hugged the rugged coast on two wheels. We leaned into one dizzying curve after another, through tropical storms—and the emotional storm our coupling caused those we loved—along the shorelines of both east and west coasts. These memories are treasures, never to be forgotten. I will grow around yet another absence in my life, as I'm learning to do with the absence of my youngest daughter.

I felt relieved to see Dad again; he heard the sad news about Butch and offered his condolences. We sat at the kitchen table, having finished one of Dad's famous grilled dinners. I pushed the plates aside to make room for my atlas and form concrete plans for the next leg of my journey before my resolve faded, and I buckled under Caroline's request to come home. Butch's memorial was scheduled for the following week, and I wanted to be on the North Shore of Lake Superior in Canada, far removed from the assemblage of mourners with their grief and drama.

Since I intended to visit the Harley-Davidson Museum in Milwaukee, Wisconsin, there was no way to avoid Chicago unless I wanted to make a giant sweep toward the southwest and add a full day to my travels. Dad and I scrutinized the atlas and discussed options, finally giving in to the fact I would be driving around the southwest side of the city. Then I did something I rarely do: I made hotel reservations in Milwaukee to shore up my resolve and guarantee that I would strike out the next morning. I planned to arrive in Milwaukee by early afternoon. Later that evening with Dad, I packed my bag and set the alarm for o-dark-thirty so I could navigate around Chicago with the least number of weekday morning commuters.

Dad had the coffee going when I awoke, and as we silently sipped the hot brew, he slid an envelope across the table. I knew it held the proverbial emergency cash Dad always put in my hands at moments like this one. No matter how old I was, Dad felt the need to make sure I had enough money in case of an emergency. I started to protest, but I caught myself. This was how he absolved himself of worry for his vagabond daughter. I said, "Thank you," hugged him, told him I loved him and would see him again in a week or so while gulping down the remaining coffee in my mug.

In the early morning darkness, Bessie and I headed out between the soybean and corn fields of Central Indiana, feeling woefully alone. I chose back roads to take me west, then north before encountering the dense traffic that would pummel me around Chicago and on into Milwaukee.

I was on Indiana SR 18, just north of Lafayette, home of Purdue University, when the sun started to rise behind me, casting a chilly pink glow around the farmland and me. I had not encountered a single vehicle since I left the outskirts of Muncie.

My thoughts bounced between anticipation of my destination and the apprehension of traveling alone. *I could turn back—the coffee was still hot in Dad's kitchen. No! No! No!* My resolve grew firmer.

Then, up ahead and to my left, something moved and caught my eye. Leaving before dawn and riding back roads increase the odds of making unwanted contact with animals. I was hyperaware and slowed the bike, keeping my eye on the movement. I soon realized it was a huge hawk sitting near the cornfield, just off the asphalt. I moved closer to the opposite side of the road, giving the bird ample room if it decided to take flight.

As I approached at a speed of thirty miles per hour or so, the hawk spread its wings and gracefully rose out of the cornfield and seemingly hovered there until I was adjacent to it on the road. I was spellbound; the giant bird looked right at me, and then flew at eye level at my pace. I looked back at the road, then back at the bird who had its head turned in my direction. We traveled side-by-side for what seemed like minutes; then, the hawk dipped its head and right wing in my direction as if to say, "Safe travels; all will be okay "and flew over my head, disappearing in the distance.

My body shook, and I felt an out-of-body experience as the morning chill intensified the feeling. I had no words for this experience. It was not the first time a bird of prey had appeared in my life during times of anxiety and loss. It had happened often enough that my friend, Charmian, encouraged me to research my spirit animal. From a variety of New Age material I found online about spirit animals, I learned that when a hawk shows up in your life, you should be sensitive to the messages it may carry and be receptive to your own intuition. When the bird of prey appears in your life, it's perhaps time to be less distracted by details surrounding you and focus on a higher perspective.

My higher perspective focused on Butch at that moment. Although I had terminated a detrimental affair with Butch, we ultimately remained friends. Butch was comical, witty, adventuresome, and unconventional. He remained loyal to my desire to ride my own bike until the end of his life. For all the angst he instigated in my heart, I will miss his easy-going manner and mega-watt smile. I will miss my friend.

A half hour or so after the hawk encounter, I decided it was time for another cup of coffee while I contemplated my relationship with birds of prey.

Bessie and I arrived in Chicago before 8:00 a.m., the loops of interstate highways already clogged with commuters. I gritted my teeth, white-knuckled the handgrips, kept my eyes open while I slogged along in the "slow" lane and watched for signs signaling my route. Chicago is one of my all-time favorite cities—but not on two wheels.

I breathed a sigh of relief when I was safely on the north side on I-95 where I could glimpse Lake Michigan. It is just under a hundred miles from Chicago to Milwaukee; the two cities practically meet in the middle with only a smattering of green Wisconsin farmland in between to mark the end of one and the beginning of another. I shook off most of my tension and enjoyed the ride up to Milwaukee. The warm summer sun and the cool air off the lake made the journey north pleasant.

My hotel was downtown near the Harley-Davidson Museum, easily navigated, much to my relief. After I checked in, I called Dad to tell him I had survived the first leg of the journey and that the apprehension I felt that morning had dissipated.

I splashed my face with cold water, changed my T-shirt, and made my way over to the museum, situated at the intersection of 6th and Canal Streets, just a stone's throw from Lake Michigan. The structure is a series of colossal steel and wire mesh cubes. The museum "campus" is laid out like a small city, surrounded on three sides by the Menomonee River and Canal. I parked Bessie amid the hundred or so bikes of every size, shape, and color lined up in neat rows in the parking lot, shed my gear, and walked toward the entrance.

As I waited in line to pay the admission, I noticed the display for the Harley-Davidson Living the Legend Rivet and Memorial Wall. The three- and six-inch rivets are engraved with a personal message and embedded in the curved memorial wall on the museum grounds. A rivet is a metal pin or bolt that joins two pieces of metal together (You also have rivets in your Levi jeans). The purchase of a rivet testifies to your commitment to living the legend—and Harley-Davidson's way of making yet more money from your commitment.

I paid my admission fee and made my way to the designated counter to purchase a rivet to be engraved. The message I gave the sales lady was simple: *Ride Free Butch* with dates for his birth and death. She explained it would be six to eight weeks before the rivet was installed. That was July of 2011, and although I received confirmation the rivet was in place on the Memorial Wall with directions on how to locate it, I have never been back to see it. A close friend visited the museum in 2018, and I asked him to take a photo of Butch's rivet. Tears sprang to my eyes when I saw the shiny silver rivet, etched with his name embedded in the red brick.

I spent a leisurely afternoon touring the museum, absorbed in the history of Harley- Davidson motorcycles. The display of gear and clothing worn by early bikers fascinated me. Heavy leather kidney belts, which protected a rider's back and kidneys, with ornate carving and funky rivet designs were my favorite. I loved viewing Bessie Stringfield's and Dot Robinson's bikes as well as the original *Easy Rider* Chopper, a customized bike with a stretched-out wheel based, pulled-back handlebars, and a patriotic paint job.

After a late lunch/early dinner in one of the restaurants on the museum property, I concluded that Harley-Davidson should stick to manufacturing motorcycles and abstain from the restaurant business. The barbecue was mediocre at best though the atmosphere was charming. I made the obligatory purchase of a destination T-shirt and walked back to my bike, ready to call it a day.

After a hot shower, I recounted the day's events on my blog and posted a few pictures of the museum. I slept soundly that night, emotionally spent and physically exhausted with only one scene briefly interrupting my slumber: a soaring hawk.

TEARS IN THE WIND PART

Loss as muse. Loss as character. Loss as life.

– Anna Quindlen, *Loud and Clear*

AFTER BREAKFAST, I MADE A QUICK TOUR OF THE Milwaukee lakefront before pointing Bessie north toward Green Bay. I planned to ride the 1,300-mile Circle Tour of Lake Superior going clockwise around the lake through Wisconsin, Michigan, Minnesota, and on into Canada, where I would then turn south, traveling down the eastern shore of the lake.

This July morning, balmy and breezy with intermittent clouds filtering the sun, was my first trip through Wisconsin on two wheels. I remember touring Wisconsin Dells, known for its numerous water-parks, with my grandparents when I was a kid. We rode the *duck boats*, all-terrain contraptions that rolled along on four wheels and then plunged its summer tourists into the water, becoming amphibious for a ride across the lake. At the lake's edge, the vehicles sprouted four wheels again to deposit their riders in front of the Cheese Factory Restaurant for a tour.

I gazed in awe at the gently rolling hills dotted with dairy farms, meticulously laid out. Immaculate green and white buildings stood in stark contrast against the blue of the horizon.

North of Green Bay, I said goodbye to the interstate; for the next several days, it would be strictly back roads for Bessie and me on the Lake Superior Circle Tour.

I crossed the state line between Wisconsin and Michigan at Iron Mountain, Michigan, to pick up US Route 2, which spans 2,571 miles and is the northernmost east-west highway in the country. Heading west, I traveled the thickly wooded road that ran parallel to the state line.

The day turned cooler, and thick clouds with a smattering of foggy rain obscured the sun. I stopped to don my rain gear and check the map. Given the cooler temps and drizzle, I chose Ironwood, Michigan, the next wide spot in the road, as a destination. It was some respectable 400-plus miles from Milwaukee and seemed like the only *large* town for miles that would have a decent hotel. I was fine with the precipitation if it didn't turn into a downpour. Bessie and I cruised along, virtually the only vehicle on the road.

As I crossed into Ironwood, about twenty miles south of Lake Superior, my hopes of finding a decent hotel vanished. With a population of 5,100, Ironwood is not exactly a thriving metropolis, although it does have some ski resorts. US Route 2 appeared to be its major thoroughfare with maybe three stoplights. As I entered the city limits, I noticed a Comfort Inn, but I rode on through the town, looking left and right for another option. Not seeing one that would qualify as a decent place to spend the night, I turned around in the nearest parking lot and headed back to the east side of town where I came in.

The Comfort Inn seemed delighted to have me as the clerk behind the desk sprang to her feet from a seated position when I walked through the double doors. She broke into a huge smile and said, "Welcome to Ironwood!"

Happy hour was underway in the lobby, which obviously had not been renovated since Led Zeppelin's II album was number one on the *Billboard* charts. One lone bearded gentleman was the sole participant of happy hour; his white shirt looked crisply pressed under a well-worn blue sport coat as if he were awaiting a lady friend. He didn't exactly look happy. I bypassed the spread of cubed cheese and cheap wine, eager to shed damp gear and take a hot shower.

As I relaxed and checked my phone for any calls, I picked up the in-room magazine that usually gives all the local history. I was curious about both Iron Mountain and Ironwood. Iron ore had been mined in both towns, but the mines were no longer operational, which may explain the towns' bleak appearances.

I learned Michigan's upper peninsula was loaded with copper. Demand for the mineral diminished after World War II, however, and many of the towns built around those mines were abandoned. Interestingly, the Native Americans, who once mined the copper, do quite nicely now by operating three large gambling casinos within a short drive from Ironwood. The town survived by trading mining for gambling in the dense and damp Michigan woods.

After a hot shower, I dressed in dry clothes and made my way downstairs to check out the local dining establishments. If the Comfort Inn was the pinnacle of lodging establishments in Ironwood, I didn't hold out much hope for a fine dining experience. I sauntered past the lone gentleman camped out near the happy-hour spread, strolled up to the front desk clerk, and inquired about a restaurant within walking distance. Before the desk clerk could answer, the happy-hour gentleman perked up and shouted across the room, "I'm going to the Bad

River Casino for dinner and gaming. Why don't you join me?" He was a decent-looking man, perhaps in his late sixties, with hastily coiffed white hair that was a little too long over his collar. Already inebriated on the cheap wine, he looked hopeful that I would be enticed by his offer. I smiled openly in his direction, thanked him sincerely for the offer, but declined. I let him know I had ridden a long distance, was hungry, tired, and probably would not make a good date for "dinner and gaming."

The desk clerk leaned over and whispered, "We don't get many women traveling alone through here." I made a mental note of that news, thanked her, and decided the restaurant situated a short walk across the parking lot would do just fine.

Ironwood was shrouded in a gray, grimy mist as I traipsed over to the Kountry Kitchen Restaurant, as if using a *K* instead of a *C* would somehow lend it distinction. The service was friendly with the food in the category of *komfort*, and I couldn't argue with the price. I ate the roasted chicken with mashed potatoes and green beans in silence, wondering about the cuisine at the Bad River Casino.

I would like to write that the *morning dawned bright and warm*, but alas, it did not. My research for this trip had warned of the nagging precipitation that hovered along the coastline of Lake Superior. My rain gear was still damp from yesterday's trip; I layered up with Under Armour cold gear and my leather chaps.

I continued my journey on US Route 2, which passed through the Bad River Indian Reservation—the Bad River Band is a branch of the Lake Superior Tribe of Ojibwa Indians—situated between Ironwood and Ashland, Wisconsin. My destination was Thunder Bay in Ontario, Canada, which lies on the western shore of Lake Superior.

I caught my first glimpse of Lake Superior near Ashland. Stopping at a park, I walked along a boardwalk into Chequamegon Bay, a Lake Superior inlet, and snapped a few pictures. The photo I took of the boardwalk disappearing into the horizon, filled with dark, angry clouds hovering over the lake, remains one of my favorites.

Outside of Ashland, I made my way onto Wisconsin Route 13, also known as State Trunk Highway. It hugs the coastline as it makes a northern swing, ensconcing the tip of Bayfield Peninsula that juts out towards the Apostle Islands National Lakeshore.

As I traveled north, the misty rain diminished, the terrain became elevated, and by the time I reached Bayfield, the sun was shining. To say that Bayfield, Wisconsin, is picturesque doesn't do it justice. Consisting of roughly 500 permanent residents and situated on the south shore of Lake Superior, Bayfield is a kaleidoscope of color. Stately Victorian homes, painted in explosions of yellow, lavender, pastel pink, and lime green sit on the hillside, their landscapes abloom with flowers. The downtown brick buildings are awash in colorful murals depicting the town's history as a lumbering town, commercial fishing port, and a region with rich, Native American history.

I parked Bessie along the busy street filled with late afternoon shoppers. Downtown Bayfield is the primary shopping district as the large, commercial malls had not infiltrated the outskirts of town to siphon business away from local merchants. I strolled around town and snapped photos of the meticulously preserved architecture and color-ful murals. My favorite was the block-long American flag, fronted by school-age children in every shape, size, and ethnic group who were celebrating education.

Bayport is the gateway to the Apostle Islands, a scenic archipel-ago of twenty-two forested islands, rimmed with sandstone sea caves, nine historic lighthouses, and whitetail deer, black bear, snowshoe hare, ruffed grouse, beaver, and myriads of other wildlife. Bayfield is one of the few destinations on my list of Places to Revisit Someday to enjoy once again the many earthly gifts the area offers.

The only way to appreciate the Apostle Islands is to take one of the cruises leaving the Port of Bayfield, or for the truly adventuresome, go sea kayaking. However, on this trip, Bessie and I were content to meander around the marina, watch the tourists, and relish a late breakfast before continuing our two-wheeled journey. An island cruise or sea kayak will be on my list of things to do when I make a repeat visit to Bayfield and the Apostle Islands.

Back on the road by late morning, I rounded the tip of the peninsula, comprised of the Red Cliff Indian Reservation, where the Red Band of Lake Superior Chippewa live, and skirted the lake in a southwesterly direction. The misty shroud reclaimed the landscape as Bessie and I headed for Duluth, Minnesota. The Twin Ports of Superior, Wisconsin, and Duluth, Minnesota, are the largest freshwater shipping ports in the world. The closer I got to the metropolitan area, the harder the cold, wet wind blew off the lake.

The foreboding lyrics of Gordon Lightfoot's 1976 hit, "The Wreck of the Edmund Fitzgerald," popped into my head and refused to leave as the skies remained gloomy.

I was thankful it was July and not November. The mist turned into a heavy drizzle as I navigated I-35 around Duluth. Huge shipping vessels were moored at the docks on the lakeside, and the crumbly, archaic buildings downtown were void of any shiny new architecture. I had no plans to sightsee, and Duluth did not make my list of Places to Revisit Someday.

I picked up US 61 heading north along the lake. It is the same Route 61, known as Blues Alley in Mississippi, where Butch and I stood at the crossroads of US 49 and US 61 outside of Clarksdale. The rain, now just short of a downpour, bordered on making the ride miserable.

The scenery evolved into spectacular despite the rain; the highway ran adjacent to the Superior National Forest, comprised of more than three million acres, and hugged the shoreline with a sweeping vista elevated above Lake Superior. Waterfalls seemed to be everywhere as signs pointed the way off the highway to one state park after another. I stopped in Two Harbors for gas and hot coffee to ward off the chill. A quick check of the map revealed I needed to journey another two-and-a-half hours to arrive in Grand Portage, where I would cross into Canada. I was impatient to get to Thunder Bay and dry out; it was another hour's trek from Grand Portage.

The border crossing into Canada was uneventful; I guess I looked more like a drowned rat at that point than a suspicious smuggler. The relentless rain had saturated my thick leather riding gloves; my numb fingers were white with cold, and my neck and shoulders were tense and achy as I gripped the handlebars. The only commerce between Grand Portage and Thunder Bay was a casino where I stopped to change American dollars into Canadian dollars.

Quite unexpectedly, tears started to flow as I stood clutching my Canadian currency in the casino lobby that smelled like stale cigarettes and the worst hangover I ever experienced. I had not shed a single tear since hearing of Butch's demise. A combination of grief, cold, wetness, and anxiety had finally found its way to the surface and emptied over my already wet face. A crying jag heaved its way up out of the center of my solar plexus with thick, gasping sobs.

Through hot, blinding tears, I grabbed the paper money the bewildered cashier thrust through the tiny hole from behind the glass window, staring expectantly past me as if he was anxious for the next customer who might be devoid of tears. I stuffed my Canadian currency into my fanny pack and quickly exited the foul-smelling lobby. As I walked back to my bike, struggling to pull on wet gloves over cold fingers, the tears kept flowing. I straddled Bessie, eager to exit the casino parking lot, swiping angrily at the tears. The highway was slick from the light rain as I made my way out of the casino parking area. It was early afternoon, but the low cloud cover made it seem like dusk; I shared the roadway with no vehicles, only the dense forest that bordered the highway on both sides.

Alone with my grief, I gave into the anguish. Great sobs rose from my chest, snot soaked into the balaclava shielding my face, and the wind took my tears while I rode closer to Thunder Bay, Ontario.

OLD WOMAN BAY

You can't stop time. You can't capture light. You can
only turn your face up and let it rain.

– Kim Edwards, *The Memory Keeper's Daughter*

THUNDER BAY, THE LARGEST CITY IN WESTERN ONTARIO,
has roughly 120,000 citizens, dominated by the highest concentration
of Finnish people outside of Finland. Aboriginals compose the second
most populous group. In my research for this trip, I also discovered that
Thunder Bay has the highest per-capita rate of homicides of any city in
Canada, which is not exactly banner news to post on the Chamber of
Commerce website.

I stopped at the first hotel—a decent looking Travelodge—I
encountered off the interstate. I felt road-weary, wet, tired, exhausted
from crying, and I wanted to get settled while it was still daylight.
Oddly enough, I had not seen another motorcycle the entire day. The

1,300-mile Lake Superior Circle Tour (there is a circle tour of all five of the Great Lakes) is popular among the traveling biker crowd, so it was unusual that I had not run across any other bikers.

I checked in, put away my gear, showered, and headed out across the parking lot to see what was within walking distance of the hotel. Not much. Thunder Bay was gritty, decaying with an abundant population of mostly indigenous street people. I didn't feel adventuresome in a city with the highest homicide rate in Canada, so I ducked into a grocery store to purchase fresh fruit, a deli sandwich, and munchies. On my return walk, I noticed the Thunder Bay Harley-Davidson dealership adjacent to the hotel, tucked off the main thoroughfare. Already closed for the day, the shop opened at ten o'clock in the morning. The only item I needed from Thunder Bay was a destination T-shirt.

I awoke early, before 5:00 a.m., as usual, although I had no plans to leave until after 10:00 a.m. I drew back the curtains to discover the thickest fog I had ever seen, and I literally could not see the parking lot. I headed downstairs in search of coffee, convinced that the fog would burn off by time to leave. Coffee service was laid out adjacent to the front desk; I poured a large cup, added the flavored creamer, and strolled over to the front windows to peer into the fog.

As I sipped the hot coffee, the desk clerk mentioned the fog was "typical" and probably wouldn't burn off anytime soon. I wandered around the main floor of the hotel, sipping my coffee and killing time until the Harley shop opened at ten o'clock.

The hotel was old, probably built in the sixties. Heavy damask curtains covered the windows, and a muddy maroon, indoor-outdoor-type carpet covered the hallways. A sign boasted of a "conference center" that was adjacent to the small regional airport. I meandered back to the restaurant, not exactly hungry, but the effort of ordering and eating breakfast would fill up the time.

After breakfast, I dressed for the ride, organized my bags, and carried my gear downstairs. I stood outside the lobby door and couldn't see a thing past an arm's length in front of me. Luckily, I had parked under the portico, but I only saw my motorcycle when I practically tripped over it. After I stowed my gear, I braved a walk across the parking lot to the Harley-Davidson store, warily choosing my steps through the seemingly impenetrable fog.

When I walked into the store, the young girl behind the counter, her well-endowed figure clad in a Harley-Davidson T-shirt and jeans, exclaimed, "You didn't ride in this weather, did you?"

"Not exactly. When does this kind of fog burn off?"

"Oh, it might burn off by early afternoon, but then it will set in again at dusk," she said.

I had checked the weather earlier, which said nothing about pea soup fog; it only mentioned warmer temperatures of around seventy degrees. Warm is relative, depending on where you live. In Florida when it "drops" to seventy degrees, I normally choose a long- sleeved T-shirt over a short-sleeved T-shirt for a ride. I had a narrow window of opportunity to make it safely to Marathon, Ontario, that day. Inching my way back across the parking lot after making my purchase, I stood next to Bessie, pondering my next move. Killing time in Thunder Bay seemed a cruel twist of irony.

I returned to the hotel restaurant for more coffee and saw two bikes under the portico; at last—two-wheel travelers! Both riders—men about my age—stood in the lobby looking lost, so I introduced myself. They had just come from where I was headed and indicated there was no fog a few miles north of town. They felt bewildered by the wall of vapor they had hit in Thunder Bay. Relieved to hear the road ahead was clear, I made plans to leave, although exiting town through the fog remained an obstacle.

Following my map, I decided to bike onto Highway 1, the Trans-Canada Highway outside of Thunder Bay, which is an east to west route across all ten Canadian provinces. Dressed in my heavy leather, Bessie and I crept cautiously across the parking lot to the access road. Just like pilots, I was flying on instruments to make it to the highway, but once I had a few miles behind me, the fog started to lift, just as my biker friends had promised. I felt optimistic.

Trans-Canada Highway is a more majestic name than the road warrants. It was still a back road, a two-lane route that gradually pulled away from Lake Superior, leaving the thickest fog behind. I traveled north to Nipigon, Ontario, part of the Thunder Bay district. Interestingly, a crater on Mars is named for this town.

I stopped for fuel and said hello to two more bikers traveling in a counterclockwise route around the lake. When making the circle tour, you must stop at each opportunity to top off your gas tank because fuel isn't always available in the small towns on Lake Superior's north shore. I would never have made it from Thunder Bay to Marathon on Bessie had I not topped off in Nipigon as there was no other fuel stop.

Nipigon Bay separates the mainland from uninhabited St. Ignace Island and Lake Superior beyond; it was a tranquil ride with cloudless skies. I felt unburdened by my grief, having left my tears in the wind as I made my way to Thunder Bay. My head was clear and the realization of achieving my ride destination as I rounded Lake Superior filled me with anticipation.

I stopped at Rainbow Falls Provincial Park, consisting of 1,421 acres, where I encountered my first *inukshuk*, a figure made of piled stones or boulders, assembled to communicate with or guide other humans throughout the Arctic region. Traditionally constructed by the Canadian and Alaskan Inuits, the native word *inuksuk* means "to act in the capacity of a human." The Inuits used them as helpers for navigation, as aids for hunters, and as clues to where food caches were stored.

Today, the inukshuk is an expression of welcome, an indication of available food and lodging, or simply a sign that you are on the right path. Seeing those unusual stone formations for the first time created for me a lifelong fascination with their shapes and meanings. They seemed to represent the balance I was seeking in my life.

The park was almost empty. I paid the small entrance fee, parked Bessie, and ventured onto one of several boardwalk paths. Although the locals considered the weather warm, I was comfortable in Under Armour cold gear and leather chaps. The sun made frequent appearances through the ever-present mist, making my solo hike through the woods pleasant.

Oddly enough, I felt completely in the present moment on my hike through the forest. The crushing grief of yesterday was gone. I felt free to grasp the brisk air, absorb the warm sunshine, and revel in my aloneness. Yes, I bore the gentle sorrow of having lost a former lover and good friend in Butch, but my grief was tempered with a triumph of the spirit. I had embarked on this journey after disengaging myself from one injurious relationship after another. I honored my instincts where the last two men in my life were concerned, walked away from the heartache, and put the experience behind me—in my rearview mirror where they belonged.

The Black Sturgeon River begins near Lake Nipigon and flows into Black Bay on Lake Superior, generating a chain of waterfalls. The worn, wooden boardwalk, slick with mist from the falling water, ended where a series of large, flat boulders created a wall for the rushing water. I stood at the end of the boardwalk as the rapidly moving water sliced through the woodsy silence; a cooling spritz from the water tickled my face.

I climbed out onto the nearest rock, which was the size of the hotel room I slept in last night, and took a seat near the edge. The intermittent sun had warmed the rocks, and I felt the heat through my jeans—a pleasant, earthy feel that I welcomed. Like a reptile warming its cold blood, I lifted my face to the sun and said a prayer of gratitude for my safe travels thus far. The clean, brisk pine smell of the woods, the sound of rushing water, the heat from the rocks—all blended to make me drowsy. I could have spent a few hours in my reptilian repose, but I remembered the fog and its propensity for moving in toward late afternoon. I hiked back to my bike, stowed my camera, and headed to Ontario's Highway 17.

Outside of Nipigon, the highway takes an easterly track, bringing travelers back to Lake Superior and the fog. I kept an eye out for service stations—there were none—and I felt thankful I had topped off my gas tank in Nipigon.

Near Schreiber, Ontario, the northernmost point on Lake Superior, the topography changes dramatically. The hard, rocky terrain dips significantly toward Lake Superior, which seems to be perpetually cloaked in fog, but an occasional breeze or a brief appearance of the sun opens a stunning view of blue water.

My next stop before Marathon, the Aguasabon Falls and River Gorge near Terrance Bay, Ontario, was barely a heartbeat off the highway. I parked in the small lot, populated with more tourists than I had seen in two days, though still a small crowd of perhaps thirty people hiking off in different directions from the parking area. I come from Central Florida, the land of seventy-two million tourists a year; therefore, I'm surprised at the absence of crowds at a "tourist attraction."

The mist off the falls made the wooden boardwalk slippery as I slowly walked to the viewing platform. I heard the roar of the waterfalls before I saw them. A distant rumble and crash of water falling from a great height slashed through the stillness of the woods. The falls drop more than one hundred feet into the Aguasabon River, which feeds into Lake Superior. Forest and fog obscured the lake, but the view of the cascading water was magnificent, second only to my first sight of Niagara Falls in upstate New York. Since I was living in the dark ages—before selfie-sticks—I waited for another tourist to gingerly walk out onto the platform so I could ask him to take a photo of me with the falls in the background.

The kind soul took my smaller camera, and after a few minutes of instruction and where to find the shutter, he managed to snap a picture, which remains one of my favorites to this day. I am smiling, happy, triumphant in heavy leather, having made my way on Bessie to this point.

As the day neared the late afternoon, the thick fog and condensation grew heavier. From Terrace Bay. I calculated the distance to Marathon, Ontario, at fifty-one miles. It would be a wet but blissfully short ride.

I smelled it before I saw it. The gory, coppery, savage aroma of death mixed with wet asphalt —the visceral smell of fresh roadkill. I slowed down, knowing that if I had to make a sudden stop, it would be slippery and potentially lethal. The odor grew stronger. Bloody chunks of raw meat and large animal parts were strewn across my path. Up ahead, I could see flashing red lights and a semi-tractor trailer rig pulled off to the side of the road. The carnage was everywhere, making the rain-slick highway even more slippery with entrails from a massive animal.

I slowed to a stop as the highway patrolman routed the sparse traffic around the worst of the carnage. Fur and guts were splattered across the front of the semi; the driver helped the trooper direct traffic. It was moose season in Canada, and I surmised the truck had hit one. *Thank you, God, it wasn't Bessie who encountered the moose. We wouldn't have had a chance.* I navigated around the mess, more than eager to call it a day.

Marathon, a tiny town of 400 souls, is tucked into a foggy cove on Lake Superior's north shore. I spotted a Travelodge as I turned off Highway 17 toward town but ventured farther off the road to see what else was available. At just past five o'clock in the afternoon, the few commercial establishments had already closed for the day. The main road into town was littered with gravel and gaping potholes that I deftly dodged for fear of disappearing into one of them.

I pulled into a little mom-and-pop motel, the Marathon Harbor Inn, near the center of town. As if to lend legitimacy to their nautical heritage, a giant rusty anchor was stuck firmly in the rock garden bordering the front of the building. An exceedingly tall man greeted me from behind the miniature counter in the tiny lobby. The proportion of both the man and the room were off, giving me a weird Alice-in-Wonderland vibe. I looked up, literally, at the man behind the counter to inquire about a room, and noticed he was very gaunt in an Ichabod Crane kind of way.

After I inquired about the availability and rate, Mr. Crane slid a registration card across the counter in my direction—a red flag, which signaled the likely absence of a computerized registration system and the internet. Before I committed to filling in the blanks on my registration card, I asked, "Do you have internet service here?" It was sketchy in Canada, even with my hotspot.

The lanky gentleman, dressed in a threadbare flannel shirt and worn trousers held up by dull, red suspenders, heaved an audible sigh. It was not so much a heavy sigh, as it was a painful exhalation of breath accompanied by a guttural sound a wounded animal might make. He looked down at me and said deliberately, "No, we do not have the internet." It was as though the weight of the modern world was on his shoulders; they slumped visibly with his admission, and it appeared that once again, he was forced to admit his little establishment was frozen in time.

It was as though I had asked for the Chippendale dancers to be sent to my room with the access code for the porn channel. I told him I needed internet access, and he nodded his head in understanding, snatched the blank registration card from my grasp, and dismissed me with a wave of his hand.

I decided the Travelodge was the best choice, so I made my way around the potholes and headed back toward the highway. I passed the Chubby Chicken fast-food stand that boasted a sign advertising the Spicy Mama competition the following weekend. I felt a genuine pang of regret that I wouldn't be around to see the winner. The only place open to buy provisions was a grocery store. The moose episode had squelched my appetite, but I always like to have water and fresh fruit with me.

The Travelodge was indeed the mecca of modernization in Marathon, and I spied three motorcycles in the parking lot. As I waited in line, I read the sign taped to the counter: *Beware of bears. It is mating season. Do not go out after dark. Do not leave food in your vehicle.* Check and check. I would not be guilty of either, which also told me why the town was locked up tight at five o'clock in the afternoon. The hotel restaurant was closed as well, but the lounge offered a meager happy-hour spread of cubed cheese and a scanty vegetable tray. I said a silent prayer of gratitude for having stopped at the grocery store.

My room was beyond comfy. I situated my gear and provisions with a sense of well-being not generally reserved for hotel rooms. After a hot shower, I pulled on flannel pajama bottoms and a heavy sweat-shirt. With the temperature down into the forties, it felt like winter to this Florida girl.

I enjoyed what Julia Roberts in *Pretty Woman* called a "carpet picnic" while I turned to my iPad for news of home. Much to my dismay, my hotspot didn't work for accessing the internet. I trudged out to the lobby to search for a hardwired computer. The small, happy-hour crowd seemed cheerful enough, and I settled into a chair in front of an ancient desktop next to the lounge.

The internet worked. I communicated with Caroline and started my blog post for the day. Glancing up, I saw a tall, portly man with a broad, pleasant smile walking in my direction. He introduced himself as Chuck; he had noticed my Daytona Bike Week sweatshirt and asked if one of the bikes in the parking lot was mine. Chuck was from Ohio and seemed eager for female company. We had a pleasant conversation in which he told me he was headed to Alaska and, in almost the same breath, asked if I would like to join him. *Whoa! Slow down, Chuck.*

"Sorry. I'm not interested in Alaska on this trip," I told him. He went on to tell me he had brought bear spray just in case he spotted a furry brown creature. He probably wanted me to know he served as an adequate protector should I change my mind about traveling with him. I agreed to a cup of coffee the next morning before we each went our separate ways. No bear spray needed.

I worked on my blog and checked messages for a few hours. It was nearly 10:00 p.m. when I looked up and saw this large bear of a man come tumbling through the front door, soaking wet, dressed in heavy riding leather. He slapped his hand on the counter and demanded a room. I wondered what kind of a dick was still riding at this hour in thick fog during bear mating season. Turns out, he would be D. Dick, the next Dick in my life after C. Dick.

I watched the man check in and inquire about a place to eat— *good luck with that, D. Dick. There might be a few cubes of cheese left on the happy-hour tray.* Then he left. I finished my blog, signed off the computer, and returned to my comfy room for one of the best night's sleep I've ever experienced on the road.

I woke up early, as usual, but I was in no hurry to go anywhere since fog still blanketed Marathon. The aroma of freshly brewed coffee and bacon wafted its way into my room, which was a good indication the restaurant was open, so I walked into the dining area, and there was D. Dick, waiting for a table. He turned in my direction, and asked, "Didn't I see you in the lobby last night, working on the computer?"

"Yes, you did. Didn't I see you come in from the fog and rain at ten o'clock?" I replied.

D. Dick suggested we have breakfast together, and I told him another biker would join us. Bear Spray Man appeared in the lobby right on cue. He looked stricken to see me standing with another man and even more so when I suggested we all breakfast together. After introductions all around, the three of us talked about our travels and shared an amiable breakfast. We contemplated the perils of departing in the fog, and it was obvious Bear Spray Man had a schedule to maintain, but D. Dick and I were under no time constraints. I bade farewell to Bear Spray Man who was bound for the Alaska-Canada Highway and Anchorage, Alaska. I heard from Bear Spray Man, aka Chuck, the following December. He sent me a beautiful wall calendar made from photos he took on his Alaska journey.

D. Dick and I enjoyed another pot of coffee while I heard all about his journey thus far. He had just lost his wife to cancer, and I shared a few sketchy details of losing someone close to me recently. I didn't dwell on my loss as his seemed more poignant. He had recently bought his Harley-Davidson and clicked off 12,000 miles in the last eighteen days—an audacious if not foolhardy undertaking. He lived in Medicine Hat, Alberta, and was going to Toronto. He was the only person I had met thus far who was traveling in the same direction as I around Lake Superior.

I agreed to travel with D. Dick that day; it made sense as we were going the same route, and I needed someone to act as *moose-buster* in the event we encountered any large animals on our journey around the north shore. I made it clear I preferred to go no more than five miles over the speed limit, make frequent stops for photos, and eat a leisurely lunch in the next town. He agreed.

Saturated with caffeine and eager to hit the road, D. Dick and I returned to our respective rooms to pack our gear, check out of the hotel, and load the bikes. The fog still encompassed the parking lot, but other biker friends told us it had cleared out a few miles down the road.

I wasn't optimistic, but I made sure D. Dick took the lead so I could follow his taillight as a beacon.

Just outside of Marathon, the roadside was crawling with bears of all sizes, rooting around in the brush looking for breakfast. *Where was Bear Spray Man now?* D. Dick decelerated, and I motioned frantically for him to keep moving. When we stopped a few miles ahead at a waterfall, he told me he slowed in the event I wanted to take pictures of the bears. At least he had listened to me.

Before I got off my bike, I surveyed the area for bears, then cautiously unloaded my camera from the saddlebag and snapped a few pictures. I took the time to build my first inuksuk on a giant boulder just off the road. It would be the first of many I have left in various places on my journeys, such as atop Pike's Peak, in Denali National Park, on the Cabot Trail in Cape Breton, Nova Scotia, and on the shore of Punalu'u Beach in Hawaii. They remind me that "I am on the right path."

The fog did indeed lift, revealing stunning views of Lake Superior as the elevation on the north shore rose dramatically over the lake. The air felt crisp, cold, and perfumed with pine, another riding-through-Christmas moment. The road gradually turned away from the water between Marathon and Wawa, making room for the 750-square-mile Pukaskwa National Park that juts out into Lake Superior. The curvy and elevated road, sandwiched between forest and boulders, is a motorcycle enthusiast's dream. The portion of the Lake Superior Circle Tour between Nipigon and Wawa, Ontario, is most assuredly one of the most magnificent rides I have experienced on two wheels.

The highway curved back toward the lake at Wawa, Ontario, which sits a thousand feet above the water with a panoramic view of the surrounding area. A giant Canadian goose, perched on a bluff overlooking a valley below, welcomes travelers to this wonderful little town, formerly a fur trading outpost on the eastern shore of Lake Superior. The goose is one of those whimsical, endearing roadside oddities such as Willie the Blue Whale on Route 66 in Catoosa, Oklahoma, or the World's Largest Peanut outside of Ashburn, Georgia, that greet tourists on their journeys.

After the obligatory picture with the giant goose, D. Dick and I parked in front of Young's General Store for my only encounter with a giant moose, one of the stuffed variety. Young's was made to look like a fur trading outpost and stocked everything from fishing tackle to dill pickles. I spent an hour or so wandering the aisles, picking up souvenirs small enough to tuck into my saddlebags. One piece I favored was a hand-carved stone inuksuk, fashioned into a necklace. Pacing the dirt parking lot and smoking, D. Dick was patient while I made my purchases.

The weather warmed to the point I shed my heavy leather jacket but not my Under Armour and chaps. We chose a local restaurant for lunch because the parking lot was jammed with cars and trucks near the general store.

I learned that D. Dick, in his early fifties, had retired from a government-type job involved with public energy/utilities. He had three grown children, although he didn't seem eager to talk about them. He grieved the death of his wife. One day she was well; three months later, she was gone. A man lacking ballast, D. Dick had tried to outrun his grief on a brand-new Harley-Davidson.

I chatted about my motorcycling life, trying to lighten the subject and find common ground. I took the opportunity to make it clear that I planned to travel back to the states that day and make the final leg of the circle to mark my journey "official." He sounded vague when I prodded him to commit to going on to Toronto, his original destination. We finished our lunch and bid Wawa adieu.

Just south of Wawa, the road descended toward Lake Superior Provincial Park and took us near the water. I stopped for photos as this is the last portion of the lake before the US border. I pulled into a small parking lot that overlooked Old Woman Bay, so named for a rock formation near the mouth of Old Woman River that resembles an old woman's face. It was also home to peregrine falcons.

Grabbing a plastic bag from my saddlebag, I headed toward the rocky shore, feeling the warmth of the sun on my back. I knelt to examine the stones, careful not to get my boots wet while I reached into the frigid water and scooped up wet rocks, shimmering brilliantly in the sunshine. Gently lapping waves at the shoreline and children's laughter from around the bend in the lake as they skittered in and out of the cold water were the only sounds.

The obsidian stones harbored no sharp edges; no matter their shape, the edges were smooth, worn by water, sand, and time. Water works patiently to shape rocks, pushing them ashore time after time as the sand and other rocks toil to make their surface smooth and their shapes unique.

We make memories in a similar fashion. Sometimes gently, sometimes roughly but always patiently, life pushes us back and forth along the shore, shaping our existence. It etches lines in our faces and grooves in the consciousness of the life we choose—or the life that chooses us.

Perhaps an Old Woman stood on this shore near the bay and, like the stones, was worn smooth by sand and other stones, all rolling together toward the shore, smoothing out her rough edges and making her shimmer in the sunlight as she cherished memories of her youth. She might remember her family, her children whose laughter rang out as they frolicked in the water. She might recollect her life before it crept into old age and became a distant memory. That was the story I created in my imagination of how the beach became known as Old Woman Bay.

D. Dick followed me to the beach, and, without direction or hesitation, started gathering stones and handing them to me. He seemed to realize the importance of my efforts in collecting rocks that afternoon along the shore. He respected my silent reverie, my focused task of choosing just the right ones to stow in my saddlebag. I thanked him and placed my earthen treasures in the deepest part of the saddlebag.

Before we climbed back on the bikes, D. Dick asked if he could "accompany" me a little further south. He wasn't quite ready to fly solo again toward his destination of Toronto. The man was pitiful in his plea, his sad demeanor heartbreaking. How could I say no? I reiterated my plans to travel south to Indiana to spend time with my dad before riding the final leg of the journey to Florida. He admitted he just wanted company for a few more days and would amend his travel plans. We saddled up and headed south for the final stretch of the journey in Canada.

The ride to Sault Ste. Marie, Michigan, where we would cross the border into the United States, hugged the coastline, and I relished each view of the expansive blue water. The French name means "the Rapids of Saint Mary" for the St. Mary's River nearby. Camping resorts, marinas, and a variety of summer cottages populated the area.

The border crossing was smooth but bittersweet because I had come to the end of my Lake Superior Circle Tour. The first thing I wanted to do was wash my bike; Bessie was sporting six days of road dirt, and I cannot stand for her to be dirty. It was also time to consider stopping for the night, and I still had D. Dick as extra baggage.

I pulled into a car wash where D. Dick and I spent several quarters ridding our bikes of the dirt and grime of travel. While the bikes were drying, I approached the subject as to which direction he would take now on his journey to Toronto. He indicated he would like to ride with me a little further. Not wanting to be rude, I mentioned that Traverse City looked like a great place to call it a day.

With a delayed start out of Marathon due to the fog and several stops along the way, it was already late afternoon, and D. Dick and I had logged more than 650 miles. Traverse City was another hundred miles. I made it clear to him that I was on the downhill run to *home*, with a stop in Indiana to see my family before traveling on to Florida.

Before leaving the car wash, I checked online and booked a room at a nice hotel near the water in Traverse City (love my Hotel Tonight app). We stopped on the north end of the five-mile Mackinac Bridge which spans the Straits of Mackinac between Lake Michigan and Lake Huron. The view was stunning; the sun glistened off the sapphire water on either side of the bridge. D. Dick snapped photos of me to commemorate my completing the circle tour. The Mackinac Bridge is the longest suspension bridge with anchorages in the Western Hemisphere, but that's not the scary part. The bridge features a grate for a surface instead of asphalt. You look down through the holes in the grate and see the water below. I was more than a little apprehensive as I started across, and the grated surface made for a bumpy ride on two wheels.

US 31 south from Mackinac City hugs the west coast of the upper peninsula of Michigan to Traverse City, situated in a nook on Grand Traverse Bay on Lake Michigan. The area is the largest producer of tart cherries in the United States. We enjoyed a pleasant ride through the fragrant Michigan woods with the water close by. I pulled into the parking lot of the hotel, looking forward to a relaxing evening. As we checked in, D. Dick commented, "It would be much cheaper to have one room with two double beds."

Uh, no, was the thought-bubble popping out of my head. I just smiled and signed for my room, leaving him to sign for his.

At dinner, Dick D. asked me if I would travel a "little ways out of the way" and ride west with him. He had decided against going to Toronto—I didn't ask why—and said he was going to head home to Alberta. I thanked him for the offer but declined. I just wasn't into this guy, and I saw the relationship already at its pinnacle. We were two acquaintances who enjoyed the commonality of the motorcycle. Period. And wasn't it just my luck to meet a guy in the middle of nowhere who appeared to want to fall in love and follow me home? I felt as though I had picked up a stray pup.

As we waited for our food, D. Dick seemed so forlorn after I had declined to amend my travel plans that I tried to cheer him up with a suggestion for his travel. I told him about the ferry from Traverse City to Green Bay, Wisconsin, and that if was headed back to Alberta, perhaps he'd be interested in taking the ferry rather than traveling around Lake Michigan. Explaining my research for the trip and how I had considered using the ferry as an alternate route, I showed him the website on my iPad as the waiter brought our salad and bread. He scrolled through the website and asked me questions as I munched on my salad. He liked the idea, and I helped him choose a departure time; he made an online reservation and would leave the following morning.

The next day, D. Dick and I shared breakfast in the swanky hotel by the water. He remained quiet, and I chattered aimlessly, trying to fill up the space between us. He was a man deep in the throes of grief, untethered, and withdrawn. Though I had empathy for this virtual stranger I had traveled with for the last few days, I felt no obligation to try and fix his emotional distress.

Truthfully, I was envious of his wife. Not that she was dead, but that she was so deeply missed by this man. I wondered if I would ever fall so completely in love with another human being that their passing would leave me emotionally shattered. Would their sudden absence in my life leave a gaping hole through which I would plummet helplessly? I doubted the likelihood, which made me a little sad.

We lingered over another cup of coffee, recounting our time together. I became eager to leave, D. Dick reluctant. I signaled the waiter for a check; D. Dick snatched it from the man's hands. I didn't protest but stood to leave. We packed our bikes in silence.

I led the way to the ferry landing; a large, modern building served as the terminal. I parked my bike, and he followed the signs to load his bike. While we were saying farewell, D. Dick made one final plea for me to go with him. The effort legitimately sounded fun, but the road was long, and I felt weary from travel. I declined, and both of us promised to keep in touch. I watched him pull his bike into the gaping jaws of the huge ferry and wave a final goodbye.

I turned Bessie south, solo once more. I had completed the Lake Superior Circle Tour, and I felt exuberant and fulfilled in my accomplishment, eager to see Dad again to share my adventures with him.

It was 137 miles to reach Marquette, Michigan, where I officially completed the "circle" part of the Circle Tour. When I arrived there by late morning, I found a spot along Lake Superior to snap a photo of Bessie and me in triumphant repose.

SEQUINS ARE NOT ADEQUATE PROTECTION

She wore her scars as her best attire;
a stunning dress made of Hellfire.

– Daniel Saint, poet

I DIDN'T SEE IT COMING. I HEARD A DEAFENING CRASH OF steel on steel on my left side. Then a soft, white light enveloped me. I heard a soothing female voice above my head, encouraging me to lie very still. "I'm a nurse. You've been hurt. I'll be with you until the helicopter arrives."

I struggled to swim to the surface of consciousness as I lay on the gritty asphalt, my brain spiraling, trying to grasp what was happening, but the soft light kept overtaking my consciousness again. Then my world went still.

A male voice broke through the mental fog. *Why is he asking me my name? Why can't I remember what it was?* His calm voice kept asking me whom he should call. *For what reason?* I wondered. I tried moving, but I couldn't. The reassuring female voice held my head in her hands with a vice-like grip, urging me not to move. Sounds of traffic, shouts, sirens, and frantic movement encircled me. I recognized the coppery taste of blood in my mouth.

I never saw the face of the female voice or learned her name; she was part of a group of bikers riding behind me on US 27, north of Clermont, Florida. The April day was the chamber-of-commerce kind we love in Florida: cool breeze, hot sun, cloudless sky, and fragrant air, void of the dreaded humidity destined to set in all too soon.

That Saturday in 2012 was my first attempt to ride after recuperating from a six-month bout of viral meningitis, which left me too weak to hold my bike upright. The virus had quarantined me in the hospital for two weeks and made me weak as a kitten for another four months. Although cleared to return to teaching three weeks after I contracted the virus, it took all my energy to drag myself out of bed each weekday to wrangle with teenagers. Instead of looking forward to weekend rides on Bessie, I looked forward to staying in bed, reading, and sleeping.

This solo ride to Leesburg was my maiden voyage from the meningitis funk, and I envisioned a day of riding, music, and food. However, I never made it to Leesburg; instead, I took my first helicopter ride to Central Florida's only Level One Trauma Center at Orlando Regional Medical Center.

I had no concept of time. As I plunged in and out of consciousness, I was incapable of comprehending why I was lying prone on the highway, my beloved Bessie, a twisted steel mess several feet away. I tried to move, but the comforting female voice kept urging me not to; her hands were gentle but firm on either side of my head. "Lie still; you've been badly hurt, and the helicopter is landing now," I heard her say over the deafening *whop-whop-whop* of the helicopter's rotor blades.

As I began to realize that it was *me* who had been hurt, and the trauma team was there to scrape *me* off the pavement, I started to thrash and protest, "No, no, no! This was not supposed to happen. A helicopter means I'm dying. No, no, no!"

The faceless angel kept reassuring me, "You will be okay, I promise. I'm a nurse, and you *will* be okay." And then she was gone.

The brisk and efficient EMTs, dressed in red jumpsuits and helmets, took charge. No matter how hard I tried, I couldn't hang onto consciousness. Someone kept telling me, "Hang on, stay with us."

I'm sorry, I can't, I thought. I heard a solid click, indicating the stretcher had been snapped into service near me. "I need you to stay with me. What's your name? Can you tell us your name?" someone asked.

The questions kept coming. Then an EMT turned to the onlookers, "Does anyone know who she is?" I was riding solo, so no one knew. The small leather bag I wore clipped to my belt loops containing all my identification had been torn off on impact. Someone had found my iPhone, but it was locked with a passcode. The calm male voice kept asking me, "What is the passcode? Who should I call?"

No one wakes up in the morning and says, "Life is going to change for me today, so let me make sure I do things a little differently." Life and death are not that tidy. Pending disasters do not send notices to your iPad while you sip your morning coffee: *Beware of assholes making illegal U-turns on US 27 N this afternoon!*

"One, two, three, lift!" I heard the EMT say. The pain snapped me back to awareness as they hoisted me onto the stretcher for the twelve-minute flight to Orlando Regional Medical Center. I let loose a piteous scream. Straps held me down, and I blacked out again as the chopper swallowed the stretcher and me whole. The EMTs tucked themselves neatly on either side of me. "You gotta stay with me. The next sound you'll hear is the rotors starting up. Stay with me," the EMT wearing a full helmet with dark glasses said. He was directly over my face, looking down.

The strap wrapped across my abdomen and clasped my arms tight against my body, bolting me to the stretcher. But somehow, I lifted my hand, bending my elbow below the strap toward my helmeted savior who took it in his, holding it tightly while he tried to keep me focused. I still couldn't speak or tell him my name.

A flurry of nurses in scrubs—no helmets—took control once we landed on the rooftop at Orlando Regional Medical Center, relieving the EMTs from their duty. As they pulled the stretcher out of the chopper, I heard a male voice exclaim, "Lord, have mercy! I will be glad when that damn bike rally is over!"

Misery came again. "One, two, three, lift!'" ordered a voice as the emergency room team lifted me from the stretcher onto the gurney. I realized experiencing pain was good; it told me I was still alive. I was fairly certain being dead meant I would have no pain.

Using a pair of scissors, one of the emergency room nurses started at my feet, and with one swift upward movement, she sliced my clothes completely off. I started to thrash and protest when she got to my almost-new Victoria's Secret front clasp, racerback, leopard print bra (MSRP $68). I guess nothing will bring a girl to wakefulness quicker than a threat to her high-dollar underwear. My complaints did not slow the nurses' brusque efficiency. As my clothes were sliced off, I was hooked up to an IV and someone kept asking me questions. I suddenly felt a warm, tranquil sensation, the first of multiple morphine shots to relieve the pain.

Miraculously, someone at the scene of the accident had found my cell phone and tucked it into the front pocket of my jeans, presumably by the owner of the calm male voice who kept asking me who should he call. The trauma team fished it from my pocket before depositing my bloody, shredded clothes in a plastic bag. Even more miraculous, I had managed to tell the calm male voice my phone's passcode, though no one yet knew my name. He figured out which name on my favorite's list was my daughter's. The accident was before the concept of ICE, the In-Case-of-an-Emergency acronym identified on cell phone contacts. I encourage everyone reading this to put ICE before your emergency contact name in your cell phone and to think twice about using a passcode. Because of this experience, I never use one now. In the event of an emergency, the person finding your phone will be able to call the ICE contact.

I wince each time I think about Caroline receiving a call from a total stranger, telling her that her mom had been hurt in a motorcycle accident and was being transported by helicopter to the nearest trauma center. She was a student in college at the time, and I am forever grateful for her roommate who drove her to the hospital. A close friend of the family, Steve, sat with her for more than five hours outside the emergency room, reassuring her that I would be okay.

I was admitted to the hospital as Jane Doe 37 since no one found my identification or thought to look at my bike registration, tucked inside the windshield bag, for information. When Caroline asked the ER receptionist for me by name, she was told no one by that name was a patient there, making her ordeal much more harrowing.

Amazingly, I suffered no broken bones. An unconscious person apparently bounces better than a fully conscious one who sees it coming and braces for impact. Despite three front teeth knocked out of my mouth with a fourth still dangling and ripping my upper lip in two, my jaw was intact. My left side bore the brunt of the initial contact with the other bike; later that night, my eye swelled shut and turned an angry purplish-black to match the rest of my flesh from shoulder to knee. I was one giant bruise on my left side. My right side was skinned from sliding along the asphalt, exposing the soft, red tissue underneath, much like what a tomato resembles with its skin blanched off.

The tank top I wore was trimmed in black sequins. Most women wear black sequined clothing to feel elegant; there was nothing elegant about sliding across the pavement that day. Before the accident, I dressed for the ride down main street—flashy, figure-hugging clothing that insisted on attention. After the accident, I adopted a more sensible, and protective approach to my riding attire.

It took the ER nurse, who scrubbed my road rash, an inordinate amount of time to remove the sequins embedded in my skin. At first, he thought the tiny particles were road dirt until he realized they weren't. "Oh, my God, girl! Those are *sequins* I'm pulling out of your flesh! I must say this is a first for me. I've never pulled sequins out of someone's skin. You went down in style, girl!" It hurt to laugh, but I chuckled anyway.

The only life-threatening injury I had was the gaping wound that started at the hairline on my forehead and ran halfway back to the crown of my head. I knew my daughter would kill me when she found out I wasn't wearing a helmet or underwear. The initial impact threw me from my bike, whereupon I landed squarely on my head in the middle of US 27, then skidded on my right shoulder, which remains permanently impinged and scarred horribly from the road rash.

By the time my daughter and Steve were allowed in the emergency room to see me, I was scrubbed, stitched, stapled, IVed, and suitably medicated to squash the pain. Caroline asked me two questions: "Mom, were you wearing underwear? Why didn't you have your helmet on?"

Do I know my kid or what? I had to plead guilty on both counts. While Caroline talked to me, Steve stood on the other side of the bed, solemnly picking gravel out of my blood-matted hair.

I had a severe concussion, which required an overnight stay in the hospital for observation. My daughter refused to leave my side, curling up in the recliner next to my bed for a restless night's sleep. At some point during the night, I gave into the pain. I dug down and burrowed into it, made it mine, embraced it, and celebrated in it. It reminded me I was alive, and I felt grateful. I refused any further pain medication after the initial ER cocktail wore off.

When I awoke the next morning, I felt like I had survived nine rounds as Muhammad Ali's punching bag, only to be knocked out in the tenth. When the nurse came in to take my vitals, she noticed I hadn't released any of the morphine drip since leaving the ER. I told her I didn't want any more pain meds. I explained that I was a recovering alcoholic, twenty-plus years sober, which made pain medication a slippery slope for me. Until I made a full recovery, I would take nothing more potent than Extra Strength Tylenol for the pain.

A physical therapist breezed into the room. "It's time to get up and take a walk!" she chirped. Before I could protest, she explained, "Once you walk a loop around the floor we are on, you can go home."

I hadn't moved since they finished putting me back together and tucked me into a narcotic's induced sleep in my room; even batting an eyelash was excruciating, and Doris Day wanted me to walk? I began reconsidering that morphine drip.

The therapist assured me again that if I walked, with her assistance, one loop of the entire floor, I qualified to go home since my other injuries were superficial. The nurse explained our first target was the bathroom, where I would relieve myself, indicating I had no internal injuries, and my plumbing was working correctly. I felt determined to ace every test and earn my free pass home. First, though, I had to sit up.

The nurse warned me I would be dizzy, but she didn't mention the earth would tilt on its axis while a fifty-pound sledgehammer hit me over the head, an accurate description of what I felt when the two women pulled me upright on the bed. Now, all I had to do was move my legs to the side—could someone please stop the spinning?

I slowly swung one leg at a time over the side, feet positioned to hit the floor, when I was hit with a wave of nausea so fierce I thought my stomach was turning inside out. Being the pro she was, the nurse was ready with the silver, kidney-shaped receptacle to catch my sickness. I gritted what was left of my teeth, pushed myself up off the bed, and planted both feet on the cold tile. With the nurse on one side and the physical therapist on the other, like bookends, I inched my way toward the bathroom.

The vertigo was so strong I felt like I was being pushed sideways by a Goliath-like hand, tipping me ever so slightly to the edge of an abyss. I grabbed for the bathroom sink; its coldness anchored me to the present, and then I looked up. The image in the mirror was horrifying but familiar, yet I hardly recognized her. My hair was matted to my head with my own blood, and my left eye was an angry swollen purple. A jagged, Frankenstein-esque laceration ran down my scalp, and my upper lip looked like it had been stitched together with one of those sewing card kits I had as a little girl. I promptly fainted. Fortunately, the nurse was there to catch me before I could do further damage to my crumpled body.

After I recovered from viewing the wretched mess that was my own reflection and successfully relieving my bladder, I was ready for the loop around the nurses' station. With the physical therapist next to me, I lurched and wobbled down the hallway, triumphantly looping the nurses' station in the center of the floor. I was allowed to go home. I grimaced as Caroline helped me dress in clothes she brought from her closet since mine had been cut off.

The nurse wheeled me from my room to the edge of the drive-through in front of the hospital where we waited for my daughter to pull her car around and take me home. Two fat, hot tears glided down my cheeks, prompting the nurse to inquire if I were experiencing pain. No, the physical pain wasn't producing the tears. Rather, it was the emotional sting of realizing how quickly we go from taking care of our children to their taking care of us.

For the next three days in my own home, Caroline fed me, changed the bandages, changed my pajamas, held me up in the shower, steadied me over the toilet, and slept beside me. When she had to return to school and work, she tenderly bundled me up and deposited me with my friend, Ann, who had agreed to further help me recuperate.

For a woman who is fiercely independent and has reared two children and looked out for herself, mostly solo, the prospect of others providing twenty-four-hour care was frightening. I learned to be humble and allow those who loved me to help me.

With my daughter supporting me on one side, I shuffled through Ann's door where she and another friend, Mickie, were waiting. The horrified look on their faces reflected how they saw my ghastly appearance as my daughter and I aimed for the nearest chair. For the next ten days, Ann, Mickie, Lin, and Arlene hovered over me like mother hens, changing bandages, plumping pillows, and helping me shower and dress. They made Jell-O, heated soup, and, best of all, found ways to make me laugh.

I am forever grateful for the kind hearts and unselfish spirits of these women. Many more friends and family, via social media and long-distance calls, bolstered my spirits.

I could have avoided the head injury, and probably the loss of my teeth, if I had been wearing my helmet. My sequined tank top was no match for rough asphalt; it was virtually sheared off me, leaving black sequins embedded in my skin. Long sleeves might have minimized the road rash and permanent scarring. I cannot say enough about wearing protective gear when riding a bike. Since my first extended road trip, I had always worn a helmet, leathers, gloves, and good boots. For some reason, that day I threw caution to the wind and shunned all protective gear.

Although my jeans and knee-high leather boots were torn and tattered during the crash, they safeguarded my legs and feet from damage. The fingerless, leather riding gloves were shredded, but their protection left the skin on my hands with only minor scrapes. I learned a painful lesson that day: *never* ride anywhere without protective gear.

Each time I climb on my bike, I say a prayer: *Circle your angels around me, God. Help me arrive safely at my destination today, as well as all those who are traveling.*

And each time I climb off my bike, I say: *Thank You, God, for another safe journey.*

The power of prayer is evident in my life.

I never learned who the people riding behind me were, those who interrupted their journey to come to my rescue. I will be forever thankful for their compassion. The saying among bikers is to never ride faster than your guardian angel can fly, and I wasn't that day.

I believe in the power of a shaman D.'s leather spirit bag I carry in my saddlebag; it's a talisman bestowing good luck and protection upon Bessie and me.

I didn't wake up one morning and think life was going to be different for me on that day because I might have an accident. Nope, what *might be* is not that tidy; life turns on a dime. You don't see or even sense a coming disaster. It doesn't arrive with a fanfare, burning bush, parting of the waters, or great epiphany. Boom! A catastrophe happens, leaving you on the pavement at the side of road wondering, *WTF?*

And, if you are fortunate enough to survive any tragedy, your outlook on life changes you both physically and mentally. You wonder, *Is this it? Is this what I want my life to be?* My firm answer to those questions is *no!*

I've been given another chance to walk a deeper walk. As my children have left home, and I've gotten older, I have vowed to live life on my terms, to color outside the lines whenever I feel like it, move in the direction that feeds my soul, and grab all the flavor I can muster from my day-to-day activities.

The accident served to deepen and redefine the conviction that my story isn't over. A whole lot more life awaits me in my middle years.

KNOCKED OFF COURSE

Every one of us is called upon, probably many times,
to start a new life.

– Barbara Kingsolver, *High Tide in Tucson*

MY DEFAULT COPING MECHANISM IS DENIAL. I MAKE
remarks like *it's not that bad; it was nothing; it was bound to happen
sooner or later; I'm fine. Really.* Denial is also the first stage in a grieving
process when you have experienced a death or profound loss.

For months after my motorcycle accident on US 27 in Clermont,
I mourned the loss of my former self and Bessie. My lifeline was
absent from the driveway; the careless bastard that made the illegal
U-turn knocked the joy right out from under me, leaving it a tangled
heap on the side of the highway. The very thing that had brought me
peace, nurtured my soul, and eased my pain was gone. Bessie was my
escape from the frightfully empty house, and now, I felt trapped within

the loneliness. My best friend was destined for the scrap heap, and I felt inconsolable.

I suffered a Grade 3 concussion—traumatic brain injury. The neurologist who examined me a week after the accident was astonished that my injuries were "minimal," given the severity of the accident and my age. Doctors, lawyers, and friends repeatedly told me, "You are lucky to be alive."

The neurologist explained post-traumatic stress symptoms and cautioned me not to expect much from myself for several months. *Months?* I halfway listened to his advice because my denial of the effects of my injuries was potent. I could not accept a disability in any form, regardless of its short-term duration.

"I feel fine, doctor," I offered in what I hoped was a convincing voice. I didn't tell him the short trip to Orlando had been torture: head pounding, sunlight blinding me, clothes chafing raw skin, stomach churning as nausea hit me from the motion sickness. I became nauseous just walking to the bathroom; riding in a car felt like I was on the dreaded Tilt-a-Whirl at the county fair.

"I have to return to work and finish the school year with my students," I said.

I hoped that mentioning my *students* needed their *teacher* would play on his emotions.

"I wouldn't advise returning to work for another few weeks," he said as he scribbled on a form, never looking me in the eye. *Weeks?* I didn't have the energy to bicker with him.

The doctor assured me my memory would return and my ability to concentrate would improve. At that moment, I could not find the words or the emotion in the dim recesses of my mind to say anything, so I accepted the return-to-work slip he signed and postdated for two weeks. I thanked him for his care, gathered my belongings, and wobbled to the waiting room where my friend, Mickie, sat, waiting to chauffeur me home.

The simple act of folding myself into the passenger seat of her car was agonizing. As I shifted gingerly in the seat, tears of frustration, tears of powerlessness, and the hot tears of anger slipped down my cheeks.

I braced myself for the waves of nausea on the ride home, pulling a hat down over my dark shades, trying to block out more of the searing sunlight. I recalled my first ocean voyage on a large sailboat and my first encounter with seasickness. The owner of the boat told me to sit on the front deck and keep my eyes on the horizon to combat the queasy feeling. I did the same as I sat in my friend's car while she drove me home.

My life was now divided into two sections: Debi before the accident and Debi after the accident. Someone had rearranged all the pieces on my life's chessboard, and I was no longer confident of my next move.

I literally hung a towel over each of the bathroom mirrors so I wouldn't have to look at my scarred, crumpled reflection. Alone, except for the daily phone calls from my daughter and a few friends, I burrowed into my down comforter in bed for the next two weeks, embracing the pain, sleeping fitfully, and losing track of time.

The doctor cleared me to go back to work at the Professional and Technical High School in Kissimmee, Florida, shortly before the 2012 school year ended for the summer, but I was terrified to face my high school students. I still looked frightful. My mouth had not healed, so I had no replacement for the missing teeth; the poorly stitched lip left me with a crooked smile, and the gash on my scalp was partially visible since my hair had been scraped off as well.

I am eternally grateful for my students' patience on days I struggled to find the words for common objects such as *book, write,* or *computer.* Or the day I stood in front of my class, filled with eager faces, and silent tears streamed down my cheeks because I couldn't deliver the lesson from Ray Bradbury's *Fahrenheit 451*, a book I had taught dozens of times and knew by heart.

The words stuck somewhere deep in my unconscious self, and I couldn't remember *why* it was so important to discuss the desensitization of Montag and his loss of human compassion. The pedagogics floated untethered, beyond my grasp.

I was so distraught I didn't notice the one student who quietly slipped out of the room to fetch the principal who kindly led me outside of my classroom to inquire if I were all right. I told him no, I was not.

Fortunately, only a few weeks of school remained until summer break. My principal knew that returning to normalcy was crucial to my recovery, and we devised a plan that would benefit the students and not tax my impaired cognitive abilities for the remaining few weeks of the school year. I created a series of comprehension questions and the criteria for the final project on *Fahrenheit 451,* which our reading coach reviewed and approved. My students were awesome; they worked with a partner each day to complete the assignments and progress toward completing their projects. I rolled around from table to table in my "rolly" chair, giving input and commenting on their work. Their projects were incredible, and our year ended on a positive note.

In May, my older daughter graduated from college. I managed to pull together a celebration to honor her accomplishments. I felt extremely proud of her, although I was fearful of her employment options. Shortly before graduating, she started working for the leasing company through whom she rented her campus apartment. It seemed like a decent job, and she decided to stay in the apartment after graduating to figure out what she wanted to do next.

Caroline's job prospects were slim. She had majored in psychology, which does not offer a lot of employment opportunities without a master's degree. I was disappointed that she was not coming home, but I supported her efforts to begin life on her own after college. Little did I know she was on a downward spiral—in reality, both of us were in a free fall to disaster, though we were plummeting into separate rabbit holes. I could not hear the pain in my daughter's voice; I could only feel my own.

The motorcycle accident robbed me of my smile, literally and figuratively. My natural smile has never been the same since losing four front teeth. I am forever grateful to my friend and dentist Dr. Linda May (Lin) for her support during such a challenging experience. It took months of phone calls and letters before my health insurance would approve the dental reconstruction surgery costs. Lin was more concerned about putting me back together and restoring some of my confidence than her compensation. She saw me a few days after the accident when she painfully removed what was left of my teeth, leaving me without four front teeth until my mouth healed and a temporary bridge could be fitted.

I was toothless for a few months, subsisting on Jell-O, mashed potatoes, and yogurt. My weight dropped accordingly, which added a raggedy, wasted dimension to my already alarming appearance. The damage to my teeth required numerous dental visits over the next several months before I had a full set of teeth again. Despite Lin's best efforts, I have never regained the genuine smile I enjoyed before the accident.

In addition to Bessie and me, the third victim of the accident was my social life, which came to a screeching halt. I had spent the better part of the previous four years building my social life around my motorcycle, but now it was gone. In the weeks after the accident, I received the usual phone calls and emails from the online dating website I was a member of—interested parties desiring to make contact. I ignored them all. I felt disfigured, unhealthy, battered, bruised, and angry. I had nothing to offer anyone.

One of the few phone calls I accepted during my April/May convalescence was from D. Dick, my erstwhile travel partner from the previous summer's Lake Superior Circle Tour. Over the past year, we had exchanged a few emails and phone calls, sharing stories of our two-wheeled travel. Nothing could be construed as romantic, and we talked vaguely of riding together again during the summer. I mentioned my desire to ride through the Canadian Rockies to Banff in Alberta, travel on the Icefields Parkway, and journey on to British Columbia.

D. Dick happened to call the day after I had my accident and was horrified to learn I was injured. He spoke with Caroline who relayed the extent of my injuries. A few days later, a florist delivered a beautiful flower arrangement to my home with best wishes for a speedy recovery. I was grateful but wary of D. Dick's intentions since my own remained solidly neutral.

The day I accepted D. Dick's phone call, he told me he had mapped out a route through the Canadian Rockies for our summer trip and called to see when I could leave. I realized right then that his intentions to travel together were not as vague as mine. I explained the extent of my injuries and the total loss of my motorcycle. Sadly, I told him, there would be no two-wheeled travel for me that summer. I could hear the disappointment in his voice as he offered options.

"I have two bikes; you can ride the other one," was one solution D. Dick offered.

"That would be wonderful and more than generous, but I have a severe concussion and PTSD. Riding a motorcycle right now would be disastrous," I explained.

"We can always ride two-up. I know you don't like being a passenger, but at least you would be riding," he continued.

"Never say never," I quipped, "but I'm just not interested in making a fabulous trip like you have mapped out as a passenger on two wheels."

We chatted a few minutes longer, and I ended the conversation with my familiar words, "It was nice talking with you. Keep in touch!"

I hunkered down lower into my depression with visions of the Canadian Rockies dancing in my head.

D. Dick's phone call ignited a flicker of hope and excitement for the prospects of traveling. I wanted to go places, to feel wheels turning under me, and the wind rushing over me. It was what I knew how to do once school ended for the summer. At least, that is what I told myself.

What I really needed to do was move fast enough to escape the feeling of powerlessness and the emotional turmoil left by the accident. May melted into June as I continued to heal and mourn losing Bessie.

One restless night, unable to sleep, I logged onto the Orbitz app to check the cost of a flight to Indiana. Although the doctor had advised against operating any motorized vehicle, he didn't rule out being a passenger. I purchased a ticket on a flight leaving in two days, and my spirits immediately lifted! I called Dad to let him know I would be visiting him.

The accident had altered my travel plans for the summer of 2012, but what resulted was one of the least planned but most serendipitous, diverse, and unusual summers I have been fortunate enough to experience.

The journey began in the Muncie, Indiana, area, visiting family and enjoying a reunion of the *Warehousian* tribe from high school. The 7th Street Warehouse served as a hangout and concert hall for teenagers in my hometown of Marion, Indiana. I contacted my niece Kiley, who lived in Chicago at the time, and she suggested I rent a car and drive up to spend time with Danny, her husband, and her, which I did.

On my visit to Chicago, Kiley, Danny, and I toured the Frank Lloyd Wright Museum and savored the Chicago blues scene. While in the Windy City, I decided to take a train to Elyria, Ohio, to visit Ann and Mickie—my surrogate mom and grandma, respectively. Each ticket I purchased at this point, including the rental car, was one-way; it was as though I had no notion of ever returning home. It was a journey of healing for my mind, body, and soul.

During my Chicago stay, I received another phone call from D. Dick, checking in to see how I was healing. I explained my travels sans motorcycle, and he told me about his recent purchase—a limited edition Forty-Fifth Anniversary Chevy Camaro SS. He explained he bought it for an investment, hoping I would agree to the motorcycle route he planned in this altered form of transportation.

"Your chariot awaits if you decide you would like to take the trip on four wheels instead of two," he offered. His voice sounded sincere.

I was stunned, speechless, and genuinely touched. I stammered, "Wow…oh, my God…unbelievable," while I collected my thoughts. If I went, I needed to define the terms of the liaison so D. Dick did not misconstrue our relationship. I didn't want to take advantage of a situation, although D. Dick was more than willing to be taken advantage of, so I ended our conversation saying, "Can I think about this on the next leg of my trip and call you in a few days?"

He replied confidently, "Take your time. I'm ready to leave when you are."

The train trip from Chicago's Union Station to Elyria, Ohio, was not the adventuresome, romantic travel of yesteryear I fondly remembered. For many summers, my grandmother and I traveled by train from Indiana to visit my uncle in Texas. On one such trip, Grandmother packed a wicker picnic basket with enough food for two days, promising we would eat in the dining car the third day. The hustle and bustle of the Indianapolis train station thrilled this little girl.

My grandmother clutched me tightly with one hand while she gripped the handle of the wicker basket with the other. We spent two nights and the better part of three days traveling from Indianapolis to Fort Worth, Texas. I was fascinated with each stop; the screeching brakes and shrill whistle jolted me awake in the middle of the night as we took on more passengers. If the train went around a curve, my grandmother would say, "Look out the window, and you can see the engine!" On the third morning, we walked to the dining car for breakfast, where the elegant waiters stood in their starched white jackets and white gloves, waiting to serve us. Toast and eggs never tasted so good!

As I waited for my train that evening in Chicago, I witnessed the dregs of humanity in the bowels of Union Station. The group assembled at the gate was a collection of the disheveled, unwashed, and unkempt, some of whom talked animatedly to no one in particular. I wondered if the apparent street people milling about the station were passengers or just wanderers looking for handouts. I was relieved when the queue started, and the street people did not line up to have their tickets checked.

The train departed Chicago around 11:00 p.m., which meant I could try to sleep on the journey. Mickie was scheduled to fetch me from the Elyria station at 5:00 a.m. I arrived in Elyria, disheveled and fatigued, not unlike the street people milling around Union Station. The young kid sitting in front of me had played music all night, and the few stops to take on passengers had a more detrimental effect on me than when I was a young child. Mickie took one look at me and said, "You need coffee!" Amen to that.

I had an outstanding time in Ohio visiting Ann's family and attending the New London Campout, a weekend gathering of friends of Bill W.'s for camping, cookouts, and fellowship. I told Ann about D. Dick's proposal of four-wheeled travel; she was wholeheartedly in favor of the adventure. Mention the word *travel*, and Ann's only reply will be, "When do we (you) leave?" I was hoping for some discourse, or at the very least a cautionary tone about traveling in such close quarters with a person I barely knew, but Ann didn't perceive any danger, only adventure. If I wanted to be convinced otherwise, I would have to seek advice elsewhere.

Rather than fly home from Ohio, I decided to drive Ann and her great-granddaughter back to Florida with me. The trip turned out to be more than an adventure since tropical storm Debbie swept across the Southeast, making our road trip wet and windy.

I called D. Dick before leaving for Florida to discuss specifics of the trip. I was concerned about the financial expectations, although he was not. I was careful to outline precisely what I could commit to moneywise, and he agreed. We talked about hotel arrangements as well, both agreeing this was not a trip with romantic expectations—it would be two fellow bikers seeking only each other's company.

I explained my inability to sit for very long, and he assured me we would stop often to stretch our legs, sightsee, and take pictures. I felt reassured and remembered that the three days we rode motorcycles together around Lake Superior had been pleasant enough.

D. Dick suggested I fly to Calgary, Canada, where he would collect me from the airport. Once again, I booked a one-way ticket, leaving in four days from Orlando with no regard for when I would return home. Although I experienced occasional vertigo, slept fitfully, and still suffered from pain in my damaged shoulder, I was healing as expected. I had convinced myself the unpredictable travel was what I needed.

I called Caroline to tell her I was home but would be leaving again. When she asked when I would return, my reply was, "I'm not sure." She seemed distant, unhappy, and vague when I asked about her work. Her answers to my questions and attempts at conversation were clipped and guarded. I chalked it up to her being frustrated with her inability to find real meaning with her life after college. Other recent graduates her age struggled with the same issues. I knew I had to let her work it out for herself though it was painful to step aside. There was nothing I could do but offer my love and support.

Any suggestion I made about further school or job possibilities was met with hostility, so I kept silent. It devastates me when I see my daughters struggle, and I'm powerless to help. I suggested to Caroline that we plan a trip we could take together during my winter break from teaching; the possibility seemed to perk her up a little. I ended our conversation by asking her if there was anything she needed or anything I could help her with. "No, Mom. I'm fine."

I replied, "I love you, and I will call when I arrive in Canada."

I packed sparingly, not wanting to lug a heavy suitcase for the next several weeks. My shoulder was impinged from the accident, severely limiting the range of motion in my right arm and causing more than a little discomfort. Once the road rash healed, I could begin therapy to improve mobility. My only relief came from alternating Aleve and Tylenol every six hours.

I checked the average temperature for the northernmost route D. Dick and I would travel; the Columbia Icefield, the largest ice field in the Rocky Mountains, lay north of Banff and bordered Banff National Park and Jasper National Park in the Canadian Rockies. I packed accordingly. It would be *cold*—twenty-eight degrees—by my Florida standards. D. Dick had told me, "There is still snow in parts of Canada. We will visit both Athabasca Glacier and Glacier National Park, so bring warm clothes!"

D. Dick's smiling face and hulking body greeted me at the receiving end of the down escalator when I arrived in Calgary. As I waited for my luggage, he fetched the *chariot* around to whisk me away on a three-week, 10,000-plus mile journey I will never forget.

D. Dick and I traveled the same roads in his 600-horsepower, limited edition Camaro that we would have done on two wheels. We cruised back roads, conquered the twisting asphalt, and admired the sweeping views. From the Columbia Icefield in the Canadian Rockies, we rode west through British Columbia where I inhaled the most breathtaking scenery I have ever experienced: jaw-dropping views of jagged, snow-topped mountains around each twisting curve. Every corner of this Canadian province features sweeping panoramic views of the Canadian Rockies and crystalline, azure lakes rimmed by old growth forests. We stopped to watch a mama bear and her cub climb a tree, moose amble down to a lake to drink, and Dall sheep perch precariously on the side of a cliff. Often, a road would end abruptly at a body of water, forcing us, the intrepid travelers, to wait for a ferry to carry us to the next remote patch of highway.

We drove to Vancouver and took a ferry to Victoria, the capital of British Columbia, on Vancouver Island. From Victoria, we journeyed north on the island through picturesque towns like Chemainus, famous for its thirty-nine murals that depict the town's history on almost every building.

The ferry at Comox deposited us at Lund, British Columbia, back on the mainland. Lund, a town named for Lund, Sweden, is the beginning of US Route 101 that runs all the way south to Mexico. We took Route 101, which hugs the Pacific Northwest and Oregon coastlines, into Northern California and drove through the majestic redwood forests to follow the Columbia River Gorge route. It is the same passage an adolescent girl named Sacajawea followed to lead the Lewis and Clark Expedition westward—along historic US Route 30, which goes across the United States from east to west. We crossed Idaho and traversed Logan's Pass and the Continental Divide in Montana's magnificent Glacier National Park.

Whenever D. Dick and I encountered motorcyclists on our journey, we looked longingly as they passed, each of us heartbroken we didn't have two wheels under us. However, the Black Chariot, as it became known, was an incredible substitute, never lacking in power or the ability to handle tight curves. D. Dick and I journeyed in companionable silence for most of those thousands of miles, punctuated by comments about the panoramic views—neutral ground, void of emotion.

During the previous summer, D. Dick had been fresh in his grieving after his wife died. This summer, he was in the depths of that grief. What must it be like to have a man who loves you so deeply that when you die, a part of him dies too? That your death leaves him so utterly devastated, he cannot fathom a life without you in it, let alone make the human connections necessary to carry on or fashion a different life? I don't think I've ever known that level of love for a man or from a man. D. Dick's silence suited me as I, too, needed to outrun my feelings.

As D. Dick promised, we frequently stopped to take photos, stretch our legs, and rest. We respected each other's privacy once we settled on a stopping point and chose a hotel. Where to eat lunch or dinner was never a problem as D. Dick acquiesced to most of my choices. It seemed as if it was too much effort for him to make decisions. Sometimes, we had a quick bite near the hotel; sometimes we ate at an upscale restaurant or popular local spot I tracked down on my Diners, Drive-Ins, and Dives app.

Our tour ended as D. Dick and I looped back east to the Canadian Badlands and D. Dick's home in eastern Alberta. I was fascinated with Red Rock Coulee and its round, reddish boulders; Dinosaur Park where Jurassic era dinosaurs had been found; and the *hoodoos*, naturally eroded twenty-foot land formations, in Drumheller Valley. We dipped into western Saskatchewan to visit Fort Walsh National Historic Site.

I agreed to stay at D. Dick's home in Alberta for a few days' rest before I scheduled my flight home. He wanted me to meet his kids, which turned out to be the worst idea of the whole trip. Not only was D. Dick still mired in the grieving process following his wife's death, his grown children were as well. Although both D. Dick and I explained my presence as merely a "travel partner and friend," his children viewed me as an interloper in their mother's house and were downright hostile during their brief visit. D. Dick was apologetic but completely clueless in how his mourning was causing his remaining family to be dysfunctional.

I called my daughter one afternoon while I was still in Alberta; again, she was distant, guarded. Then she said the one thing that resonated deeply, "Mom, you've never been away from home this long."

I felt bereft. I needed the comfort of *home*; I was tired of traveling. I assured her I would be home within the next few days. At dinner that night, I told D. Dick it was time to return to Florida. He seemed ambivalent, which was convenient. I made sure he was available to make the six-hour round trip to the Calgary airport from his home in Medicine Hat, Alberta, before I bought a ticket. At the airport, I thanked D. Dick warmly for the travel opportunity. We half-heartedly promised to keep in touch.

I returned to Florida in late July, a month before school was to start, feeling better physically and somewhat satiated from my trip. I soon realized, however, that the travel was just a postponement of the depression that follows a denial of one's circumstances.

Unfortunately, I now faced the details of my decision to bring legal action against the other biker who was at fault in my accident. My hospital bills, dental reconstruction, and the total loss of my bike amounted to a significant sum of money despite what my insurance covered. Endless legal hassles with my children's father over the years had left me loath to seek an attorney or enter a courtroom again for any reason.

I crumpled under the logic, however, and before leaving for my trip, I sought the advice of an attorney acquaintance I had known for years. He was happy to take my case, and he promised me the moon. What I experienced over the next five months was victimization of a different kind.

After denying how horrendously the accident affected me, I encountered the next stage of grief—anger. I was angry because the other biker who caused the accident was unhurt. Thankfully, his nine-year-old daughter, who was riding with him, was treated and released at a local hospital. I was mad that he had a small child on the back of his bike, but I consoled myself with the knowledge that the girl's mother would be just as angry as I was, and the man who caused my pain would have his own grief to bear.

I wanted to extract a price as payment for my anger, pain, and loss. The attorney I contracted with promised to "get as much as possible" from the guilty party to compensate me for the damages I incurred. I believed his hokey television commercials; I believed in his experienced ambulance chasing, and, in the end, I believed he would say anything, provided he received his percentage of the settlement.

Five months later when the settlement was concluded, and I had wiped the slime off my hands, he magnanimously absolved himself of his fee due to "our friendship" over the years. I walked away with just enough money to buy a new bike and considerably less than the "six-fig-ure-settlement" that he intimated at the beginning of our discussion. My health insurance company negotiated a compensation with the heli-copter service and the hospital, eliminating a hefty balance that would have crushed me financially. I seethed. I grumbled endlessly to anyone who would listen. My anger became a mania that bubbled just under the surface, spilling over with the slightest provocation.

Looking back, I don't recall many specifics about August through November of 2012. The anger gave way to depression. I was Alice in a long, dark free fall down the rabbit hole, except there was no smiling Cheshire cat or a Hookah-Smoking caterpillar to soften my landing. I had a few follow-up phone calls from D. Dick, but basically, we never saw each other again after our summer sojourn.

Depression descended on me, enveloping me in a soft, dark place I nestled into and damn near didn't recover from. The descent was slow. Like Alice, I floated downward with deliberate attempts to grasp what was familiar in my surroundings. I prayed. I asked God for help but cursed Him for my circumstances.

I was quick to dissolve into tears—long crying jags, originating in my core and graduating to heaving sobs of misery. I barely saw Caroline; our conversations were brief, both of us struggling. I disconnected from social media, the dating website, and all attempts at mingling with other humans outside of my teaching associates.

I did what I had to do to teach, to connect with students and colleagues, but my heart wasn't in it. I left work, drove home, disrobed, donned pajamas, and crawled into an unmade bed, hunkering down with a book or movie until I had to get up and do it all over again. Weekends afforded me forty-eight hours in bed to wallow in my depression.

My thoughts—they tormented me. I had survived a bad accident, but why? Life was tenuous; what would I do with the life I had left? I knew I would ride again, but when?

I was drowning in regret and guilt—for my younger daughter's absence, for the struggles my older daughter was apparently wrestling with, the loss of my bike. I bemoaned stupid things I may or may not have said—all the times I was a bitch, all the times I must have been an embarrassment to my daughters. I hated the pain I had caused, the fear I generated, the idiocy, the lapses in judgment—and on and on. Hunter Thompson said it best: "The Edge...there is no honest way to explain it because the only people who really know where it is are the ones who have gone over." I was teetering on the edge.

A few close friends continued to reach out to me, aware of the dark place I inhabited. Their attempts to draw me out were met with remarks such as, "I'm fine. Really." Ha! They knew better. And I knew better. I was that little girl whistling in the dark, trying to pretend I wasn't terrified of the shadows.

Friends strongly suggested I rely on AA's Twelve Steps of Recovery that rescued me from the depths of alcoholism a couple of decades before. I needed to reach a level of acceptance—the final stage of the grieving process—with the altered circumstances of my life. Unfortunately, grieving is not exactly a linear process, nor does it fit into a definitive time frame.

I awoke from a fitful sleep one night, switched on the light, grabbed a book from the *favorites* stack on my nightstand (not to be confused with the *current* books I'm reading), and prepared to read myself back to sleep. The book was Robert Pirsig's *Zen and the Art of Motorcycle Maintenance*—a worn and tattered copy I had had since the seventies. (The books in my *favorites* stack have been read multiple times.) With middle-of-the-night reading, I randomly open a book and start wherever my eyes land. I don't want to follow a plot line—I only want the words to lull me back to sleep.

Instantly, familiar words became new and flew straight to my heart: "One of the most moral acts is to create a space in which life can move forward." I had been knocked completely off course by this motorcycle accident, and I had forgotten how to get up and move forward. It really was simple—I needed to create a space for me to heal. Misfortune and loss are givens in this life, and I couldn't go to bed and never get up each time the two landed inside my hula hoop.

That night, as I read Pirsig's words again and again, a calmness settled in my core, nudging aside the anxiety that had been a constant companion since the accident. My limbs relaxed as I succumbed to a heavy drowsiness.

I awoke to the gift of a different outlook, an epiphany. I vowed to shake off the bulky vestiges of my depressed state and start moving forward with my life, post-accident. I vowed to walk a deeper walk and to live in the moment with no regard for the past and no worries for the future. I took a stringent moral inventory, and I vowed to reach deep within and find a softer, gentler me—one who was worthy of the life I had been given.

Thanksgiving break. I called Caroline to see if she could take some time off over the winter holidays; we were going on a road trip!

My daughter and I met to plan our trip, deciding to fly out to San Francisco, a city neither one of us had experienced before. We would travel over Christmas break, and both of us wanted to attend a performance of *The Nutcracker* by the San Francisco Ballet. I scoured the travel websites on Cyber Monday, seeking the most bang for my buck regarding travel options. I put together a fabulous package for nine days of sightseeing, reserved rooms at a wonderful hotel on Fisherman's Wharf, purchased ballet tickets, and booked first-class airfare.

We rang in the 2013 New Year in San Francisco, and the trip turned out to be one of the best I have ever enjoyed with my daughter. We toured Haight Ashbury with a whacked out, aging hippie tour guide, took a ferry ride to Alcatraz, sipped Gevalia coffee, and ate chocolate croissants as we overlooked the bay. We snapped selfies at the Golden Gate Bridge as we flirted with a group of young male Italian tourists, bought books at City Lights Bookstore, and toured virtually every museum. The highlight of the trip was the San Francisco Ballet's performance of *The Nutcracker* at the opulent opera house.

After my daughter and I returned from California, I spent some time with my friend, Ann, before returning to school after winter break. She casually mentioned my dating life and wondered when that aspect of my life would return to normal. I laughed out loud, spewing a mouthful of coffee.

"Normal? There was nothing ever *normal* about my dating life," I reminded her.

"But you were having fun and meeting some interesting people," she gently persisted. I appreciated her genuine concern for my happiness in that respect.

"Fun?" I hooted. "More like a parade of dreary, humdrum Dicks. No, thank you.

Besides," I continued, "I canceled my membership to the dating website."

Ann's face was crestfallen. "But why?" she whined.

"Are you whining? Don't whine; it's unbecoming of someone your age," I chided. I explained I just didn't have the energy anymore for the tedious process and frequent disappointment of online dating.

"I've reached a level of acceptance with my aloneness that I'm comfortable with," I half-heartedly offered, hoping this would end the conversation about my dating life—or lack of. "In fact, I find myself quite good company!"

Amused, but undeterred, Ann plowed on. "I saw an advertisement recently for a new dating website for people over fifty. I think you should try it."

"Oh God. *Seniors*? Great. Now I can expect a parade of dreary, humdrum, limp Dicks. No, thank you!" I said.

"Come on, what do you have to lose?" she continued. "It's called OurTime.com. Why don't you sign up for a few months and just see what happens? Maybe you were on the wrong websites before."

I had to agree with Ann on that last point. The quality of potential candidates on the websites I searched was questionable more often than honorable. Ann is a hopeless romantic; she believes in magical adventures of love with fairy tale endings. I, on the other hand, am a realist who still holds out hope for a miracle. More out of exasperation than compliance, I agreed to give it a try. That appeased Ann, and when I left her, visions of romance danced in *her* head.

I wanted a partner in life—that was a certainty. After two failed marriages and a trail of broken relationships, I wasn't exactly confident in my ability to attract the right guy. Perhaps what I needed to focus on was becoming the kind of person I wanted to attract in my life.

That softer, gentler me logged onto OurTime.com, browsed the offerings, read the terms and conditions, and paid the fee. It was a new year—2013, and I was full of renewed optimism with a different attitude about life in general. I tweaked my profile biography, uploaded my photos, and clicked *publish*, once again casting my lure into the murky waters of online dating, hoping to catch love. Vonnegut's words in *Cat's Cradle* hovered in my mind: "There is love enough in this world for everybody, if people will just look."

SOLITARY

If I were a drink, I would be a white chocolate cappuccino
with whipped topping;
if I were a song, I would be bluesy and raw.
If I were a photograph, I would be black and white,
with sharp contrasts;
if I were a road, I would be curvy and challenging.
If I were a shoe, I would be a well-worn pair of black leather
cowboy boots with fringe.
If I were an article of clothing, I would be a soft pair of
denim jeans that hugs
every curve and feels like an old friend when you slip them on.
If I were a book, I would have a happy ending;
if I were a bird, I would be a sandhill crane—they mate for life.
If I were a moment in time, I would be breathless.

– Debi Duggar

ALONE IS SUCH A FORLORN WORD. I PREFER *SOLITARY*, AS in a chosen course for one's life: She finds herself centered in the calm of her *solitary* life. I also relate to the following synonyms for alone: *incomparable, solo, insulated*, and *unique*. I especially like *unique*. That's my word—the definition of *alone* that I own. The best compliment I have ever received was when a female friend called me *unique*. Unique is someone who buys her first motorcycle at age fifty-four and then proceeds to spend most of her time riding over hill, over dale (or was it Dick?), and everywhere in between—*alone*.

I can do a mental run-through of my past and recall the times and the infinite number of hours I have spent in solitude. And it doesn't make me sad; the thought itself is both comforting and melancholy.

From an early age, I felt different from others, as if I didn't fit in anywhere. I didn't see myself as defective; it was more like I was functioning in a different dimension—apart and remote from everyone else.

My earliest memories of grade school and on through middle school are uncomfortable. I couldn't wait to leave school and take refuge in my bedroom with my books. I loved the solitude of my books then, and I love the solitude of my books now.

The face of solitude morphed into another kind of difference when I entered high school. It was the decade of Peace, Love, and Rock 'n Roll. The availability of drugs and alcohol made it easy to isolate, to seek seclusion, and I grasped the opportunity with both hands. The late sixties proved fertile ground for experimentation but not without its irony in terms of single women. Just as I would recoil from a hot flame, I recoiled from the accepted norm that I should marry and reproduce once I graduated from high school. I was branded as *different*—not in a good way but *different* in a not-so-good way because I bucked cultural expectations.

I am a seeker, not a conformist. I viewed the confines of marriage as limiting in scope, suffocating in breadth, as well as impossible intellectually. I still do. Psychologically, I equate marriage with authority, and I have issues with authority.

I have two children by my second husband; once we procreated, I couldn't see any meaningful life for me within the confines of the marriage. Therefore, I raised my daughters alone, getting by with a little help from my friends.

When both of my daughters left for college, my single life, however, closed in on me more acutely than ever. My cherished solitude, sans my children, became a double-edged sword that cut a swath across my heart. I had to learn to let go of them and the life we had shared. Undoubtedly, it wasn't about being alone; instead, it was about navigating another passage in life. It's like a rebirth. We redefine ourselves as we age, as our parents grow older, as our children age; we emerge on the other side of that rebirth, changed.

I chose to live a solitary, un-partnered life. I have had, and continue to have, productive relationships with some wonderful men. And those men who stay in my life are rare creatures of the opposite sex who are not intimidated or otherwise emasculated by my presence. They know precisely when to ebb and flow in my life, and I adore them for their perception.

Traveling solo on Bessie has been the euphemism for my traveling solo through life. It's just easier; the older I get, the better I like *unencumbered* as not only a state of mind but a state of being. I have no fear of eating alone, sleeping alone, or traveling alone. It is the fear of *being* alone and being lonely that often creates desperate women, and desperate women compromise their true selves.

Within the heart of my solitude over the years, I have forged an authentic self. I have learned that I am the curator of my dreams. I know what feeds my soul. With stunning clarity, I have shaped my beliefs, attitudes, and values and proceeded to live a life built on that foundation. I have become comfortable in my skin.

When I meet the man who walks into my life and compliments it, not complicates it, I will be sure of him because I am sure of myself. But I don't wait around for that to happen; I choose to travel solo, comfortable with my own company.

ALL IS RIGHT WITH MY UNIVERSE

Let yourself be silently drawn by the strong pull of
what you really love. It will not lead you astray.

–Jalal ad-Din Muhammad Rumi, Persian poet

I WRAPPED MY LEGS AROUND ALL NINETY-SIX CUBIC
inches of my pre-owned Road King, ignored the colossal knot of apprehension lying in the pit of my stomach, fired the V-twin engine, and
rolled out of my driveway before 8:00 a.m. After eleven months of
two-wheeled deprivation, I bought Bessie Two in March of 2013. I
would like to report buying Bessie Two was easier than buying Bessie
One, but alas, I cannot. You don't need a penis to buy a motorcycle, but
I'm confident it helps.

After months of recuperation and financial wrangling to receive compensation for my motorcycle accident in 2012, I embarked, with cash in hand, on a quest to find a Bessie Two. The settlement helped my overall financial picture somewhat, and I agreed with the bank to put my house on the market in a short sale to get out from under an upside-down mortgage. From those two monetary outcomes, I squirreled away enough money to consider a pre-owned replacement bike. The planets were beginning to align.

When I went shopping for my first bike in January of 2008, I knew little about motorcycles, but I knew I wanted to travel. This awareness is half the battle when searching for a new mode of transportation. From October to January, I visited various Harley-Davidson dealerships in Central Florida, wandering up and down the aisles of shiny bikes while an all-male sales staff stood around, looking at me while I surveyed bikes. One lone salesman in the Brandon, Florida, dealership sauntered over but never asked any questions about what I would like in a motorcycle. "You need to buy a Sportster. A lot of women buy Sportsters," he boasted.

"Not any of the women I know," I offered unapologetically. "A Sportster is too small for me; I like to travel." Now right there, the salesman should have grasped that tidbit of information and turned it into a selling point. But no, he was determined to promote the Sportster as the best option for a woman.

"They are lightweight," he said. (Which meant I would get blown off the road by a passing semi.)

"They are easy to handle." (Which translated to the misconception of a woman's ability to ride a cruiser class bike).

"We sell a lot of Sportsters to the ladies." (And to *really* small men).

"They come in pink." With that remark, I was out of there.

Only when I took along a male friend who spoke fluent man language and had the proper appendage was I able to communicate my wishes to the salesman and purchase my first Harley-Davidson.

Fast forward five years to February 2013, and, unfortunately, not much had changed. Dealerships had yet to figure out how to sell a motorcycle to women. Realistically, Harley- Davidson will have to transcend generations of motorcycle clichés to reach the female market. Nearly naked pin-up girls with ample bosoms and bikini-clad bike washers appeal to the male customer. But women continue to wait for the day to see scantily clad firemen with rippled torsos draped over the fender of a new Street Glide. Or a bare-chested hunk astride a new Road King, beckoning seductively, "Put something exciting between your legs, ladies." Instead, Harley-Davidson designed a line of pink-themed clothing and moved the potted plants closer to the door. Lame. Really, lame.

As I shopped for Bessie Two this time around, I was confident in my knowledge of motorcycles and boasted nearly 100,000 road miles of experience on Bessie One. I devoted eleven months to researching the bike of my dreams while I recuperated from the accident. I knew what I could afford, and I had cash in hand. Unfortunately, still no penis.

On a gorgeous, sunny Saturday afternoon, I strode into the dealership nearest my home. The receptionist warmly greeted me, and then I turned toward the showroom instead of the display of pink clothing and nice potted plants near the door. No one approached me as I gazed at the new bikes in the showroom. I walked outside and cruised up and down the rows of pre-owned motorcycles. Still, no salesperson approached, although three salesmen watched me intently. Exasperated, I walked over to the knot of salesmen and asked, "Which one of you needs to sell a bike today?"

Of course, they all did, but the dealer had some sort of salesmen hierarchy in play, and one of the men jerked his thumb in the direction of another guy and announced, "It's his turn."

The salesman with the black shirt (whose name I have forgotten) introduced himself, limply shook my hand, crossed his arms over his chest, and stared at me. No qualifying questions, no small talk or jovial banter—he just stared. Undaunted, I began the conversation,

"This is my second bike. I logged over 180,000 miles on my first," I offered bravely.

"Uh-huh," he grunted.

"I totaled my Softail this past April," I said defiantly.

And no lie, Mr. Congeniality responded, "Were you on it when it was totaled?"

That one single eyebrow of mine arched involuntarily over the rim of my sunglasses in disbelief. I pulled my sunglasses down a tad to stare Mr. Congeniality in the eye. "Yes. I was."

I boldly pushed my mirrored aviators back into place thinking, *If this guy steers me towards the Sportster, I'm going to get hateful.* I plowed on.

"I'm looking for a pre-owned Road King or Street Glide. Model year 2009 to 2010, black, and low mileage, of course." My voice was strong and sure as I spoke these words.

"I have a brand-new 2013 on the showroom floor I can show you today," he offered.

"I don't want a 2013. I want a pre-owned bike that I can afford, and I intend to pay cash," I restated.

Over the next few weeks, I said the same thing to three different salesmen at this dealership.

Mr. Congeniality reluctantly showed me a couple of pre-owned Road Kings; they were not black, and one of them had exceedingly high mileage. When I pointed out the excessive number of miles, he directed my attention to the nice-looking luggage rack and once again declared, "I can put you on a brand-new Road King today." I had the distinct feeling he wasn't listening.

"No, that's not what I want. Why don't you take my phone number and look for a pre-owned bike that meets my specifications," I replied.

He dutifully jotted down my information in his little wire-bound notebook, and I walked off the lot. Two weeks went by, and I still didn't have a bike. I experienced similar fruitless encounters at two other dealerships in Central Florida.

I returned to the first dealership, walked into the showroom, and asked for the sales manager. The friendly receptionist—someone should please put her to work selling bikes to women; she would make you a fortune. She is genial, confident in her position behind the counter, and helpful—pointed me in the direction of a glassed-in cubicle where a burly man sat behind a desk. I stood in the doorway until he looked up.

Unfortunately, his eyes didn't get any further than my cleavage, and I inquired,

"Where will I find George (Mr. Congeniality)? He's had my phone number for two weeks and hasn't called about a bike yet."

Still staring at my cleavage, the sales manager cooed, "Honey, if I had your number, you can bet I would have called before now." (If he could have only seen the snarky thought bubble popping out of my head.)

Before I could respond, Mr. Congeniality walked over, looking surprised that I had returned and perhaps startled that I was serious about buying a bike. He admitted he had not located a pre-owned bike that met my specifications and steered me in the direction of the new motorcycles. I decided to humor him and agreed to a test drive on both the Street Glide and the Road King. I already knew I wanted the Road King, so after our demo ride, I remarked, "I would need to have the

Road King lowered so my feet are flat on the ground. Perhaps swap out the shocks to Street Glide shocks."

"If you're going to do that, you might as well buy the Street Glide," he responded.

We switched bikes, and I rode the Street Glide. I didn't like the Street Glide, although the height was right. I told him I didn't care for the weight the fairing added to the front end. He countered by cranking the stereo full-blast as if deafening music would compensate for a heavy front end.

We returned to the dealership, and I began a conversation with all three salesmen. "I want the Road King lowered."

"Then you might as well get a Street Glide."

"I don't like the Street Glide," I told them.

"Let's put a short reach seat on the Road King and see if that helps." They did, but It didn't change anything.

"I don't like how the seat looks. I want the Street Glide shocks put on the Road King," I said.

"That's gonna cost ya about $600. Why don't you go over to the apparel section and buy a nice pair of boots with a really thick heel to give you some height?"

I left the dealership and did not return. Two salesmen and the sales manager were incapable of listening to my requests and selling me what I wanted. A week later, on my way home from an overnight stay near Brooksville, Florida, I decided to stop at the Tampa Harley-Davidson dealership and try again to buy a bike. The guys there restored my faith in humanity.

I headed directly for the area marked *Tent Sale* where the pre-owned bikes were displayed. It was early, not yet 9:00 a.m., and I was the only shopper. An older gentleman, whom I will call Frank, approached me with a warm smile, introduced himself, and asked me if I wanted coffee.

"Yes! Yes, Frank, I do want coffee. Thank you." As I sipped the hot brew, Frank questioned me to determine what I wanted. I explained in detail my previous experience on Bessie One, the accident, and my desire to purchase a pre-owned Road King. Frank nodded, listened intently, and commented when appropriate.

"I like to call them *pre-loved*," Frank said as he steered me toward the one black, 2009 Road King under the tent.

"Let's take it for a test ride. Ready?" Frank was more excited than I was, as he clapped his hands together, smiled broadly, and motioned for me to follow him into the building to sign the waiver for a test ride. Frank grabbed two helmets, and I followed enthusiastically back out to the lot where someone had pulled the Road King up to the front of the building for me. Frank straddled the Road Glide that he would ride; I pulled the helmet on and straddled the Road King. I followed Frank out of the parking lot and down Dale Mabry Highway, thankful for the light Sunday morning traffic.

Somewhere on that short test run, I fell in love, not with Frank, but with Bessie Two. She *spoke* to me, just as Bessie One did.

Frank and I returned to the lot. I hopped off, pulled off my helmet, and with a big smile declared, "I'll take it! But there are some adjustments I want you to make."

Frank was all ears, clutching his clipboard and ready to make notes on the sales order.

"I want Street Glide shocks installed to lower this Road King about an inch."

"No problem. We can do that at no charge."

"I want the stock handlebars switched to fourteen-inch, mini-ape hangers," I continued.

"No problem. Let me get the parts guy over here to measure your reach."

"I want the floorboards, highway pegs, handgrips, and primary case switched to Willie G chrome accessories."

"No problem. Let's head over to the parts department so you can tell them what you want."

Instead of three guys standing around ignoring me as they had at other dealerships, I faced three guys with clipboards, writing down everything I requested to be put on my bike. Three hours later, I was still smiling, happily clasping the sales agreement for a *pre-loved* Road King that not only met but exceeded my expectations—to be delivered in two weeks. No penis necessary.

The only way for some people to conquer fear is to ride right over it. Other than a few short test rides, this marked the first time in eleven months I enjoyed my own motorcycle beneath me. My arms shook as I rolled out of my driveway and cautiously made a right turn. I was hypervigilant.

I cruised ever so slowly the short distance to my mechanic's shop, X-Tech. When I pulled into the parking area and switched off the ignition, I finally exhaled. I was still shaking when I climbed off the bike. Jerry, my mechanic, checked Bessie Two from fender to fender, took her for a test ride, and proclaimed her a "damn fine ride. You did good, girl; you did good!"

Then he suggested, "I think we need to drop it another inch for you though. I want to see your feet flat on the pavement. I should put an extension on that kickstand too. It's a bitch to try and find it underneath the frame." Jerry is slightly shorter than I am, so he understood the importance of customizing the bike to fit.

I mentioned that I thought my pipes could be a little louder, and he responded with a wink, "Of course they could!" I planned to drop Bessie off during spring break for the necessary adjustments.

I left Jerry's shop, feeling triumphant and headed out of town to bond with my new bike on the familiar back roads of the Green

Swamp Wilderness Preserve, a 110,000-acre-recharge area for the Florida aquifer. Leaving traffic behind, I found my rhythm with the bike *thump, thump, thumping* underneath me. The sound was reassuring and familiar.

I approached the curves on Green Pond Road cautiously. The Road King is approximately eighty pounds heavier than my Softail was, which means the balance is different. Because of the added weight, taking a turn, embracing a curve, and stopping work differently with this motorcycle than with Bessie One. The Road King frame is longer, and the gas tank is larger. The decision to replace the stock handlebars for mini-ape hangers was a good one; rather than reaching over the gas tank, my arms rested comfortably above it.

The cool March wind took my fear that day and scattered it over the lush landscape of the Green Swamp. I tackled the curves with increasing confidence, trusting my instincts and the machine. The sun hung in a brilliant blue sky, warming my face as the wind rushed over me.

I took pleasure in the scent of flavored oxygen as I rode through the orange groves, fruit trees dense with blossoms. I turned down Old Glade Road, a desolate, flat, newly paved, straight piece of asphalt, bordered by swamp and cow pastures—the perfect place to explore sixth gear (Bessie One had only five gears). When Bessie Two hit eighty miles per hour, I let out a *yee-haw* at the top of my lungs—and I cried. I cried tears of joy, frustration, fear, and relief. The accident did not permanently rob me of my passion—only temporarily.

By the time Bessie Two and I had clicked off 140 miles, we were one. My injured shoulder was screaming, however, and my neck was torqued from the tension; my hips ached. Although I had returned to the gym a few months after my accident, regaining my physical strength would take more time. Wrestling a bigger motorcycle required better upper body strength. It was time to end the maiden voyage and turn toward home.

I pulled into my driveway, maneuvered the bike into its spot, checked the odometer—196 miles total—switched off the ignition, and said a prayer of thanks. I unfolded myself from the bike, straightening out the kinks and getting my balance.

I took a soft cloth and some cleaner from the saddlebag and began to gently rub the bugs off the chrome. With Zen-like concentration, I worked my way around the bike, restoring the chrome to its gleaming, unblemished state. I knelt to polish the primary case and saw my face reflected in the chrome. It was glowing; I was genuinely smiling. My soul had been nourished, and I had fallen deeply in love with another Bessie. The planets aligned. All was good in my universe once again.

LIKE A LOVER, ONLY BETTER

The test of the machine is the satisfaction it gives you. There isn't any
other test. If the machine produces tranquility, it's right. If it disturbs you,
it's wrong until either the machine or your mind is changed.

– Robert Pirsig, *Zen and the Art of Motorcycle Maintenance*

APRIL 2013. THE LEESBURG BIKEFEST, BILLED AS THE
"world's largest three-day motorcycle and music event," loomed on
my calendar. The previous year, I had set out to enjoy the ride to the
event, but I never made it to Leesburg.

As Bessie and I cruised around town near the first anniversary
of my accident, I decided to stop by X-Tech's, Inc., in Winter Haven to
see my mechanic, Jerry, and his wife, Xanda.

"Hey, Jerry. Are you guys riding up to Leesburg next weekend?"

"Nope. Don't plan on it. Are you?"

"I don't know. I haven't decided yet."

Jerry jerked his thumb toward Bessie and with his gravelly
smoker's voice, declared, "You need to get on that bitch and ride it to

Leesburg. Stare that demon down and overcome the fear. Ain't nuthin' gonna hurt ya."

And there it was from a Sprocket-Wrench Prophet—my fear laid bare. Since taking ownership of Bessie Two the second week in March, I had stuck close to home, making cautious trips on familiar back roads and avoiding places in Central Florida known for heavy traffic. I was still taking baby steps, allowing unspoken fear to dictate my riding destinations. I was fearful of traffic, being in another accident, and of losing my life.

Jerry is a classic *old-school* biker, barely five feet four inches tall. He resembles Billy Gibbons of the rock band ZZ Top with a scraggly gray beard hanging midway down his chest and stringy locks of hair that get lost in the collar of his X-Tech's work shirt.

Jerry has wrenched bikes for so long that grease is permanently embedded in his fingers and hands. His speech is succinct, and he doesn't elaborate on what he says or mince words. He has a raunchy sense of humor that works around only motorcycle garages and biker bars. Most women would find his sexist attitude offensive, but I find it endearing. Xanda, who works alongside him at their shop, is a saint for putting up with him.

During the past five years, Jerry and I have developed a solid friendship, built on ornery sexual banter and our love of motorcycles. *Get on that bitch and ride; stare the demon down* is exactly what I needed to hear from someone like Jerry. He knew me and how I loved to ride. He respected me for the miles I had logged solo and realized the accident had set me back.

I hugged him, waved to Xanda, and pulled out of the parking lot, determined *to stare the demon down.*

The following Friday, I rode Bessie to downtown Winter Haven to meet friends for dinner at a local Thai restaurant. I didn't breathe a word to anyone about my plans to go to Leesburg that night. (Traveling on my motorcycle when it's dark is something I rarely do.) Why I decided to make the trip to Leesburg at night made for an interesting hypothesis though. Was it because there was less traffic on the road, so I was in less danger? Or, because I could sneak up on my worry in the dark? Or, because no one would see me if I failed to master the fear?

I left the restaurant with the familiar knot of apprehension lying in the pit of my stomach, but the Sprocket-Wrench Prophet had thrown down the gauntlet with his words, *Get on that bitch and ride*. I felt ready. I hit the back roads, purposely avoiding US 27, the scene of the accident.

It was a gorgeous spring evening to ride; the warm sun was dropping in the west, trading places with cooler air, thick with the fragrance of orange blossoms. The road grew crowded with other bikes as I neared Leesburg on US 441. I cruised past Gator's Dockside and Gator Harley-Davidson without stopping; their parking lots were clogged with motorcycles and bikers having a great time. I was on a mission. I planned to amble down Main Street, the center of biker activities in Leesburg, and then head home.

Leesburg Bikefest in Lake County, Florida, has grown tremendously since its inception in 1997. It isn't the size of Daytona Bike Week, but the Leesburg party attracts 300,000 people for the three-day festival. I could sense the rumble and excitement a mile away. I glided into the stream of motorcycles exiting off US 441 to make my way down Main Street with no trepidation as I eased Bessie into the throng of other bikers.

All kinds of cycles and bikers in full party mode not only lined the street on both sides, but they were also parked single file in the middle of the street—creating a tight space to navigate Bessie. It's always a thrill to ride down a Main Street of any bike event—it's the equivalent of walking the red carpet for Hollywood stars.

Partygoers jammed the roadway, hooting, hollering, whistling, and snapping photos. Bessie and I commanded a good deal of attention as we moved slowly from one end of Leesburg's Main Street to the other. All too quickly, the heady rush of riding among fellow bikers was over, and I found myself at the intersection of Main Street and US Highway 27—*Bloody US 27*.

If fear is the demon, then Highway 27 is the head of the dangerous monster. I was obligated to take this route home and cross the intersection where *it* happened. Full-on dark had arrived, and I was starting to question my sanity—not the first time I had done that and probably not the last. Undaunted, though, I squeezed the throttle and headed south toward home.

Traffic was light, and the night air was refreshing. As I approached Clermont, my hands clutched the handgrips a little tighter. There were two voices in my head now, keeping time like a metronome, chanting the mantras:

> *Stare the demon down.* (Jerry)
> *I won't let anything hurt you.* (Butch, my former riding partner).
> *Stare the demon down.*
> *I won't let anything hurt you.*

The cadence of the voices quickened as I approach the intersection, my heart pounding in my ears over the roar of Bessie Two.

The official Lake County police report marked the intersection of US 27 and SR 19 as the site of the collision. I have always maintained it was two intersections south of that point since that was the last location I recall before being hit. It doesn't matter. This stretch of asphalt is where the demon dwelled. The voices continued:

> *Stare the demon down.*
> *I won't let anything hurt you.*
> *Stare the demon down.*

I concentrated on driving, checking left, right, and ahead for obstacles, and prayed the light at the first intersection would stay green. Only when I cleared the intersection did I allow myself to exhale. I took deep, gulping breaths of the cool night air to avoid hyperventilating as I navigated the next two intersections. Oddly enough, there were no flashing lights, no clash of metal on metal, no screams, no soft white light—just me and Bessie Two cruising through the intersection whereas a year prior, Bessie One and I were literally knocked off course.

Success! I was still upright and breathing. I fist-pumped the chilly night air and shouted "Yes!" to the wind. I left Clermont's city limits and squeezed the throttle, eager to get home.

At nearly 10:00 p.m., I pulled into my driveway; relief flooding my consciousness. I sat on Bessie, listening to the soft tick of the engine cooling and the familiar night sounds of my neighborhood. A dog barked in the distance, the cicadas chirped a symphony, and the sultry sound of a Latin rhythm emanated softly from my neighbor Julio's bedroom window.

With my hands still gripping the handlebars, I said softly, "Thank You, God, for safe passage." As I climbed off Bessie, I felt lighter. A weight had been lifted, and with the toe of my boot, I snuffed out the demon that was holding me back from really enjoying my new ride.

Springtime and love are synonymous. After I stared the demon down, I spent the rest of the 2013 spring falling in love with Bessie Two. I designated Thursday as my start-the-weekend-early ride night. I watched the clock in my classroom tick sluggishly toward the end of the school day. Each Thursday, once the kids were dismissed, I raced home, anticipating the evening as I would anticipate time with an energetic lover. Only better.

I practically turned my car into my neighborhood on two wheels and screeched to a halt in the driveway. As I unlocked the back door and stepped inside, I kicked off my shoes, peeled off the teacher clothes while racing through the dining and living rooms, leaving a swath of discarded garments behind me. It took me two minutes to pull on jeans and a T-shirt, grab my boots, and head back the way I came. What I wanted to eat for dinner determined my destination. The simplicity of the effort was enchanting.

I continued to ride, mostly alone. I half-heartedly engaged in the online dating website, participating in a few email conversations or absentmindedly skimming the *prospects* for someone who might look interesting. My friend, Ann, was right about one thing: the OurTime. com dating website was different from the other sites I previously joined. Most of the men in this one were either working professionals or comfortably retired and pursuing a variety of activities with energy and enthusiasm for life. I noticed an absence of sleaziness and requests for nude photos or crude sexual connotations.

Unfortunately, the men who rode motorcycles were scarce, and that remained a *non-negotiable* point in my dating criteria. However, I managed to connect with a few nice guys that resulted in an agreeable encounter or two, such as an enjoyable lunch date or a companionable ride.

I did link up with two men—both riders—whom I deemed worthy of a further investment of my time. One had the distinct disadvantage (for him) of living in North Carolina; the other resided fifty miles from my home. All my life I have been attracted to men who are in some way unavailable, and a lot of miles between us often creates that restriction. If a prospective lover or partner is geographically distant, I can keep him there.

I was seeking a partner, not a Siamese twin. I have never wanted to be joined at the hip with a man, and I'm well aware that my desire to have a partner *and* solitude are in direct conflict with each other. Nevertheless, I remained persistent and undaunted in my pursuit of the *perfect man* who would embrace this inconsistency. As it turned out, E. Dick, the prospect who lived close to me, was not that man.

It is deliciously ironic that E. Dick appears as *E* in the alphabetical sequence of Dicks. His name is close to the word *edict,* which can be defined as a *proclamation* or *an act.* He was unquestionably an act. From our initial email conversations, I knew he rode a motorcycle and that he was intelligent, witty, cultured, and a published author. E. Dick had a keen sense of humor too.

Ostensibly a nice guy, E. Dick and I hit it off splendidly on our first meet-and-greet, otherwise known as the *scratch-and-sniff.* He was attractive, funny, worldly, and I sensed he was only slightly intimidated by my adventuresome spirit. He challenged me with his engaging intellectual capacity. Throughout a long lunch, we apparently became sparring partners in some cerebral competition concerning *who knows more about a given topic than the other*, which became exhausting by the end of lunch. I wasn't sure if I had *won*, or if there was *supposed* to be a winner. In hindsight, the intellectual turf war was a red flag, signaling a frightfully insecure man attempting to compensate for his inadequacies.

For three months, E. Dick and I volleyed back and forth with our quasi-attraction, trying to find common ground. The liaison was not exclusive, as I continued to communicate off and on with North Carolina man, although I felt he did not demonstrate a sincere effort— his lack of emails or phone calls noticeable—in developing a relationship, so I pursued other impressive prospects.

E. Dick loved art, the theater, and writing, which is where we found the most common ground. Although he owned a motorcycle and rode, he didn't ride as I did. While he was interested in my adventures on the bike, he didn't possess the confidence to do the same.

I felt curious to learn about his writing experience, and I shared my desire to write this book, which nurtured long conversations about what he had written as well as the mechanics of publishing and marketing a book. All I can say for the purpose of this book is that E. Dick was a businessman. Evidently, his business was moderately successful, if *success* equates to a stylish home in a fashionable location like those in charming Orlando suburbs where the Yuppies move in and spend a fortune renovating an eighty-year-old house, which features chic, original art (abstract, dark, angry), and a classic Jaguar coup. I found E. Dick challenging, intriguing—and downright arrogant.

Early in any possible liaison with a man, I'm the kind of woman who wants to know if the physical aspect of the relationship will be as satisfying as the exhilarating rides, intimate lunches, or stimulating conversation. Most of the time, I am woefully disappointed. Or, the reverse happens. Physical intimacy is wholly satisfying, but all other aspects of our affinity are boring and dreary. I always strive for balance.

E. Dick was "like the flesh and blood equivalent of a DKNY dress. You know it's not your style, but it's right there, so you try it on anyway," to quote *Sex in the City's* Carrie Bradshaw. Before trying on the dress, E. Dick and I had all the right ingredients for a pleasurable tryst: lovely afternoon ride on the motorcycles, hearty lunch, verbal foreplay, and mutual desire. Unfortunately, I discovered the root of his insecurities and persistent efforts to over-compensate intellectually. To borrow another line from *Sex in the City,* this time from Samantha Jones:

(Breathlessly) "Ok. I'm ready. Put it in."

(Her lover) "It is in."

The relationship shriveled after E. Dick and I both realized and agreed that the dress didn't fit. No worries. I had met a fascinating man who provided useful insight for my writing project—and another story to tell.

I felt content to spend time with my favorite companion, Bessie, enjoying our solo rides around Central Florida. In the spring of 2013, I began planning a celebration for Caroline's upcoming graduation from college and pouring over the atlas, scouting out a summer's road trip with Bessie Two. I decided my route might just take me through North Carolina.

MENTAL MASTURBATION

Always go with the choice that scares you the most, because that's the one that is going to require the most from you.

– Caroline Myss, *New York Times* best-selling author

IN PREPARATION FOR MY 2013 SUMMER ROAD TRIP—AND Bessie Two's maiden voyage—I honored my spirit biker-sister Bessie Stringfield by tossing a penny onto the United States map in my atlas. This ritual determined Stringfield's destination point for what became known as the Penny Tours, and I do the same for my extended ventures on two wheels. Abe Lincoln landed on Pennsylvania near the Ohio border, charting my itinerary.

I decided to make a loop, departing from Florida, going to northeastern Georgia, to Tennessee, Kentucky, Indiana, Ohio, the Virginias, and Carolinas. I wanted to ride the most challenging back roads in the Southeast, and Pennsylvania could easily be added to my route. If only I'd known this journey would introduce me to the man who would terminate the alphabet of Dicks in my life, I might not have procrastinated in getting ready to go.

For a month leading up to my departure on June 21, I went through endless mental masturbation, which can be defined as the act of engaging in an infinite cycle of overanalyzing and questioning your motives, usually to avoid taking action in your life. Theoretically, I looked forward to my summer excursion after ending another dynamic school year with a great group of students. Filled with pride and admiration, I also sat in the cavernous university auditorium at Caroline's graduation while grateful tears slipped down my cheeks as I watched her collect her diploma. I even acted cheery to her dad and his wife during family photo shoots and the post-graduation luncheon. A year had passed since my accident, and I felt physically and mentally strong again. For all practical purposes, life was good.

However, a hard nugget of what I called *self-doubt* remained. While I poured over the atlas, I kept questioning and rationalizing whether I should go or stay home, which cast a pall over my plans. An endless list of reasons to not go flew back and forth in my mind:

After taking Caroline to San Francisco for her graduation gift, maybe I just need to save money this summer.

Perhaps I could put the money I would spend on this trip in a vacation fund and take an exceptional trip this winter.

I can use the money to buy furniture.

Other voices taunted me:

You might not return home.

What if there's another accident? Think about how your daughter would feel when she got that phone call again.

Those mountain roads you've chosen are dangerous.

What if your vertigo returns while you're riding?

I was having lunch with my friend, Julie, one afternoon, blithely voicing my reservations. It was one of those maybe-I-shouldn't conversations you have with a close friend because you know she will see right through your bullshit and set you straight.

When Julie heard enough of my maybe-I-shouldn't line of thinking, she squared off over our burger and fries, leaned into the table, her face little more than arm's length from mine, and in a quiet voice said, "But it's what you always do in the summer."

And there it was—my truth, lying right there on the table between the salt shaker and ketchup. Friends who love you hold your truth. In my case, the revelation was that I was terrified to embark on this trip solo, yet even more terrified to stay home. Friends who don't want to see you dangle from the edge of whatever cliff you are about to go over place honesty right before you. It is not their opinion, nor is it a bunch of empty words crafted to make you feel better. Once it's plunked in your lap, you are obligated to pick it up and examine its validity.

My friend, Ann, knows me as well; in a series of phone conversations, she, too, placed truth in front of my eyes:

"You're not thinking about canceling your trip, are you?"

"But you always set off on an adventure in the summer!"

"You're not still afraid to travel on Bessie, are you?"

Her last statement was not a challenge—it was a gauntlet I needed to run through.

The feeling that I would never return home once I left on this trip dwelt in a spider-webbed corner of my psyche. I knew there are no safety guarantees on the road; in a split second, my course could be altered, my life changed. Fortuitously, a twist of fate *might* change my life, leaving me transformed—the reason I ride in the first place. The fact was, I needed to feel the fear, which is why I chose the most challenging roads in the Southeast for this trip.

I awoke before dawn on June 21, experiencing the familiar *resfeber—the* anxiety, and excitement of a traveler's heart before a journey begins. I took pleasure in drinking a cup of strong coffee, meditating, and praying—a must-do ritual before getting on my motorcycle. I moved about the house quietly—Caroline was still sleeping—pulling on my gear. I adjusted the pack attached to the backrest on the bike, and although it was humid, I donned my light jacket, knowing I would feel cool once I got on the road.

I left my daughter a note, telling her I loved her and that I would call when I stopped for the night. I couldn't resist tiptoeing to her room, cracking open the door ever so slightly, and briefly watching her sleep— no longer a small child but a college graduate. I whispered, "Mom loves you." I turned, walked through the kitchen, checked to make sure the coffeepot was turned off, and locked the door behind me.

Under cover of morning's small hours, the distant street lamp cast an eerie glow at the end of the driveway as I engaged in another ritual. I tied my bandana around my head just so, placed the helmet on my head, and clipped the chin strap in place. Next, I pulled on my leather gloves, adjusting each finger so the seams didn't rub, zipped my jacket, and settled the collar. My compulsive *gear ritual* is critical; it provides the illusion I have a semblance of control as I begin any journey on two wheels.

I straddled Bessie, set her upright under me, clicked the kickstand in place, bowed my head and prayed, "God, ride with me today and help all of us who are on the road to arrive safely at our destination. Circle your angels around me, Butch." Only then, did I feel justified to flip the ignition switch, hoping the thunderous sound of the engine didn't wake Caroline. Butterflies flew in formation as I drove out of my drive and headed north.

Although the weather appeared ominous in other parts of the country, the weather gods smiled as Bessie and I navigated Interstate 4 through Orlando just as the sun was coming up. We headed east on I-4 to merge onto I-95 near Daytona Beach. A few miles north, we became immersed in a mixture of fog and smoke from a nearby fire. Luckily, it dispersed north of St. Augustine.

We made easy progress until just south of Savannah, Georgia, where I stopped to slip on the hot and bothersome rain gear. The shower was light and brief, and as quickly as I had paused to put it on, I stopped to shed the rain gear and stow it in my saddlebag. Just a few more interstate miles and the beloved back roads would become my primary highways.

I picked up US 25 north of Statesboro, Georgia, and could hear the lyrics to "Statesboro Blues" start in my head. It's a Piedmont (plateau region in mainly the Southeast between the Blue Ridge Mountains and the Atlantic Coastal Plain) blues song, composed by Blind Willie McTell in 1923. I'm a rabid blues fan and take every opportunity to absorb the history and geography that gave birth to the musical genre.

McTell called Statesboro, Georgia, home—hence the song's title. Blues musician Taj Mahal recorded a contemporary version of "Statesboro Blues" in 1968, which inspired Duane Allman to learn to play slide guitar; he was a natural. However, the song did not become popular until the Allman Brothers Band recorded it on their first live album *At Fillmore East* in 1971. The brothers, who were living in Macon, Georgia, at the time, embossed the song with their unique brand of southern rock. I doubt Blind Willie would even recognize his tune. *Rolling Stone* ranks the Allman Brothers' version ninth on its list of 100 Greatest Guitar Songs of All Time.

I cued the song on my iPod, and with the familiar guitar riffs of Duane Allman amplified in my ear, I embraced the country routes of southeast Georgia. The humid air was fragrant with the antiseptic smell of Georgia pine as Bessie and I made our way to Augusta, where I planned to end the day.

Listening to the soul-searching rhythms of "Statesboro Blues" as I meandered through Georgia's blues history brought back memories of Butch. He, too, was a rabid blues fan. Our 2007 trip to Clarksdale, Mississippi—considered ground zero for the blues—was a memorable pilgrimage to the heart of the Mississippi Delta. US 61 runs 1,400 miles between New Orleans and the town of Wyoming, Minnesota. Known as the Blues Highway, its historical markers guide the intrepid traveler to points of rich musical interest along the way.

Butch and I accessed the Blues Highway north of New Orleans. It was a sweltering ride through loamy Mississippi farmland on a two-lane highway. In Clarksdale, we paid our respects to the musical genre at the Delta Blues Museum and knelt at the altar of the Ground Zero Blues Club; we stood at the "crossroads" of US 61 and US 49 where legendary blues guitarist Robert Johnson allegedly sold his soul to the devil and sat in the very room where Chicago artist Howlin' Wolf (Chester Arthur Burnett) slept. Many other blues musicians have called the area along US 61 in Mississippi home: B.B. King, Robert Johnson, Muddy Waters, Charley Patton, Ike Turner, and Sam Cooke, to name a few. The Blues Highway runs north to Memphis where a young Elvis Presley from Tupelo, Mississippi, would change the face of rock and roll music forever.

Known as the Empress of the Blues, vocalist Bessie Smith lost her life in a car accident on this highway in 1937. We visited the Clarksdale Riverside Hotel, formerly an African-American hospital in the early twentieth century, where she died. Adventuresome travelers can sleep in the hotel for a mere $40 per night. As Butch and I stepped into the bleak front parlor, an ancient black man—his face a series of deep creases, his faded blue eyes piercing—rose arthritically from his chair to greet us. He inquired as to whether we would be spending the night because "we only take cash." We declined but said we wanted to see where Bessie Smith died. He obligingly gestured toward a small room off the main hallway, indicating we were free to look inside. Who knew if it really WAS the room where she died, but Butch and I were enthralled nonetheless.

For many black musicians who lived in the repressive Jim Crow South, US 61 served as an escape route to move north to cities like Detroit, Chicago, New York City that were full of musical promise and a better way of life. Both *road* and *travel* are popular themes in blues music, representing a *way out* or the ability to *pack up and go,* leaving any troubles behind. Bob Dylan's classic album *Highway 61 Revisited* immortalized the highway for a younger generation of music lovers.

Music and memories swirled in my head as I navigated around Augusta to SR 28, which connects to the Savannah River National Scenic Byway, where I would begin the second leg of my journey the next day. The memories were like an emollient for my soul, tamping down the fears and easing the anxiety. My hotel outside of Augusta was just off SR 28 and within walking distance of several restaurants.

After checking in, I started unpacking my bike when I discovered the latch to my left saddlebag was broken. It wasn't a major issue, but it could be if I didn't fix it. After fumbling with it for several minutes, I deemed it beyond my ability to repair and decided I needed to locate a Harley-Davidson dealership first thing in the morning. With a broken latch, there was nothing to secure the lid to the saddlebag, and a stout wind could loosen it, possibly breaking it off entirely.

I called Caroline, content to hear the relief in her voice when I told her I had arrived safely at the first day's destination. Tomorrow, I would venture to northeast Georgia; the road beckoned me toward the challenging twists and turns I sought to bolster my flailing self-confidence and give me clarity.

LOOSE GRAVEL

I have always known that at last I would take this road,
but yesterday I didn't know that it would be today.

– Ariwara no Narihira, Japanese Courtier and Waka poet

I HAVE SPENT MOST OF MY ADULT LIFE OPERATING AT FULL
tilt with the attitude of *how fast can I get there,* or worse, *how quickly
can I get away.* Ironically, it took a fast-moving, 800-pound motorcycle
and a skid across a highway to slow me down. So, I was not in a hurry
to arrive anywhere on my first extended trip as I leisurely packed my
bike the second morning of my odyssey. A solid night's sleep attributed
to my sense of well-being on that morning.

This trip was all about the journey and bonding with Bessie Two
on some of the most demanding roads in the Southeast. What makes
a back road something to conquer? It's the curves, elevations, surface
conditions, and weather, which combine to make one hell of a ride on

two wheels. A challenging highway seems to be a metaphor for life as well; when I've successfully navigated an arduous, twisting road, I feel like I've tackled the obstacles that might be blocking my journey in life as well.

My morning began on the Savannah River National Scenic Byway, a 100-mile stretch of meandering road along the Savannah River that outlines the border between Georgia and South Carolina. I borrowed a paper clip—yes, a paper clip—from the hotel's front desk clerk and secured the broken latch after my bags were packed. I made a mental note to include duct tape in my tool kit on the next trip. Duct tape and WD-40 are crucial; if it won't move, and you want it to, use WD-40. If it moves, and you don't want it to, use the duct tape. And before I departed, I located the Harley-Davidson dealership in Anderson, South Carolina, on the map.

The weather was clear, and forecasters promised sunshine; humidity's clammy cloak draped itself around me as I merged onto SR 28 north. Bessie and I rambled through gently rolling farmland sprinkled with historic churches, their white spires crowned with crosses poking toward the heavens. Cows grazed lazily on the grassy slopes; some glanced up as I passed by.

Small towns like McCormick and Willington, South Carolina, are no more than charming wide spots along the way, frozen in time. Oddly, the tiny little towns, nestled snuggly along the Byway, afforded me a sense of comfort, a familiarity to my travels that morning. The country road looped through the densely-wooded Hickory Knob State Park and Resort, which ironically sports an eighteen-hole golf course, and the 371,000-acre Sumter National Forest. The thick foliage made it difficult for the sun's rays to penetrate, creating a surprisingly cool ride for a summer day in the deep South.

Little traffic interrupted my peaceful reverie as I glided along the flowing hills and gentle curves, at one with machine and nature. The mental masturbation of a few days ago gave way to an affirmation of why I ride in the first place. The rhythm of riding along a gently meandering road is hypnotic and soothing to my soul. I inhaled deeply of the lush verdant landscape while visually drinking the picturesque towns. All too quickly, I arrived at the point where I would leave the Scenic Byway and turn west to pick up SR 29 to Anderson.

The service manager at Timms Harley-Davidson dealership in Anderson replaced my broken saddlebag latch in record time and refused to charge me. While I waited, I met Charles Timms Sr. who opened the dealership in 1948 after returning from World War II. That same year Harley-Davidson introduced the Panhead model motorcycle, so named because the redesigned rocker covers (part of the engine) looked like upside-down roasting pans.

Mr. Timms, about five feet five inches tall, had a twinkle in his eye as he said he was intrigued that I was a "woman out there riding alone." Mr. Timms had to be in his eighties; his face crinkled from age and sun damage, his hands gnarly from arthritis. I shared a few of my road stories with him. He told me he didn't work anymore—his son and two grandsons operated the business, but, he continued, "I show up every day after breakfast to make sure things are running smoothly." And yes, he still rode his motorcycle.

Before I said goodbye to the charming Mr. Timms, I visited the apparel shop to score a destination T-shirt. With a new latch securing my saddlebag, I was ready to merge onto the super slab (I-85) west to SR 11 near Gaffney, South Carolina.

South Carolina SR 11 is the Cherokee Foothills Scenic Byway, which winds through the southernmost peaks of the Blue Ridge Mountains and gently bends through peach orchards and picturesque villages. The 112-mile, two-lane highway—once used by Cherokee Indians and French fur traders—abounds with antique shops, roadside farm stands, and charming little bed-and-breakfast inns.

I picked up SR 130 in Georgia and headed north through the Nantahala (Cherokee word meaning "Land of the Noonday Sun") National Forest, where the fun really begins for a motorcyclist. Steering through the *twisties*—bending, curvy roads—felt exhilarating. State Roads 28 and 11 were tame in comparison. I came up behind three bikers traveling together on a narrow mountain artery and tackled the curves with them for more than two hours. I wasn't sure where we were going, but it was great fun going there.

The trio stopped at the first gas station, and I pulled in behind them to introduce myself. They lived in the area, and I was surprised to learn we were in North Carolina, somewhere near Franklin. I chatted with the lone woman, Amy, who uttered that familiar phrase to me for the second time that day: "You mean you rode all the way from Florida—by *yourself*?" She confessed she was envious and hoped to "just take off and ride" someday. I encouraged her to do just that as her husband gave me the side-eye while quietly sipping his soda and puffing on his cigarette. I got the distinct impression hubby didn't approve of women riding alone, although Amy rode her own bike. Probably with his permission.

I said farewell to my fellow riders and decided it was time to find a place to spend this Saturday night; Bessie and I were deep in the mountains where darkness fell quickly. Highlands or Walhalla, North Carolina, where I could find lodging, was still an hour's ride on treacherous mountain roads.

US 64 west is chocked-full of gut-wrenching switchbacks and ten-mile-per-hour curves that require a rider on a fully loaded touring bike to stay upright while steering it sharply uphill or downhill. (May the centrifugal force be with you!)

Then it happened. I made a wrong turn at an unmarked fork in the road, confident I remained on US 64, going west.

After manipulating a few more agonizing curves, the unthinkable followed: the asphalt turned into gravel—*loose gravel* on a steep, narrow road with a sheer drop-off to my right. Not good. I knew I had to keep moving forward. The second I stopped and tried to put my feet on the ground, odds were my foot would slip on loose gravel, and I would topple, laying the bike down, or worse, sliding over the edge and tumbling down a steep ravine with no bottom in sight.

My heart raced. Sweat ran down my back toward the waistband of my jeans, and twilight descended on the mountain. I slipped and slid up the mountain for at least three miles before I spotted two pickup trucks parked to the left side.

As I approached, I saw a group of teenagers, two boys and two girls, doing God-knows-what in the middle of nowhere, but I wasn't there to judge. They appeared clean-cut jocks and cheerleader types out for a little afternoon fun. I felt no "danger" vibes from the four teens, only the predicament I was in on a dangerous mountain road. I slowed near the trucks, taking the chance that if I stopped and stumbled, four strong bodies could help me right my bike. The teens turned cautiously in my direction—the sweet smell of pot wafting in the air—and eyed me slowly.

"I'm sorry to interrupt your party, but I could use some help," I said over the thump-thump-thump of my engine, more than a little frantically.

"Cool," was the collective response from four stoned teenagers as country music played softly from a radio in one of the pickups.

"Where you headed?" the blond boy asked.

"Highlands," I replied.

"Oh, man, you missed it. It's like, back that way." Captain Obvious gestured in the direction I had just traveled.

"Yes. I know. I need to turn my bike around, and I could use your help."

"Sure. What do you want us to do?"

They were going to need a lot of direction to keep me from going over the side of the mountain. All four of them took a swig from the bottles of beer in their hands as if to fortify themselves for the task at hand. They set the bottles near the back bumper of one of the trucks and seemed eager to assist. Eagerness could get me killed, however, so I explained how we were going to accomplish the task.

I positioned one of the girls, her long blond hair fell in a silky river down her back, almost reaching the waistband of her Daisy Dukes, near the edge of the roadway and the threatening drop-off. I told her to watch that I didn't get too close to it while one of the boys slowly pushed me backward, my feet slipping in the gravel. The other couple positioned themselves near the other two as back up in case our original plan failed.

All four were focused and hyperalert as if my life depended on their assistance—and it did. I pulled forward, my muscles taut with tension, and turned the front wheel slightly. With my boots scooting on the gravel and blonde girl standing with her feet apart, arms out wide to her side as if she were ready to catch me if I fell, I repeated the process—basically a very tight three-point turnaround—until the bike's front end pointed down the mountain. A hoot and holler cheer erupted from the four teenagers as they sensed "we" had accomplished something critical on the mountain that day. They high-fived each other; I was terrified to let go of the handlebars for my high five, but the relief on my face was enough for them. One of the boys slapped me on the back; the other one made a beeline for the bumper of the truck where his beer was getting warm.

I said a silent *thank You, God,* as I exhaled, calmed my shaking hands with a few deep breaths. I shouted a heartfelt "Thank You" to the teenagers and headed back the way I came. I traversed the treacherous switchbacks again, this time in a downward direction. When I got to the point where I had made the wrong turn, I double-checked to be sure I was on US 64. Bessie and I drove into Highlands, North Carolina, before daylight faded.

About an hour past the gravely turnaround atop the mountain, I stopped at the nearest hotel, a rustic-looking lodge, and parked my motorcycle. I climbed off, wobbled around, and darn near lost my balance I felt so weak-kneed. I took deep, cleansing breaths as I pulled off my helmet and gloves, reminding myself all was okay.

As I paced the parking lot of the lodge, shaking off the tension, I reminded myself: I did not drop the bike, I did not slide off the mountain, I did not skid headfirst along asphalt nor did any other tragedy befall Bessie and me. I managed, I took charge, I calculated the situation, and I resolved it without harm to life or limb. And on top of that, I gave four stoned teenagers a good story to tell for weeks to come.

Life is fraught with "loose gravel," unexpected events that can throw a person off course. How we negotiate the loose gravel shapes our outlook and determines our contentment in life. Bessie and I came to find a challenge, and this experience more than qualified. Tomorrow, we would run the Gauntlet in northern Georgia.

DRAGON SLAYER

Brave [wo]men did not kill dragons. The brave
[wo]men rode them.

Adapted from *Game of Thrones*

SUNDAY MORNING DAWNED BRIGHT AND FULL OF PROM-
ise. Bessie and I, still feeling triumphant after we avoided plummeting
down a North Carolina mountain yesterday, were eager to get on the
road early. The invigorating crisp air rushed into my room as I lugged
my pack out to Bessie.

I dug my leather chaps and heavy coat out of the saddlebag; it
would be a nippy ride until the sun breached the Blue Ridge. I had
made an advanced reservation at the Copperhead Lodge outside of
Blairsville, Georgia. It is operated by bikers, for bikers, and is a central
starting point for the Gauntlet, advertised as 133 Miles of Smiles for
its demanding twists and turns; it loops through northeast Georgia.

I chugged down a cup of hotel coffee and promised myself I would
stop for breakfast farther down the way. If the caffeine didn't jolt me

fully awake, I knew the cold air would finish the job as Bessie and I left Highlands, North Carolina, in our review mirror.

I took US 64 West to US 441 South into Georgia. The northeast corner of the state is nestled in the Blue Ridge Mountains and the Chattahoochee National Forest, which cover eighteen north Georgia counties. I fell in love with the region my first time through the area about five years ago and had returned many times to enjoy the Georgia mountains.

I rode the eastern portion of the Gauntlet before checking into Copperhead Lodge. As promised, I "smiled" as I negotiated fluctuating elevations and tight turns that curved through the mountains. As I traversed the eastern portion of the Gauntlet, I stopped for lunch—I know, I skipped right over breakfast—in Dahlonega, Georgia, a quaint little town situated around an old-fashioned town square; antiquated buildings sat neatly in rows across from a grassy park. The area around this town is the heart of Georgia wine country.

Tourists—many of them bikers—roamed the sidewalks, enjoying the variety of unique goods and services Dahlonega offered. My nose followed the luscious smell of barbeque a few blocks off the main square where I tucked away a plate of sweet, tangy barbeque with generous sides of collard greens and mac 'n cheese at the award-winning Smokin' Gold BBQ. I have gone back for that Southern cuisine lots of times over the years, and I've never been disappointed with the quality of their food.

Copperhead Lodge is a massive stone and wood structure, nestled on the side of a hill overlooking dense forests. Cabins, for rent or sale, dot the meadow along the road leading up to the lodge; faux rustic, modular homes with small garages just right for a motorcycle or two, sit on a grassy knoll overlooking the lodge. Along the edge of the parking area, several bikes rested in the biker-parking-only spaces. A generous verandah with a stone fireplace and wicker ceiling fans sat off the restaurant side of the lodge, overlooking a substantial pool area.

I parked Bessie in a designated slot, traded my helmet for my Harley-Davidson ball cap, and felt the peace of quiet surroundings. A bumblebee buzzed among the wildflowers in the meadow, sampling the red, purple and yellow blossoms which bordered the sidewalk while a cacophony of bird chatter arose from the trees. The sun became beastly hot with heat waves visible across the vast expanse of meadow.

Copperhead's main room had vaulted ceilings that soared upward, supported by rustic wood beams as thick as an elephant's leg. Laughter mingled with tinkling glasses and music in the bar. I checked in, met the owners (who later divorced and sold the lodge) and motored around to the back where each room faced the woods. Bessie was the only Harley-Davidson cruiser among a gang of BMW (Beemer) motorcycles. Same species, but a different breed of riders. I don't trust a motorcycle that doesn't make noise; they don't appreciate one that does.

After stowing my gear in the small but comfortable room, Bessie and I headed back out to the main road to explore the area. Blairsville is one of the larger towns in this Georgia area with approximately 1,000 year-round inhabitants. Most small mountain towns swell in numbers when summer tourists come, seeking a respite from the summer heat in Florida. About half of Florida's population own summer homes in northeast Georgia. Although the morning mountain air is usually cool, summer afternoons in Northeast Georgia can be just as beastly as Florida.

I grabbed a few provisions at a local grocery since I checked the menu at the lodge restaurant and found it lacking. I returned to the lodge, intent on grabbing a book and nestling into one of the comfy sofas strewn about the verandah. My BMW neighbors, who gathered outside their rooms, eyed me as I noisily eased Bessie into her slot.

Six men, one woman. They were from Louisiana, and we chatted amiably for several minutes after which they invited me to join them for breakfast and a ride the following morning. Breakfast yes, ride no. I wasn't interested in sharpening my floorboards on the switchbacks while trying to keep up with a herd of Beemers. We confirmed a time to meet for breakfast, and then I grabbed my book and kicked back on a verandah sofa for a pleasant evening of reading.

Thankfully, the Beemer group were early risers. We congregated outside the row of rooms, packed our bikes, and commiserated over the fact there was no coffee available at the hotel until after 8:00 a.m. Since Copperhead's nightly rates were the highest in the area, one would at least expect to find a small coffeepot in the room.

Although the sun was rising, heavy gray clouds blocked my favorite sunrise colors of pink and orange. Rain dominated the forecast. I retreated to my room to stretch before saddling up. My right shoulder carries the residual damage from the accident—an impinged shoulder that stiffens during the night and is doubly painful after riding all day.

I followed the group to a diner in town, and as we situated ourselves at the table, I gravitated towards the woman, whose name was Ellen, and sat down next to her. Ellen rode her own bike as well, and we shared similar stories regarding our introduction to riding, solo travels, and our age. I savored other bikers' stories and purposely avoided telling them about my gravel road experience from the previous day. Beemers would have relished such a challenge as uphill on a gravel road and would have made it there and back with no qualms.

We finished breakfast, exchanged cards with contact information, and bid farewell. I planned to finish the western half of the Gauntlet, collect more "smiles," and then travel north to slay a dragon—or at least its tail.

The Gauntlet is 133 miles of winding curves and *twisties*, not found on a GPS, that snake through the northeast Georgia mountains.

The area is heavily wooded with several large recreation areas situated around beautiful lakes and populated with vintage small towns that cater to our kind of biker crowd. Well-maintained roads are marked, which makes the ride doubly enjoyable. Although the clouds hung heavy in the mountains, the rain never materialized.

I navigated SR 180, zigzagging up Brasstown Bald, the highest point in Georgia at 4,783 feet. On a clear day, the observation deck at the top of the mountain offers sweeping views of four states and the skyline of Atlanta. However, on the day I rode the tram to the top and climbed the stairs to the observation tower, half the mountain was swaddled in cotton-like clouds, blocking a view of anything but more clouds.

As I headed back down the mountain, the precipitation was so heavy I couldn't tell if it was raining or if I was just surrounded by rain clouds. Either way, it made for a slippery ride while maneuvering hairpin turns. Once I arrived at the bottom of Brasstown Bald, the weather was clear; two deer rustled in the adjacent bushes as I rode by.

I doubled back west to merge onto Gumlog Road at the northern tip of Lake Nottely, built by the Tennessee Valley Authority during World War II, and south to Nottely Dam Road. I encountered few bikers; perhaps the threat of rain had kept them away.

I was still "smiling" when I hit Skeenah Gap Road and SR 60, the southwest portion of the Gauntlet loop. The tight curves took every bit of my concentration; I had to be sure I did the right amount of braking and throttle. The scenery along the Gauntlet is a bucolic feast for the eyes: deep, cool forests, meadows that dip and roll, picturesque farmhouses, scenic overlooks with ample places to stop and drink in the view, and miles of wildflowers. The ride felt incredibly relaxing despite my having to stay focused on the demanding route.

My favorite part of the ride was on the twelve-mile Wolf Pen Gap Road, which is the same as SR 180. Its hairpin loops never stopped on the two-lane back circuit; I was barely out of one before I leaned into the next one. Suddenly, six Beemers (not the group from Louisiana) flew right past me, their boxy machines silent except for an annoying *zzzzzzzzt*. I was on a narrow mountain road with death-defying twists, a double yellow line, and caution signs signaling twenty-mile-per-hour *blind* curves. And these people were whizzing past me, which is precisely why I declined to ride with the Beemer group from Louisiana. I appreciate the fact that there are all kinds of motorcycles and cyclists; what I don't appreciate is when *their* agendas on *their* bikes jeopardize *my* safety on *my* bike.

I'm reminded of a biker philosophy: *It is the twisties, not the super slabs that separate the riders from the SQUIDS.* In motorcycle slang, SQUID is an acronym for Stupidly Quick, Underdressed, Imminently Dead. They are the reckless bikers who ride beyond their abilities, ride without proper gear, and endanger the lives of others on the road. A biker doesn't have to possess all these characteristics to qualify as a SQUID—just one will do.

Wolf Pen Gap Road ends at US 129 and completes the western portion of the Gauntlet. I executed a celebratory fist up and shouted *yeehaw* to no one in particular to celebrate having *run the Gauntlet.* Skillfully maneuvering the slippery slope a few days before and now conquering the challenges along the Gauntlet dissolved any remnants of the fear I felt prior to the beginning of this trip. I headed back to Blairsville to gas up, check the map, and journey north on US 129 toward Deals Gap, North Carolina.

The meandering highway between Blairsville, Georgia, and Murphy, North Carolina, is reminiscent of a bygone era when *slow* was the acceptable mode of travel. Dense outcroppings of tiger lilies—showy combinations of orange and yellow blooms, their black stamens in the center were like eyes that followed me as I passed them—lined large portions of the route. Their long stems bowed in the wind. It seemed every home near the highway was surrounded by massive blooms of hydrangeas, heavy with every conceivable shade of blue, purple, and pink blossoms that drooped toward the ground.

Deals Gap is a mountain pass on US 129, along the border of North Carolina and Tennessee, and is on the periphery of the Great Smoky Mountains National Park. The southern starting point of the Tail of the Dragon—its eleven-mile stretch boasts 318 curves—is considered the premier destination in the United States for motorcyclists and sports car enthusiasts.

Other than mentioning *woods*, don't ask what the scenery was like along the Dragon, as it is impossible to do any sightseeing. The tight, continuous twists and turns demand every ounce of a motorcyclist's or driver's concentration to avoid becoming a statistic to be added to the Dragon Death Map, a macabre, four-color map of the highway available in the Deals Gap gift shop and on tailofthedragon.com. It details all the points along the route where someone has lost their life. The Dragon is most assuredly the ride of a lifetime, and once completed, separates accomplished riders from SQUIDS.

I planned to ride the Tail of the Dragon on a weekday when there was less chance of traffic, especially Beemer or sport riders who felt it their duty to see how fast they could cover the 318 snaky turns. I stopped at the Deals Gap Motorcycle Resort, a bare-bones motel, restaurant, and gift shop, catering to the fearless souls who come to slay the Dragon. It is customary to have your picture taken under the Tree of Shame, a large tree festooned with wrecked motorcycle parts which have been picked up along the route from riders who underestimated the Dragon. I asked a nice-looking gentleman, sporting several Harley patches on his leather vest, to snap my picture. I snagged a commemorative T-shirt, stowed my purchase, checked to make sure my pack was secure, and rolled Bessie onto the asphalt, ready to slay the Dragon. My confidence was fortified having triumphantly completed the Gauntlet.

The tight *twisties* began immediately; no time to ease into them, and no time to let down my guard one iota. I vowed to take it slow and stay in second gear. Most accidents on the Dragon are a result of speed, inexperience, or a deadly combination of both.

I nearly had the road to myself, and I enjoyed an exhilarating ride, which commanded my concentration and the skill set I had developed over the years. The Dragon is like a thrill ride at the county fair: anticipation creates that fluttery feeling in the pit of your stomach while the dips, curves, and elevation electrify every nerve ending.

I ignored anyone in my rearview mirror and focused solely on the next curve: clutch, shift, brake, repeat. Only once did my floorboard scrape the pavement as I pointed the front of my bike into a curve; the noise and subsequent sensation in my stomach felt like a jolt of electricity. Eleven miles flew by, and I was almost tempted to turn around and do it all over again!

I stopped on the north end at the Harley-Davidson store to do a little victory dance in the parking lot; two men standing across the lot next to their bikes smiled as I gyrated, arms in the air. They probably guessed why I was celebrating but had no idea of the mental masturbation that precluded the victory dance.

Considering where I was a year ago from this point, riding again was a gift; running the Gauntlet and Slaying the Dragon were priceless presents to be treasured.

At this juncture in my summer-of-2013 trip, I was six days from home, slowly making my way to Indiana to visit family and friends. My dad was expecting me, although he knew better than to pin me down to a specific time and day. I said farewell to the glorious twisty mountain back roads and pointed Bessie north.

Unfortunately, the ride between Knoxville, Tennessee, and Central Indiana was inundated with summer storms. What should have been a ten-to-twelve-hour journey on Interstate 75 became a two-day ordeal. It was impossible to dodge angry black clouds and torrential rain, regardless of the route I chose. My original destination, in keeping true to the spirit of Bessie Stringfield's Penny Tour, of Pennsylvania would have to wait for the return trip.

After two days of the worst riding conditions I had ever experienced, I finally arrived safely at Dad's house. He was ready with the garden hose to wash off Bessie's road grime while the Dragon Slayer took a hot shower and dried out.

Later that night, I showed Dad the GoPro video of my journey on the Gauntlet and the Dragon. I had mounted the tiny camera on the roll bar near the front of the bike and close to the road. This position affords a daring angle to the viewer of all the twists and turns the Dragon had to offer. A few minutes into the Dragon footage, my Dad looked at me and exclaimed incredulously, "My God! You did *that*?"

"Yes. Yes, Dad, I did."

SALVATION IN THE HEARTLAND

The only difference between the saint and the sinner is that
every saint has a past and every sinner has a future.

– Oscar Wilde, *A Woman of No Importance*

SHORTLY AFTER GRADUATING FROM HIGH SCHOOL, I LEFT
Marion, Indiana, my birthplace, the small, rural, and provincial place
I couldn't wait to escape from; however, it has always been home: "The
dark ancestral cave, the womb from which mankind emerged into the
light, forever pulls one back," wrote Thomas Wolfe in *You Can't Go
Home Again*.

My dad retired in the 1980s, after which he and my mom moved
forty miles to Muncie, Indiana, to be closer to my brother and sister.
Muncie was never *home* to me, but Dad's house is where he had "to
take me in" as the narrator in Frost's poem "The Death of the Hired
Man" suggests.

The morning after I had conquered the Gauntlet and slain the Dragon, I sat in Dad's kitchen, sipping coffee and listening to the clocks tick. He had a clock in every room, and some rooms, like the kitchen, had several. *Tick* and its answer, *tock*, resonated in stereo throughout the house. The sweep hand made its perpetual revolution, jerking the minute hand to attention every sixty seconds; it pushed the hour hand slowly toward its next position. It served as a foreshadowing, a synchronized countdown of Dad's life—an audible inventory of time spent, minutes wasted, and the precious few minutes left.

I was reminded of Pink Floyd's song "Time" as the minutes of that dull day ticked away while I sat resolutely in Dad's kitchen. The ticking clocks would drive me crazy, but I didn't live there—I was only visiting.

I felt the need to escape less than twenty-four hours after I arrived. I love my family, and on the dysfunctional meter, my family pegs just slightly right of *average*. Back when I drank copious amounts of alcohol, our dysfunctional meter remained on the right, the *extreme* right. Sobriety and age have their merits, I suppose.

Before the clocks ticked away any more precious time, I decided to take Bessie for a spin around Delaware County and over to Marion, my old hometown, for a look around.

The country roads of the rural farming communities of East Central Indiana are laid out in perfect patchwork squares. The verdant fields of corn, soybeans, and tomatoes were sliced into neat squares by strips of asphalt. Muncie is home to Ball State University and Ball Memorial Hospital, named in honor of five prosperous Ball brothers who are recognized mostly for their production of home-canning glass jars. Despite the ebb and flow of manufacturing in the area, Muncie has thrived with the presence of the university.

I crisscrossed the county on a series of back roads, their surface crawling with black tar snakes—jagged black lines of patching tar—scarring the asphalt. The tar snakes heat up in the summer sun, creating slippery patches for two-wheelers. Emerald cornstalks topped with yellow tassels stood tall in fields of flat land on both sides of me; the air was fragrant with a grassy, fertile smell.

An old, dilapidated barn caught my eye, and I slowed Bessie to a stop. My boots crunched on the loose gravel near the shoulder of the road—the only sound as I climbed off the bike to inspect the barn. I love old barns and possess several dozen photos of them in every size, shape, and stage of decay. I love the rough texture of the wood and how the original bright red paint softens as it fades and blends into the grayness of the wood; the little odds and ends left behind suggest its story and that of the family who inhabited the property. Things such as a row of cloudy, empty canning jars atop a sagging shelf, their lids corroded or a scythe left hanging on a wall, its long, wooden handle shiny and smooth from use; its once sharp blade now rusty from neglect.

I pulled my Canon 5D out of the saddlebag, adjusted the lens, and strolled toward the barn, looking for a *no trespassing* sign or other indication I should not inspect the grounds. The sun felt fierce in the still air. An orange-breasted Baltimore oriole hopped under the shade of an overgrown slippery elm tree and pecked at the ground for grubs or worms. Cicadas pierced the summer silence with their screechy, incessant hum.

I walked to the side of the barn where an overgrown patch of white asters and white and gold blooming goldenrod contrasted beautifully with the faded red wood. A rusty basketball hoop, minus its net, hung lopsidedly from one side of the barn. I envisioned a tall, lanky farm kid endlessly tossing a basketball toward the hoop, his dreams of playing for one of many basketball-crazed big ten schools not yet a reality. When you grow up in Indiana, you learn to love two sports—basketball and auto racing. As I snapped several pictures of the exterior of the barn, I inhaled the sweet summer air.

Bessie and I traversed the county roads from Delaware County, named for the Delaware Indians, to Grant County toward Marion. I passed through Fairmount where its claim to fame remains James Dean, the iconic fifties bad boy. Dean was born in Marion, and after the family moved to California for a few years where his mother died, his dad sent young James back to nearby Fairmount to live with an aunt. He graduated from Fairmount High School and went back to California with his dog, Max, to seek fame and immortality in Hollywood.

The tiny farming community is a mecca for fans who make the pilgrimage to visit the James Dean Gallery and plant lipstick-laced kisses on his headstone in Park Cemetery. Thousands of Dean devotees come every year to the James Dean Festival, featuring classic cars, music, and motorcycles. Preserving his legacy is a full-time occupation for Grant County residents.

I rode in on the south side of Marion, slowing as I passed the home where I grew up. I felt dismayed when I looked at the decay of a once stately, two-story house that had been my home. It seemed smaller.

I glanced up at the second story where my bedroom window faced the street. Two south windows overlooked the roof of our sunroom. On summer mornings, I used to crawl through the window to the gently sloping roof, spread a beach towel on the warm shingles and sunbathe with Jimi Hendrix or Carlos Santana playing on my turntable.

I hoped the lilac bush was still in the backyard—the one I loved that grew just outside the dining room window. During the summer when the windows were open, the extravagant floral fragrance of lilac blossoms filled the house, mingling with the sweet summer breeze. My mom always clipped several branches of blooms and put them in a hefty vase in the center of the dining room table; their vivid lavender color lent a cheerfulness to our home.

Indiana Wesleyan University, a private Christian liberal arts college, has consumed my old neighborhood like a giant amoeba sprawling over the south end of town. The compact, single-family homes, like the one my grandparents had, are gone, replaced with dormitories and other brick academic buildings. The 345-acre campus appears to be the sparkling jewel for an otherwise deteriorating hometown.

As I rode toward downtown, I looked for familiar landmarks but found the blight of decay everywhere. Large parts of south Marion where I grew up were just gone or razed, no longer useful or recognizable. I suppose if you grow up in a town, stay there, and age with it, it's like seeing your reflection in the mirror. The aging and decaying come gradually, and you either choose not to notice, or you reach a level of acceptance with what you see. But when you don't view your reflection daily, even a glance proves startling. Everywhere I turned, I asked myself, *What used to be there?*

The courthouse, its imposing presence perched in the center of town, was one of the few buildings in downtown Marion I recognized. Although it was a weekday, the square was sparsely populated, and I slipped into one of the vertical parking spaces fanning out around the courthouse.

Dad wanted me to see the murals on the Community School for the Arts building on the east side of the square on Adams Street. Notable Hoosier portraits, two-stories tall, adorned the side wall, where its dazzling swath of color brightened the dreary downtown. James Dean is there, and so is native Jim Davis, creator of the lovable feline character Garfield. Cole Porter, whose musical *Kiss Me Kate* won a Tony Award, smiles at all who pass by; he wrote other musicals, scores for movies, and hit songs such as "Night and Day."

Another new and fun addition to downtown was the Squealers on the Square—life-size pig statues, decorated with a festival of colors, which occupied several corners around the courthouse. One squealer was painted with a modish Andy Warhol kind of theme with James

Dean's face. Another statue is a "Pig-casso," festooned with Picasso's trademark geometric patterns in a kaleidoscope of color. There is even a pig that resembles Garfield the cat. The Harley pig is mostly black, and its face and upper body are an explosion of yellow and red Harley flames.

My hometown and Harley-Davidson have had a long and intimate connection. In 1916, Lawrence Ray Weishaar, a Class A Racing Champion in the 1910s and 1920s, began racing on the Harley-Davidson Wrecking Crew team. He achieved his most significant victory by beating the standing record of eighteen minutes in the Marion Cornfield Classic Road Race.

The team's mascot was a small live pig, which Weishaar took for a ride on his victory laps. The little squealer and Weishaar became so popular that Harley's cycles became known as *hogs*. The nickname for a Harley-Davidson evolved into the acronym for membership in the Harley Owners Group, *HOG*, which boasts over a million members worldwide. Marion hosts an annual Hog Daze Motorcycle Rally each year in August to commemorate the shared history and motorcycles.

I strolled across the square, my heart heavy as I looked at the new Vietnam War Memorial. The Vietnam War dominated my childhood and adolescence, ending in 1973, the year I graduated from high school. My biological dad did three tours in Vietnam as did several boys I grew up with. The Marion boys killed in action (KIAs) are listed first on the three-dimensional granite obelisk, followed by those who served and returned home. I gazed up to the top of the list and read the names silently, recognizing many—and one in particular. He and I dated shortly after he returned from 'Nam. I had heard he died in a house fire several years ago, along with two of his children. His name is etched in granite now, preserved for posterity.

I remember several vets in our group of high school friends who came home, burdened with the atrocities of a futile war fought over policies we didn't understand, and they turned to drugs and alcohol to temper their post-traumatic stress disorder (PTSD) and anger. I don't know a single Vietnam soldier who returned the same person as he was when he left. Tears stung my eyes as I recalled the boys I knew, and I said a prayer of gratitude for their service. I wondered how many other small-town squares across America are adorned with granite memorials to men and women who fought in what history has deemed a senseless war in southeast Asia.

I stood near Bessie and gazed around my hometown square one last time, feeling like a stranger in an unknown land. Suddenly, from two blocks away, a loud, though familiar, voice pierced my quiet reverie. It shouted, "Debi Tolbert (my maiden name), is that you?"

I looked over to see Bubba Jones, (not his real name), hurrying to my side of the square, his substantial body hurtling toward me as fast as he could go. I was astonished anyone recognized me since I had on a hat and mirrored aviator sunglasses. I had not seen this person in decades. He reached my side of the square and enveloped me in a bear hug, nearly knocking me off my feet. Trying to reclaim my balance and extricate myself from his grasp, I exclaimed, "Wow! Bubba, is that you? How long has it been?"

"Damn, Debi. You look great! Wow! What are you doing downtown?" bellowed Bubba, his big, doughy face uncomfortably close to mine. He acted as if we ran into each other weekly while strolling around downtown. Bubba and I went to school together from fourth grade through high school, and he tormented me every single one of those days. Perhaps *tormented* is too harsh a word, although that is how I felt at the time. In today's school culture, we call it "bullying," which seems a little harsh to describe Bubba's teasing ways and constant, unwanted attention in my direction. My mom assured me that if boys *teased* you, they actually *liked* you. Thanks, Mom.

Several years after high school, Bubba and I reconnected through a mutual friend, and I learned what a sweet person he had become later in life. He and I quickly caught up on four decades of adulthood, and then I made a motion to leave, anticipating the boob-crushing, farewell bear hug that was imminent. Bubba never disappointed.

Once freed from Bubba's grasp, Bessie and I cruised out North River Road, which meandered along the Mississinewa River whose muddy brown contents spilled over the dam near the entrance to Matter Park. I felt happy to see a new walking trail along the river; elegant old homes that surrounded the hospital area showed no signs of decay. What Central Park is to New York City, Matter Park is to Marion—sort of.

In my youth, the park was a much-anticipated family destination for amusement rides and cotton candy. I spent untold summer afternoons at the public pool, learning to swim, and later, discovering what the attraction between boys and girls meant. In my adolescence, the park was a summer and fall meeting place for bored teenagers with too much time on their hands. I parked Bessie in the lot I used to hang out in like all other bored teenagers and walked up the hill toward the center of the park.

I stood on the hill overlooking the river; its muddy water flowed slowly, and summertime greenery covered the banks. I peered down toward the area where the kiddie rides used to be, long gone now. Closing my eyes, I recalled hearing calliope music from the magical carousel, beckoning eager children with fistfuls of tickets to climb aboard. I pictured delighted boys and girls on brightly painted horses, frozen in a perpetual gallop, as parents clutched smaller children to keep them in the saddle.

As a little girl, the other kids and I experienced pure joy as we sat in the two-person speedboats, six of them attached to a turnstile-type device that churned the boats around in a large circle. It didn't matter where you steered, each boat followed the other as they floated in a large, swimming pool type carrousel full of water while smiling children clanged the bell attached to the dashboard of the craft.

The cable cars—so high in the air! How daring I felt to climb into the cage-like car for a ride suspended above the park, swinging dangerously close to the river, then back down again into the noisy center of the concession area. Memory took me to the cotton candy vendor who always did a brisk business; each child pleaded with their parents for a nickel to buy the sweet, melt-on-your-tongue spun sugar. A perfect cloud of pink, sticky confection, twirled around a paper cone, served as the reward for being good. A miniature locomotive pulled a train that chugged along the diminutive tracks to all points of interest in the park. What a golden time to be a kid!

The park also housed animals—poor wretched beasts, caged and forlorn. I could never forget the baboons—monkeys too—their nasty smell overwhelmed the exotic animal enclosure. I felt embarrassed to see their exposed, red bottoms while they absentmindedly picked fleas off each other, seemingly oblivious to humans watching from the other side of the bars. The fetid odor of a dirty animal sitting in a cage where someone doused the cement floor with Pine Sol to make it smell clean still burns my nostrils. To this day when I smell Pine Sol, I get a flashback of the baboon cages at Matter Park—like something out of a Stephen King novel. I do not wax nostalgic for the animals at the park, but I do for the kiddie rides. Happily, the "exotic" animals were removed from the park along with the kiddie rides many years ago.

As I walked back to where Bessie waited for me, I realized the park had been transformed several times over the years to accommodate the needs of the community. The band shell was still there near the ancient swings and slide atop the hill. A stunning formal garden area had replaced the softball fields, and the tennis courts had been relocated. The pond where my friends and I ice-skated in the winter was now surrounded by an urbanized children's play area.

Matter Park remains the idyllic backdrop for family picnics, community events, and yes, bored teenagers seeking a respite from small-town life. My small-town soul felt nourished as I fired up Bessie, breaking the woodsy silence of the park, and made my way back to Delaware County.

Sunday—recognized as a church day in the Heartland. Dad was eager to take me to his church, and I felt pleased to accompany him. My parents didn't start attending church until my mom became very sick, about ten years before she passed. I'm grateful they found a spiritual home, which proved to be a solid support system for Dad.

I journeyed up from the South—land of the Baptists—to where the *true* Christians reside. I don't exactly agree with the doctrine in the house of God where my dad chose to worship, but it was impossible to ignore a bass-playing, Bible-thumping preacher who referenced the Doobie Brothers and Elvis from the pulpit while vehemently suggesting, with a mega-watt smile on his face, that if you don't believe in *his* God, well, you don't really *believe*. The congregation shouted *Amen!* He cited the 3Ms—Muslims, Mormons, and movie stars (Scientologists)—his examples of heathen belief systems that do not meet Christian standards.

The pastor opened his sermon with the patriotic notion that America needed to get back to its Biblical roots—what this country was founded upon. And if you forgot your copy of the King James Version of the Good Book, you had only to keep your eye on one of two giant screens located at either end of the stage where the scripture electronically scrolled for your reading enjoyment.

I'm sure the pastor also learned in seminary that America was established on religious tolerance—remember the Pilgrims? They arrived in the New World to escape religious persecution in England. It surprised me that my liberal dad was so enraptured with this brand of religion; I made a mental note not to drink any Kool-Aid served in the fellowship hall.

Like John Irving's character John Wheelwright in a *Prayer for Owen Meany,* I grew up with a church-rummage faith, patched together by friends and relatives on any given Sunday. We lived smack-dab in the middle of a Wesleyan Methodist community, but I don't remember my parents (it would take a terminal illness to propel them toward the Lord) or grandparents attending church or providing any religious instruction.

My siblings and I always had shiny new Easter outfits, but whether we made it to church in those clothes depended on the kindness of other people. I do remember neighbors, relatives, and classmates who invited me to attend church services with their families. My mom readily agreed, and in hindsight, it was probably because (a) she didn't want the wrath of some Wesleyan God coming down around us on Harmon Street, and (b) if I was shuffled off to church on Sunday morning, then she had one less kid to tend to. She was a working mom during the sixties and had little time to do more than what was necessary for us siblings.

This approach to religion exposed me to a patchwork of denominations in our community. Living at the epicenter of the Methodist community meant that multiple families invited me to attend church. The Methodists had a lot of rules and thou-shalt-nots: no short skirts and makeup, little to no laughing, and no fraternizing with the opposite sex. From the pulpit, the minister hurled warnings about the evils of drinking and smoking at a congregation who never seemed to smile. At a young age, I intrinsically knew I didn't fit in with the Methodists. Nevertheless, each time I received an invitation, my mom or grandma dressed me appropriately and waved me down the driveway.

I attended the Episcopal church across town, another part of my religious patchwork; it seemed only good Episcopalians lived *across town*, not in south Marion where I cohabited with the Methodists. They found it critically important to *dress up* to be in God's presence, which dictated girls donned hats and little white gloves. Women wore makeup, and I saw a lot of their knees exposed, so they were not as strict as the Methodists. I didn't understand the frequent kneeling, standing, and chanting, but the congregation was always smiling, so I guessed the ritual was gratifying to them.

However, what I loved most about the Episcopalians was the social after the service. Everyone was invited to meet in the church basement where tables sat, brightly decorated with checked tablecloths and flowers. Coffee, hot chocolate, and mounds of buttered cinnamon toast awaited hungry worshippers. No one seemed to care if you returned to the toast table for seconds or even thirds. You didn't get that with the Methodists.

Once or twice I attended a Catholic service. It was located *across* town, too, and the Catholics even had their own school system. I never felt comfortable with them. Like the Methodists, they preached several thou-shalt-nots, but individually, they didn't seem to wholly buy into the practice. Unlike the Methodist preachers, Catholic priests saw no real sin in drinking alcohol or smoking.

But why did the Catholics need their own school system? Perhaps it was the concept of "abstinence," which, apparently, didn't work too well since Catholic couples seemed to produce several children. Were their children so pious they didn't require "normal" education? Or were non-Catholic children so heathen the Catholics didn't want their children contaminated? Alas, the Catholics didn't like me too well either since, even at a young age, I was cynical and inquisitive.

By the time I reached high school and my teen years, free will had firmly taken hold, and my parents stopped parceling me out to evangelical families for religious instruction. It was never a conscious decision on anyone's part; the invitations to join other families for church seemed to stop, and my parents never questioned why. I didn't decide on a church home until after my first daughter was born, and I was pregnant with the second. Because I was a parent, I wanted to be responsible for nurturing my children's religious instruction, making sure they didn't experience a similar patchwork faith like what I grew up with.

When I started shopping for a place to worship, experience told me not to seek the Methodists, Episcopalians, or Catholics. I married into a family of Southern Baptists and Seventh-day Adventists, so I checked those two denominations off my list as well. I knew I would not survive the Baptist teetotaler belief and attending church on Saturday with the Adventists was just plain weird. I chose the Presbyterians; they seemed the least religious of any denomination.

I dragged my toddler and my pregnant self to the two different Presbyterian churches in Winter Haven trying to decide which one would be more comfortable. As a product of the Baptist-Seventh-day-Adventist marriage, their father refused to attend services with us. I chose Hope Presbyterian Church in Winter Haven because Dr. Tom McGrath embraced my toddler and me the very first Sunday by saying, "Children are always welcome in our sanctuary." Dr. McGrath and I remain friends to this day, although I no longer attend formal services.

I brought up my daughters, Caroline and Mallory, in a Presbyterian church home; they went to Sunday school, church preschool, Wednesday family night activities, youth group meetings, and holiday celebrations. I allowed the professionals to indoctrinate my daughters with God's word, but I reserved the right to believe as I saw fit. I have always been more spiritual than religious. I believe and trust in a Higher Power and still uphold that miracles are possible.

One evening as I picked my daughters up from their youth group meeting, Caroline asked me, "Mom, do we have to go to youth group anymore?"

After a brief discussion about the whys and wherefores, I told her, "No, you don't. Not if you don't want to." She was thirteen, and Mallory was twelve. That was the end of our weekly attendance at church. But we never left God; we each found our own personal relationship with a deity, unfettered by formal participation in ritual.

My thoughts drifted back to the present while I sat beside my dad in the church of his choosing, worshipping a God of *my* understanding. Worship is worship regardless of the building—or absence of one—or the person in the pulpit. Sometimes my prayers seem complicated, sometimes they're timid or vague, and periodically, they're a simple request for help or a thank-you for blessings. Regardless of the intention or enthusiasm in which my prayers are delivered, I know God hears those prayers. My dilemma this Sunday was that I sat in church thinking about riding my Harley-Davidson instead of meditating on God.

My visit to Indiana was ending, and Sunday service in the heartland seemed the perfect place for this sinner to ponder the past and look forward to the future. The pastor called for anyone seeking God's salvation to come forth and be saved as the reformed rock musicians on stage played churchy accompaniment. A few people walked timidly to the altar where there was a laying on of hands, prayers, and murmurings of approval from the congregation. Parishioners passed tissues along the pews for those so besotted by God's grace, they were moved to tears.

As the new converts went to the altar, I reflected on my visit home and all the years I had been away, moving around, chasing fulfillment, only to find it right here where I started. After the big cities and fast-paced life lost their appeal for me, I settled in a small town in Central Florida, much like my hometown, where I have lived more than half my life and raised my daughters. I am a small-town girl at heart with small-town values. Perhaps the heartland was the altar where I found my peace. It took many years of constant relocating and thousands of miles of travel for me to discover that everywhere I went—big cities, small towns—there I was. It's not about geography. Rather, it's about the heartland restoring my emotional mindset and recreating my salvation.

Footnote: Like many northern towns, both large and small, Marion has struggled to redefine itself after much of the manufacturing departed or closed. Lest I leave my reader with a negative impression of my hometown, please know that city leaders have put many positive initiatives into place and continue to do so as hardworking friends and family play key roles in revitalizing and preserving the integrity of Marion, Indiana.

IT'S NOT ABOUT POTATO SALAD

What is that feeling when you're driving away from people and they
recede on the plain till you see their specks dispersing? —It's the
too-huge world vaulting us, and it's good-bye.
But we lean forward to the next crazy venture
beneath the skies.

– Jack Kerouac, *On the Road*

MONDAY MORNING, BRIGHT AND EARLY, I SHARED A FINAL
cup of coffee with Dad and outlined the travel plans that would eventually take me home to Florida. The ticking of the clocks filled lapses in
conversation as we sipped our cup of joe. Since Mom died in 2005, my
relationship with Dad had deepened into one I cherished. I had urged

him numerous times to winter in Florida with me, but the pleading fell on deaf ears. He refused to venture too far from home, choosing his solitary, routine existence instead and filling the days with maudlin music and his clocks, ticking away the moments that made up a dull day.

I wanted to tell him how grateful I was for the unconditional love he had shown me over the years. I wanted to thank him for the life lessons I learned under his parentage. Most of the lessons were difficult, not because of the way he delivered them but because of the way I defied them. It was not until I became a parent myself that I understood what my dad had tried to teach me.

I wanted to admit to him that my journey in life would not have been as complicated or as turbulent had I listened and followed his directions. I would not have gathered a truckload of missed opportunities if I had taken his advice decades ago. The inability to accept these facts about myself, let alone give voice to my faults, kept me silent that morning.

It is a sad fact that most of us don't learn what our moms and dads try to teach us until we have endured so much pain and heartache that we silently shout *Uncle!* We then relinquish our defiance to embrace the lesson.

Dad was a patient man. Although the words were never spoken between us, I knew he understood my heart. I pray that the way I live my life today and the way I have raised my daughters represent the amends I've failed to utter.

For what would be the last time, I hugged my dad, told him I loved him, backed Bessie out of his driveway, and watched his waving hand disappear in my rearview mirror. If I could have glimpsed into the future, I would have sat much longer in his kitchen, gratefully enduring the ticking of the clocks and sipping one last cup of coffee.

I left Indiana just before sunrise; the fields along SR 35S were shrouded in a chilly mist that seeped into my light jacket, prompting a series of uncontrollable shivers. The rising sun painted the green fields with pink and orange, my favorite morning colors. *There is no better alarm clock than sunshine on chrome,* I thought as I headed south, patting the gas tank as if Bessie were a living steed, deserving of my affection. A comfortable melancholy set in, and I said a prayer of gratitude for this visit home.

Anticipation eventually took precedence over my melancholy mood while I mentally reviewed my end-of-June plans for the next week of travel. In keeping true to my Penny Tour destination and riding in the spirit of Bessie Stringfield, I looked forward to visiting Fallingwater in Pennsylvania, the home Frank Lloyd Wright designed for the family of Pittsburgh department store owner Edgar J. Kaufmann, Sr. It lies forty-three miles southeast of Pittsburg. And I aimed to traverse Skyline Drive in Shenandoah National Park and Monticello in Virginia, before arriving in Greensboro, North Carolina, for a prearranged rendezvous with North Carolina Man.

The first three destinations had been on my Bike-It list for a few years; the fourth destination in North Carolina would be a welcome detour on my itinerary. North Carolina Man and I had engaged in several phone conversations over the past month, establishing an easy rapport that boded well with me. He seemed genuine, voiced interest in my travels on two wheels, and was not aggressive. I tend to be the aggressor in relationships—making the first move, making the bold suggestions, and generally leading the way. Most men find this a turn-off, but North Carolina Man did not seem to mind.

During one such conversation we had while I was at my dad's house, I suggested he and I meet face-to-face for lunch or dinner on my journey back to Florida. I indicated my travel plans could easily be amended to include a stop in the Tar Heel State. He readily agreed, suggesting the Harley-Davidson dealership just off I-40 in Greensboro, North Carolina, would be convenient.

Although the sun had begun to warm the air toward late morning, the chill I started with as I left Marion earlier lingered. On the east side of Dayton, Ohio, I spied a Bob Evans restaurant. I'm not a fan of chain restaurants, but hot coffee is hot coffee, and I needed an infusion—pronto. Easy off the highway, easy on my route. I wasn't seeking a dining experience—just hot coffee and a light breakfast.

I claimed the only remaining seat at the counter with the local farmers and a few truckers. I nodded a good morning in their direction. The counter was littered with the previous customer's leftover breakfast, so I waited for it to be removed. Several more minutes ticked by.

Two waitresses stood behind the counter at the opposite end from where I sat, brashly discussing their displeasure with their jobs. After more time passed, I inquired loudly in their direction, "Could I please get this cleared and have a cup of coffee?"

The dark-haired waitress, who looked like she had applied her makeup with a spatula that morning, snarled something unintelligible as she ambled in my direction. Scowling, she slammed dirty dishes into a dishpan under the counter as if the crockery was to blame for her lot in life. She gave a half-hearted swipe across the Formica with a soggy rag from underneath the counter and then turned her back on me.

I still didn't have coffee or a menu and what little patience I possessed was dwindling. I loudly said to her ample backside, "This might be a good place to open a restaurant." The men at the counter lowered their heads and stifled their chuckles.

With startling agility, Wanda the Waitress grabbed a menu, the coffeepot, and a cup, slapping all three down in front of me. I glared right back at her and rattled off my order without even looking at the greasy menu. When my order was ready, she slammed my breakfast plate—along with the check—on the counter with the same angry gusto I assumed she had with everything else in her life.

I enjoyed the hot coffee and breakfast while Wanda continued to complain about her job to whomever would listen. After the other nicer waitress ran my debit card, instead of a monetary tip, I wrote on the back of her receipt, "Here is my *tip*, Sugar. Find another line of work." I walked out, knowing my comment would be insufficient to prompt change. Someone like this waitress who is so miserable with their life is probably comfortable in their misery.

Spiritually, I understand that travel is supposed to be about the journey, not necessarily the destination. However, on that day, the destination to Fallingwater in Mill Run, Pennsylvania, took priority over the journey. I have had the pleasure of traveling extensively on Ohio back roads, so I decided to take I-70 east to Pennsylvania in the interest of time. Fallingwater was a good eight hours from where I endured breakfast outside of Dayton. The weather was warm and dry by the time I merged into the light traffic on the interstate.

I slipped into a reverie that only my motorcycle can induce: the vibration of the engine, the rush of the wind, the roar of the motor seduced me at seventy miles per hour. I remembered I had traveled this same route three summers ago on my way to Lakewood, New Jersey, from Grafton, Ohio for a job interview. Educational software companies are always reaching out to teachers to serve as consultants for their products. I was recruited for the possibility, although I did not apply for it; I half-heartedly agreed to an interview.

When Achieve3000 offered to fly me to Lakewood for the interview, I declined, indicating I would be traveling on my motorcycle at that time and would ride on to New Jersey.

Traveling on the Pennsylvania Turnpike, which begins at the Ohio state line and ends at the New Jersey border, was like riding across 360 miles of speed bumps. The road was rutted with frost heaves and uneven pavement due to poor construction. My wheels seemed to maintain a rhythm of *bump, bump, SLAM, bump, bump, SLAM* across the wretched toll road. My hands ached from gripping the handgrips, my arms were stiff and sore from the tension, and my teeth ached from the jarring and slamming. When I reached the tollbooth at the end of the Turnpike, the attendant stated I owed forty dollars in tolls.

I bellowed back, "Forty dollars? There is no way I will *pay* to ride that god-awful, poor excuse for a road!" Indignantly, I went on to rationalize, "Forty dollars? I will have to pay my mechanic $90 per hour to tighten every nut and bolt on this bike after almost 400 miles of slamming on decrepit asphalt! Not to mention several visits to my chiropractor to straighten *me* out!"

The attendant wasn't even stunned or offended. He simply handed me a form to complete and send to a Harrisburg address, explaining why I refused to pay the toll. End of story.

A side note, though, to my interview. It went well, and I was offered the job at three times my teaching salary. I declined on principle, however. Why would I want only *two* weeks of vacation each year when teaching offered me a whole summer? That would seriously interfere with Bessie's and my time together.

Coming out of a motorcycle-induced road reverie is startling. In his book, *Ghost Rider: Travels on the Healing Road*, Neil Peart, my favorite saddle tramp, calls it a mental groove: "...drifting away into the zone, thoughts far away while the main brain handles the road." You realize you have been hurtling along at seventy miles per hour while mentally zoning out until traffic or weather demands total focus.

By mid-afternoon, I had left the Ohio roads behind and was now on the dreaded Pennsylvania toll highway. If there are asphalt roads in hell, they are modeled after Pennsylvania roads. Or perhaps the inspiration for AC/DC's album *Highway to Hell* was inspired by a trip the band took across the home state of Punxsutawney Phil.

I connected with SR 51 south, grateful to leave the super slab but wary of what I would encounter on Pennsylvania's secondary roads.

The Allegheny foothills is gently rolling farmland interspersed with pine forest. Bad roads aside, the geography is pastoral and gratifying for the traveler.

Following my GPS directions to Fallingwater, I connected with SR 201, a steep, twisty, secondary road that took me deeper into the mountains. The small towns, which looked tired and worn down by a fickle economy, had once been part of a thriving steel and auto-related industrial belt.

I crossed a treacherously rough railroad track, where deep crevices ran parallel with the track, and I had to steer Bessie at an angle to cross so I didn't lose my tire in the gaping crack. On the other side of the track, I encountered a detour sign—not good. The last thing I wanted was to be rerouted onto a substandard, secondary Allegheny mountain road. I twisted and turned with the detour signs, deftly dodging the abundance of potholes filled with loose gravel and ended up in a tiny town called Bowen.

I slowed to almost ten miles per hour to cross yet another railroad track—probably the same line I maneuvered across several miles back—and *boom*! On the opposite side of the track, I hit a pothole so deep it stopped my bike, and my rear tire came to rest in the cavernous hole with the bike frame nearly touching the highway. I had to twist the throttle and gain torque to pull up out of the black hole, only to start sliding in loose gravel. I managed to keep Bessie upright and quickly pulled over into a parking space near the curb. The town was virtually deserted as I climbed off, spouting expletives in the direction of the giant pothole. I didn't see any pedestrian activity on the street, and my savage cursing as I paced the sidewalk near my bike didn't bring anyone out of the storefronts to investigate.

I crouched down to inspect Bessie, fully expecting to see her frame cracked in two or the wheel bent beyond repair. It was at this point I decided my return to Pennsylvania was probably one of the worst ideas I had had in a while—Penny Tour be damned. I couldn't see any visible damage and prayed my tire wouldn't go flat a few miles down the road; as deserted as the town appeared, I doubted there was a tow truck within a couple of hundred miles. My instinct was to scrap my plans to visit Fallingwater and get the hell out of Pennsylvania.

I slowly wound my way back to SR 201, treating Bessie as if she were an injured comrade on the field of battle. I arrived in Connellsville, another small industrial town built along the Youghiogheny River. I knew I was less than fifty miles from Fallingwater, but my resolve to check it off my Bike-It list was wavering. I was bone-tired from the jostle across the Pennsylvania Turnpike, and the pothole from hell served to shake my confidence only slightly. I knew if I had to overcome one more obstacle that day, it would suck the joy right out of my trip to Fallingwater.

I attempted to follow the route signs in Connellsville, but they were so numerous—three signs stacked atop each other indicating all three route numbers were legitimate—and the traffic so congested that I ended up going in circles. Each time I circled back to SR 201, I encountered side streets strewn with gravel that had escaped from gaping potholes. Out of frustration, I pulled into a Wendy's parking lot to get my bearings. I was drained. Since leaving my dad's house, I had clicked off nearly 400 miles within seven hours. And I was still not where I intended to be.

I asked two different local people getting into or out of their cars in Wendy's parking lot the best way to get to Fallingwater and received two different answers. The second guy I asked looked at me, pointed at the bike, and said," You don't want to take that thing up there!"

'Nuff said, Mister. That was all I needed to hear.

I decided Fallingwater would have to remain unchecked on my Bike-It list until a later date. I retreated to Wendy's restroom to wash my dusty hands and throw cold water on my face. I felt dejected. I looked into the mirror and asked myself, *What would Bessie Stringfield have done?* That fearless soul would have marshaled on and found Fallingwater; at least, however, I had made it to Pennsylvania where my penny originally dropped.

While I ate a soggy salad that tasted more like the plastic it was served in than a vegetable, I scanned the state map in my atlas and chose a direction. Although I felt dejected, I congratulated myself on not taking any more chances with the wretched roads. It was amazing that I had managed to stay upright thus far. As I stood next to Bessie, pulling on my helmet and gloves, I realized she looked dejected as well. She was dirty, tired, and bruised from the miserable roads. I threw my leg over the saddle and mouthed a silent prayer that we would make it to our destination safely. I headed over to I-40 south—out of Pennsylvania.

Within a few miles, I encountered workers repairing sections of the interstate. I was grateful Pennsylvania was overhauling its deplorable roads, but the repair work meant I now had to dodge loose gravel *and* hot tar. Traffic was down to one lane, so vehicles were halted to allow the opposite lane of vehicles by.

As I stopped and started with the one-lane interstate traffic through the road construction, thick, angry storm clouds were building in the east. Once free of the roadwork, I pulled into a nearby rest area to don rain gear. Gripping the handlebars, I gritted my teeth, and rode directly into the storm. The temperature dropped significantly to a wet chill; rain lashed at Bessie and me, the wind gusts whipping me sideways. Fortunately, I traveled out of it as quickly as I entered it; thirty minutes down the road, the wind and rain stopped.

I firmly believe any day I'm on Bessie is a good day, but my patience was being tested on this day. One of the few obstacles not thrown my way that day was pestilence unless you count Wanda the Waitress back at the Bob Evans in Ohio.

Although it was about an hour before I usually started looking for a place to spend the night, I decided Bessie and I had had enough. It was time to call it a day. Shortly after the downpour, I pulled into a Hampton Inn off I-40, climbed stiffly off the bike, and hobbled toward the entrance, my hips stiff. I pulled off my helmet and gloves, unzipped my rain jacket, and walked up to the check-in desk. The smiling woman behind the counter said, "Welcome to Hampton Inn! Do you have a reservation?"

I admitted I did not but hoped that wouldn't be a problem.

She said, "No problem. If I could just have your driver's license and credit card." Thank goodness. I proffered both from my waist pack and glanced over at the promotional sign near the counter. "Frostburg, Maryland! Maryland? I thought I was further south in West Virginia," I exclaimed, looking at the concierge as if it were her fault I wasn't in West Virginia.

She looked up from her computer, gazed over the top of her glasses at me and said, slowly, "Nooo, this is Maryland. Do you still want a room?"

"Yes, of course. I'm sorry; it's been a long ride."

She processed my reservation, handed my plastic back to me along with the room key, and mentioned that the warm chocolate chip cookies would be available around 6:00 p.m. I felt like I was home.

I hefted the pack off the back of the bike, dug in my saddlebag for my iPad and toiletry bag, locked the bike and lugged it all to the room. Once in my room, I turned the water on in the bathtub, stripped off wet rain gear and sweaty clothes, leaving them in a dingy pile next to the bed. I sank into the steamy water up to my chin, giving my sore arms and shoulders some relief from the day's ride. Tomorrow was the Fourth of July, and I planned to savor my time on Skyline Drive, going south through the Shenandoah National Park in Virginia, as soon as

I figured out how the hell I ended up in Maryland. I planned to spend Independence Day at Monticello, the birthplace of Thomas Jefferson.

I slept well; no visions of potholes tormented my slumber. The hour before sunrise is my customary departure time. The chilly morning air startled me, but then I realized I was in Frostburg, Maryland. I dug the heavy leather jacket and chaps out of the saddlebag and slipped back inside the lobby for another cup of hot coffee. I touched base with North Carolina Man, informing him of my current location and destination today. I confirmed our plans to meet in Greensboro on July 6. I had no qualms about calling at such an early hour since he was a morning person like me—a plus on his side.

Leaving Frostburg, I traveled I-68 for a short distance to SR 51 south into "Almost Heaven" West Virginia. State Road 51 in the Blue Ridge Mountains is as smooth as a baby's bottom with hills, dips, curves, and very little traffic. This was the challenge I sought, not the torture of dodging potholes on two wheels. I topped the first rise and saw the ribbon of highway unfurled before me as it cut a swath through dense forest, undulating in the morning light and beckoning me onward. I performed daring, tummy-tickling dips on the downhill, downshifted for the climb upward, and repeated the ride all over again. I was giddy with excitement, like a kid on her first two-wheeled bicycle, screaming *Whee!* all the way downhill. Two wheels gave me freedom and a sense of control over my life. I leaned into the curves and bent forward, head-rushing into the sloping runs.

State Road 51 meandered through Oldtown and Paw Paw, West Virginia, named for the pawpaw, a wild fruit which grows in abundance throughout the region; a stunning panorama of rolling farmland surrounded the road on each side.

At the state line into Virginia, SR 51 connected with SR 127, and then I took SR 522 and SR 340 toward Front Royal, Virginia, and the northern entrance to Shenandoah National Park. I could have easily gotten lost with the multiple switchbacks, route changes, and elevations through the thick forests. Which is why I try to visualize my routes each day. Although a biker may remark, "You are never lost on two wheels," I wanted to be sure it didn't happen to me.

As I pulled up to Shenandoah National Park's entrance, I noticed an unexpected absence of tourists. I hail from the land of Mickey Mouse who fills multiple theme parks daily with thousands of tourists who pay top dollar to wait in endless queues. On Independence Day, Disney parks are packed shoulder to shoulder, stroller to stroller with sunburned tourists. Here I am in one of our Founding Father's backyards by myself and about to "ride the Sky," one of the Top 100 Most Scenic Drives in America—unencumbered by sweaty tourists. Once I paid the modest fee, I stopped to affix my GoPro camera to my helmet. (My dad was so enamored with the videos from this tiny camera!)

Skyline Drive is a 105-mile road atop crests in the Blue Ridge Mountains and runs the length of the Shenandoah National Park between Front Royal to Rockfish Gap, Virginia. President Herbert Hoover, whose rustic, summer home is in nearby Rapidan Camp, commissioned the road to be built in 1931. The Drive curves and climbs almost immediately after entering the Park. Over seventy scenic overlooks, protected by low stone walls, provide convenient stops where tourists can enjoy staggering views of the Shenandoah Valley spread out in every direction. Although the Park has a few campgrounds, I saw few mega RVs that plague motorcyclists on remote mountain roads.

Completing the Skyline Drive takes about three hours at the posted thirty-five miles per hour speed limit. No more than thirty minutes after I biked onto the Drive, dark clouds began to gather. At 3,300 feet, you are virtually *in* the clouds, the mist clinging to the sides of the mountain like the cottony, faux spider web material available at Halloween.

I pulled off at one of the observation points and put on my rain gear. The mist at this altitude was enough to dampen my clothes and boots. With no other cars at the overlook, it was as though I had nature's mural to myself. The view and sense of seclusion overwhelmed me. I stood motionless and listened; I heard the soft tick of Bessie's engine cooling, the drip of condensation on greenery, the hum of the cicadas, and a lone bird, perhaps calling to a mate. I thought of the anonymous saying I had read, "Sometimes you find yourself in the middle of nowhere. And sometimes, in the middle of nowhere, you find yourself." These moments of solitude among nature's elements are my *soulscapes*; I see a landscape or vista that is so encompassing, so deeply felt that it nurtures my soul, like a sunflower turning its buttery blossoms to follow the sun's journey across the sky.

I tilted my face upward, to feel the wetness on my skin and smell the rich, loamy scent of the forest. There was little to no wind, the still air swollen with moisture. Reluctant to leave my *soulscape*, I ambled back to Bessie and pulled rain gear out of my bag as if someone hit the slow-motion function on a movie camera. I tugged the bright orange pants over my boots and jeans; their color was almost an assault on the subtle, muted tones of the trees. The rain gear is horribly hot and sweat pooled into every crevice it could on me as I swung my leg over Bessie, eager for some wind to cool me down. I flipped her switch, her engine shattering the tranquility.

As if donning rain gear were a cue, the drizzle began a few hundred feet down the road. I was grateful for the thirty-five miles per hour speed limit; rain on a hot highway makes for a slick surface. Skyline Drive is a slow, meandering ride on a good highway with gentle curves and impressive elevation in the Blue Ridge Mountains. The drive's distinction as one of the Top 100 Scenic Roads in America is richly deserved.

I encountered a doe and her little spotted fawn, like a whimsical gift from the pages of a children's book, around one corner and then a mama black bear and two cubs, feasting on the berry bushes that covered the shallow ravine. I noted mama bear's massive size, larger than Bessie and I combined.

By the time I arrived at the south end of the Park, the drizzle had turned into a downpour with gray clouds blocking any sunlight. I was unenthusiastic about joining the traffic throng that zipped to and fro on the highways outside the Park.

I stopped in Rockfish Gap to check my map and decided to travel closer to Monticello, Thomas Jefferson's home, located near Charlottesville, Virginia. The relentless rain made navigation treacherous at best. As I neared Charlottesville, traffic became congested with holiday travelers, and I exited off Interstate 64 to gas up and scout the area for a place to spend the night. I pulled up to a pump, fished my debit card out of my waist pack, and swiped the card. It was declined. Knowing full well there was no reason for the decline, I swiped again. Then the annoying message *please see attendant* popped up.

The gas station/convenience store was packed with people, and I waited my turn to see the attendant. She swiped my card a third time—no deal. I thought briefly about arguing with her, but she dismissed me as if I was a pesky fly invading her counter space and looked past me to the next customer in line. I had to back up and say, "Excuse me, I will pay cash for the gas," before she brought her attention back to the poor biker lady whose card was declined.

I don't carry much cash when I travel, and at that time, I did not have a credit card with me, only my Visa debit card. I pay travel expenses in cash via my debit card and always have a substantial reserve set aside for any bike-related emergency.

I stood at the gas pump, filling Bessie's tank, perplexed and anxious. Cars waited to take my space at the pump, so I had to find a different place to make a phone call to my bank—and it was still pouring rain.

I navigated to a nearby McDonald's, also teaming with holiday travelers, most of whom had several small children in tow. The noisy dining area, adjacent to the plastic ball pit and brimming to capacity with boisterous children, was a stark contrast to my soulscape experience just a few hours ago. There was nowhere to sit, and even if I had found a seat, the noise level would have handicapped any phone conversation.

I went back outside and stood under an overhang near the rear door, adjacent to the dumpster, the constant rain pounding on the pavement. I searched online for my bank's phone number while mentally reviewing all the reasons my card was not accepted at the gas pump. (A few years after this incident, banks introduced convenient apps for smartphones that makes banking as simple as a few swipes.)

I heard a recorded message with the first few numbers I called, reminding me it was a holiday weekend and that my bank would be happy to help me out the following Tuesday.

Anxiety gave way to panic as I visualized having to spend a soggy night sleeping near this dumpster at a Charlottesville's McDonald's. I longed for the days when the president of the local bank was the guy I went to high school with, and I had his mom's phone number somewhere in my directory. That guy wouldn't mind taking a phone call on a holiday and helping a customer in a bind. My current bank used to be that kind of monetary establishment until the late 1980s when banks started selling their souls to bigger banks and moving further away from their local customers. I could swallow my pride, call Dad or my brother, and yell, *Help!* Instead, I kept making phone calls, until, miraculously, I connected with a live person. After answering several questions, giving her my account numbers and my blood type, she ascertained I was indeed the account holder, and she was willing to help me.

"I see your card was deactivated because we had a breach of security at one of our processing centers," she told me. She seemed annoyed. In her mind, deactivating my card was a perfectly logical action to take given the circumstances.

Feeling exasperated, I asked her, "Exactly what kind of a breach?"

The bank associate explained to me that thousands of account numbers had been stolen from the bank's retail customers, and if a customer made a purchase at a retail outlet, such as Target, with their debit card, then those cards had been compromised. The bank's solution was to deactivate all debit cards and issue new ones. She assured me mine was in the mail.

"I'm traveling, and because *your* computer base was compromised, you deactivated my card without any notification!?" I blurted. I was trying not to piss off the only person standing between me and a night near the dumpster.

"It's for your own protection," she said defensively. Intellectually, I appreciated the gesture, but emotionally, I was too upset to be grateful.

"We sent you an email six days ago, notifying you of the situation. Did you respond to the email?"

"No," I had to admit, "I saw no email."

Begging forgiveness, I knew this woman was either going to help me or destroy me. I pleaded with her to reactivate my card, going so far as to detail my dire situation. She reminded me it was a holiday, but she offered to make a few phone calls and see what she could do to help me.

"Do you mind holding?" she asked. What choice did I have?

Elevator music played in my ear while I was placed on hold. By now, I had slid my backside down the gritty wall of the McDonald's to sit on the semi-wet pavement like a vagrant waiting for a handout. I had shed my rain jacket but still had the bright orange bibbed pants on over my jeans. I felt like a leftover McChicken someone had wadded up in the paper wrapper and tossed toward the dumpster, missing it by a few feet.

The oppressive humidity, the persistent rain, and the dumpster smell added to my misery. After what seemed like an eternity, my savior returned to the line with good news. "We will reinstate your card, and it will be good for another ten days."

Ten days, yes! I would be home before then, and my new, uncompromised debit card would be waiting for me. I thanked her profusely for her help, wished her a happy July Fourth, or what was left of it, as it was nearing the dinner hour.

I gathered up my water-logged dignity and stood up from my squat on the pavement. Loping across the parking lot toward Bessie who waited patiently in the pouring rain, I climbed aboard and cautiously set out on the slick pavement to find the nearest hotel.

I swung into the parking lot of a Hampton Inn, just a few miles from the entrance to Monticello, and, thankfully, by then the rain had subsided. Before unloading the bike, I called my daughter. I knew she was attending a barbeque at her dad's house with her cousins, her stepsister and stepbrother, and their children. She was in a happy mood, and I could hear the kids laughing and splashing noisily in the pool in the background. I pictured the near Norman Rockwell scene with aching clarity: Dad at the grill flipping burgers, stepmom busily covering the picnic table with a red-checkered tablecloth and placing flag-themed paper plates and napkins on it. And my daughter relishing the extended family atmosphere.

Guilt tormented me as I stood in the Hampton Inn parking lot, cell phone in hand, pacing on the damp pavement under the portico, still dressed in my plastic rain gear. I have always felt guilty because I could not give my daughters the close-knit family atmosphere they craved. Since I divorced their dad, it was just we three, and when my younger daughter left, our family shrank to two. My eyes stung with tears as I remembered the forlorn feeling when I had to drop them off for holidays and return home alone. Conceiving and birthing children was easy. Building and maintaining a family unit was apparently impossible for me.

Caroline detected the melancholy in my voice and asked, "What's wrong, Mom? You sound tired."

As I tried to hold back tears, I rehashed the highlights of my day— biking in the downpour, the stint near the dumpster while my debit card snafu was rectified, and the guilt I felt because I wasn't home preparing a festive holiday meal that looked like it fell off the cover of a *Martha Stewart Living* magazine.

"I don't know, honey. Sometimes I question what propels me to strike out on my own like this and wander. Why do I push myself? Why do I put myself in harm's way?" By now, I was pacing and whining like a school girl. Exasperated, I grumbled, "Maybe I should just be home making potato salad like all good moms on July Fourth."

"No, Mom. You are not like other moms. You are way cooler. None of my friends' moms travel on their Harley during school vacays," she explained with the logic she developed somewhere around twelve years of age. A logic that always seemed mature for her years. At times, I often felt like *she* was the parent, and I was the errant child who needed a gentle but firm reminder of my inherent goodness.

Caroline's words placated me for the time being. I vowed to reexamine my guilt later when I wasn't tired and wet. I outlined my travel plans over the next few days, reassuring her I would be home by the middle of the week. I told her I loved her and before we said good-bye, she said, "By the way, Mom, I hate potato salad, and if you were home making that right now, I would *really* be concerned. I love you; ride safe."

My daughter was right. This trip has been about the journey back from a bad accident—a journey outward and away from the safety of home to recapture my lost confidence on two wheels. It has been about finding control, gleaning satisfaction from the journey, and discovering new vistas with Bessie Two. It was not about potato salad.

SURRENDER

Sometimes what seems like surrender isn't surrender at all. It's about what's going on in our hearts. About seeing clearly the way life is and accepting it and being true to it, whatever the pain, because the pain of not being true to it is far, far greater.

– Nicholas Evans, *The Horse Whisperer*

THE DRIVE UP TO THE GROUNDS OF MONTICELLO, THOMAS Jefferson's plantation home outside of Charlottesville, Virginia, was stunningly beautiful. The landscape along the steeply curving narrow road looked as if a skilled artisan had chiseled it. In addition, the dreary, relentless rain of yesterday gave way to a glorious, sun-drenched day; the morning air was cool with the promise of warmer temps as the day progressed. My spirit had been fortified with a good night's sleep and an uplifting conversation with my daughter.

I reached the top of the hill and turned into the postage-stamp sized parking area that rolled and dipped in every direction. Finding a flat surface to safely park Bessie was a challenge. As I climbed off the bike and stowed my helmet, a woman, roughly my age, parked her Prius and strolled in my direction. We greeted each other with a friendly, "Good morning!" After grabbing my camera, I went over to the reception area to purchase a ticket. I purposely had avoided visiting Monticello on Independence Day because I didn't want to encounter a crowd and was pleased to see a manageable number of people lining up to buy tickets on the day *after* July Fourth.

Travel is always a pilgrimage of sorts, whether it's focused on literary, historical, or musical destinations. I seek places where my favorite authors lived, worked, or wrote about in their novels, preferring to visit historical sites over shopping or dining in gourmet restaurants. I stop at historical markers along highways, most in random, out-of-the-way places, to read about the significance of that patch of land or strip of road.

Discovering the locations of places on famous album covers or the burial sites of my favorite dead musicians is another quirky habit I have. When my girls were small, our summer travels introduced them to history. For a college graduation gift, I took Caroline to San Francisco, and I remember her asking me, "Mom, are we going to see where any dead poets or musicians are buried on this trip?"

Monticello was a double bonus as it was a historical site and the home of one of my favorite authors, Thomas Jefferson. America's Colonial period molded our history when the fledging thirteen colonies fought for independence from Great Britain, and great minds like Jefferson's, Adams', and Washington's shaped a new government.

I was dismayed to learn the early tour had been sold out, and the next tour would not occur until 12:45 p.m. I planned to leave the area by that time to travel toward North Carolina; there was a man I planned to see about our future. I pleaded my case to the woman at the ticket counter and pointed out I was only one, not-too-large person, so was it possible to squeeze me on that first tour? She was sympathetic, made a few adjustments on her computer, reissued my ticket, and suggested I hurry over to the shuttle waiting area just behind the reception building. I scooted over quickly and claimed my space on the benches that lined the small courtyard.

I spotted the gray-haired woman I had seen in the parking lot earlier and made my way to the space next to her. We introduced ourselves; her name was Pat, and she was from the Chicago area.

As Pat and I waited for the tour guide to collect us from the waiting area, I learned that we were sisters in sojourning. Seventy-year-old Pat had retired from her job the previous year, 2012, had sold or stored all her worldly possessions, including her house, and embarked on a tour of the United States in her Prius that she lovingly called Prudence. I was stunned and drawn to her like a moth to a flame. It has been my experience that kindred spirits never fail to find each other in the most unusual of circumstances. I told her about my travels on a Harley I called Bessie, which prompted Pat to ask a barrage of questions.

Chattering like two excited schoolgirls on their first solo trip away from home, Pat and I boarded the shuttle to take us up the hill to the plantation. Pat had left Chicago ten months ago, determined to work her way through the same travel bible I used, *National Geographic,* which described the Top 100 Most Scenic Drives in America. She was a member of the Unitarian church, which provides a network of homes where fellow church members can stay on their travels. The Presbyterians don't do that; it would be too much like a commitment.

Since I rarely encounter other women on two or four wheels who are traveling solo, it was exhilarating to meet Pat and share experiences.

When our small group disembarked on the grounds of the magnificent plantation, Pat and I squelched our conversation to listen to the tour guide. A feature article in *Southern Living* says that "Thomas Jefferson's astounding home and gardens reflect his skills as an architect and gardener, not to mention his boundless curiosity." We climbed up the steps of the columned portico at the west entrance, our necks craned to the sky to get a better look at the magnificent dome that crowned the entrance to the mansion.

Like a flock of curious children, our group followed the tour guide as she led us from one spacious, well-appointed room to another. Skylights permitted natural light to fill the house, bathing rooms and their furnishings in various golden hues, depending on the time of day.

In 1768, when he was twenty-six years old, Jefferson began construction on his home on land he inherited land from his father; it wasn't completed until forty years later in 1808 due to Jefferson making countless design changes and remodeling.

According to our tour guide, except for the glass in the windows, which was imported from Europe, every raw material used in construction came from Jefferson's estate. The bricks and nails were baked and forged on the property; timber was harvested from the forests, and stones were quarried from surrounding mountains.

The entire structure boasts forty-three rooms and spans 11,000 square feet, excluding pavilions and rooms under the terrace. Our tour ambled through the highlights of the living quarters where sixty percent of the furnishings are original. Exquisite handmade chairs, mahogany tables, gleaming parquet floors, gilded mirrors, and an extensive art collection that hung in tiers on most of the available wall space—all grace this home.

Brocade curtains throughout the house and a silk counterpane with fringe on it in Jefferson's bedroom were designed by him. I was fascinated with the master bedroom and the library. Our third president was a master of efficiency; his alcove bed is situated between his office and his actual bedroom. An obelisk clock positioned at the foot of the bed enabled him to awake with the sun, and his furnishings were arranged in areas for maximum efficiency.

The library is an octagon, a favored architectural shape for Jefferson, that overlooks the gardens and aviary. Over the years, Jefferson's library has boasted upward of 20,000 volumes. When the British burned the U. S. Capitol in 1815, Jefferson sold over 6,000 personal volumes from his library to replace what had been lost in the Library of Congress. Monticello's library has approximately 6,000 titles, which are replicas of his original volumes.

I would love to have excused myself from the tour, ordered iced tea from a gloved butler, selected a few volumes, kicked back in one of several easy chairs, and enjoyed an afternoon of reading. Alas, the tour came to an end, and our guide hustled us out of the main house onto the verandah.

A breathtaking view of the Blue Ridge Mountains stretched out before us as we stood on the verandah. It was dominated by the Peaks of Otter from which Virginia sent stones to be part of the Washington Monument.

Magnificent vegetable gardens, meticulously cultivated in an endless variety of plants and colors, lay below the hill on which Jefferson's home rests. The rows were designed more like a formal garden than a mere garden patch with every vegetable row straight as an arrow. The spaces between them had an equal amount of rich, dark soil, and the plants were arranged from the tallest to the shortest. Narrow dirt paths bordered each side of the terraced garden where caretakers and guests had equal access to the profusion of plant life. Guests could purchase seedlings and dried seeds, descendants of Jefferson's original garden, in the gift shop.

While others in the tour group milled around in the gift shop, Pat and I moved ahead and struck out on our own to tour the remaining grounds and continue our conversation. Pat was a little taller than I and took off at a purposeful stride for Mulberry Row, Monticello's slave quarters. She wore sensible shoes and light, airy summer clothing that didn't hinder her loping gait. A drawback to traveling on two wheels is the clothing and shoes you are stuck with when you stop to do something like tour the grounds of Monticello. Not only did I have a tough time matching Pat's generous stride in my knee- high leather riding boots, but I also had to hike uphill before we headed downhill. My denim jeans and black T-shirt were stifling as it was July-in-the-South hot. Experience has taught me to pack a pair of sneakers to wear for sightseeing.

Pat and I made it to the back of the plantation where the slave quarters stood in welcome and ample shade. While Pat read information signs and offered commentary, I caught my breath and wiped the sweat off my face with a bandana.

The paradox of Monticello is that the author of the Declaration of Independence, which promotes life, liberty and the pursuit of happiness for all, was a slave owner. It seems Jefferson's idea of liberty extended to only wealthy white men. Women and enslaved people were omitted from the equation. Jefferson would be surprised at how far America has come, though we have so much further to go to fulfill his original intentions.

At any one time, approximately 130 slaves lived at Monticello and worked the 5,000-acre plantation. After touring Mulberry Row and from what I know about Jefferson's beliefs, I concluded that if one were a slave, it was better to be at Monticello than on most other plantations. He brought in skilled artisans to teach their crafts to enslaved men and women; financial incentives rather than punishment encouraged loyalty and productivity. Furthermore, Jefferson promoted education, and many of his slaves traveled to Europe with him, gaining knowledge and expertise, which they brought back to Monticello.

The broiling sun moved to its highest point in the sky, indicating it was past noon as Pat and I walked back toward the reception area and gift shop, which ended our time together. I wanted to browse the books in the gift shop before riding out to Appomattox, and she went off to the restaurant to sample the menu. Pat promised to visit Florida on her journey, and I promised to give her a ride on Bessie if she did. We exchanged cards, embraced with a hug of solidarity in recognition of each other's intrepid spirits, and parted company.

I spent a leisurely hour in the bookstore, finding it darn near impossible to decide on any one title to take home. I opted instead for a T-shirt that read, *I Cannot Live Without Books. Thomas Jefferson.*

My only disappointment on this memorable visit was the absence of school age children at Monticello. I saw mostly people my age and older. I guessed the Magic Kingdom in Florida was bursting at the seams on this holiday weekend; families would be lined up in endless queues, waiting to ride through the Hall of Presidents where kids would *ooh* and *aah* over the animatronic replicas. Hopefully, the same kids will have a chance to visit Monticello and Mount Vernon where real Presidents walked the halls.

I went back to the parking area, checked my map for directions to Appomattox, which was less than an hour's drive down the road, and headed south on Virginia's SR 20.

The road to Appomattox Court House National Historic Park is curvy, hilly, and shaded. The tourism and travel slogan says *Virginia is for Lovers*, and though I can't vouch for the truth in their advertisement, I can confirm its roads are custom-made for bikers. The elevations dip and tumble, giving you an old-fashioned tummy tickle when you crest one hill and dive down the next. I thought about my new friend, Pat, and hoped she had as much fun in Prudence, her Prius, as I did on Bessie, my Harley.

On Palm Sunday, April 9, 1865, General Robert E. Lee surrendered to General Ulysses S. Grant in a village named Appomattox Court House, Virginia, in a private home owned by Wilmer McLean. The surrender signaled the end of the Southern states' attempt to create a separate nation as well as set the stage for the more powerful federal government we know today.

The village has been restored, and volunteers in period clothing give living history tours of the grounds. The Park is situated in a vast field of rolling hills, dotted with restored Colonial buildings. No neon signs direct tourists to the area nor do trams bustle people from parking lot to ticket booths. The only indication I was still in the twenty-first century was the paved parking area.

As I maneuvered Bessie into a spot and climbed off, I heard a voice behind me shout, "Did you ride that thing all the way from Florida?"

I pulled my helmet off and turned to see who was asking. An elderly couple was walking in my direction toward the village entrance.

"Yes, and then some," was my reply. The man looked to be in his seventies; he was tall and gaunt with gray hair sprouting from underneath a Cubs baseball cap. He stopped to chat a moment, reminiscing about his younger days when he rode a motorcycle. Conversations like this one always end the same: "I had to quit riding because of my hips (knees—insert whatever ailment here). Enjoy it while you can!"

"Thank you. I plan to do just that," was, and still is, my reply.

The sun was set to broil in the clear blue sky as I made my way toward the Colonial period dwellings, clustered together amid shade trees. A packed dirt path with fences running along both sides led me through the meadow; the toes of my black leather boots gathered a fine coating of dust.

The path ended at the stately Appomattox Court House Visitor Center, located in the reconstructed courthouse building. (Note: Appomattox Court House is the name of the town, not the name of the courthouse; Court House, is two words, which are capitalized.) I showed my annual U.S. National Parks pass at the entrance; the pass is without a doubt the best money I've ever spent on travel. As I wiped the sweat off my neck and forehead with my bandana, I picked up a map of the premises and walked around the museum-like interior, relishing the frigid, air-conditioned room. Vintage photos of Colonial life and maps covered the walls of the reception room. I took my time examining the articles, reluctant to leave the chill of the interior for the sweltering heat outside.

History should be experienced from geography and museums, not textbooks. When my daughters were small, we spent our summer vacations traveling as far as we could go in any direction on my teaching salary, visiting museums and our national parks. One of my favorite photos of them was taken at Petersburg National Battlefield in Virginia. They are dressed in Confederate soldier garb and toting muskets. The siege of St. Petersburg was the longest military event of the Civil War with upward of 70,000 casualties and, ultimately, the decline of General Robert E. Lee.

On this day in Appomattox Park, attendants and volunteers strolled in period dress, mingling with visitors to answer questions. They remained in character, speaking as if it were the 1840s and their little renovated village was still the thriving outpost it once was. I wandered over to Clover Hill Tavern, the oldest building in the village, where a rowdy group of "villagers" had broken into song on the front porch.

Past the Plunkett-Meeks Store and post office, the footpath led me to the Bocock-Isbell House and the local jail. Further out was the McLean House, the site of the actual surrender of General Lee to General Grant. The visitor center attendant previously informed me that the interior of the house was closed due to renovations, but I decided to make the trek anyway to inspect the grounds.

I was a lone traveler on the packed dirt path that guided me to the dignified, two-story brick home at its end. "There is nothing moving," as my grandmother used to say to describe a hot, still, summer day. It was so quiet I could hear the bees as they buzzed among the patches of wildflowers, sampling the veritable buffet of blossoms that lined the fence. A chorus of birds, darting from branch to branch in the trees, serenaded me with their chirruping and cheeping. I imagined that if I stopped and stood still, I could hear butterflies flap their wings as they flitted to and fro in search of nectar. Once I left the immediate area of the village, the only human sound I noticed was my boots crunching small pebbles with each step I took on the walk.

I wondered if General Lee walked or rode on horseback to the McLean House. How humiliating—or perhaps humbling—it must have been to trudge down a path, packed hard by heavy, dusty riding boots, walk up the front steps, and surrender an entire way of life.

I wandered around the grounds of the house, thinking a lot about the meaning of *surrender* in my own life. Anything I've ever had to give up, either foolishly or desperately, has been pierced with claw marks because I tried to hang on to it. Surrender is a paradox; it takes a tremendous amount of character to say, "I surrender," but only in relinquishing power over whatever it is that needs to go does anyone find complete freedom.

For General Lee, surrender meant to cease warring with an enemy and submit to their authority. For me, surrender has meant to give up, to lose, to abandon myself entirely to something greater, more powerful.

In 1993, I surrendered my addiction. I admitted defeat and acknowledged an all-inclusive hopelessness while being held captive by drugs and alcohol. For twenty-four years of active addiction, my life spiraled in and out of control, careening toward one personal disaster after another. The 12-Step Group, of which I remain a member in good standing, suggested completely yielding to a power greater than myself if I desired a clean and sober life. I learned that surrender is the intersection between acceptance and change. How many times did I stand at that intersection—much like blues legend Robert Johnson standing at the crossroads where he met the devil—struggling to let go of a destructive force and accept God's grace.

As I perched on a worn, wooden bench under the shade of a huge oak tree, I wondered how many mothers unwillingly gave up their sons to die in the war between the North and the South.

Although I never willingly surrendered my younger daughter, I have submitted to the loss. I have stopped fighting the heartache created by her absence. Instead, I stand forlornly at the intersection, choosing acceptance, praying for change. The memories I have of her crush me: her laughter, her copious amount of soft blonde hair, and the sprinkle of freckles across her nose.

The heartache is a physiological reaction that starts in my chest, clamping my heart like a vice grip, the pain radiating down into my gut, melting my leg muscles to the point I need to sit down for fear of toppling over. It is a *fight or flight* response, sending spasms of grief, albeit briefly, along every nerve ending, creating the desire to run fast—in any direction—to escape the pain. I surrender to the feeling until it passes, and I accept her absence, dreading the next inevitable bout of heartache.

Slowly, inescapably, we all surrender our youth, like the elderly gentlemen in the parking lot who had to relinquish his riding days to bad hips. The lyrics to Jackson Browne's "Pretender" play in my head as he sings about all of us who start out so young and strong and then eventually give up our youth to old age. I witnessed first my grandparents and then my parents surrender their youth as I myself aged. Thankfully, aging is gradual until one day an illness or an accident prompts us to literally yield to its limitations. I recall the many aspects of youth that I readily relinquished: a lack of confidence, the need to please everyone, the awkward feelings, the financial struggles, and the lack of direction.

However, claw marks will become visible if I am forced to surrender my independence or my ability to ride Bessie!

By my calculations, General Lee was only fifty-eight years old when he surrendered his troops at Appomattox—old by Colonial standards—but the same age I was when I stood on the grounds of the McLean House. I don't consider myself old because my life really began the day I embraced a sober lifestyle, which puts me emotionally now in my early twenties! I doubt, however, General Lee's surrender at fifty-eight left him feeling liberated. On the contrary, Lee was a pariah among his former friends and associates in Washington, D.C., so much so that ten months after the surrender, he is quoted as saying, "I am now considered such a monster that I hesitate to darken with my shadow, the doors of those I love, lest I should bring upon them misfortune."

As bees buzzed from one sweet, succulent blossom to another in the honeysuckle vines and shrubs bordering the small brick outbuilding behind me, I tried to decide if I had ever surrendered to romantic love. Lust, yes. Love—not so much. An all-embracing submission to love would have required a commitment on my part to remain true to him, regardless of the circumstances. I am the first to admit that when the going got rough in past relationships, I was the one to move on to whomever was next—especially during my alcohol and drug days.

My practice was to give up the relationship before I gave myself to it. When I matured and my two girls came along, I genuinely desired a lasting bond with their father, but he and I were doomed from the start. He married a drunk, and when I became sober, he did not like me as a clear-headed woman. And frankly, as a sober woman, I did not like him very much either. For four and a half years afterward, I stayed with him, trying to make the marriage work for the sake of our girls.

I reached a time in our tumultuous relationship when I concluded single motherhood would be far more beneficial for my children than their living in a perpetual battleground our home resembled. I conceded defeat in marriage, but I did not abdicate my children's chance at a peaceful coexistence if their parents lived separately. I wondered if Mrs. Lee was happy in her marriage. Did she think less of him for surrendering his troops to General Grant so the war could end?

Reluctantly, the hallowed grounds of Appomattox forced my attention back to my present. Before I stood to leave, I lingered a minute longer, feeling lazy from the heat and my rambling thoughts. I inhaled deeply of the honeysuckle's perfume. *The South is so fragrant,* I thought as I closed my eyes and said a prayer of gratitude for my journey thus far.

I pushed myself up off the wooden bench and walked slowly around the McLean house to the dirt walkway. Judging by the position of the sun, it was nearing late afternoon. I don't wear a watch when I travel; it seems an intrusion on my time. I could have looked at my phone, but pulling a digital device out of my pocket amid a Civil War site seemed unpatriotic. My shadow stretched long behind me as I walked, as if it were reluctant to surrender to our departure as well.

I walked back through the village, waving farewell to the rowdy crowd of tavern guests talking with tourists on the front lawn. I was happy to see Bessie waiting patiently for my return, as if she were a flesh and blood steed instead of a steel horse. Turning south out of the parking area, I noticed the sun starting to paint pink and gold strokes as it began its decent in the West.

It was time to seek shelter for the night. Tomorrow was officially the start of our trip home.

36.0726N, 79.7920W

Arrange whatever pieces come your way.

– Virginia Woolf, *A Writer's Diary*

IT'S A FUNNY THING ABOUT MY JOURNEYS ON TWO wheels. Each time I twist the throttle, I never know if I am traveling away from my destiny or rushing headlong toward an indefinite calling. The morning after my visit to Monticello and Appomattox, I awoke to anticipate not only the day's travel but also a strong feeling that I was hurtling toward a new chapter in my life.

An intriguing new relationship simmered on the back burner, waiting patiently to be explored. My contact with North Carolina Man had been consistent, no matter where I was. We talked each evening after I settled for the night in various locations. He demonstrated a genuine interest in my solo travels with no hint of intimidation. It was encouraging and refreshing to connect with a man who was not threatened by my independence or otherwise felt emasculated because I chose to travel alone.

I made plans to meet this man in Greensboro, North Carolina, en route to Florida. He suggested we meet at the Harley-Davidson dealership because, as he told me, "It is convenient to find just off I-40, and if you are comfortable after we meet, we can go to lunch from there." I liked that Harley-Davidson would be our common denominator and a safe place to meet a man I knew from only our email correspondence and phone conversations.

I reminded myself of Debi's Criteria for a Life Partner list I created when I embarked on dating websites' adventures. I would not be swayed from, nor would I compromise my criteria. I had the distinct impression North Carolina Man was working from his roster of standards and would not be deterred either, which made him that much more interesting.

When we talked on the phone, we shared basic information about ourselves, revealing commonalities that felt familiar and comfortable. He was easy to chat with, preferring that I carry the conversational ball while he listened and responded with an anecdote or comment of his own. He was quick to laugh and see the humor in situations. His relaxed phone demeanor suggested that he didn't take himself too seriously and wore life like a loose garment. He had worked in the same industry for three decades, still owned property in Maine although he lived in North Carolina, and was affable in talking about his future dreams—all pluses that rocketed him to the top of my requirements for a life partner candidate.

The blue skies were brilliantly sunny as I cruised toward Greensboro, praying fervently that something—like inclement weather—would not happen to screw this meeting up. I was a little too self-critical as I dressed that morning: *Does the white shirt show my love handles? Should I wear foundation on my face to hide the brown spots?* In the end, I said to hell with the makeup foundation and figured if my love handles showed, he would either like them or not.

I followed the voice of Google Maps in my headset as she guided me to the Harley-Davidson dealership just off I-40 outside of Greensboro. I slowly navigated the frontage road, expertly dodging a few potholes while scanning the parking area for my lunch date. Not seeing anyone who appeared to be looking for me, I pulled into a space near the main Harley-Davidson building, killed the engine, and climbed off Bessie. I pulled off my helmet and desperately tried to ruffle my short hair out of the helmet head crunch that leaves it plastered to my head. Hanging my helmet over the handgrip, I sucked in my gut as I rearranged the white shirt over the top of my jeans and stole a glance at my reflection in the window of the dealership. I resembled a wind-blown woman who had just biked 180 miles—without foundation—to meet her mystery guy for lunch. It would have to do.

I turned to see a man standing near a picnic area adjacent to the main building, waving tentatively, his motorcycle nearby. I also realized he had been watching the entire episode of me trying desperately to look presentable, for which I quickly hoped I hadn't appeared too vain. We previously had exchanged pictures, so we knew vaguely what each other looked like. I waved back and strode across the parking lot to where he was standing.

North Carolina Man had a slighter build than his photos suggested, but otherwise, I recognized him. He stood a foot taller than me; thin, light grayish hair appeared to be rapidly receding from his brow. Wire-rimmed glasses gave him a dated look, but his smile was genuine, and he was looking at me as if he had just won the lottery. He extended his hand and said, "I'm Paul. I'm glad to meet you—finally!"

"Hey, Paul. I'm Debi, and I would prefer a hug, not a handshake."

He was somewhat startled when I pulled him close for a quick embrace, his hands alighting awkwardly around my waist, exactly where I perceived the love handles to be, and said, "I'm happy to meet you as well."

I caught a whiff of Old Spice aftershave, which was good; I don't like men who take a bath in aftershave so thick it sticks to your face after a quick hug, leaving the odorous smell lingering hours afterward. He smelled familiar, like my dad. I stepped back after our hug, held him at arm's length and commented, "Thank you for looking just like your photo!" He chuckled. I felt an instant fondness for this man; I had no flip-flopping stomach or head-over-heels feeling. I saw just a wholesome goodness that held promise.

I sat down on the bench and patted the space beside me, indicating Paul should do the same. We made small talk, breaking the ice, stealing furtive glances at each other, and connecting our voices with our faces. He asked about my ride; I inquired about the proximity of our location and where he lived. We chatted amiably for thirty minutes or so, and then he asked me, "Do you feel okay going to lunch with me?"

I resisted the urge to giggle because the way he posed the question seemed to indicate he might have thought I had reservations about my safety in his presence, which was utterly absurd as there was no way this man could be threatening even if he tried. His desire to put me at ease superseded his need to impress, which, in turn, impressed me.

I replied, "Ready when you are. I will follow you since I have no idea where we are going." I walked back across the parking area to my bike, wondering the whole time if he was the type of guy who liked to watch a woman recede. I pulled Bessie around to the picnic area, falling into line behind his pearl white Harley-Davidson Classic. The irony of his owning a *white horse* was not lost on me; in mythological events, a warrior or god-like figure on a white steed symbolized triumph over negative forces. Perhaps it was an omen, maybe a coincidence, or better yet, my wild imagination.

Bessie and I followed this knight in shining armor around several twists and turns through somewhat heavy Saturday traffic on the outskirts of Greensboro. It was clear he was trying to decide where to go for lunch, so I was a little surprised he didn't pre-plan which restaurant to go to as our many phone conversations led me to believe he was a planner. Since he didn't inquire about choices I might have had for lunch, I imagined he was now in a real tizzy, asking himself: *What does she like? What does she not like? Is she a vegetarian? Should I stop and ask? Is she allergic to seafood? Damn, I should have asked her before we took off!*

Finally, after half an hour of dodging traffic and a couple of dizzying turns, Paul pulled into an Olive Garden parking lot—safe choice! Who doesn't like Italian food? As I dismounted Bessie and dug a hat out of my saddlebag to camouflage my helmet hair, he said, "I hope this is okay."

"It's perfect," I replied. I didn't say it, but I was further impressed that he spurned the customary biker bar with scantily clad waitresses and blaring music in favor of—the Olive Garden.

In the months ahead, as Paul and I became better acquainted, he would relegate all such decisions to me, and when my apathy toward such matters reared its ugly head, forcing him to decide for both of us, I labeled it the Olive Garden call.

The hostess showed Paul and me to a booth near the window and placed the menus on the table as we scooted into seats across from each other. She inquired about our drinks. I ordered water; he ordered iced tea, another plus.

Paul and I previously had the conversation about my recovery from alcoholism; when I'm interested in a potential partner, I am upfront about that aspect of my life. He was not put off by my revelation as most men had been and knew I tolerated only a moderate amount of alcohol in the people I associated with. In the same conversation about alcohol, he admitted that he never drank a beer while on his bike, saving any alcohol consumption for after his ride, if at all. This is an easy comment to "say" when the relationship consists solely of emails and phone calls. I must see you in person to make sure you walk the walk.

We scanned the menus, both claiming not to be "very hungry." Other than salads, I don't recall what Paul and I ate. We made small talk, mostly about my trip over the last few weeks. As we chatted, I kept waiting for the lightning bolt to hit, or my twat to do a flip-flop, signaling, "This is the guy!" But there was no such sensation. Paul was a plain, vanilla-flavored, nice guy—the type I usually discount as too boring to be a good match. He had no grit, no rawness, no bad-boy persona, which were attributes I thought I needed to see in a man to make life interesting. I doubted Paul had ever found the edge of the wild side of life, let alone walk it.

A raging dialogue started in my head while I listened to Paul describe his forthcoming ride to the Sturgis Motorcycle Rally in South Dakota with his group of friends:

> *He is boring.*
> *No, he is a nice guy,*
> *He is not the big, burly guy you usually like.*
> *No, he is gentle and kind.*
> *He smells like your dad.*
> *Why is that such a bad thing?*
> *His bike is white.*
> *For God's sake, Debi, don't be so shallow.*
> *He lives in North Carolina.*
> *You got me there. That's a problem.*

And, so it went, me at war with myself over this gracious guy who ordered a salad and iced tea for lunch at the Olive Garden.

Paul and I talked about our pasts and shared some notes about each of our children; he asked about my teaching, I asked about his work, we lamented over previous relationships and why they didn't work out, and we discussed what a future might look like with the right partner.

Our conversation was amicable, and it didn't feel like an interview as previous meet and greets have been. All the pieces seemed to fit into place, except one. I pointed out the considerable geography between us for any kind of traditional dating scenario and reiterated that I was not interested in a long-distance love affair. Been there. Done that. And, I was not interested in moving. His reply?

"I can live anywhere."

"But what about your job?" I pressed. Being employed was at the top of my criteria list for a partner. I wasn't interested in supporting anyone but myself.

"I travel for two or more weeks at a time, and I'm only home on weekends. If I'm an hour's drive or less from a major airport, my company doesn't really care where I live."

And there it was. The lightning bolt struck, the earth tilted slightly on its axis, my twat did a flip-flop, and I was in *LOVE*! Seriously? With a man who comes home only a few times a month, maybe even less?

In all my years of dating and searching, I had never met a man who was so attractive. Please don't think me shallow for that last thought. Believe me when I say, this kind of setup was a win-win situation for both of us.

In the years since his divorce, Paul found it difficult to date any woman seriously for this very reason—he was out of state or out of the country more than he was home. Most of the women who were initially attracted to him quickly lost patience and interest when they realized he was not one hundred percent available all the time. Conversely, for me, his lifestyle fit my lifestyle perfectly.

As Paul and I lingered over the remnants of our lunch, we agreed there was enough interest between us to pursue a possible relationship. He was emboldened enough to suggest I accompany him to the Sturgis Motorcycle Rally, located in the Black Hills of South Dakota. Although he was a man after my own heart in terms of suggesting an adventure on the spur of the moment, I had to decline. But, not before I did the mental gymnastics in my head: *Can I run home, repack, make it back here before they leave? Will I make it back to Florida from North Dakota in time for the first day of school? Do I have enough money to do this?*

I explained to Paul that my school year started in two weeks, about the time his group would leave for Sturgis. It would be impossible for me to make the trip.

Paul asked about my plans for the remainder of the day, indicating there were lots of great back roads to ride near the area. It was already late afternoon, and I told him I needed to travel east to pick up I-95 south. I planned to spend the night near the interstate and arrive home in Florida the next afternoon.

"Do you mind if I ride a little way out of town with you?" he asked.

This guy was so polite, so well-mannered, and almost timid with his intentions; I said a silent prayer that I would not scare him off with my spirited independence and naturally assertive manner.

"That would be great!" I replied as we made our exit from the restaurant. "I'm sorry I don't have the luxury of staying in the area longer to ride those back roads, but I promise you, I will return to do just that," I offered. He beamed.

Bessie and I followed Paul back to I-40 east and then several miles on the interstate toward Raleigh-Durham. It was a gorgeous sunny day—the sun hot, the air warm, and not a cloud in the sky. The area was hilly with deep green forests; I could imagine good twisty back roads running through the hills. After an hour of interstate travel, I thought Paul was going to escort me all the way to I-95, but then he exited to a rest area, which I assumed was our farewell point.

Paul pulled into a parking space, and I pulled Bessie up, snug beside him. "Do you have a hotel in mind for this evening?" he inquired, as we both pulled off our helmets.

"No, I usually just ride until I'm tired; I don't make reservations in advance."

Paul looked at me and said, "I would feel better if I knew you had a specific reservation for this evening." I bristled slightly at the protective posture he felt comfortable adopting but adjusted my response so as not to sound defensive:

"I can look at a map and tell you about how far I'll continue to travel. It's already late afternoon, and I usually stop before 5:00 p.m. That should get me close to I-95 south," I explained as I dug my iPad out of my saddlebag to check the map and hotel availability.

Paul and I walked up to the picnic area and sat down in the shade. I accessed my map and chose a point near I-95, pointing it out as I handed Paul the iPad. "Here. This looks like a good place to stop for the night," I said while I excused myself to visit the ladies' room. When I returned, he said, "You're all set."

More than a little perplexed, I said, "With what?"

"You have a reservation at the Hampton Inn in Smithfield for this evening. They have your name under my Hilton Honors points reservation. It's on me. I appreciate you making the trip to Greensboro to have lunch with me. It's the least I can do," he explained.

"Wow! You really don't have to do that," I stammered. "I'm capable of paying for my room."

Shut. Up. Just. Shut. Up. Debi! He is aware of the fact you can pay for your own hotel. Just say thank you to this sweet guy.

Paul was still seated at the picnic table, clutching my iPad, gazing around furtively as if someone was going to give him the correct answer to my overly defensive comment. I quickly corrected myself and jokingly said, "Gosh, I have a man who is paying for my hotel room, and he is not even suggesting he accompany me. That's a new one!"

He smiled, obviously relieved, and said, "I would be happy to join you, but I think we can save that for another time."

"And so we shall. I've had a wonderful time getting to know the person behind all of our emails and phone calls," I said. I touched his shoulder lightly. "Thank you for lunch, and the unexpected treat of a hotel reservation!" We slowly walked back to the parking area, as neither one of us wanted the afternoon to end.

Before we departed, I asked a bystander to snap our photo with my iPhone. I stepped close to Paul, and he placed his arm around my waist and pulled me close. In the picture, I have one arm around his waist, the other arm outstretched, clutching Bessie, the vehicle that had brought me to this point, this latitude and longitude where I met the man whom I would soon deem my *perfect partner*. Paul planted a quick peck on the cheek before he released me to don my helmet and gloves. I saddled up, backed Bessie out of the parking spot, and waved goodbye while he stood near his bike, watching me depart.

Several weeks later, I printed the picture and put it in an ornate silver frame with sparkling bits of mirror embedded in the silver. It sits on my desk in my classroom today, a shimmering reminder of how life can turn on a dime if we open ourselves to the possibilities of what the universe may offer.

I rolled into my driveway on July 7 with 3,858 miles accumulated on Bessie Two. I switched off the ignition, and while I listened to the soothing tick, tick, tick of the engine cooling, I said, "Thank you, God, for safe travels on this journey."

When I set out on this journey on June 21, I was seeking to rediscover my confidence to ride my motorcycle. Last year's accident had robbed me of that. But I had regained my ability to handle my bike and squelched the all-too-familiar fear that had become a frequent flyer with Bessie and me. I felt triumphant; my confidence had been restored, and the fear, which had begun to cling to me like a bad smell, had all but disappeared or moved to the back seat.

With each daring hairpin turn I encountered, I gained clarity for the challenges in my life. I chose the most defiant roads in the Southeast to help me recoup what I possessed before my accident. And I did.

I am now confident I can accomplish most anything my heart desires; I can endure any crisis long enough to arrive at the other side. Obstacles, like pot-holes, will continue to pop up in the road of my life. But I know that what I must do to meet them is to be alert, to engage the clutch, downshift when necessary, brake to remain safe, ease up on the throttle, and navigate the next blind curve with assurance—because I will have clarity on the downhill run.

At the end of each journey astride my Bessie, my heart knows I made the right decision to ride, to travel, to challenge myself, to flirt with danger, and to conquer my fears. I find a piece of my soul lying out there on the concrete ribbon. It might be a part that needs reclaiming or a piece that needs to be discovered, or perhaps it is a piece of my soul reminding me that life is beautiful despite the rough gravel patches.

CHARLESTON

It was a good moment, the kind you would like to press between
the pages of a book, or hide in your sock drawer, so you
could touch it again.

– Rick Bragg, *All Over but the Shoutin'*

THE WINDS OF CHANGE WERE SWIRLING ALL AROUND ME,
blowing gusts from every direction. I returned from my summer of 2013
road trip with renewed energy and sporting a refurbished self-confidence after riding Bessie Two on some of the most challenging roads
in the Southeast. I also met North Carolina Man. Fresh vigor and a
recharged self-confidence would serve me well with the challenges I
would have to face as the year trundled toward its end.

Before Paul and I could make plans to meet again after our initial
meeting in Greensboro over the summer, he was assigned to a project
in France. Paul is a service engineer with a company that maintains

the machine tool industry all over the world. At the start of our relationship, Paul spent five months rebuilding machines in a factory that supplied the off-shore drilling industry in a small coastal village on the Mediterranean Sea in the south of France.

Ours had become a whirlwind romance, played out on two continents. A long-distance courtship, transpiring between wireless towers at odd hours, framed our getting-to-know-you conversations—all condensed into four months. The six-hour time difference between France and the US dictated he call on his lunch hour just as I was finishing breakfast and before my commute to school.

Long talks on the phone are candid and often revealing, but they lack intimacy. I don't simply listen to words. They're meaningless without facial expressions or the subtleties of body language to communicate true feelings and opinions. When you say, "I'm looking for someone to spend the rest of my life with," I want to see the message in your face, the look in your eyes, and whether your gestures match the tone of your words. When you claim, "I'm not a big drinker," I wish to spend at least forty-eight hours with you to determine if you speak the truth. I interpret your silences because I can hear everything you don't say in words. Most importantly, I need to look you in the eye when you tell me you love me.

Paul arranged to fly to North Carolina from France in September. The time he was on American soil would give us forty-eight hours to say hello in person and plan a future rendezvous. I suggested we meet in Charleston, South Carolina, since it was about halfway between where each of us resided. I would ride up from Central Florida, and Paul would travel down from Greensboro, North Carolina, once he returned from France.

By the fall of 2013, a sale was pending on my house. Both eager to get out of the upside-down mortgage as well as move on with my life, I was in limbo, trying to decide where I would go next. The old house represented a lifetime of living for me; it was the place I finally unpacked my belongings, planted shrubbery, and settled into for the first time in my life. I lived more years in that house than I had anywhere else. The prospect of my empty nest status felt forlorn as well. Although my daughter, Caroline, had graduated from college, lacking any job prospects, she moved back home. I was delighted; she—not so much. I encouraged her to apply to nursing school and vowed to help her as long as she lived at home to save money. We struck a deal.

I had spent twenty plus years raising my girls and managing our lives together, but I knew I had to set about creating the next chapter of my life. Bessie would again be the vehicle that would guide me toward a fresh start, new home, and captivating partner.

Charleston, South Carolina, is a great ride destination from Central Florida, and as it turned out, a charming place to fall in love. It is an antebellum jewel nestled along Charleston Harbor overlooking Fort Sumter where the first shots of the Civil War rang out. A visit to Charleston is like stepping back in time where history comes alive and makes it impossible to forget our country's divided past. Vintage colonial homes sit beside the cobblestone streets of Old Charleston proper.

The waterfront with its seawall, known as the Battery, is lined with stately mansions painted in a profusion of pastels as if a child with a bucket of sidewalk chalk colored recklessly outside the lines. Regardless of the season, a cornucopia of blossoms festoon Charleston's parks, doorsteps, tiny brick-walled courtyards, and tree-lined streets. The heady perfume of gardenia, magnolia, jasmine, dogwood, and honeysuckle mingle with salty air, infusing every corner of the city. A visit to Charleston is a vacation for all five senses and a respite for one's soul.

As much as I anticipated visiting one of my favorite southern cities, seeing Paul was foremost in my thoughts. We left our respective homes the Thursday before Labor Day; Patriot's Point in Charleston Harbor, where the naval and maritime museum is located, was our destination.

Bessie and I meandered north on Florida's US 27 and connected with US 19 that cuts through the heart of the Ocala National Forest. It is still rather easy to stick to the less crowded back roads in Florida, which makes traveling at a leisurely pace quite enjoyable. North of Palatka, I turned west to pick up US 301 going north to avoid I-95 traffic snarls near Jacksonville. US 301 skirts the Okefenokee Swamp to the east, and with only a few minor jogs, an adventuresome traveler can savor a relaxing back road excursion along this highway through Florida, Georgia, and the southern part of South Carolina.

I crossed the Savannah River, the border between Georgia and South Carolina, and then headed southeast to US 17 that slips quietly through the marshy Low Country and into Charleston from the east.

My olfactory senses kicked into overdrive. One doesn't *see* the Low Country of South Carolina first—one *smells* it immediately. Rising from the marshes, the salty fecundity swirled around me and drenched me with a moist richness that can only be explained as *ripe*. It's as if this piece of earth, not Sub-Saharan Africa, is the womb from which all mankind was born.

One of my favorite authors, Pat Conroy, eloquently paints his beloved Low Country in *The Prince of Tides:*

> To describe our growing up in the low country of South Carolina, I would have to take you to the marsh on a spring day, flush the great blue heron from its silent occupation, scatter marsh hens as we sink to our knees in mud, open you an oyster with a pocketknife and feed it to you from the shell and say, "There. That taste. That's the taste of my childhood."

The traffic thickened as I approached Charleston proper, a bustling, modern city that sits apart from the Civil War era buildings on the waterfront. I navigated Bessie around the bypass and across the majestic, cable-stayed Arthur Ravenel Jr. Bridge toward Patriots Point. As I crossed the Cooper River, I saw the *USS Yorktown*, moored resplendently as the centerpiece of Patriot's Point as if she were the reigning monarch of Charleston Harbor. Fort Sumter's silhouette sat poised in the distance.

Bessie and I rode up under the portico of the Holiday Inn at Patriot's Point, which stood across the street from the harbor. I didn't see another bike, which indicated I was first to arrive for our rendezvous weekend. I checked with the front desk to discover that Paul had left instructions for me to check in, but I chose instead to wait outside and clean Bessie.

Without the wind in my face, the stifling humidity quickly produced a sticky film of sweat on my skin as I worked to rid Bessie of bugs and road grime. Within a few minutes, I heard the familiar *thump, thump, thump* of a Harley-Davidson rounding the corner into the hotel parking lot.

Paul 's face lit up with a smile when he saw me standing next to my bike. He pulled into the space next to mine, stiffly climbed off, discarded his helmet and opened his arms wide, beckoning me into his embrace, happy to make a flesh and blood connection after months of phone conversations. He was more handsome than I remembered. My arms stayed around his neck, his around my waist for what seemed like minutes before he reluctantly let go and said, "I left instructions for you to check in when you arrived. Have you been waiting long?"

"I arrived about twenty minutes ago," I told him. "I opted to get the road grime off Bessie instead."

"Ah," was his only reply, as he peered around me and looked at my bike, as if it were foreign to him that I would choose to clean my bike instead of checking in to an air-conditioned room.

Paul turned and walked inside to register us into the Holiday Inn. It was then that I realized I was still holding the spray bottle of a quick detailer in one hand and a rag full of dead bugs in the other. *Nice,* I thought. I glanced over at Paul's bike, coated with dead insects too, so I sprayed it down and started cleaning off his bike as well. Paul came strolling back outside, holding two plastic room keys but stopped dead in his tracks when he saw me scrubbing his incredibly dirty bike.

"What are you doing?" Paul stood behind me, staring incredulously.

"I'm cleaning your bike; it's a mess," I replied.

"You don't have to do that," Paul said defensively as he grabbed a spare rag lying on the bench next to the bikes. He started cleaning off the filthy mess with me.

"I know. But I just can't stand for a bike to be so dirty," I told him, more than a little apologetically. For an instant, I thought I might have overstepped my bounds—a man's or a woman's bike is sacred. Not just anyone can touch it, let alone clean it. Months later, after Paul and I settled into domesticity, he told me that the bike-cleaning incident was the clincher for him. He decided then and there that any woman who looked like I did, rode her own motorcycle, and didn't shy away from cleaning *his* bike was a keeper.

We unpacked our gear, and while I protested, Paul collected both my bags for the trip up to the room. I tried to make it clear, without sounding bitchy, that I carted my own luggage, but he wasn't hearing it. As he juggled four small bags toward the elevator, he managed to hand me a room key and tell me, "You can get the door." I decided my opinion was a conversation for another time.

I had instilled in my girls not only a love of travel but also the need to be responsible for their own belongings when we traveled. I told them they could pack anything they wanted for a trip so long as they could still carry their own luggage. I remember our plane trip to California and two pre-teen girls struggling valiantly through the airport with enormous duffle bags, stuffed to the gills with things they just couldn't live without. Thankfully, their duffle bags had wheels, or they never would have made it to Los Angeles and back.

Paul and I would have several of these tug-of-war moments when his gentlemanly character clashed with my independent disposition. He took all my protests in stride, smiled, gently laid his hand on the small of my back and opened the door for me anyway.

The hotel room was a suite with a combination bedroom and sitting room. I expected an awkward moment or two as we settled into a weekend together, but I didn't anticipate what came *next*.

"I thought I would get a suite, so I could sleep on the pull-out couch," Paul said by way of explanation as he set our bags down, placing his hands awkwardly on his hips as if they were suddenly foreign appendages to him.

I looked at him and shuddered as I remembered C. Dick saying the same thing to me. "Why would you want to do that?" I uttered, dejectedly.

Paul stammered as his arms dropped limply at his side, "I… don't really want to, but… I didn't want to assume anything." Now he looked dejected and downright embarrassed; his arms flapped helplessly as he looked around the room, hoping to find a quick solution to the situation.

Within ten minutes, the Gentleman Biker had clashed with the Liberated Biker Chick at least three times. I made a mental note to shift gears and enjoy Paul for who he was: a nice guy with impeccable manners and a sense of priority where I was concerned.

"Well, I don't want you to sleep on the couch," I declared emphatically as I picked up my bags, plopped them on the bed, and started hanging T-shirts in the closet. His face flooded with relief as he smiled and started rearranging his gear.

"Okay then, that's settled," he said. He, too, began unpacking.

Now that the sleeping arrangements were established, we stowed our gear, went back to the lobby for coffee, and talked about our respective rides to Charleston. In that brief conversation, I ascertained that Paul was a fan of back roads—but only if someone else led the way. As a solo rider, he stuck to the interstates. He admitted to a case of jet lag, having arrived back in the US from France only a few hours before he left home in Greensboro to travel south. The coffee was so strong that it seemed toxic and capable of peeling off the top of your scalp. I wasn't sure if the coffee or my proximity to Paul was creating the tingling I felt in every extremity.

I pulled a map of Charleston from my bag, spread it out on the table between us, along with my list of things to see and places to eat, for Paul to inspect. I quickly told him that if he needed to rest this afternoon and evening after all the travel, I would be perfectly fine with that option. Afterward, I realized he wasn't about to admit he wanted to rest when we had only forty-eight hours together. He would fly back to France from Greensboro the following week. The purpose of the weekend was to get close to each other, but I had to know if he was also interested in sightseeing, one of my passions when I travel. I purposefully had jammed our two full days' itinerary with every appealing spot I could find to visit in Charleston. I had to know whether Paul could "keep up with me," regarding how I liked to travel. He did not disappoint.

I wanted to show Paul the South I had come to love and call home. Although he currently resided in North Carolina, Paul is a Massachusetts northerner through and through, having spent only a few years below the Mason-Dixon line. My objective in creating an itinerary for this visit set the pattern for our future travel; Paul lovingly refers to me as his "cruise director."

Paul didn't shy away from my plans. When he saw the USS *Yorktown* was on my list, he said, "I've always wanted to board that aircraft carrier," as if he were a small boy of twelve.

Charleston is a place to indulge all five senses, especially taste. Low Country fare is dense with local, fresh seafood, seasoned with southern zest and served with gusto. The Folly Beach Crab House is a two-story, waterfront eatery that was congested with locals and tourists alike on this holiday weekend. Large ceiling fans in lieu of air conditioning pushed salty, humid air about with little effect on the fierce humidity. I ordered Carolina Crab Cakes with a side of fried green tomatoes; Paul opted for a grilled chicken sandwich. Immediately, a red flag went up: *He doesn't like seafood!* I soon learned that Paul is a simple, meat and potatoes kind of guy whose eating choices often collided with my adventuresome spirit in all things, including food. Over the years, however, I have coaxed him out of his rut, tempting him to try fresh seafood along with a variety of Asian cuisine.

I persevered in working through my list of Charleston restaurants, hoping Paul would find something on the menu he liked, such as creamy shrimp and grits at Moe's Crosstown Restaurant, a crunchy fried grouper sandwich at Red's Icehouse overlooking Shem Creek, and melt-in-your-mouth chicken and waffles at Jestine's Kitchen. We found common ground with shrimp dishes, and after his first taste of savory shrimp and grits, he was hooked; we both enjoyed good old-fashioned burgers and southern barbeque.

Paul and I joined the queue of tourists that snaked around the ticket kiosk and continued up the gangplank to the gaping jaws of the USS *Yorktown*. The sun was relentless, the humidity suffocating as we inched our way at glacial speed toward the leviathan anchored in the murky waters of the harbor.

Once inside the ship, tourists are free to walk unaccompanied through the museum-like exhibits. One of my favorite photos is of Paul sitting in an F-15 fighter jet, gripping the joystick, smiling up at me and saying, "I've always wanted to fly one of these!" There was that twelve-year-old boy again!

We climbed down into the bowels of the ship that housed the crew. It was hot and close quarters. I looked at Paul and said, "I need to be topside where I can breathe." He didn't hesitate to grab my hand and find the stairs leading up to the deck. I inhaled the salty air deeply; fetid or not, it relieved the queasy feeling I had below deck.

Paul and I finished our tour of the ship, walked back down the gangplank to wait on the boat to take us to Fort Sumter. I told Paul that I liked to take short, informational videos of my travels, which I kept on file to show students. He enthusiastically embraced the role of videographer after I showed him how my Canon 5D recorded video.

Paul endeared himself to me that weekend with the little things he did like placing his hand on the small of my back to usher me through an open door, taking my hand and leading me out of the lower deck of the ship when I felt queasy, and demonstrating interest in the videos for my students.

The short boat ride for twenty or so tourists to go out to Fort Sumter in Charleston Harbor was windy, and the small craft bounced and bobbed on the grayish, white-capped water. A sharp, briny wind whipped over us, causing those of us wearing caps to either take them off or clutch the top of our heads to keep them on. The water's cooling effect tamed the heat only slightly.

We disembarked on the small wooden pier that stretched out into the water a short distance from the entrance to the fort. I was struck by the fort's "smallness." I guess I felt that a place so significant should be bigger, more impressive.

Paul and I ambled around the crumbling structure, reading the plaques, snapping photos, and dodging the relentless wind that buffeted the tiny island. Before our boat was scheduled to leave, I handed Paul the camera and told him I wanted to do a short video that explained the significance of Fort Sumter in US history. And this is one of those "sock-drawer memories"; he took the camera, gazed at our surroundings and suggested, "Maybe we want to move over there (gesturing towards the brick wall that makes up the exterior of the fort) to get out of the wind. Plus, it's better light." I fell in love with a man who recognized the advantages to placing me in "better light."

As the weekend in Charleston ended, neither of us had any doubt that our separate paths would now merge into one. During the hours together, we shared amiable conversations over dinner and comfortable silences when talk lulled. There was no tug-o-war over where to eat or what to see, primarily because Paul acquiesced to my desires, a pattern that would serve us well when we traveled in the future.

Paul was right when he told me he wasn't a big drinker, and when he did drink, it was after we settled the bikes for the night, and it was usually one beer. His is not a concept I understand, but it's one I admire. After the initial discussion about where Paul would sleep, we discovered the *dress fit* in all the right places. I was relaxed with Paul—no pretense, no high expectations, and no hurry to move on to whatever was next. His unassuming demeanor and refreshing absence of baggage was a welcome addition to my life. The destructive pattern of overlooking "nice guys" in my life was about to end.

When Paul and I discussed the possibility of cohabitating and how it might affect our families, Paul was careful to say, "Of course, your daughter is welcome in my life—whatever we decide." He already knew Caroline had returned home after college, and I had agreed to help her with nursing school as long as she lived with me.

On Sunday morning, Paul and I lingered over our coffee, each of us feeling a promising contentment. We were reluctant for the weekend to end, but our respective responsibilities called us home—in opposite directions.

We rode together to I-95 where Paul turned north, and I faced south, bidding farewell for another month. We planned to meet in October for Biketoberfest; I would be taking a virgin to Daytona.

LETTING GO

I WALKED SLOWLY ACROSS THE WORN HARDWOOD FLOORS like a woman in a dream in the near-empty house I had occupied for over sixteen years in Florida. Their familiar creaks groaned under my feet. My footsteps echoed off the walls, naked of the accouterments that make a house a home and softens its sounds; the photos, books, plants, pillows, and almost all the material objects had been relocated to the *new* house.

Dust bunnies, long hidden under the couch, swirled across the hardwood and settled in a new place, much the same as I will. I looked around at the walls with no pictures, the dusty floors, the empty bookshelves, and barren cabinets as a wave of melancholy hit me so hard, I had to close my eyes and slump down, cross-legged on the floor for fear its weight would crush me. I closed my eyes and opened my heart to recollections from the past.

I hear the echo of my girls' voices the day we moved in; they were four and five years old, excited and eager to claim their new home. They ran through the vacant house, their footsteps on the hardwood—not so worn then—resonating off the walls. Their shouts and laughter reverberated back and forth as they investigated their rooms.

I see myself as I stand in the minuscule kitchen of this antique bungalow, wondering how it was all going to work for us. The girls' father and I had separated, and our divorce was pending. I had no job, no education, and two young children. I was terrified.

Sixteen years later, I had two grown children, three college degrees, and a secure career. My daughters are educated, and my life is full. This place sheltered us through it all, bearing witness to the struggles, victories, heartaches, and the triumphs.

Words from Van Morrison's "Brown Eyed Girl" float into my reverie: "Cast my memory back there, Lord...." With my eyes still closed, I lifted my arms and embraced the memories of our living here, pulling them close, breathing in the air of all those years, filled to the brim with laughter and tears.

The need to go versus the desire to stay tugged at me from every direction. Even now while my partner waits patiently in the driveway, ready to whisk me away to the next chapter in my life, I feel uncertain. The moving van is loaded.

I squished my eyes closed a little tighter and a little longer, unwilling to leave as tears slipped down my cheeks. I hear once more the soft murmurs of my girls, reading to each other as we lay on the bottom bed of their bunk, the streetlight outside their window casting a warm glow.

I listen to their eager voices as they awake Christmas morning and rush to the shining tree to see what Santa had left beside the fireplace.

I pay attention to the melody of many "Happy Birthdays," celebrated around the chipped and pockmarked dining room table. I hear the back door slamming umpteen-million times as we went about our busy lives.

My ears pick up the sound of tap shoes drumming a rhythm on the wood floors as my older daughter practiced her dance. I remember soccer cleats squeaking across the dining room floor on the way to a shower, and the scuffle of pristinely polished dress shoes that my Junior Reserve Officers Training Corps (JROTC) cadet wore.

I hear the distinct clip, clip, clack, clack of high heels on hardwood, as I snap pictures for prom, homecoming, and graduation, all happening too soon as the years sped by. And yes, the sounds of tears, shouts, and frustration that go hand in hand with parenting mingle with the happy noises.

I opened my eyes, looked around lovingly at four empty walls as I got back on my feet and said one last goodbye to the old house. I slowly left a well-lived home; you might say we wore it out! I mentally packed up the memories—some literal—as Moms are keepers of those by nature, but on most days, I will see them figuratively when memories are all I have.

I inhaled the last remnants of our lives there, wiped the tears from my eyes, dusted myself off, and walked out into the sunshine of new day.

MY WINGMAN

No road is long with good company.

– Turkish Proverb

IN NOVEMBER OF 2013, PAUL AND I MADE AN OFFER ON A home in Central Florida. He was prepared to move from North Carolina to Florida, where we would start a new life together. Many said our whirlwind courtship and decision to cohabitate six months after we met was moving our relationship along too quickly, but Paul and I both agreed it was an event that took over fifty years to happen—naysayers be damned.

While waiting until the sale was finalized, I arranged for Caroline and me to stay in my old home for a few months, renting it back from the new owner. In March of 2014, we moved into the new house; Paul would join us in April once his company released him to work from a home base in the Southeast.

My daughter and I began the arduous task of scraping off wallpaper and painting the interior walls. The house was built in the late eighties when wallpaper and wallpaper borders were "in vogue." I detest wallpaper; I like it even less when I must scrape it off. Except for the great room, every wall was swathed in pinkish, mauvish, art-deco-themed wallpaper.

I had kept only the essentials of furniture I owned, vowing to buy new pieces once we finished the cleaning and painting. Caroline and I camped out in the living room on folding chairs and slept on mattresses tossed on the floor in the bedrooms. The work of transforming the house took her mind off her father's dire medical condition. Several decades of smoking had taken their toll; his heart was giving out as were his scorched lungs. He lived close by, and she visited him in the evenings. His numerous hospitalizations and near-death episodes left her wrung out emotionally.

The father of my daughters passed away the first part of April. The news sent my older daughter into an emotional tailspin, which I felt helpless to fix. All I could do was watch, offer support and a safe place to land. As for my younger daughter, Mallory, I had no idea how her dad's death affected her since I had no contact with her. I wanted to be a source of support for Caroline in her grief; however, the tumultuous history her father and I shared made it difficult for me to muster any sympathy at his passing. I encouraged her to spend time with her older sister and brother, her dad's children from a previous marriage, and other members of her father's family. I am grateful for their enduring support and love for my daughters.

Paul left his apartment in North Carolina, sold his house in Maine, packed his belongings in a U-Haul, and arrived in Florida near the end of April. I could placate the naysayers and say that Paul and I had a difficult time adjusting to our living arrangements—but we did not. Paul did struggle to adapt to the Sunshine State for a variety of reasons, but as a couple, we eased into domesticity without a hitch.

Paul and I embarked on numerous road trips in and around his new Florida home. Probably the most significant adjustment Paul had to make in his move was not having his close-knit group of friends around him; they had filled their weekends with shared riding experiences. I tried to compensate by packing our weekends with riding adventures. He was astonished to discover a diversity of landscape, rolling back roads, and an interior devoted to agriculture and cattle. Paul discovered that Florida was not all beaches and tourists slathered with sunblock. He liked that we could leave the house on our bikes and within ten minutes be on a leisurely secondary road, virtually void of traffic, surrounded by fragrant orange groves or strawberry fields. Paul claimed his favorite trip that year was the ride south to Everglades City and Chokoloskee Island. Again, he was amazed by the stark beauty of the vast Everglades, void of the crowds of tourists that flock to Orlando or the beaches. He was delighted to visit the Smallwood Store, established in 1906 by Ted Smallwood, on Chokoloskee Island, where he asked questions about its history and heard the story of Edgar J. Watson, the outlaw entrepreneur who lived in the Everglades at the turn of the century. I loved watching Paul's astonishment when he saw an alligator.

Seeing the familiar in a new light through someone else's eyes is always refreshing, and so it was for me when Paul and I traveled my adopted state.

I took him to Circle B Bar Preserve in Polk County, went on a nature walk, and visited the Audubon Center near our home on one of our many trips around the state that first year. Circle B is rife with gators that amble along the swampy preserve, occasionally crossing paths with tourists who hike the nature trails. Paul was like a kid playing I

Spy: "Look! There's another gator over there! I spy one sunning himself right there; see it?"

I knew the true test of the durability of our relationship, however, would be the summer road trip I planned for us to take as soon as my school year ended in May. I targeted several destinations to check off my Bike-It list. My main desire was to ride to the top of Pike's Peak in Colorado, one of several 14,000-plus-foot pinnacles in the Rocky Mountains.

I decided that from Florida, we would first head west to Austin, Texas, to ride through the spectacular Texas Hill Country and then turn north to Fort Worth to visit my family. From there, Paul and I would travel north through the Texas Panhandle and a portion of historic Route 66 and proceed to Colorado Springs. My niece, Kasey, was living and working in Denver, and we wanted to fly Caroline to Denver where we would all meet for a mini-family reunion.

I longed to cross the Rockies, check out the Anasazi cliff dwellings, and, time permitting, pick up Route 66 again in New Mexico. I outlined the schedule for Paul one evening as we sat enjoying the view from our Florida room, and he wholeheartedly embraced the itinerary. It would be a pattern for all our future travel—I planned the trips, and Paul agreed to what I suggested. I had finally found a man who complimented my life rather than complicate it. My wingman had arrived!

On Friday, June 6, I spent the morning in my classroom—sans students—finalizing grades and stowing books away for safe keeping. It had been a tough but productive year in which my students performed spectacularly on the standardized reading test. I left for the summer break with a profound sense of accomplishment because they had demonstrated significant learning gains.

Earlier in the school year, I had applied for and was accepted into the academic coach's pool for the county in which I worked. Each school has one or more academic coaches who perform a variety of duties aligned with a school's improvement plan. A literacy coach, for example, is responsible for tracking data, working with classroom teachers to improve student performance, training new teachers, and promoting reading and writing skills.

My new position would take me out of the classroom, a prospect I had mixed feelings about, but I had decided I owed it to myself to advance toward a possible administrative position. As I prepped my classroom for the summer, I was sad knowing I would not return to this school I loved so dearly.

I left campus before noon and made the commute back to Winter Haven to switch my packing skills to Bessie. Paul and I were going to leave the next morning on the first leg of our journey west.

Caroline joined us for dinner that night as Paul and I discussed our travel plans. My daughter thoroughly embraced mine and Paul's domestic partnership. She was a skeptical child at best, so I knew her quick acceptance of Paul was a good sign. The fact that he was only home on the weekends made the arrangement less stressful for all three of us while we learned to cohabitate. "I hope you are ready to leave at oh-dark-thirty, Paul," my daughter teased. "That's just how she rolls."

She was a seasoned traveler with her mom and a veteran of many oh-dark-thirty departures. When my girls were small, we left on camping trips in the wee hours of the morning; I knew they would sleep while I clicked off a few hundred miles. When they finally awoke, rubbing the sleep out of their eyes amid a pile of blankets in the back seat, their first question was, "Where are we, Mom?" The second question was, "Are we having donuts?"

The only time I allowed them to eat donuts was on a road trip. All three of us looked forward to the sugary, gooey, yeasty goodness of a Dunkin' Donut—with hot coffee for me and cold milk for them.

I glanced at Paul, who wasn't yet accustomed to my daughter's teasing, and said, "We won't be leaving at oh-dark-thirty. I have compromised with a 6:00 a.m. departure time." Caroline glanced at Paul, lifted her left brow approvingly, and uttered, "Uh-huh. She must really like you if she is willing to leave on a road trip so late."

I cracked up; Paul chuckled warily, not yet used to mine or my daughter's often snarky sense of humor. I'm okay with a 6:00 a.m. departure if I can watch the sun come up from the saddle. I knew the group of people Paul traveled with over the last few years were not early morning risers. He had called me at 10:00 a.m. on a weekend the previous summer while he was on his way to Sturgis Bike Rally. I asked, "How far have you traveled this morning?'"

He replied, "Oh, we haven't left yet."

"What?! It's ten o'clock! I would be at least 200 miles down the road by now!" I told him.

Since I'm a sunrise person, Paul and I rather quickly established a pattern during the early months of our cohabitation; I'm usually the first one up, sipping coffee, and reading the newspaper a good hour or more before Paul awakes. He shuffles out of bed, mumbles a "good morning," then slurps coffee for at least ten minutes before he ventures into conversation with me.

On the morning of our departure, I was awake a good two hours before the alarm went off. I tossed and turned in the soft comfort of our bed, warm and familiar. My mind was racing with details: *Did I remember this? Did I check that? Do I have that covered?* The familiar *resfeber*, the Swedish word for travel anxiety, made it impossible to sleep. In addition to my usual anticipation for a road trip, I'm not going to lie—I felt a touch of anxiety at the prospect of a wingman. I adored Paul, but I just wasn't convinced we could sustain the adoration for a two-week, 24/7, several-thousand-mile road trip.

I crept around the house softly to not wake Caroline or Paul as I made last minute preparations. I carried my toiletry bag to the kitchen and sat it near the other bags waiting to be carried out to the garage. I checked the contents of my waist pack: ID, credit card, Burt's Bee's lip moisturizer, cash, and a switchblade. I rechecked the pantry, making sure there was enough cat food for the person who would take care of the fur babies after Caroline left for Denver. I poured another cup of coffee, lifted the garage door, and pulled a deck chair out to the driveway to sit by Bessie.

As I sipped my coffee, I sat very still and absorbed the "silence" of the morning. A spastic squirrel scampered up a tree; the cows across the road stamped their hooves, exhaled audibly, and one or two lowed softly while the mockingbirds trilled their morning song. I checked the weather forecast on my iPhone app, noticed the time and knew the alarm would be waking Paul in a few minutes.

Technically, Paul had thirty minutes from the time he awoke to prepare to leave. However, I was already standing in the driveway, tapping my toe and feeling anxious for fear I would miss the first luminous light tinged with pink and gold as the sun peeked over the eastern horizon. I would have been up for an hour before I engaged a wingman, and I would have been forty minutes down the road by now.

As Paul backed his bike out of the garage, I tiptoed into my daughter's room to kiss her goodbye. She was awake, and I told her we would see her in a week in Denver and that I would call her in the evening. I hugged her tightly, kissed her cheek, and told her I loved her. "Love you, too, Mom. Ride safe."

I gave my wingman, who was packed and waiting by the bikes right on time, a high five, straddled Bessie, and the V-twin engines roared to life simultaneously.

Paul and I merged onto US 27 north just as the first rosy tinges of the morning sun were blooming in the east. With no rain on the horizon, our ride north through Florida promised to be postcard perfect.

BOUDIN BALLS AND HOT SAUCE

A woman has got to love a bad man once or twice in her life,
to be thankful for a good one.

– Marjorie Kinnan Rawlings, Florida author

AS THE SUN MOVED SLOWLY TO ITS MID-MORNING POSI-
tion in a flawless cobalt sky, Paul and I made our way north on US 19.
The sleepy little southern towns—Homosassa, Inglis, Otter Creek,
Ellzey—whooshed by as we enjoyed the morning ride, void of any traffic
save the occasional pickup truck. When my stomach started to rumble,
I scanned each small town we rode through for a possible breakfast
stop. If the restaurant parking lot was full, it was a strong endorsement
the food was good.

Just outside of Chiefland, Florida, I spied a full parking lot at Betts
Big T Restaurant and pulled into the dusty, gravel parking lot, careful
not to slip-slide in the loose rock. I circled back in a partial U-turn, so

our bikes pointed out toward the road, making it easier to exit a gravel area. The look of relief on Paul's face told me it was a good idea to stop for sustenance and a restroom break. As we had logged the miles together, and even on short weekend runs, I knew that by mid-morning Paul needed a second infusion of caffeine, and so did I.

Although the parking lot was full, the cavernous dining area easily accommodated another two diners for breakfast. The walls were covered in old, knotty-pine paneling with intricate crown molding joining the walls to the ceiling. A middle-aged woman whose bleached blonde hair was whipped into a frothy "do," greeted us. Her name tag, that read "Fran," was pinned to her ample bosom.

"Morning, y'all! Just the two of ya? Right this way, hon."

She led us to an enormous booth near the front window and slapped the menus down on the table. "I'll be right back with your coffee," she promised before we even told her we wanted coffee. Fran was a pro.

The red leather banquettes showed their age. Not tacky, just well-used. The wooden bench-type seat had been worn to a shiny patina with age, and I felt a slight indention where countless diners had sat. I wondered how many butts over how many decades had slid over the wooden benches to wear them down to such a beautiful, rich mahogany color.

Betts is the kind of place where the sweet tea is so sweet it can make your teeth ache and still warm enough from the brewing that it promptly melts the ice in the glass as it's poured. The coffee is high octane, the fluffy biscuits can put your grandmother to shame, and the waitress calls everyone, "Hon." Fran asked, "Whatcha gonna have, hon?" as she plucked her pencil out of the blonde froth of hair and scratched our breakfast requests across her tiny order pad.

Betts was a bustling truck stop along US 19 before Interstate 75 siphoned off the truckers. That would explain the immense interior; at one time, the establishment offered gas, trucker amenities, a full-service station, and a small restaurant. As the gas and service station customers dwindled, Betts restaurant grew to make up for the deficit.

I ordered scrambled eggs, grits, and a biscuit with endless refills of coffee. I doused my eggs with a liberal shot of Crystal Hot Sauce—an ever-present condiment on any good southern restaurant table—and squelched the grumbling in my tummy. While Paul finished his breakfast, I glanced at the map.

Our route would be a repeat of the forgettable trip I made with C. Dick in 2011 (See the chapter, "C. Dick Run."). Although I loved North Florida, I was not going to stop at any of the same spots I did in 2011. I planned to bypass the charming little town of Sopchoppy and avoid the turnoff for the barrier islands of the northern Gulf coast.

A little beyond Perry, Florida, SR 98 west slices through the thick pine and oak forests of North Florida. The swampy, fertile air was humid, clogging my nostrils as sweat trickled down my back. My Under Armour heat clothing with its patented wicking technology was no match for an oppressive summer day.

Paul and I stopped in Apalachicola to hydrate; the summer sun was out in full force. Boss Oyster, one of the best places to enjoy salty, Apalachicola mollusks, is a great place to go if you stop during a month with "R" in its name, and this time, it was not. When the hostess asked if we wanted inside seating or deck seating, I was torn between the slogging, barely detectable air conditioning and the pleasant Gulf breeze. We chose the deck overlooking the bay with its rich, salty marsh smell wafting along with the soft, gentle wind only slightly cooling my moist skin.

I made a plea for water before I excused myself to find the ladies room. The hostess, who appeared not to sweat, gestured in the direction we just came—outside. The outside wall facing the street enclosed a narrow door labeled "Ladies Room." I stepped inside the smallest bathroom I've ever seen. Port-o-potties are roomier. The tiny bathroom was barely big enough to change your mind in and had no air conditioning or a window for ventilation. It was like a sweatbox; my clothes were so soggy with sweat that I had to peel my jeans down, then gyrate comically to get them back up. On the upside, the outside air felt a tad bit cooler after I left the sweatbox.

When I sat back down at the table, the waitress placed two large tumblers of ice water on the table. Like a toddler, I grabbed mine with both hands and chugged it down before I ordered a fried grouper sandwich with a side of coleslaw and requested a full pitcher of water. I felt as dry as the Sahara Desert.

It was late afternoon, and our goal was to ride to Fort Walton Beach before Paul and I stopped for the night. The pitcher of ice water was an oasis for my parched system; the breeze cooled and relaxed us as we finished our lunch, and I felt myself surrender to the heat. I handed Paul the iPad and asked him to find a hotel in Panama City, just sixty miles up the road. I knew, however, it would take us more than an hour to navigate the slow, coastal traffic. North Florida beaches are spectacular, so different from the east or west coast beaches. People love to gaze at them as they drive along.

As Paul and I rode through Mexico Beach, we slowed with the other traffic to gawk at the turquoise waters lapping at the white, sugar-sand beach. Approaching Panama City, I stopped to put the hotel address into the Google Maps app to get a visual on where we needed to go so I could watch for signs. This was before Bluetooth headsets, which are lifesavers when you are trying to navigate on a motorcycle.

I missed the hotel twice because we were in a run-down industrial section, surrounded by tire repair shops, pawn shops, and assorted other local storefronts. It wasn't our typical "hotel area." On the third try, I saw the Holiday Inn tucked back behind a Wendy's restaurant. As I passed it, I glanced over and dismally realized it was the only restaurant I could see in the immediate area.

After a much-needed shower, Paul and I started on foot to scope out other restaurant possibilities. We saw an Applebee's sign on the horizon and trudged about five blocks. As I sank into the cushy leather banquette, I exhaled slowly, grateful for the icy air conditioning. As the waitress brought water and menus, I looked at Google Maps and realized we had traveled 477 miles—and were still in Florida. I wasn't so much hungry as I was thirsty, and we both ordered a specialty salad. Next, I checked the Weather Channel app, which indicated severe weather across our route going west. I made a mental note to leave the hotel in the morning with rain gear on, not stuffed in the bottom of the saddlebag. Paul and I finished our dinner in companionable silence as we glanced at the news or weather on one of several televisions in the dining area; we warily watched the weather forecasters predict rain across the South and to the west.

Paul and I left before sunup the following morning, rain gear on, expecting a wild ride. Thankfully, the weather forecasts were all wrong. By the time we reached Destin and Fort Walton Beach, we were boiling in the nylon rain clothing. We were on US 98 west, a scenic secondary road through North Florida, except in the summer when it's clogged with beach traffic. I'm confident the giant sea turtles lumbered from the beach to the water faster than we were traveling on US 98.

I whipped into a gas station, shed the rain gear, discussed an alternate route with Paul, and hydrated. I wanted Paul to see Destin Beach, rated by *US News and World Report*'s travel section as one of the World's Top 50 Most Beautiful Beaches. But, I didn't want to spend yet another travel day trying to escape Florida. We endured the traffic snarl for another hour, gripping the clutch-brake-clutch, never shifting past second gear as the sun baked me, and sweat rolled down my neck, pooling somewhere in my cleavage until we reached the turnoff for Destin Beach.

The first time I walked out onto the beach in Destin, I was mesmerized. Translucent white sand, like quartz, with an ever-so-slight tinge of sparkling pink, lent a magical quality with the consistency of fine sugar. On a bright, sunny day, the Gulf water is a clear, jewel-toned green, as if Poseidon himself scattered precious emeralds atop the waves, making them dance and sparkle under the subtropical sun unlike the cobalt blue waters off South Florida and the Keys.

Paul and I wrestled our bikes into a tiny parking space, surrounded by large beach homes, built on postage-stamp-sized lots, that towered over the beach road and blocked any view of the Gulf. I was relieved to step off the bike, free of the heat from the V-twin between my legs. We crossed the boardwalk to the beach while scantily clad beach-goers stared openly at our jeans, boots, and long sleeves. Not exactly appropriate beach attire on such a sweltering day, but we were staying only a minute! We trudged a little way through the white-pink sand, Paul in awe of the splendor. I snapped a few pictures of him standing on one of the world's most beautiful beaches, looking ridiculous in boots and jeans. We walked back toward the bikes, eager to feel a breeze on the road, albeit a hot one.

After enduring the traffic bottleneck on US 98 west, I decided to travel north to pick up Interstate 10, which would take us away from the beach congestion as well as traffic around Pensacola and Mobile, Alabama. At least on I-10, there is little traffic, and just as we thought, we made good time—until wham! The cars and trucks in front of us came to a complete standstill on the two-lane section of I-10 that spans Mobile Bay.

A slow-moving sea of overheated vehicles slugged along the seven-mile bridge with water on either side adding to the heat and humidity. While we sat suspended high above Mobile Bay, the sun switched from slow bake to broil. With my boots on the hot pavement as I was astride a giant beast that was pumping out thigh-scorching heat,

I tried not to think about fainting. Or, our bikes overheating. When that happens, we don't go anywhere until the engine cools.

As we crept along at two miles per hour, squeezing and releasing the clutch ever-so-slightly to move forward, my brain felt as if it were boiling; sweat poured down my back. I envisioned arctic ice, penguins, frozen glaciers, and mountains of snow as I conjured up a frigid phantom wind blowing across my face. It was a blistering, thirty-minute crawl across the bay. The congestion loosened when two lanes became four again. Cars sprinted in every direction, jockeying for position as if they were competing in the Daytona 500.

Unfortunately, I-10 is one of the dullest highways in the lower forty-eight states except for the bridge across the mighty Mississippi River. We stopped at the Mississippi Welcome Center inside the state line, and as I pulled my helmet off, I heard a loud voice behind us, "Hawgs are runnin' hot today, ain't they?" Now, I'm a fairly friendly person but only when I'm doing the approaching. As a woman who has primarily traveled alone or with two daughters, I'm automatically wary or unfriendly when strangers approach. Paul, on the other hand, talks to anyone. Not just talks but draws them in, sidles up to them, seeking conversation. As the two men walked toward us, I hung back, replacing my helmet with the Harley hat and scanning the building for a restroom sign. I felt like I needed a shower, but a splash of cool water would suffice.

I returned to find Paul still talking to the two men who were also on touring Harleys. While Paul sought the restroom, I was left to pick up the conversation with our fellow bikers. They had traveled down from Ottawa, Canada, to ride through the South. Every other sentence was a complaint about the unbearable heat, which I had to agree with after we had inched our way across Mobile Bay. I said, "Yes, down here, we wear the weather." I replaced my cap with my helmet, indicating I was preparing to leave. I suggested they might want to return in the winter months to enjoy what the South has to offer bikers, and then I bid them safe travel.

I checked the map before leaving the welcome center; we needed to ride to Lake Charles, Louisiana, to remain on schedule to meet my daughter in Denver. I detested being held to a schedule, but when we factored Caroline into the travel equation, there was no avoiding a timetable. It would be a 500-plus-mile day in soupy southern heat and humidity.

As I-10 runs primarily through the swamps of Florida, Alabama, and Mississippi, there is little opportunity for sightseeing or finding something other than fast food to eat. Paul and I exited off the interstate at a bit of a town called Gautier, Mississippi, seeking someplace to eat lunch. I noticed a crowded parking lot at a restaurant named the Country Gentleman. Visions of shrimp and grits, mac 'n cheese, or fried chicken with a side of collard greens danced in my head as we entered the restaurant. Imagine my disappointment when the menu was all *Greek* food! The décor was eclectic at best, featuring a plethora of roosters and cast-iron skillets scattered randomly on the walls, and a dizzying array of fishing nets full of seashells hung from the ceiling. I felt the Country Gentleman was facing an identity crisis but consoled myself with the fact it was better than a burger at Wendy's, or worse, McDonald's. I concede it was a tasty lunch with fast, friendly service despite their identity crisis.

As Paul and I bumped and thumped along the Louisiana section of I-10, I can only assume the department of transportation borrowed Pennsylvania's *Road Construction Primer* as those were the only other roads I've traversed in such deplorable condition. The pavement was stripped and wavy on the right lane and patched with loose gravel on the left lane. Going the interstate speed was impossible. My shoulders took a beating, my legs vibrated as bad as the bike's, and my rear end was numb. And, the insufferable heat and a monotonous landscape added to this misery. As late afternoon approached, the rosy glow of travel anticipation had faded from my cheeks. I hit the wall. It was time to stop. Blissful, I saw the sign for Lake Charles, which indicated we were only fifty-three miles from our stopping point for the day. As I endured those last several miles, I mentally said *thank you* for safe travel thus far and another false severe weather forecast.

Sunrise over Lake Charles, Louisiana, was smeared with chemical and refinery plants belching thick smoke over the watery landscape.

Paul and I were well-rested the next morning. Our bikes were clean, and we were ready for Texas. We took an exit off I-10 and picked up US 90 west again—another old, secondary road that the interstate had sucked the life out of. The first establishment we saw showing any signs of life was a "Gentleman's Club," advertising twenty-five to thirty sexy women. I chuckled at the number equation. I guess the number of sexy women willing to dance topless in the Louisiana bayou varied from night to night. Or, once the "gentlemen" patrons sobered up in the daylight, at least five of the women were not very sexy at all. We saw funky, abandoned filling stations and houses turned into antique stores selling bits and pieces of a bygone era. The road was not in any better condition than the interstate, but I was willing to overlook the gravel-filled potholes to enjoy the towering oak canopy that shaded the broken asphalt and the sweet, fragrance of magnolia blossoms.

As Paul and I cruised along the shaded back road at a moderate speed, expertly dodging potholes, we passed several signs, some crudely homemade, others more professionally styled, publicizing homemade boudin balls. My curiosity got the better of me. We passed three road-side eateries, which were barely more than ramshackle wooden stands, advertising boudin balls. I vowed to stop at the next one. Unfortunately, the next sign I saw was the Texas state line, which shattered my hopes of tasting them. I wondered whether they were solely a Louisiana delicacy.

Eager for a short respite, Paul and I pulled into the Texas Welcome Center, where we snapped a photo with the state sign, something we do each time we cross a state line. The sign in front of my parking space told me to Beware of Snakes. Well, damn! I flash backed to a trip with my girls several years ago when we traveled the Gulf Coast, headed to South Padre Island, Texas, to see Kemp's ridley sea turtles.

The girls and I stopped for the night to camp on Galveston Island. Once the tent was up, the girls changed into their bathing suits, eager to go for a swim after being cooped up in the car all day. As we approached the boardwalk from the parking area to the beach, the signs warned Beware of Poisonous Snakes. A refreshing swim never happened. In addition to fearing the snakes, we endured a tropical storm during the night that nearly blew our tent into the next state.

I stepped lightly on my way to the restroom, checked the stall and under the toilet seat thoroughly before ascending the porcelain throne at the Texas Welcome Center. While I waited for Paul, I searched for boudin balls on my iPhone. It seems they are a South Louisiana delicacy, a sausage made of pork and rice. The sausage is removed from its casing, mixed with rice and seasonings and then rolled into balls, dipped in breading, and deep fried. A variety of dipping sauces add flavor and spice. I was sinking into a boudin-ball depression, thinking I had completely missed my opportunity to try the tasty Louisiana tidbit. On a brighter note, however, we had avoided the snakes and had resumed our ride toward Beaumont, Texas.

Paul and I glided onto US 69 north out of Beaumont, choosing to bypass the Houston crush of traffic and make our way to Austin on back roads. The posted speed limit in Texas is seventy-five miles per hour, even on the secondary roads. It was nice to haul ass on a good road without fear of being stopped. Just north of Beaumont, we connected with US 190 west, a fabulous ride through the Sam Houston National Forest. The forest is thick with both shortleaf and loblolly pine trees, dogwood, hickory, birch, and a variety of oaks. The pungent, woodsy smell was intoxicating.

Just outside of Livingston, Texas, I spotted a billboard promoting Shrimp Boat Manny's restaurant, and their specialty was—boudin balls! Manny must have been a Louisiana Cajun transplant to East Texas, and he brought his boudin balls' recipe with him. It was my lucky day! We gained an hour once we crossed the Texas state line, but our body clocks told us it was lunchtime. I whipped into the parking lot and noticed the ominous black clouds forming in the west—the direction Paul and I were traveling toward. I chose not to worry about the clouds right then; I had visions of boudin balls dancing in my head!

Shrimp Boat Manny's suffered no identity crisis; they advertised Southern Louisiana Cajun Cuisine, offered up amid funky, nautical décor with a genuine saltwater smell that permeated the interior. Bright red crustaceans flitted about in a giant aquarium near the hostess stand, tempting diners with their aquatic ballet. It was barely past a late breakfast in Texas, but the hostess seated us with a cheerful, "Welcome to Manny's!" The menu featured Crawfish Etouffee, Red Beans and Rice with Sausage, Dirty Rice and Boudin Balls. I ordered the latter two with sweet tea from a spunky waitress who had more enthusiasm than the hostess. I liked Manny's a lot.

The waitress returned with two giant tumblers of sweet tea, mine was spiked with fresh lemon, and she promised a refill when we finished these. Little did I know that I would need several refills after just a few bites of the boudin balls. There is spicy, and then there is Cajun spicy, and it's wise to know the difference.

The spunky waitress placed a heaping plate of dirty rice with two large, golden brown pork and rice sausage balls perched on top in front of me. She topped off our sweet tea, asked if we needed anything else, and left us to our lunch. Unwittingly, I sprinkled a few dashes of Crystal Hot Sauce on my dirty rice, just for flavor. I cut through the first ball;

it was crispy on the outside, juicy and moist on the inside. I dipped it in the accompanying sauce and savored the deep-fried goodness. The second bite was just as delicious as the first.

Then, the Cajun spice kicked in; I felt light-headed and broke out in a cold sweat all over. Paul laughed as I fanned my open mouth while he commented that his sausage rice and beans were just right. I gulped the tumbler of tea, sucking on the ice cubes until the waitress saw my distress and brought a pitcher of water with two glasses of ice. As she set the liquid down that would cool the fire in my digestive tract, she looked at me demurely and declared, "They're a little spicy, aren't they?"

Dorito's are a little spicy. *Pace Picante* sauce is a little spicy. *These?* Those boudin balls were capable of spontaneously combusting right there on top of the rice! But, I couldn't resist the savory goodness. Although my tongue and most of my taste buds were numb, I finished the tasty delicacies, left only a smidgeon of the rice, and washed it all down with a gallon of water and at least half a gallon of sweet tea. My eyeballs were sweating by the time I finished.

As Paul and I stood in the parking lot behind Manny's, my taste buds utterly numb from Cajun spice but my sinuses clear, I reapplied sunblock with a wary eye on the darkening sky. I checked the weather on my phone, and red, angry patches were moving across the radar, directly toward us. I walked over to Paul to show him the radar when a loud clap of thunder shook the sky, and a cold wind blew across the parking lot; dirt and debris swirled around us like mini dust devils. We pulled our rain gear out of the saddlebags and prepared to suit up for a wet ride. Within seconds, the temperature dropped twenty degrees. The sky turned night-black.

We grabbed our rain gear and ran back to the covered porch that surrounded three sides of Shrimp Boat Manny's. As Paul and I tugged our waterproof clothing on over our jeans, the wind whipped the rain in sideways; tiny needles blasted our skin. I watched the radar, and it looked like the worst of the weather would pass us in ten to twenty minutes. We waited on Manny's porch, my tongue still numb from the Cajun spice.

As the rain slackened, Paul and I cautiously exited the parking lot. I turned west toward Huntsville and boom! It was as if the storm did an about-face, engulfing us in thick sheets of rain. A deluge of Biblical proportions. I couldn't even see enough of the road to tell if I were still on it. Worse, I couldn't see a place to pull off to the side. I feared if I stopped, whatever vehicle was behind me, other than Paul, would slam right into us. I switched on my hazard lights and prayed the torrential rains would end. We made it to the outskirts of Huntsville, Texas, where we stopped at the first gas station, pulled under the skimpy canopy near the pumps, and got out of the downpour.

Paul and I huddled under the canopy like drowned rats; the station didn't have a convenience store, just a walk-up cashier's window. We waited at least an hour until I could see on the radar that the angry red patches were turning green, disappearing completely a few miles down the road. We were wet and uncomfortable.

I cleared off my glasses, wiped off the windshield, and slowly pulled out of the parking area. By the time we reached College Station, Texas, the sun was shining again. We stopped to change out of our rain suits and when I checked my email, I noticed a message from a school principal back home who wanted to interview me for their literacy coach position. I took a minute to call the school secretary, explained I was traveling, and if we could conduct the interview via FaceTime or Skype, I was interested.

Our destination was Austin, Texas. Outside of Bryan, Texas, we drove onto SR 21 that would take us to US 290. Remarkable secondary roads cut through vast ranchlands, gently rolling hills, and tiny towns like Dime Box, Old Dime Box, and Whoop Stop—hardly wide spots in the road. As we neared Austin, a drizzle began and forced us to stop once more and get into our rain gear. We hit downtown Austin during rush hour, inching our way along the interstate in the slick drizzle.

Just before sunset, Paul and I arrived at the Holiday Inn in downtown Austin. As I stood under the hotel portico, peeling off my dampened rain gear, I realized my previous anxiety of embarking on an extended road trip with a companion no longer existed. My wingman stayed just inside my left rearview mirror, didn't grumble or fuss when I exited for sightseeing, and went along wholeheartedly with just about anywhere I chose to eat. Was I so naïve I thought our travel or companionship would always be easy? No. But for this trip, at this juncture in my life, it was a welcome change.

After registering with the front desk, Paul walked back toward our bikes with a smile on his face despite the rain. Waving the plastic room key at me, he said, 'Let's get out of this rain, change into dry clothes, and find some barbeque for dinner!'

APPLE PIE, CADILLACS,
AND BARBEQUE

Ninety-nine percent of the world's lovers are not with their first choice.
That's what makes the jukebox play.

– Willie Nelson

I WAS A BABE IN ARMS WHEN MY GRANDMOTHER FISHER
packed me up along with a picnic basket of fried chicken and canned
peaches for my first trip to Texas. My uncle Dale had made the Lone
Star State his home after he served in the army in Korea. We spent three
days on the train from Indianapolis, Indiana, to Fort Worth, Texas, to
visit her son and introduce him to his brand-new niece.

My grandmother and I made the trip by train several times when I was a child. Years later, I traveled with my parents to the Lone Star state in a '67 Chevy station wagon with the windows rolled down and hot, dusty air blowing through the interior. I've gone on my own to visit my Texas kin several times over the last few decades. I like to think I've been just about *everywhere* in Texas, always one of my favorite destinations. I don't think I really fell in love with Texas, however, until I visited the Texas Hill Country in the summer of 2014. Austin and the surrounding Hill Country was the last piece of Texas geography for me to explore.

Paul and I arrived in Austin on a Monday, but I don't feel a rainy Monday night exploration of the Live Music Capital of the World is a fair assessment of a thriving, party town. We headed downtown to eat at Stubb's Bar-B-Q, which was first opened in 1968 in Lubbock, Texas, by C. B. "Stubb" Stubblefield, a former United States Army staff sergeant and Korean War veteran. He later closed that location and opened the present restaurant in Austin.

When yet-to-be-famous country and blues artists like Tom T. Hall stopped by Stubbs to "sing for their supper," word of the tangy, sweet barbeque and smokin' hot live blues traveled fast. We found both to be true on our visit.

Stubbs, a multi-level eatery housed in a former industrial-type commercial building, offers restaurant and outdoor seating, a live music venue, and a pool hall. Even on a rainy Monday night, the place was packed. My combination plate of chicken, pork, and brisket did not disappoint. The music wafting up to the dining level from the concert hall was contemporary country and blues by a local group—a nice accompaniment to our dinner and precisely what I expected to find. After trying all four flavors of Stubb's tangy, sweet barbeque sauce, I became a devotee. A bottle of Stubbs is an ever-present condiment in my fridge.

After dinner, Paul and I walked toward the Sixth Street Entertainment District of downtown Austin. It is roughly eight-to-ten blocks long and a few blocks deep on either side, and live music radiates from virtually every bar and restaurant. It was 9:00 p.m. and drizzling rain. A few people, probably tourists like us, were strolling along the street, peering into open establishments while seeking their brand of music.

Paul and I sauntered into a few bars and were disappointed when all we found was head-banging music, appreciated by a decidedly twenty-something crowd. It wasn't the country blues I anticipated. The last club we visited before heading back to the hotel offered a decent blues guitarist, and when he stopped for a break, someone slipped a few quarters in the jukebox to play Willie Nelson. "Blue Eyes Crying in the Rain" is a song I can relate to on a rainy evening in Austin.

The following morning, Paul and I wrestled our bikes out of Austin on the clogged interstate in rush-hour traffic. On a positive note, though, the rain that had plagued us for the last two days had stopped, giving way to an oppressive, dry Texas heat.

US 290 west led us away from Austin, directly into the Texas Hill Country. Wide-open highway, seventy-five miles per hour posted speed limit, little to no traffic, and clear blue skies made the ride pleasurable. We stopped at Dripping Springs, Texas, and bought a map of the region and planned to make a loop through the Hill Country before traveling north to Fort Worth to visit my family.

Pedernales Falls State Park was nearby, so we took a detour to see it. Hailing from Florida where sightseers go everywhere, I expect every attraction to be jammed with tourists, which was not the case at this state park. After a leisurely drive off US 290 west, we crossed the Pedernales River and noticed flash-flood warning signs. The parking area was almost deserted as we situated the bikes and walked to the small rest area to buy water from the soft drink machine.

When I am riding in extreme heat, I make it a habit to down a bottle of water each time I stop. Following the signs to the falls, Paul and I hiked a short distance on a well-marked trail down to the river. Another sign alerted us again to the possibility of flash flooding:

> WARNING: The water in the river can rise from a placid stream to a raging torrent in a few minutes. If you are in the river area and notice the water rising or getting muddy, leave the river area immediately. Flash flooding is common in the Texas Hill Country. Please be alert to weather conditions.

I couldn't decide which was worse: poisonous snakes or flash flooding. We spent a few quiet moments sitting on the decking overlooking the falls, which were not exactly *falls* by my definition, but water coursing gently over large limestone formations. Paul and I studied the map of the region and decided one day in the Hill Country would not do it justice, so before we exited the state park, I called my aunt and uncle in Fort Worth to delay our arrival another day.

When I started planning this trip months ago, I consulted *The Most Scenic Drives in America*—one of several travel bibles I own—and discovered several roads in the Hill Country that qualified as must-rides. The road markers were a dizzying array of "farm roads" that changed numbers with every turn.

Our drive through the Hill Country was serene at best; Paul and I rarely passed another vehicle. The back roads meandered through sculpted hills that once trembled with the hooves of horses and longhorn cattle. Tiny towns resembled cowboy-themed movie back lots along the landscape. Just outside of Blanco, Texas, we stopped to hydrate and wash down the bikes. They were covered with thick dust and had not been washed since we left home. It's just bad karma to ride on a dirty bike.

The call from the Florida principal who wanted to interview me for the coaching position showed up on my "missed call" list again. We stopped in Boerne, Texas, an idyllic town settled by German colonists, to find a quiet place to make a phone call. It was bustling with shoppers and tourists. The Cibolo Creek meanders through the town, and I made a turn down the main drag and spied a coffee shop that looked perfect for refreshment and conversation.

After finding a parking spot a few blocks away, Paul and I trekked back to the coffee shop in our boots, jeans, and long sleeves, looking unquestionably out of place on a hot Texas day. Although the interior of the shop was packed, the patio area was not. I called the school secretary to suggest an interview via Skype since I would not return to Florida for a few weeks. While I was on hold, Paul brought me an iced coffee and a bottle of water. I confirmed a Skype call for the following morning. It was the first time I have never worried about what to wear on a job interview; I had only Under Armour heat gear and jeans! I don't even carry make-up on a road trip.

Leaving Boerne behind, I was enthralled by the acres and acres of wildflowers that blanketed the Hill Country landscape; their vivid blooms stretched to the horizon in either direction. It was like riding through an impressionist painting. The innumerable hues gently waved and bent in the dry breeze as we passed. I was disappointed we were too late to see the spectacular bluebonnets, which blossom from February to April, depending on the amount of rainfall. Mental note: Return for the bluebonnet bloom.

Our route wound through vast ranchlands with ornate gates protecting the ranch road from trespassers. Elaborate ironworks atop towering gates spelled out names like Otter Creek Ranch, Twin Boar Ranch, and Circle R Ranch in ornamental script unique to the family it represented. Roads led to a copious array of trees off in the distance, veiling a family home in greenery. My mind wandered for several miles as I tried to imagine life on a ranch in the Texas Hill Country. I saw a sign for Luckenbach, Texas, which started an earworm of Waylon and Willie songs in my head.

Our destination was Medina, Texas, to indulge in a slab of apple pie topped with hand-churned vanilla ice cream and homemade apple cinnamon sauce—positive proof that bikers will travel hundreds of miles on a twisting back road to savor good food.

Medina was literally a wide spot on SR 16. There was a bar, a post office, the Apple Store (not the swanky anchor store selling Steve Jobs' devices) and a dozen houses that we saw along the "main" road. I guess a person can get drunk, mail a letter, and eat apple pie, all within walking distance of home.

The Apple Store is a part of Love Creek Orchards; the original owners, Baxter and Carol Adams, planted the first apple trees in 1981. They retired in 2007 and sold their beloved apple orchard and store to Bryan and Stacie Hutzler. What started as a roadside stand in front of the stone house to sell sweet red apples blossomed into a patio café and gift shop. I had read about their legendary apple pie—voted the Best Apple Pie in Texas—in a magazine while waiting in my doctor's office a few months ago. I noted the name and location in my ever-growing list of places to see and compelling places to eat that I keep in Notes on my iPhone. The owners claimed, "Five pounds of apples go into every pie." I grew up eating pie virtually every day from the master pie-maker herself, my grandmother. I decided it was a challenge I could accept, even if it meant traveling to Medina, Texas. I was there to determine if, in fact, the Apple Store truly had created the Best Apple Pie in Texas.

The small, stone house sat among a cluster of trees in deep shade, an instant reprieve from the Texas heat. The second I walked through the screened door—no air conditioning—with the tinkling bell to announce a visitor's arrival, I was swathed—no drenched—in the aroma of fresh-baked apples and cinnamon. As the screen door banged lightly behind Paul, I stopped just inside the door on the worn hardwood floor, closed my eyes, and inhaled deeply. The rich, buttery smell was enough to make any pie lover swoon. The tiny, older woman, dwarfed by an intricate display of apple craft items, chuckled. She said, "We get that reaction a lot!" I indicated we were there for the pie, and she pointed toward the back of the house and said, "Just follow the smell." No problem. We passed through two small rooms, jam-packed with items that looked like apples, smelled like apples, sported apple appliques, and were made of apples. However, I had come for the pie, not the gift shopping.

At the back, near the exit to the patio, the biggest, fattest pies I had ever seen sat on a table. The golden dome of the crust was a good six inches above the rim of the pie dish. Thick, juicy pie wedges, at least a quarter of the pie, were sliced and ready for the taking. We were directed to serve ourselves. For the briefest of seconds, Paul and I considered sharing a piece. Then the woman at the pie table suggested we top our pie with a scoop of vanilla ice cream and a ladle of the homemade apple cinnamon sauce, and we dismissed all thoughts of sharing. She didn't have to ask me twice.

The back of the house opened onto a vast covered patio, festooned with a red and white theme. We carried our slices of pie to a table near the edge of the patio in hopes of catching a cross breeze. The ceiling fans did little to restrain the stifling heat. By the time I sat down, my ice cream was already melting.

The first bite was darn near orgasmic; in fact, I went into a sugar-induced-semi-coma as I savored each sweet, juicy, flaky bite. Paul and I didn't utter a word. We ate. Just as I was seriously contemplating another slice, a woman approached our table and asked if we wanted something to drink. She was about our age and sported a Harley-Davidson destination shirt. "Yes, water would be great to wash down this sugary goodness," I replied, and in the same breath, I asked, "Do you ride?"

Long story short: She grew up in St. Petersburg, Florida, visited Texas to ride the Hill Country over eight years ago, and never left. That's how good riding and apple pie are in Texas. We chatted with our server as we finished our pie and took notes from her riding experience in the area.

Paul talked me out of a second piece of pie, but I went back inside to buy a jar of the apple cinnamon sauce to take to my aunt. I stood in front of the pie table, legitimately trying to figure out a way to strap a pie box on the back of Bessie, but alas, it was not feasible.

Fortified with pie and ice cream—and yes, it absolutely was THE BEST apple pie in Texas—Paul and I planned to tackle a portion of the Three Sisters ride, better known as the Twisted Sisters, that connects three Hill Country ranch roads—335, 336, and 337—in a one-hundred-mile loop. I knew we would not have time to cover the entire loop on this trip. We would save the challenging road for when we returned to see the bluebonnets.

I asked our server at the Apple Store which abbreviated route to take. We shortened the Sisters on her recommendations and decided to add SR 16 between Medina and Kerrville, Texas, which would be our stopping point for the night. The route followed canyons and climbed jagged, steep hills; the roads offered many tight, twisty curves with sheer drop-offs alongside and not much in the way of guardrails. The geography in the Hill Country is totally incongruous with the flat, infinite plains in the rest of Texas. In one fifteen-mile section, I counted approximately sixty-five curves!

The asphalt was old in some sections with gravel patches. The route is a blissed-out ride for an experienced rider, but I would caution a novice rider to go slow and not be distracted by the stunning vistas that pop into view around every curve. Mule deer stood in clusters, munching on whatever was growing alongside the road. They didn't appear disturbed or spooked by our passing.

After a few hours of the thrilling, curvy ride, we ended up in the small town of Kerrville, tucked into a deep valley in the Texas hills. I stopped at the first gas station, pulled off my helmet, and, like a little kid who just stepped off the roller coaster ride, called over to Paul, "Wow, let's do that again!" And, I believe he would have accepted my challenge had it not been so close to sunset. Between the apple pie sugar rush and the exhilarating ride through the Hill Country, I was beyond gleeful. I have never ingested a mood-altering substance that made me feel any more euphoric than a challenging, pulse-pounding ride on two wheels.

Our hotel was perched on an incline on the north side of town; a Subway sandwich shop sat adjacent to it. Before checking in, we grabbed a couple of sandwiches to eat in the room. After a long, hot soak in the in-room hot tub, Paul and I were spent; we slept like the dead that night.

While Paul went downstairs for breakfast the following morning, I set up my iPad for my Skype interview. After connecting with the middle school principal in Kissimmee, Florida, I apologized for my somewhat "unprofessional" appearance, and we both had a good laugh. He presented a challenge, which, unfortunately, I have never had the courage to back down from—a struggling school population comprised of second-language students and a not-so-friendly neighborhood. After an hour of questions and answers, I told him I was interested in the position, and he agreed to call me the following Monday morning. Little did I know that it would be one of the worse career decisions I ever made.

It was late morning for us when Paul and I rode north to Fort Worth, Texas, where my aunt Dorothy and uncle Dale warmly greeted us. Their splendid hospitality has never disappointed. Paul was treated to a grand tour of the Old Fort Worth Stockyards, a Texas Longhorn cattle drive, a rodeo, and a delicious Lone Star barbeque. I loved reminiscing with my uncle about my grandparents and visiting with my cousins. I was reluctant to leave the pleasant family vibe, but Paul and I were expected in Colorado within the next two days. The morning we left, Uncle Dale made a Texas-sized breakfast that included eggs over easy, crispy bacon, biscuits with homemade strawberry jam, pecan waffles with syrup, and fresh fruit—which held us halfway to Amarillo!

Unlike the journey through the Hill Country, the six-hour ride north from Fort Worth to Amarillo was along wide-open plains. We traveled secondary roads to the outskirts of Lubbock, then took Interstate 27 north to Amarillo. Winds from Oklahoma to the east and from New Mexico to the west blew hot and dry across the Texas Panhandle. They were consistent, relentless to the point we were traveling at an angle. The bikes tilted precariously as Paul and I struggled to keep them perpendicular to the road. It was a stark contrast to the joy-inducing curves and elevations in the Hill Country. This was flat-out, balls-to-the-wall riding. It took every ounce of concentration to keep Bessie moving northward.

We stopped in Plainview, Texas—aptly named as there is a "plain view" of the Texas Panhandle in every direction—to gas up and rest. I walked inside the convenience store to buy water, and when I came back out, Paul was slumped up against the side of the building, his rear end on the sidewalk, his legs straight out in front of him—a picture of pure exhaustion. It was another three hours to Amarillo. If not for the fact we were to meet my daughter in Colorado Springs in two days, I think we would have stayed right there in Plainview for the night. Regardless of the protective mask I wore, my face was on fire from the wind and sun. Dust clogged my throat and nostrils, and my arms were shaky from the tension. I felt like Paul looked.

I rarely find travel boring, especially on two wheels. However, when the monotony of the ride sets in as it started to do 300 miles south of Amarillo, one of the things I do for relief is read signs. Road signs, billboards, cross-street signs—any sign that grounds me and pulls me back to focus on the road. Some riders, like Paul, listen to music like from a big dashboard stereo, blasting music. I prefer the sound of the wind in my ears.

It was impossible to miss the giant billboards advertising The Big Texan Steak Ranch on historic Route 66 in Amarillo. The billboards challenged would-be visitors to a free, seventy-two-ounce steak with all the trimmings if they could eat it in one sitting. The colossal signs popped up every fifty miles, luring travelers with the promise of the best steak in Texas, a shooting arcade, live music, a brewery, gift shop, and motel. The Goliath cowboy on the billboards, adorned with a ten-gallon cowboy hat, red-checked western shirt, and leather chaps beckoned weary travelers with a huge Texas smile and a lariat as if he could reach out and rope them in. By the time we reached the outskirts of Amarillo, I was convinced The Big Texan Steak Ranch would be our destination for dinner. I had enjoyed the Best Apple Pie in Texas, why not the Best Steak in Texas?

Our destination hotel, yet another Hampton Inn—our home away from home—was a few blocks from Route 66, the Mother Road, which we planned to ride west on the following day. I spied The Big Texan as we entered Amarillo. There is nothing, *nothing* so satisfactory after a day of riding in hot, dusty conditions as a shower. I stood under the hot spray as the water pounded over my shoulders and watched the sweat and dust form grayish rivulets and swirl toward the drain. The soothing heat loosened the tension in my upper body.

While Paul showered, I went downstairs to inquire about The Big Texan Steak Ranch. The last thing I wanted to do was climb back on Bessie and travel six or eight miles in the direction we just came from to eat. To my surprise, the person behind the registration desk said The Big Texan would send a car for us and deliver us back to the hotel. All I had to do was call the reservation number and provide our location. Done! I went back upstairs and hurried Paul along; he was none too crazy about going anywhere for dinner, but I promised him, "It will be fun!"

As Paul and I waited under the portico of the hotel for our ride, I glanced down the parking lot and spotted a vintage El Dorado Cadillac limousine with honest-to-goodness longhorn steer horns as a hood ornament and The Big Texan logo emblazoned on the side panels make the turn. The car, which was at least a block long, pulled up to Paul and me and out stepped the cowboy from the billboard! He was dressed in the same ten-gallon hat, red-checked shirt, leather chaps. He greeted us with a big, "Howdy, folks," as he tipped his hat in my direction. Yee-haw! This WOULD be fun!

Paul and I climbed in the back seat of the El Dorado, which was the size of a small living room, grinning like two teenagers who had managed to sneak out for the night. Our driver entertained us with the history of The Big Texan as he expertly navigated the rush- hour traffic around Amarillo. Once inside the cavernous building, we were ushered into the gift shop to "wait" on our table and then through the maze of activities designed to keep patrons spending money. Paul and I took our turn at the shooting gallery, sat in the Biggest Rocking Chair in Texas, shuffled through the dance hall, and finally wound back around to where we started. Magically, our table was ready.

The dining hall was two stories high; the second story overlooked the main floor seating area. In the center of the large open space— *everything* in Texas is big and wide open—was a small, raised platform with a table for four—the "arena" for the seventy-two-ounce steak challenge. Like gladiators of ancient Rome, brave diners ascend the platform, armed with knife and fork, to slay the meat. The humongous steak is served with shrimp cocktail, baked potato, rolls, and butter. If the challenger consumes the meal in one hour, it's free. Alas, no takers the evening we were there.

I ordered a petite size barbeque brisket; Paul opted for loaded potatoes, which we decided to share as our exhaustion and the day's heat had squelched our appetites. While Paul and I waited on our meal, I watched a strolling trio of musicians make their way around the upper deck, serenading diners. When they made it to our table, and as I enjoyed my brisket, I requested "Mamas Don't Let Your Babies Grow Up to Be Cowboys" by Willie Nelson and Waylon Jennings. At the chorus of the song, the entire upper deck joined in, belting out the lyrics, and swaying to the music, glasses raised. Waylon and Willie would have been proud. The food was tasty, and I regretted we were not famished as this would have been the place to really tie on the old feed bag.

Paul and I waited contentedly on the expansive side porch for our Texas limousine to whisk us back to the hotel. As we snuggled into the sumptuous back seat, we both agreed The Big Texan made the arduous ride north worth our while.

The following morning dawned bright, clear, and hot. While Paul finished packing in the room—I am always waiting on him to pack—I carried my bags to Bessie. Several other bikes had joined us during the night, and two were parked near mine. The conversation with one of the men—their women were passengers—went like this:

Me: "Good Morning!"

Male Biker: "Good morning. You know, if you had a rolling pack, it wouldn't be so difficult to carry your gear out to the bike."

Me: "Thanks. I do just fine."

Male Biker: "You know if you had one of these gel seats like I have, your ass wouldn't get so tired."

Me: "Thanks, but this ass doesn't get tired" I reached around and slapped my own ass.

Male Biker: "I hope you have something to go over your ears; the wind is really bad."

Me: "Thanks. We did just fine riding up from Fort Worth yesterday."

About that time, Paul walked up. Male Biker shouts, "Good Morning," and turns back to his partner. Honestly, some men just can't help themselves when they see a competent female rider.

Paul and I cruised over to US 66 to travel the Mother Road, so named as it was legitimately the first interstate to connect Chicago, Illinois, with the West Coast in Los Angeles County, California. We would ride Route 66 west before turning north to our destination of Colorado Springs before the end of the day. I love the history of Route 66, which was the major thoroughfare from Chicago to Los Angeles in the fifties and sixties. It was constructed in 1926 when a changing, increasingly mobile America sought "fast," convenient travel. Roadside motels, diners, and tourist attractions sprang up along the highway, welcoming travelers from the Midwest to the West Coast. Decommissioned in 1985, Route 66 was soon overshadowed by faster, wider interstates. As cities burgeoned and interstates sprawled around the old highway, large portions of the historic highway—especially in the Midwest—were consumed to the point of it becoming almost nonexistent. I had traveled Route 66 on two wheels before—from Oklahoma City, Oklahoma, to Santa Monica Pier, but Paul had not, which is why we made this minor detour on our trip.

Oklahoma, New Mexico, and Arizona have the most drivable sections of the original Route 66 alignment of any other states but beware: In some places, the pavement ends abruptly at a dirt road. Interstate 40, east to west, runs parallel to the original road in many sections of Texas. The roadside attractions along Route 66 continue to be sought-after- stops for adventuresome travelers seeking an almost cult-like, spiritual connection to a bygone era. One of those attractions is Cadillac Ranch, about ten miles west of Amarillo.

I swung into a Home Depot parking lot, and Paul gave me a quizzical look as he climbed off the bike. "We need spray paint," I yelled. "I'll be right back." Still wearing my helmet and gloves, I purchased a can of pink Day-Glo spray paint. I waved it in front of Paul before securing it in my saddlebag with the declaration, "For the Cadillacs." He had never experienced the oddity that is the Cadillac Ranch.

Stuck in the sometimes dry, sometimes muddy dirt field west of Amarillo on the old Route 66 were ten Cadillacs, lined up and buried nose-down, tail fins up—the only elevation visible on the horizon. The Caddies ranged from a 1949 Club Sedan to a 1963 Sedan de Ville. They had been half-buried in the Texas dirt—as art—longer than they had been on the road.

The Cadillac Ranch originated in 1974 when a group of San Francisco art hippies, who called themselves the Ant Farm, migrated to the land owned by Amarillo millionaire Stanley Marsh III. Marsh commissioned a piece of original art that would baffle the locals, and the resident artists came up with a tribute to the Cadillac tail fin.

Just off Exit 60 on Interstate 40, spray-paint-wielding tourists and Route 66 devotees were parked alongside the dusty, almost-gravel road adjacent to the ranch. The Sahara-like wind blew red, gritty dust around the corners of my sunglasses and stuck to my ChapStick lips. Undaunted, I made my way to the rustic, arched gateway that created a narrow opening in the fence surrounding the property. Off in the distance, perhaps the equivalent of a city block or so, were the graffiti-emblazoned Cadillac tail fins jutting skyward, their nose ends forever lost in the sunbaked Texas dirt.

I headed out toward the line of cars, clutching my can of pink Day-Glo spray paint; Paul trailed behind me still wondering what the hell we were doing in a field of dirt with a crop of dead Cadillacs. I tried to explain, "It's about art. It's about anarchy. It's about anti-authoritarianism. It's about the spiritual connection with the Mother Road." My explanation fell on deaf ears because all that Paul could see were tourists defacing already defaced classic cars with spray paint in the middle of nowhere Texas. Nonetheless, I appointed Paul to take pictures since he legitimately "didn't get it," while I gleefully attacked the nearest car with my pink paint. The feeling of unbridled abandon as you destroy public property is difficult to describe.

How many times have you been in a ladies' room in a seedy dive bar (well, maybe you haven't, but I have) and as you perch—gingerly— on the toilet seat, you notice all the graffiti that has been written on the stall walls? Usually, you read remarks like *Doris is a bitch, Ralph is my soul mate,* and *for a good ride, call Mike,* with a variety of obscenities scrawled across the stall walls. Each time, I sit in one of those bathrooms, I long for a black Sharpie in my bag to add my witticism to the wall art, but good manners and the lack of a Sharpie stop me.

Spray painting half-buried Cadillacs goes way beyond restroom stall graffiti. I spent a good hour moving from one car to another, adding my pink art to layers upon layers of existing artwork while Paul snapped photos, bewildered yet fascinated with the process.

I walked back to our bikes after an hour of enthusiastic vandalizing with the euphoric feeling I had just "screwed the man," or something like that. I was ready for the last leg of the adventure for the day.

US 385 north is a remote secondary road with loose gravel and Texas-size potholes in places. Vast wind farms have sprouted up along the northern Texas plains, the enormous wind turbines stretching skyward along the ridges. Their blades furiously slice the searing wind. There was virtually no traffic and an alarming absence of gas stations.

I kept glancing at my fuel indicator and gauging the distance from the last road sign I recalled passing. Factor in the wind resistance—which increases fuel consumption—and I could really be alarmed.

Paul and I passed small towns, which were void of service stations and merely wide spots in the road. Dalhart, Texas, held promise for refueling, and as we coasted into the small town on fumes, I was grateful. While I refueled Bessie, gusts of wind whipped through the parking lot, nearly knocking the bike and me over. Paul and I finished putting gas in our tanks and then pulled the bikes to the side of the building to block the wind while we rehydrated and rested.

US 87 going toward Raton, New Mexico, is a deserted strip of highway surrounded by open plains. Just when I thought the wind could not get worse, it did. It was violent and persistent. It was brutal, consistently howling from the west, pushing our bikes in the direction it wanted them to go. The only thing I can compare it to is Hurricane Charley in 2004 which ripped up the center of Florida as a category four storm. I stood in the bedroom of my old house and listened to it howl for what seemed like hours. I watched fifty-foot pine trees bend like matchsticks under the gale-force winds.

My white knuckles gripped the handlebars; my head ached from the tension in my neck and shoulders. Paul struggled as well. I could see his bike at a precarious angle in my rearview mirror.

Gas stations continued to be few and far between, adding more apprehension to our ride. The heat, the rapacious wind, and the many miles caused tempers to flare between Paul and me. It was my first glimpse of another side to his personality, a side I didn't particularly care for. A couple of times on that day as we battled our way to Colorado Springs, I thought about the bliss of traveling solo. I would still have to face the elements, but no one would be with me to whine or complain about them. I learned a long time ago that if you desire to travel, especially on two wheels, you should probably go with the flow.

The wind plagued us into Colorado, diminishing just south of Pueblo where the mountains to the west presented a barrier. The ride north from Pueblo, sans wind, was refreshing with the crisp scent of pine forests replacing the acrid air of Texas. Our hotel was downtown Colorado Springs, and I was never so glad to see the sign for our exit as I was that day. A hot shower did wonders for our attitudes.

I called my daughter, who had arrived safely in Denver, and made plans to see her the following day. She and my niece would travel to Colorado Springs to ride up Pikes Peak with us. As Paul and I walked the few blocks to dinner, a welcome mountain breeze soothed our parched skin, music wafted from several of the busy eateries, and I felt at peace with the universe. Little did I know that within a few short hours, my peaceful, easy feeling would be shattered.

CURVES GIVE ME CLARITY

The Edge...There is no honest way to explain it because the only people who really know where it is are the ones who have gone over. The others—the living—are those who pushed their luck as far as they felt they could handle it, and then pulled back, or slowed down, or did whatever they had to when it came time to choose between Now and Later.

– Hunter S. Thompson, *Hell's Angels: A Strange and Terrible Saga of the Outlaw Motorcycle Gangs*

THE SHRILL SOUND OF MY CELL PHONE AT 4 A.M. (MDT) jolted me out of a deep, tired sleep. Paul and I had just completed an exhilarating ride through west Texas hill country and turned north to Amarillo where brutal heat and wind had made riding our motorcycles difficult. We cruised into Colorado Springs, nestled in the foothills of the Rocky Mountains, late in the afternoon.

It was my brother David on the phone, delivering the startling news that our dad was dead. One deliberate—or random—act can change the course of life itself.

On the day before Father's Day in June, my dad called 911, lay down in the bed he had shared with my mother for nearly fifty years, placed the .22 caliber pistol under his chin, and chose to end his life, leaving those of us who loved him to wonder *why*.

It is impossible to make sense of such a selfish, illogical act. When my brother said, "Deb, Dad is dead," I had assumed, given his age, it was a heart attack or maybe a stroke that had taken him, so I was fairly calm. Then my brother said, "There's more." *What more can there be when your dad is dead?* My mind raced to all the possibilities: *Had there been a home invasion or burglary? Had someone shot him? Had there been an accident? Had he fallen somewhere? Had he been in a car accident, or had a car hit him while he was walking?*

My brother's voice came through the phone I held next to my ear, "He shot himself." I was speechless. The news didn't fit with any of the scenarios that I would qualify as "acceptable." My brother, too, was in such shock that the details he gave me sounded like matter-of-fact information.

Dad shot himself. My mind went blank, my brain kicked into autopilot, my emotions froze. "He did *what*?" I asked incredulously, hoping the connection was bad, and I didn't just hear my brother tell me our father had shot himself.

"I know it's hard to believe," was my brother's detached response. He quickly told me what few facts he had from the police, indicated he was headed over to Dad's house at that moment and directed me to stay put so he could tell me any new developments as he learned them.

"Is Paul with you?" He wanted to be sure I was okay.

"Yes, yes, he's here," I replied feebly. He ended our conversation, leaving me holding my cell phone as if it were a poisonous snake. I stood, disoriented and trembling, in the dark hotel room, feeling as though the conversation had been a bad dream.

Dad was a man who seemingly had it all: a loving family, three successful children, six awesome grandchildren, a comfortable retirement, a nice home, a dedicated church family, and good health. Perhaps, Dad somehow thought he didn't have enough.

My dad left a note with detailed instructions on who should be called and the type of service that he wanted upon his death. He added a single line of script to his family, telling us that he loved us.

Dad's call to 911 seconds before pulling the trigger, alerting law enforcement to his intended deed, insured none of his loved ones would have to witness his last gruesome action: finding him dead from a self-inflicted gunshot wound. He made sure we would not have to live with that memory seared into our psyche. It was his final act of love for us.

Before I could put my phone down and assemble my thoughts, Paul had already kicked into high gear during the brief conversation I had with my brother. He dressed, went downstairs for coffee—I didn't notice him leaving the room—and returned to hold me, while I repeated over and over, "No, no, no, no!" I couldn't cry; bewilderment is not an emotion that requires tears as an accompaniment. Paul held me tight in his arms, mumbling soothing words, words I couldn't hear, nor can I remember. He was just as dumbfounded as I was.

After taking the first sip of the scalding hot coffee Paul put in my hand, I ran to the bathroom and threw up watery bile that burned like poison. As I gripped the sides of the toilet to steady my shaking arms, I kept repeating, "This isn't happening right now! This can't be happening."

For a couple of decades, when I was much younger, I traveled in the wrong direction and went down an endless road of alcohol, drugs, and destructive relationships. I survived. However, my twenty-four years of sobriety hung in the balance at that moment; I instinctively wanted a drink—not coffee—to numb my feelings, to provide an escape from this nasty reality.

I hung my head lower over the toilet, the faint smell of disinfectant adding to my nausea, closed my eyes, said a prayer, and picked up my phone. While huddled on the cold tile in the bathroom, I called my lifeline, Ann, to deliver the news about my dad and admit my need for a drink. Her first question was, "Are you okay, and is Paul with you?" After hearing that he was in the next room, she laid truth in my lap succinctly: "When has a drink ever solved your problems?"

The question is an alcoholic riddle of sorts; if you solve it, then you can drink. Only I never could solve it. Drinking only complicated matters and exacerbated whatever troubles were already present. I knew that, which is why I called Ann—I wanted to hear that message again. She told me to pull myself together, stay in the moment, pray, and do the next right thing—another alcoholic riddle. I got up and ran cold water, splashing it on my face several times, trying to feel something—anything.

I had to call Caroline and my niece, Kasey. We had flown my daughter the previous day to Denver, where Kasey was living at the time. They were to meet us in Colorado Springs and ride up Pikes Peak with Paul and me.

When I stepped out of the bathroom, Paul was already packing and relaying what he thought we should do. I asked him to give me some time to process the awful news and speak with my brother again before we made plans. Being the sweet man that he is, he agreed. Paul was just as bewildered as I, wondering how he should react when his partner's dad had just committed suicide. That's not something covered in etiquette rules. He had never met any of my family before now; he was treading unknown waters with this new, dreadful set of circumstances.

My whole body trembled when I called Caroline and Kasey in Denver to tell them that their grandfather was dead. I tried to soften the blow as I spoke to my daughter who had just lost her own father two months before this latest tragedy.

In that first moment of relaying the devastating news to her, anger hit me like a punch to the gut. Not sadness. Not grief. Just pissed at Dad: *Why would you do such a thing to your family? How do you just check out from life when you seem to have so much to live for?* I wanted to scream, I wanted to run, I wanted to get ahead of the impending waves of sadness and grief.

I told Caroline we had to alter our plans and that she and Kasey should stay in Denver until Paul and I could get there and make further travel decisions. She agreed. I told both how much I loved them and assured them that their grandpa loved them as well.

The sun finally rose in Colorado Springs; I wasn't operating in darkness anymore. The faint rays of light crept through the sheer curtains and cast an eerie glow on the gear- strewn hotel room. *Why does tragedy always strike in the dark?*

I managed to robotically pull on yesterday's T-shirt and jeans that lay crumpled on the chair next to the bed. Paul steered me toward the door, suggesting I needed coffee and food. I was incapable of making the simplest decision. As I stood in the elevator for the descent to the lobby, I tried to feel something, anything, but there was nothing—nothing but bone-numbing tiredness and a pulverizing headache from lack of sleep.

Paul kept making plans to head east. "I'll pack the bikes after breakfast, and we can leave after you've had a chance to wake up. We can be in Indiana within two days, I imagine."

His words sounded hollow as they bounced around in the tiny elevator. I looked at the breakfast offering in the light, cheery dining area, and my stomach did a flip-flop. I mechanically scooped up the rubbery-looking eggs, grabbed a muffin, and walked over to a table by the window. Paul brought more coffee and more plans. He was talking non-stop.

As I sipped my coffee, praying it would stay down this time, I gazed at him with a vacant look in my eyes. I was listening but not hearing. I knew he was trying to be helpful and control the situation by making plans for me.

Somewhere in the middle of the eggs that were cooling on the table in front of me and Paul's would-be arrangements, I decided I was going to ride to Pikes Peak as planned—*today. Dammit!* My dad's selfish act was not going to interrupt my vacation and my intention to ride Bessie straight up that 14,000-foot summit.

I interrupted Paul's breakfast monologue and stated in my hoarse voice, "I want to ride to Pikes Peak today as we planned."

He stopped eating, stared, and asked, "Are you sure?" At that moment, I was never more certain of anything in my life. I didn't want to give credence to the cliché *Dad would have wanted me to* because right then, what the hell did I know about what Dad wanted? I felt confident, though, that Dad would genuinely be embarrassed if he knew how much disruption his suicide had caused his family. That's just how Dad was; he never wanted to inconvenience anyone.

Our goal would not involve my daughter and niece, however. I decided the trip was too risky with their riding two-up and my shaky emotional state. I called Caroline and told her we would be in Denver sometime before nightfall and that Mom needed to ride. Bessie saved my life on more than one occasion when I felt my life was unraveling at the edges and imploding from the center. I was standing at Hunter Thompson's Edge, and I had no intention of going over just yet. I needed to feel the wind on my face and connect with the elements. Today was no exception. My daughter, knowing this about me, acquiesced, told me she loved me, warned me to be careful, and asked me to call when we were on our way to Denver.

I went through the all-too-familiar motions of packing my gear, hauling it downstairs, and securing it on the bike. David had called again to relay what little information he had discovered by talking with the police, which wasn't much. There was still no reason as to *why*, and there never would be. Paul just listened to my end of the conversation. Thankfully, he didn't ask questions for which I had no answers. Paul's way of comforting me was to make himself useful.

I assured my brother that Paul and I would be with our girls in Denver before nightfall to help them prepare to get to Indiana once he had made Dad's funeral arrangements.

I started to resent the fact that Dad's choice to end his life set in motion an extraordinary number of things his loved ones now had to take care of. It was the butterfly effect. Dad's "relief" from the pain of living created major internal chaos for his family and a mournful, lengthy checklist of tasks to do. It would fall upon my brother and sister, Jodi, who had always lived close to our parents, to settle the details. It was my responsibility to travel homeward, something I had done for years.

I checked the atlas, noted where we were in relation to where Paul and I planned to travel that morning. That small act of checking the map gave me a center from which I could operate. It was concrete and visual; it was a destination. All my life, I have loved maps. I sleep with an atlas by my bed. I passionately study maps and the history of cartography in our country, even when I'm not going anywhere.

I plugged the destination *Pikes Peak* into my iPhone, pulled on gloves, situated the headband on my forehead, adjusted my sunglasses, buckled my helmet under my chin, and fired up the V-twin. This pattern of getting ready to ride made me feel "safe" again, albeit briefly. Biking is about ritual and process for me. I want my gear to be in order, comfortable, practical, and serve its purpose. Only then do I feel I'm in control of something, no matter how small. If there is chaos in my mind, the ritual provides order. If there is emotional pain, it produces a calming effect. If all is well, it confirms that indeed, all is well. The energy from the V-twin engine sent a signal to my spine and brain that the trip would be okay: just twist the throttle, move onto the open road, catch the wind, and make the journey.

I followed the GPS directions toward Pikes Peak on this clear, hot, eighty-five- degree morning. The mechanics of managing Bessie helped me focus on staying upright: throttle, clutch, shift, brake, repeat.

Paul and I stopped a short distance west of Colorado Springs to ride through the Garden of the Gods, a "garden" which contains nineteen tall, spectacular red rock formations, formed a few million years ago when dinosaurs walked the earth. The formations lie between Pikes Peak and Colorado Springs. It seemed I was passing through a Flintstones' cartoon, yet it was a comforting reality to be among the geological wonders.

The area is a 1,364-acre public park, but, unfortunately, several years ago, someone thought it would be a good idea to build houses in the area. Nestled among the giant red rock configurations is a suburb of Colorado Springs. The homes, mostly large structures that seem to "honor" the environment with their architecture, appeared to be more like distorted assaults on the majesty of the rocks.

I am a Taurus, an earth sign, which means I am most comfortable in the elements. When tragedy, trauma, or just plain melancholy hits, I derive comfort and energy or life force itself from nature's components—wind, sun, water, or rocks. On this day, I wanted to feel the wind wash over me, and the sun warm my skin to help me make sense of a senseless act.

Paul and I paid our fees, a mere ten dollars each, to ride the Pikes Peak Highway, nineteen miles of paved road to the summit. The first sensations that hit me were the smells: fresh-cut spruce and pine and the crisp mountain air that grew colder as we climbed in elevation. It felt like I was in Santa's village. The fragrance evoked memories of past Christmases and my dad.

As the highway meandered through gently curving forest, I thought of all the Christmases when I was a kid and how Dad kept the spirit of the holidays alive and preserved the illusion that yes, there really was a Santa Claus.

Dad was a hardworking, blue-collar union man who assumed the responsibilities of a family at a young age, which was typical of many who married in the mid-fifties. I was three years old when he married Mom; he legally adopted me and never questioned the validity of the parental bond. I never knew my biological father. The man who wed my mother was the only father I ever knew; he raised me, instilled in me the same Midwestern values he grew up with, and he was the dad who served up love and discipline in equal amounts.

The dropping temperature pulled me out of my reverie and into the moment. Paul and I stopped halfway up to admire the mountain views and layer on more clothing; it was eighty-five degrees at the lowest elevation to Pikes Peak and close to thirty-two at its summit.

The Pikes Peak Highway at the point we pulled over, about eight miles from the entrance, was leisurely curvy, nothing too challenging. I climbed off Bessie, pulled my heavy leather and gloves out of the saddlebag, and layered up for the ascent. Paul did likewise.

The view was astonishing—the air clear and fresh. The shock of the last few hours began to hit me hard. Why would anyone want to voluntarily check out of a world so full of stunning vistas and possibilities? The tears poured—hot liquid running silently from my eyes, partially blurring the majestic panorama of the Colorado Rockies.

I still couldn't separate grief from anger though, so I looked for something that would ground me, and my glance landed on loose rock in the ravine next to where Paul and I had parked the bikes. I climbed down the shallow gulf and hauled up an armful of flat, dusty rocks the size of dinner plates. Paul just watched, afraid to interrupt my efforts at putting my world in order.

I constructed the base for an inukshuk, using the large flat rocks and then plunged into the ravine again, my boots slipping on the loose gravel, to find smaller rocks to stack on top. My pockets loaded with stones, I clawed my way up the ravine again, my leather gloves gripping the dirt to assure my footing.

I was wholly focused on creating the inukshuk for my dad on a ledge overlooking the ravine on one side and the sheer drop-off down the mountain on the other side of the road. Paul seemed to sense my act was a solitary one; he stood at the side of the ravine, checking the road for traffic.

Inuits and other peoples of the Arctic region had constructed these rock statues—some in the shape of a man, others like pyramids—to indicate that "someone was here on this spot" or that "this is the right path to wherever you're going." The inukshuks were also built to alert travelers of a place where they could take shelter or seek food in the dangerously cold Arctic winter.

I had to do something to make sense of the helpless feeling I had, to feel something tangible that I could hang my emotions on. I started piling rocks on the narrow ledge, but they kept slipping off, and each time one fell, the tears streamed hotter on my cheeks. For every stone that dropped, I returned to the ravine to find the right combination that would stack solidly and stay put. Sensing my frustration, Paul began to pick up rocks too. He never asked, "What are you doing?" He simply helped, searching the gravel along the pavement for suitable rocks and quietly sensing I was engaged in a critical task.

I finally got several rocks to balance on each other, rising about two feet high. Standing back from my creation—my jeans dusty with the reddish dirt and my face streaked with the same red dust—I swiped at my tears with dirty gloves and announced to Paul, to the wind, to the universe in a husky voice, "This is an inukshuk for Dad." I silently said a prayer, praying Dad was on the right path. What path are you allowed to follow in the afterlife when you take your own life?

I snapped a photo, and then I cried once more. I kicked the loose gravel with the toe of my boot and gave into my anguish. I bent over, put my hands on my knees, and howled with fear, grief, and sadness while Paul stood aside, his back slightly turned, and allowed me space for this private heartache.

When I had spent my allotment of tears and sorrow for that moment, Paul turned, clutched me close to him, and held on tight until I was ready to be released. "Are you okay to ride?" he asked, my well-being his only concern. I assured him I was. I turned, climbed on Bessie, fired the ignition, shifted into gear, and gritted my teeth for the challenging ten-mile-per-hour switchbacks as we climbed higher in elevation.

The icy wind took my tears, as it had done so many times before when I was consumed with grief and sadness and dispersed them behind me. I dislike crying. I don't like how I look before, during, or afterward. I equate weeping with weakness. It seems an unstoppable evil. Over the years, I have found private places to purge my tears and pain. I especially never wanted my young daughters to see me weep; I was afraid they would sense my tears as evidence of my inability to provide for them or keep them safe.

I kept an old chest of drawers in the shed behind the house. When the frustrations and challenges of single motherhood overwhelmed me to the point of tears, I went to the shed and beat the old chest of drawers savagely with a hammer. I would cry and howl, striking the old wood as hard as I could, my hands vibrating with the impact. This escape helped quell my anger and frustration, so it did not explode sideways at my daughters.

The shower was another great place to purge pain: the rushing water masked the sound of sobbing. I could beat the wet tile with my fist while the water spiraled my tears down the drain. Afterward, I could lay my cheek on the cold tile and find relief and peace.

The car was another haven where I found comfort. Sitting in the driver's seat, I would turn up the music and pound the steering wheel while I sobbed and howled as much as I wanted to.

However, the best place I've discovered to soothe my heart is on my motorcycle. Riding is a solitary activity anyway, so I locate a deserted back road and unleash the pent-up hurt.

How many tears has the wind swept away for my younger daughter? How many tears did the wind claim when I heard the news of Butch's death? And how many countless tears has the wind possessed over the last eight years as I struggled with loss?

Before I could squander any more grief for my dad, the highway became more challenging and took all my concentration. The dense pine forest had disappeared—so had the leisurely curves. To my right was the sweeping landscape of the Rocky Mountains, sans guardrails; to my left were the stone faces of the mountains, dusted with snow.

It was still early Tuesday morning with very little traffic on our ascent. Paul and I had no time to relax into a straight piece of asphalt until another ten-mile-per-hour switchback appeared. Traveling so slowly on a fully loaded, touring class bike means a rider is very close to "falling over." You must downshift, brake, make the turn, and then, before you actually could tumble over, you have to throttle, shift, and throttle again. The process was a rush: I was one with the machine, one with the elements. The icy air piqued my senses, and I was euphoric.

The Pikes Peak Highway is the second highest paved road in the United States, and Mount Evans, also in the Colorado Rockies, is five miles taller than Pikes Peak. The last four miles to reach the crest took all the concentration I could muster—no time to panic, no way to back out. Go big or go home!

Paul and I rounded the last switchback and boom! There was the 14,115-foot summit with its freezing wind--colder than a witch's tit.

My hands were nearly frozen to the handle grips despite the gloves; I was stiff with cold and fear. Jubilant in my accomplishment, I climbed off Bessie, gave Paul—who was right behind me every mile of the way—a high five, and we both started digging in our saddlebags for additional heavy leather gear.

The snowy summit was breathtaking and must have appeared the same to Katherine Lee Bates when she saw this view in 1893. The landscape became her inspiration for composing the hymn "America, the Beautiful."

Between the challenging ride and spectacular scenery spread before us, I forgot the tragedy of the moment. We became tourists, snapping pictures and marveling at the wonder surrounding us on the trip up. We headed into Pikes Peak Summit House for hot coffee and some of its world-famous Pikes Peak donuts. They are melt-in-your-mouth fried dough confections, well-worth the ride. After we made a few quick purchases, we bundled up, ready to ride down.

Suddenly, it hit me—I needed to be with my daughter and my niece.

After completing the journey down the mountain, Paul and I headed north for the hundred-mile trip to Denver on I-25, a wretched strip of highway where vehicles fly by, oblivious to the seventy miles per hour posted speed limit on botched pavement. Very quickly, I started to panic—it has happened frequently since my accident in 2012—in the heavy, fast traffic and chilly crosswinds.

I turned my focus inward, willing myself to grip the handlebars, suck it up, and ride. The closer we got to Denver, the denser the congestion became. I was navigating through traffic on unfamiliar roads—and then it started to hail. Yes, HAIL! Chunks of ice pelted us as we dodged cars and trucks and tried to keep our eyes on the directional signs.

The hail and wind became so heavy that Paul and I took the closest exit and found shelter under some trees in a residential area. We waited twenty minutes or so, watching incredulously as the hail rained down. We had been battling dense traffic, a construction zone, unfamiliar and wet roads—and now, unbelievable weather conditions.

After waiting until the weather improved and then enduring a frightening ride around Denver, I saw the exit for the highway that would take us to my niece's house. But I exited north instead of south. As soon as I did, I realized my mistake and motioned to Paul to pull over—and about this time, it started to rain and hail *again*. We were on a residential side street, out of traffic. I put the kickstand down, stumbled off the bike and crumbled, just like a cookie dunked in hot coffee. I had a mental meltdown, sobbing, hyperventilating, and shouting, "WHY? WHY? WHY?"

Poor Paul. He bent down, put his hands under my armpits, and tried to pull me upright. He held me tight and repeated, "Breathe, you're okay. Just breathe."

Paul called my daughter and Kasey, told them where we were, and asked them to come and escort us to her house. While we waited, I paced the sidewalk like a caged animal, clenching and unclenching my fists, struggling with "fight or flight" level anxiety. After about twenty minutes, Kasey's SUV turned the corner; she stopped behind the bikes, and all three of them tumbled out—Kasey's boyfriend, Hunter, included. I was a sniveling, shaking mess. Both Caroline and Kasey stopped short just outside their car with startled looks on their faces, afraid to move. Paul talked me down with the common-sense reminder that I had to suck it up and ride because he couldn't ride two bikes.

I grabbed Caroline and Kasey for a group hug, assuring them I was okay. Poor Hunter, who walked over to Paul to introduce himself, was meeting Kasey's crazy aunt Debi for the first time. I steeled myself for the short ride to Kasey's house, following her SUV as if it were my lifeline.

Halfway there, we heard sirens coming at us from all sides. I panicked again, not able to breathe, and stopped in the middle of the traffic snarl and blaring sirens. *WTF!? Could any more challenges come my way today?*

I looked in my rearview mirror and saw emergency lights flashing on both sides; I didn't know which way to go or if I should even move. I sat paralyzed in the middle of traffic, the sirens screaming past; first, a large firetruck, then an ambulance and several police cars whizzed by. The noise was deafening as they skirted the traffic stopped at the intersection.

Once the emergency vehicles passed, I remained frozen, cars honking in frustration behind us. Paul yelled over the cacophony of horns, "Deb, move. Turn. It's okay!" I spied Kasey's SUV pulled to the side, waiting on us. She pulled into her driveway, Paul and I followed. Shaking and sobbing, I parked Bessie, climbed off, and Caroline took charge and began giving me directions—bless her heart:

"Mom, take your gloves off, now your helmet, and put your helmet on the handlebars."

"It's okay. Hunter will get your tour pack; just walk toward the garage."

"You're fine. Take your boots off before we go in."

"We will get what you need from the bike; just sit down here at the counter."

I did as I was told, and the shaking subsided. I sipped cold water, waiting on Paul and Hunter to carry our gear into the house. Somewhere in all the activity of unloading the bikes, the girls decided we needed food for dinner, and they made up a list.

Caroline handed me a towel to dry off. Unable to trust my legs to hold me, I felt incapable of going upstairs for a shower. Paul and Hunter, list in hand, went for provisions, probably happy to be relieved of the drama that swirled around us.

As I perched on the bar stool at the counter, I spoke quietly with my daughter and niece who had questions about their grandfather I couldn't answer, but it was good to talk. We called my brother in Indiana, and, remarkably, he already had completed Dad's funeral arrangements, now set for Thursday. I got online and rerouted my daughter's flight from Denver to Indianapolis. My niece finalized her travel plans just as the boys walked in with food for dinner.

Hunter took charge of dinner, fired up the grill, made burgers, and functioned as the perfect host for the morbid reunion. Over juicy burgers and cold beverages, Paul and I determined we needed a day of rest—off the bikes—before we did a marathon 1,100-mile ride from Denver to Muncie, Indiana. We decided to leave at oh-dark-thirty on Monday morning. We also concluded we would celebrate Father's Day tomorrow with the only father in our group—my partner, Paul, by taking a foray into the nearby mountains with the kids and having lunch.

I fell into a fitful sleep that night on the narrow twin bed in my niece's spare room. Paul, who can sleep anywhere, was sound asleep on the floor on an inflatable mattress. I prayed, "God, give me the strength to process this tragedy, stay strong for the ride ahead, and be brave for what lies before me when a parent commits suicide."

FATHER'S DAY

Parents rarely let go of their children, so children let go of them. They move on. They move away. The moments that used to define them—a mother's approval, a father's nod—are covered by moments of their own accomplishments. It is not until much later, as the skin sags and the heart weakens, that children understand; their stories, and all their accomplishments sit atop the stories of their mothers and fathers, stones upon stones, beneath the waters of their lives.

– Mitch Albom, *The Five People You Meet in Heaven*

INSTEAD OF CALLING DAD TO WISH HIM A HAPPY FATHER'S Day that Sunday morning in 2014, I was reading his obituary my sister-in-law, Jacquie, had drafted for the *Chronicle-Tribune*, my hometown newspaper. The effort was unsettling and wholly unnatural at best, but she wanted my approval.

After I had awakened, I kissed my partner Paul and wished him a Happy Father's Day. Next, I kissed my sleeping daughter; her warm, sweet sleep-smell enveloped me as I leaned over the blowup mattress she occupied on the floor. Caroline had recently lost her father in April—and now this tragedy with her grandfather had hit her hard. I whispered, "I love you," and made a silent promise that, somehow, we would get through this day with a smile. Sluggish with grief and worn-out from anxiety, all of us were slow to rise that morning at my niece's house.

My niece, Kasey, didn't drink coffee—another wholly unnatural circumstance—which meant there wasn't even a coffeepot in the house. Paul and I are rabid coffee drinkers. I prefer to drink my first scalding cup of java just seconds after my feet hit the floor in the morning.

It was 5:30 a.m. in Belmar, a sleepy suburb of Denver. Paul and I groggily pulled on street clothes, intent on finding the potent, hot elixir of life. We left Kasey's house as quietly as possible so as not to wake the non-coffee drinkers. The forty-degree mountain chill blasted the sleep from my face, causing me to shrink deeper into my leather coat while we stood near the deserted street and scanned the residential area for an open coffee establishment on Sunday morning.

Paul and I knew the Chick-fil-A we spotted would not be open on Sunday, so we didn't even bother to head in that direction. We decided our best chance to find coffee might be somewhere in the multilevel Target a few blocks away, where we could *buy* a coffeepot, coffee, and filters. Alas, it did not open until 8 a.m. I figured we would be in severe caffeine withdrawals by then, incapable of making our own brew.

Paul and I silently trudged back across the commons and found a Panera Bread a few blocks up the main road. We hurried toward the unlit sign as if it were an oasis in the desert, beckoning us with the promise of caffeine. The sign read, "Open at 7 a.m."; it was 6:45. I had hope. For the next fifteen minutes, we paced the sidewalk in front of Panera like addicts waiting for the methadone clinic to open—hands stuffed in the pockets of our heavy leather riding jackets and collars popped up around our necks to ward off the chill. We stared straight down at the sidewalk or sneaked furtive glances toward the locked door—still unable to speak. No one should have to endure all this physical activity and frigid weather without first ingesting caffeine.

Our heads snapped to attention, and our silent march halted when Paul and I heard the crack of a dead bolt lock sliding open. The door to Panera swung outward. An overly chirpy twentysomething greeted us with a hearty, "Good Morning!" Our panic was over, baby!

Paul and I scurried inside and ordered two large coffees with the directive to leave room for creamer in both—for starters. We shuffled back outside, each clutching the coffee cup as if it were life itself, and settled at a table, anticipating the rising sun. I took two scalding gulps, and relief flooded my body as I leaned back in the chair with my face tilted toward the barely-over-the-horizon sun. I fired up a chocolate Tatiana, ignoring the sign that said, "No Smoking." I rationalized my defiance by claiming to no one in particular, "We *are* outside, and no one else is here." Smoking chocolate cigarillos is a nasty habit I indulge in only under extreme duress. Once the nicotine hit my bloodstream and mingled with the caffeine, I knew all would be right with the universe for that moment.

Paul and I were in no hurry to return to the quiet, sleepy household, so we savored our morning wake-me-ups as the sun warmed the air. The caffeine and nicotine loosened our tongues, and we began to talk at last. For fear of reactivating my anguish, Paul and I kept the conversation neutral. We both agreed Hunter, Kasey's boyfriend, was a great guy, her new home was adorable, and she seemed happy—positive comments in an otherwise heartbreaking set of circumstances.

Paul's cell phone rang; it was his son Jay; he stepped away from the table with his coffee to talk. I was relieved to have the space at the table alone for a few minutes. I savored the caffeine and nicotine like addicts relish their next fix.

After finishing our first round of coffee and Paul had chatted with his son, I went back inside, ordered four more large coffees and a dozen bagels to take back to the kids for breakfast, silently hoping no one else drank coffee, and I would have at least one more tumbler of energizing joe for myself.

When Paul and I returned to the house around 8:30 a.m., I laid breakfast out on the kitchen counter. Caroline, Kasey, and Hunter slowly made their way downstairs. The girls were rumpled from sleep, their shoulders curling forward in a protective posture. Hunter, like Paul, was unsure of his role in our family's tragedy, hanging back but available if we needed him. Paul and I sipped our second tumblers of coffee while the kids picked at the bagels, answering my questions concerning the day's plan in quiet, one-word responses.

"I think we should drive into the mountains today."

"Okay."

"Maybe we could take a picnic!"

"Sounds good."

"Have we finalized your travel arrangements for tomorrow?"

"Yes."

The five of us lapsed into grateful silence until everyone had sufficient time to become fully awake.

Thankfully, Kasey started thinking like a tour guide and suggested we take a ride into the mountains to visit Buffalo Bill's grave atop Lookout Mountain in Golden and then go for a walk in Dinosaur Park, about seven miles from Golden. Paul and Hunter decided to ride on two wheels. Hunter is a sports bike enthusiast, but we love him anyway, and I opted to ride with the girls on four.

While I rerouted Caroline's return flight from Indiana to Florida, leaving the next morning, Kasey packed juice, soft drinks, and snacks in a cooler like an attentive mother. She is my brother's youngest child and reminds me so much of his younger self. Kasey has had a phenomenal career in the corporate world, meeting with success that few twenty-six- year-olds experience. We loaded the car with what we deemed essential for the day's outing, and off we went; the guys on bikes followed behind us.

Lookout Mountain is due west of Denver proper, about a thirty-minute ride from Kasey's house. The road leading up to the Buffalo Bill Museum is part of the Lariat Loop Scenic Highway where people can view the spectacular Rockies. Although I was just a tad bit jealous of the boys on bikes enjoying the warm sunshine, crisp air, and winding mountain road, I felt safe in the car with Caroline and Kasey.

The life of William F. "Buffalo Bill" Cody is the stuff cowboy legends are made of—their adventures popularized in newspapers and dime novels in the mid to late 1800s. His relationship with Colorado started in 1859—he was only fourteen years old—when he made his first trip to the state as part of the Pikes Peak Gold Rush. Also, Cody became a Pony Express Rider during this period until he had to return home to take care of his mother.

The museum displays exhibits from Buffalo Bill's Wild West show for which real cowboys and cowgirls are recruited from nearby ranches to perform. Cody, a world-renowned entertainer, led a colorful life and died in Denver in 1917. The museum and gravesite are a testament to Cody's dedication to the Native Americans, their way of life, and the Wild West he loved.

We spent a leisurely morning touring the museum and grounds. We laughed, our grief forgotten for the moment as we took pictures of each other posing in the cardboard cutouts of Buffalo Bill and Annie Oakley.

Dinosaur Ridge, a segment of the Dakota Hogback in the Morrison Fossil Area National Natural Landmark, is a short drive from Lookout Mountain and is one of the world's most famous dinosaur fossil localities. The rocks were formed as part of the Morrison Formation of the Jurassic age, and it is where Arthur Lakes discovered dinosaur bones in 1877. Vehicle traffic is prohibited from driving to the site where fossils can be viewed, so after we parked, the five of us hiked the mile and a half up the paved trail. I felt grounded among the ancient rocks; their solidness made me feel safe and protected in the warm sun. The physical exertion of hiking the gradual slope upward energized my tired body. Although the contents of the park are fascinating, I'm not sure if we were all that excited to examine dinosaur tracks, stegosaurus bones, and trace fossils, but the effort distracted us from the foreboding sadness that tomorrow would bring. We hiked back to the car and bikes, intent on a tour of Red Rocks Amphitheater before settling down for lunch.

Red Rocks Amphitheater, which can seat over nine thousand people, is a spectacular outcropping of well—red rocks. Formed millions of years ago, they provide a natural, acoustically perfect stage. Musicians of every genre, from opera stars to the Canadian rock band Bare Naked Ladies, have performed here. The Beatles played at Red Rocks in August of 1964, and, ironically, it was the only show on their North American tour that year that did not sell out.

I still remember the Beatles appearing on the Ed Sullivan Show the previous February of 1964. I was one of seventy-three million people who tuned in to watch the Fab Four twist and shout on stage, their first live performance on US soil. I was in love with Paul McCartney, and for me, the rock and roll genie was unleashed from the bottle from that moment on. On this day at Red Rocks, I had to be content with visiting the museum, which featured all musicians who have performed in the amphitheater, including the Beatles. As morning crept into the afternoon, our touring came to an end, and we agreed to eat a late lunch in Golden.

I remember breezing through Golden, Colorado, in 1973 when longhaired, Earth-Shoe-wearing hippies, clad in jeans and tie-dyed shirts, populated the area. Golden now seemed a little more grown-up and urbanized.

Kasey, Caroline, Paul, Hunter, and I settled in at a hole-in-the-wall, fifties-style burger joint called Bob's Atomic Burgers, just across the street from the Coors Brewery. Bob's burgers are homemade, hand-shaped, juicy, and delicious. We gathered around one of the outdoor tables kissed by the sun, grateful for the chance to rest.

As the five of us recounted our day and enjoyed our burgers, I suggested we go around the table and relate a funny story about our dads. I told the story of my dad trying to teach me to drive in 1970. He had a lavender (yes, lavender)1966 Chevy Impala that he coveted. A utility pole stood tall at the end of our driveway on Harmon Street.

After Dad pulled the car through the drive and down the alley to the side street behind our house, we switched places, so I was behind the wheel, and he was in the passenger seat. I drove at a snail's pace through the neighborhood, practicing my stops, using the turn signal, and negotiating the turn like a pro. Dad made sure I stayed put long enough to look both ways at every stop sign.

The lesson was deemed a success, and Dad directed me to head home and pull in the driveway. As I came down Harmon Street toward our house, I slowed to negotiate the turn into our drive. Dad said, "Slow down! Don't hit the pole!"

WHAM! I panicked, accelerated instead of braking, and hit the pole head-on at about fifteen miles per hour. The lavender metal made an awful crunching sound. I cried, "No, no, no!" as the car came to a dead stop.

Dad kept saying, "It's okay; no one is hurt. It's okay."

A week later, my dad paid $300 for a 1963 Volkswagen Bug that he deemed "my car." We often reminisced about that incident, and the years did nothing to soften the hilarity of the moment. It was classic.

Paul told the story of his dad, and the kids all shared stories that were equally humorous. The laughter warded off any sadness that we would have felt while celebrating Father's Day under such a grim set of circumstances.

We returned, pleasantly exhausted, to Kasey's house by early evening to organize ourselves for the tasks and trips ahead. Paul and I collected our gear and loaded the bikes, intent on starting just before sunrise the following morning. The girls packed their bags for their early but separate flights, though they would land at Indianapolis International Airport within hours of each other. Hunter was driving them to the Denver International Airport Monday morning.

Paul and I decided to travel a straight shot through Kansas, Missouri, and Illinois on I-70, arriving in Indiana late Tuesday, provided the weather gods were with us, and we had no mechanical failures. I dreaded the thousand-mile trip and this kind of unpleasant riding experience. We discussed other options, such as flying to Indiana, returning to Denver, then riding our bikes home, but none of them made the trip any easier for either of us.

Paul had to return to work the following Monday, so we had no other option for traveling together but to head east to Indiana on our bikes. No one plans for a tragedy. If there had been a way to have avoided this ordeal, I would have taken it, but tragedy called the Dutiful Daughter back to the role she had played before—sometimes well, sometimes very poorly.

I lay my head on my pillow for what would be a fitful night's rest. In the quiet darkness, Paul already asleep, I listened to the kids settling down for the night. My emotions were adrift in uncharted waters. The death of our parents is one of life's inevitable passages for which we are never truly prepared to negotiate. My mom died years ago of a smoking-related disease; there was no shame in her passing. But, my dad took his own life; I felt abandoned, angry, and ashamed. And I felt a more profound shame for feeling ashamed.

Closing my eyes, I repeated the Serenity Prayer, written by Reinhold Niebuhr: "God, grant me the serenity to accept the things I cannot change; courage to change the things I can; and wisdom to know the difference," over and over.

HOMEWARD BOUND

Part One

O lost,
And by the wind grieved,
Ghost,
Come back again.

– Thomas Wolfe, *Look Homeward, Angel*

THE STATELY SKYLINE OF DENVER AND THE MAJESTIC
Rocky Mountains grew ever smaller in my rearview mirror as Paul
and I traveled due east on a chilly Monday morning. It was the day after

Father's Day in June of 2014. Within a few hours, the Colorado mountains had flattened to gently rolling hills until the topography became level with the dreary and monotonous horizon as we neared Kansas. This is the kind of ride that separates the "riders" from the "wannabes." It was interstate travel with grief as my passenger. Not only did I dread crossing Kansas, but I also hated the thought of thirty-plus hours of solitude astride Bessie. Too much time to think.

The western Great Plains are barren, hot, dry, and wide open, which enables the unleashed wind to buffet adventurers to and fro. I had traveled from east to west in Kansas on two wheels before, so I knew what to expect. Paul did not. As soon as we left the eastern Colorado grasslands and crossed into Kansas, the wind pummeled us sideways on an almost deserted Interstate 70—except for the semi-tractor trailers that pressured us when they whizzed by.

Paul's Harley-Davidson Classic has a large faring (biker dashboard); my Road King has a detachable windshield. The crosswinds had caught the faring, whipping the front of Paul's bike mercilessly as he fought to keep it on the road. Each time a wind gust hit, he made the mistake of slowing down, which caused him to lose stability and gave the wind more power. In my mirror, I could see a fast-approaching tractor trailer barreling down on him at seventy miles an hour.

With increasing alarm for Paul's safety, I watched in my rearview mirror as thirty-mile-an-hour wind blasts sent Paul perilously close to the semi, and, as it moved out around to pass Paul, another gust of wind whipped him sideways. He slowed as the semi passed, the wind taking full advantage of his slow speed. I motioned for him to speed up, my arm shooting in the air, signaling "come on!" to no avail.

I had no problem keeping Bessie upright and traveling a safe, interstate speed. I could only surmise that a combination of the faring problem and inexperience caused Paul's plight. A little over three hours into our journey, I took the next exit off I-70, and Paul followed. We pulled into the lone gas station around 9:00 a.m.; dust swirled around our bikes as we stopped near the side of the building.

I should have known that the last thing the crippling male ego needs to hear at a time like this is how he should ride his motorcycle in the adverse conditions Kansas produced. However, lack of sleep, trauma-induced anxiety, and my focus on getting us to Indiana quickly and safely unleashed my sharp tongue and short temper.

Paul climbed off his bike, tugged angrily at his helmet strap, and growled,

"Why in the hell are you going so fast in this god-awful wind?"

Startled by his accusation, I didn't check my tone before responding. "I'm going the speed limit. Any slower and the wind will knock us over for sure. Why are you slowing down to forty miles an hour on a fucking interstate?" I shouted, as I jerked my helmet off and stomped over to the ladies' restroom.

All I needed was a reason to vent the anger that had seethed just below the surface since four o'clock Saturday morning when I accepted the phone call from my brother announcing our dad was dead. I returned to find Paul pacing the dirt between our bikes, looking like a storm cloud. As I pulled my gloves on, I suggested, "You need to stay the speed limit. When a wind gust hits, lean into it; you are only jeopardizing your safety when you slow down."

"Don't tell me what I need to do on my fucking bike," Paul sharply replied, as he leaned over my bike, jabbing his index finger in my direction.

"Then cowboy up and ride, dammit," I tossed over my shoulder as I hit the starter, the roar of the V-twin drowning out whatever verbal insult he hurled in my direction.

Somehow, Paul's inability to keep the Classic on the road was my fault, or at least it seemed that's what Paul believed. I spewed gravel as I tore out of the dusty parking area, winding out first gear, pipes roaring, a perverse sense of satisfaction blooming in my chest. I pulled onto the interstate without looking in my rearview mirror to make sure Paul was there. My thoughts began to tug at me.

When a parent dies by suicide, you begin to question every interaction you ever had over the preceding years. You hit the rewind button and try to analyze every phone conversation, every face-to-face discussion you had with your parent. You question whether you were a good daughter, although I had been informed that I couldn't determine that. Only my dad could decide if I was a good daughter. He frequently told all his children how proud he was of them and how much he loved them. But since he never said to me specifically, "Deb, you are a good daughter," I assumed that yes, I *was* a good daughter.

You rack your brain for "signs" that this kind of tragedy was coming down the pike to shatter your family, shatter your illusions, and literally shatter your world. Perhaps I saw its probability more clearly than my siblings. Distance—living in Florida rather than Indiana—gave me clarity.

A few summers ago, after a trip to Indiana to visit Dad, I mentioned what I had observed to my brother David: "Dad seems depressed. He doesn't move too far from home, and the joy seems to have disappeared from his life." My brother didn't see what I had noticed because he interacted with our dad more frequently.

Every single attribute Dad possessed—kindness, loving nature, supportive spirit, strength—were in direct opposition to suicide's characteristic: a selfish, cowardly act inflicted out of desperation and a sense of hopelessness. Although I knew Dad never really adjusted to losing Mom, from the outside looking in, I did not detect his loneliness. Never in a million years would I have imagined he was capable of taking his own life.

The harsh, acrid wind belted me sideways, jolting me out of my trance. The sun's insidious heat rays, though masked by the constant wind, burned nonetheless. My face felt scorched, my nostrils dry, and Paul and I were only a couple of hundred miles down the road on a 1,500-mile journey. I glanced in my rearview mirror to see Paul, a mere speck, a mile or more behind me. But I didn't care. I gritted my teeth, leaned into the wind, and maintained an even seventy miles an hour, going due east.

An unexpected gift from my mom's passing several years ago was the opportunity to develop a closer relationship with Dad. It seemed all his emotional energy had been connected to her: keeping her happy (an impossible undertaking) and being the gatekeeper when unpleasantness or disharmony occurred. A decade before her demise, Mom was sick with one illness after another. Dad retired and spent his days managing her medications and medical care, catering to her every whim and wish with no concern for his own well-being.

Mom and Dad's life together became very narrow; they relied on a few church friends and my sister and brother for any social interaction. Dad's fidelity to her was baffling to me; he saw Mom in a light none of us could fathom. I wanted to believe his devotion and even his withdrawal from his extended family were decisions he made because he loved her so much. But, I never could reconcile that belief with what I observed between them.

Many years ago, her narcissism demanded that he sever ties with his own family in Ohio; she consumed him. As the gatekeeper, he was tenacious when he thought one of us siblings might challenge her perception of herself or her relationship with us. Nothing was permitted to upset Mom. No unpleasantries were permitted to befall her. And certainly, no truths about her behavior were to be spoken about; Mom's perception of truth was the gospel.

My dad was not my biological father, but he legally adopted me when I was three years old, soon after he and my mother married in 1958. However, from birth to age nine, I lived with my grandparents,

Dorothy and Clayton Fisher. I knew my parents lived elsewhere in town and that I had a little brother and sister. Mom and Dad visited often. I never questioned the arrangement; it was my "normal," because I was very content with my grandparents.

For reasons unknown to me, my mother decided I should be part of her family, so she removed me from my grandparents' home when I was nine. My grandmother was heartbroken and cried as she explained to me that I had to live with my parents during the week so I could go to the right school. Apparently, the school district discovered my grandparents did not have legal custody over me. They had insisted she produce proof of legal guardianship so I could attend a nearby school, or, if not, I had to attend school in the district my parents were zoned for.

My grandma assured me I could spend each weekend with her, and I recall waiting patiently by the front door after school on Fridays, relief flooding my body when I saw my grandfather's truck pull into the driveway to fetch me.

I remember being devastated at this upheaval in my life, although what does a nine-year-old know about devastation? In retrospect, it was the beginning of a downward spiral, crippling me emotionally for decades to come.

As the unpredictable gusts of wind pounded me sideways on the interstate and my nostrils filled with dust, I longed to click my heels together, like Dorothy in *Oz*, and magically transport myself home to Indiana.

My thoughts drifted back to the day in 1965 when I discovered a tattered cardboard box stuffed in the back of the hall closet. Mom and Dad and us three siblings had moved to a large, two-story home, and I was directed to stow boxes of our winter clothing in the upstairs' closets.

I pulled the tattered box, about the size of a milk crate, out to make room for more boxes, and a worn, paper folder—the kind with clasps in the middle—caught my eye. It had my name on the front, written in my mom's flowery handwriting, and my date of birth. Only it wasn't my name as I knew it—yes, it was my first name, but the last name was *Dudley*.

After I was born, Mom had created dozens of these folders with photos for every milestone of my life: first birthday, the baby contest, first car trip, Uncle Dale, and so on, with captions and long narratives to accompany the photos.

I opened the folder, and there was a picture of me, surrounded by cousins. I was seated at my grandma's kitchen table. In the center of the table was a birthday cake and noise makers; we were all wearing those silly pointed birthday hats and sporting huge grins on our faces. It must have been my third birthday. Glued onto the page was a newspaper clipping announcing the birthday celebration of *Debbie Lynn Dudley*.

I abandoned my chore with the boxes and went downstairs to find my mom. She was seated at the kitchen counter, smoking, when I walked in with the folder in my hand. She glanced at the folder, and her facial expression grew dark. She said, "Where the hell did you get that?"

"It was in a box in the closet," I admitted guardedly. Even at a young age, I knew I was treading somewhere she didn't want me to go. She snatched the folder from my hands, shouting, "Give it to me!" She left the kitchen, yelling for my dad, "John!"

I wandered back upstairs, bypassing the boxes, and walked into my bedroom and shut the door. I felt a sense of dread; I sensed I had done something wrong, but I wasn't sure what it was. I remember wanting to run, wanting to hide, wanting to avoid whatever truth was in that dog-eared folder with the strange last name.

I was trying to organize my books on a shelf in my new bedroom when Dad walked in with a gentle expression on his face. I will never forget the words he spoke that day as the sun filled the second-floor bedroom, dust motes dancing in the warm rays.

"Your mom was married before she married me," he began with no prelude and little emotion as if he were reading from a script. "Dudley is the last name of your real dad, and it was your last name until I adopted you legally."

I sat motionless on the bed as Dad stood towering over me, delivering the sparse explanation of my parentage. "He didn't love you," Dad continued. "He agreed to let me adopt you if he didn't have to pay child support anymore. Your mom and I felt it was best you didn't know, and now that you do, we won't speak of it again because it upsets your mom." He gave me a single pat on the shoulder and murmured, "Your Mom and I love you." He turned and left the room.

Something foul and unspeakable took up residence in my soul that day. I hated him; I hated my mother. I believed I was "unlovable" and "unwanted" from that moment on. The repercussion of those words on a ten-year-old psyche would not be sufficiently understood for a few more decades, but on that day, I opened a Pandora's box, filled with self-loathing, anger, and self-destruction.

I caught Paul's frantic waving in my rearview mirror, bringing me back to the present as he motioned me to exit the interstate again. It was a welcome respite from the ache of recollection.

I pulled up to the first gas pump as Paul went around to the opposite side. I knew he was spitting mad by the way he jerked his bike into position next to the pump. As I climbed off Bessie and fished my debit card out of my waist pack, he stepped over the cement island between the pumps and started talking straight in my face. I listened to his tirade about the wind, my pace, and my riding—liberally laced with verbal insults and accusations—for about sixty seconds, and then I unsnapped my helmet, set it on the bike seat, pivoted, turned away, and walked into the service station to find the restroom.

I stood in front of the bathroom mirror and fumed, my fury barely contained. *Who was this guy? How dare he start this crap under any circumstances, especially the ones we were forced to deal with right now?* Paul was about to find out that I was in no mood to tolerate his juvenile antics.

I stormed out of the restroom, crossed the parking lot, and filled my tank. Paul was apparently in the restroom. I capped my tank as he stalked back to his bike. After digging the atlas out of my tour pack, I tossed it over the concrete island like it was a Frisbee. It smacked him in the chest and fell to the ground.

"I suggest you find a way back to Florida that is more suitable to you," I angrily said, "because I'm not going to listen to you whine all the way to Indiana. I'm sorry you can't keep your bike on the road, but I'm expected at my dad's funeral on Thursday. How dare you start this crap with me now?" My indignation didn't slow his tirade. It only added fuel to whatever fire had started in him.

"You would like that, wouldn't you? Me leaving you in Kansas," he replied.

"YOU? Leaving ME?" I laughed. "Don't flatter yourself. I was riding solo long before you came along, and I won't hesitate to do it again."

And then Paul and I were off on the kind of round and round argument couples have when emotions take hold, pride is at stake, and each partner is as obstinate as the other. He scooped the atlas off the ground and started to hand it to me.

"Don't bother," I scoffed. "I know my way home from here," as I buckled my helmet in place and prepared to leave. Paul quickly stuffed the atlas in his tour pack and hastily buckled his helmet, almost as if he were afraid I would leave without him. Which I had every intention of doing.

The episode ended with both of us screeching out of the gas station parking lot where a few bystanders were robbed of the fun of watching our roadside drama. If anything was different, it was that my angry challenge to him to find his own way back to Florida made Paul more determined to keep pace with me—wind be damned.

The past inched into my present again as the monotony of the interstate settled over me. I remembered the beginning of sixth grade. I felt shame. I felt defective. I felt as though I didn't belong. My mother had a secret, and somehow, I was responsible for her disgrace and interrupting her life. I was obliged to keep the secret as well. I became skillful at keeping secrets, and until the day she died, she never uttered a word about my biological father.

My own grandma never mentioned my birth for fear my mother— her daughter—would cut ties with her and prevent her from seeing me. My dad never treated me any differently than he did with my brother or sister, and initially, I didn't question his love for me. The words *stepdaughter* and *stepdad* or *half-brother, half-sister* were never used. Mom did her best to erase her teenage mistake, eliminating my biological father completely and his large, extended family. I spent the next four decades trying to connect the dots and, eventually, discovered several aunts—my bio-dad's sisters—and multiple cousins who were all aware of my birth circumstances.

My arms ached from gripping the handlebars and doing battle with the brutal Kansas crosswinds. My mind was numb from lack of sleep, the livid exchanges with Paul, and the distressing memories I had allowed to run riot since my Dad's demise.

It was late Tuesday afternoon, and we had been on the road for over eight hours—and still less than 400 miles from Denver. At this rate, we would not make it to Indiana until sometime Wednesday.

As we neared Salina, Kansas, I made the decision for us to stop for the night. I scouted an exit that offered lodging, signaled to Paul, who was still behind me, and pulled under the portico of a Hampton Inn. Not waiting for him to ask questions or start the argument all over again—whatever it was that we were arguing about—I wearily walked inside to register, still wearing my helmet and gloves. Paul followed and finished the registration while I returned to Bessie and retrieved my tour pack. We didn't speak.

I resented Paul's anger, his emotional withdrawal from me at a time when I needed comforting the most. Yet, I understood his anxiety as well. Paul was just as tired as I was, just as bewildered by the tragic set of circumstances we were both operating within, and he was traveling toward an unplanned destination where he was a stranger to everyone, as they were to him. I tried to keep this aspect of the anger between us at the forefront of our reality.

Happy hour, with a plentiful appetizer selection, was in full swing. Although neither of us felt very happy, I needed food before I needed a shower. The appetizer selection was a convenient alternative to finding a restaurant and battling the wind again. We filled a plate, chose a seat in the cramped, noisy area adjacent to the lobby and ate in silence. Tears slid down my cheeks—no doubt leaving a wet trail through the layered dust on my skin—and dripped onto the table in front of me. I sobbed quietly as I ate the pasta casserole, tepid and tasteless. Paul refused to look me in the eye; his attention was solely on the food he put on his plate.

After going to our room, taking a shower with more agonizing silence between Paul and me, I called my brother. He affirmed the funeral plans for Thursday, commiserated with me over the travel conditions I related—I left out the part about mine and Paul's heated exchanges—and told me to take our time and be safe. I fell into a fitful sleep after praying tomorrow would be a better day.

HOMEWARD BOUND

Part Two

She wasn't sad anymore;
she was numb
and she knew
somehow,
numb was worse.

– Atticus, poet

ALTHOUGH MY HANGOVER THE NEXT MORNING WAS OF
the emotional variety, it possessed all the trappings of a genuine alcoholic bender: splitting headache, blurred vision, nausea, and a muddled,

disconnected feeling. I stood in the shower for what seemed like hours, praying the scalding water would revive me enough to feel human again. It didn't. Paul's knocking on the door snapped me back to our reality. We traded places in the tiny bathroom, each of us grunting, "Good Morning," which I assumed signaled the argument was over. He was kind enough to fetch coffee from the lobby while I was in the shower. I slugged back the first cup, waiting for the caffeine to alert my brain that it was okay to wake up.

Paul and I packed our bags and trudged to the lobby for breakfast; I drank mine, but Paul tucked into a sizable meal of the rubbery mess the Hampton Inn called scrambled eggs, along with chunky potatoes simmered in grease, toast, fruit, and yogurt. It made me nauseous just watching him eat. Our conversation was non-existent.

We didn't need to check the map because I-70 would once again be our route east. My only concern was how many more miles we had to travel until the persistent wind stopped.

I walked outside while Paul finished breakfast. The temperature had already climbed to near eighty degrees, and the sun was barely up over the horizon. If there is one thing consistent about this part of Kansas, it is the wind that blows at least ten miles per hour every day. I stood in front of Bessie, my whole being numb, and wondered how long the wind would plague us today.

After Paul finished eating, he and I got on our bikes, and as we merged onto I-70, we were immediately walloped by a gust of wind coming from the south, nearly pushing me into the traffic lane to my left. I gripped the handlebars, leaned right, and pulled Bessie into the merge lane while maintaining a safe speed. Paul was directly behind me. The ride was a repeat of yesterday for the next eighty or ninety miles.

As we neared Topeka, the topography started to change; flat, dusty plains gave way to vivid green hills and deep ravines, perhaps the inspiration for L. Frank Baum's naming the fictional capital of *Oz* the Emerald City, where the Great Wizard resided. The lush, verdant bumps of elevation slowed the brutal wind. I thought of Dorothy and her ruby slippers. To leave the Emerald City and escape the Wicked Witch, all she had to do was click her heels together and chant, "There's no place like home."

I settled into the monotony of the ride, hypnotized by the broken white lines flying past in a syncopated rhythm, as I chanted over and over, *There's no place like home...there's no place like home...there's no place like home.* My thoughts took a detour down another road in my head.

The day in late 1969 when I discovered drugs, alcohol, and rock 'n roll was a twisted sort of liberation from the self-loathing I learned to take comfort in. Rebellion was the vehicle I used to take revenge on my mom and dad's secrets and lies. Smoking pot freed my mind, mellowed my angst. Alcohol made me brave and beautiful. The friends I discovered along with the drugs and alcohol formed a nucleus around the music that spoke of love, war, protest, and rebellion.

At the age of fifteen, I became every parent's worst nightmare. I lied about where I went, who I was with, and just about everything else I could lie about. When I was caught—which was often—I jutted out my chin, crossed my arms over my chest, and took whatever punishment Dad handed down. The consequences steeled my resolve to find new ways to lie, break the rules, and hurt my parents.

With each drug-fueled, drunken episode, I begged my mom to tell me the truth about my parentage, about my biological dad and the circumstances of my birth. There is nothing more pitiful than a slobbery teenage drunk bouncing off the walls, pleading, and crying for an explanation—an explanation that never came. Those oft repeated scenes ended with my mother retreating to a corner of whatever room the confrontation took place with her cigarettes, tearfully claiming *she* was the victim while Dad ushered me to my bedroom, saving the punishment for the next day when I sobered up.

The punishments had little effect on my drinking, drugging, and defiant behavior in my teens. Worn down by trying, I believe my parents reached a point of resignation and acceptance somewhere around my senior year of high school. They had my younger sister and brother to focus on. At the age of fifteen, I started working at Osco Drug Store for $1.10 per hour, thirty hours a week. The conditions for driving the Volkswagen Bug Dad bought me was that I had to pay the insurance and buy gas.

I managed to get involved in a work-study program during my senior year of high school, where I went to school a half day and worked a half day, making $1.30 per hour at a Volkswagen-Mercedes dealership in Marion, my hometown.

I missed one of the insurance premiums, and my dad took the car away for six months. I had to ride the city bus to work or anywhere else I wanted to go. I learned what it meant to be a "functioning alcoholic" while I earned an income to maintain the lifestyle. It was a pattern I repeated for the next few decades.

Perhaps any other stepparent would have given up on such a problematic young girl, but Dad never did. He seemed committed to saving me from myself, and I am grateful for his love and loyalty.

After my mom died, Dad was very open about the troublesome years all three of us shared. He regretted the way he and Mom had hidden the truth of my parentage. He wished Mom had not alienated me from my biological dad's extended family. I learned I had attended school from elementary years on with numerous first cousins who I had no idea existed. Dad worked side-by-side for years with one of my aunts who was prohibited from contacting me.

The scope and intensity of my mother's wrath was astonishing. Only after becoming a parent myself did I begin to understand why she chose to treat me as she did. Not only do we parents go to any length to help our children, but we also realize that all we ever can do is give our best with the knowledge and awareness we have of any situation. My parents did the best they could, given the culture and times they lived in; divorce and single motherhood were social stigmas for a woman in the 1950s. My mother simply wanted to erase her indiscretion and pursue a life free of anyone's judgment in the only way she knew how—through deception.

The interstate widened, and traffic became dense as Paul and I neared Kansas City, first in Kansas and then in Missouri. We crossed the Missouri River that separates the two Kansas cities, and if I could have done a happy dance, I would have. Nevertheless, I did an energetic fist pump to indicate my delight in leaving Kansas behind.

As I navigated the loop around the south end of the city, I resented the "balls-to-the-wall" ride we had been forced to make. Kansas City, Missouri, is home to some of the best blues, jazz, and barbeque in the Midwest, and we did not have time to stop and partake. Missouri is also home to Mark Twain and includes a generous swath of the historic 2,448-mile Route 66, neither of which we would see on this trip.

Paul and I merged back onto I-70 east—another stick-straight, wide-open stretch of asphalt that slices across Missouri—which was taking us closer to our destination. To reach Muncie Indiana, on this day would require a good eleven to twelve hours of hard riding to cover more than five hundred miles. Our plan was to get as close as possible before we called it a day.

Traffic snarled around St. Louis; construction hazards were everywhere, and then it began to rain. Not a downpour, but a slow drizzle that created slick highways and treacherous conditions for two wheels.

Paul was trying to signal me to stop; I knew he wanted to put on rain gear, but I ignored him and crept around the St. Louis metro area, dodging orange construction barrels and bumper-to-bumper traffic.

The rain and humidity were uncomfortable but nothing like yesterday's bashing winds. Since leaving Salina in the early morning, we had stopped only for gas while grabbing snacks, drinks, and a bathroom break on the run.

I was beyond exhausted—I was numb. My fingers had no feeling from gripping the handlebars, my ass had lost all feeling from non-stop riding, my hips and shoulders hurt from anxiety-induced tension, my mind was numb with anger toward my dad's selfish act and the unanswered question of *why*.

It was nearing late afternoon, and both of us were wet, hungry, and beyond tired. About fifty miles east of St. Louis, I spied a billboard for a Hampton Inn, one of the hotels we liked. Exiting the interstate, we headed down a sparsely traveled, two-lane road, a cornfield on either side of us. *Corn!* I was closer to home.

Paul and I spent the night in Highland, Illinois, a tiny little town settled by German-Swiss migrants, on SR 160, south of the interstate. It was less than 300 miles from my brother's house near Muncie, Indiana. I called David to tell him where we were and when to expect us tomorrow. Our conversation was brief, almost terse, as we were both beginning to come to terms with our anger over our dad's decision. My brother sounded as tired as I felt. I fell into another fitful sleep, the rhythm of the road still pounding out a cadence in my head.

THE GATHERING

Part 1

Our job from this point forward is to practice acceptance.
Acceptance does not require that we understand.
Because we do not.
Acceptance does not require the answer to the
question, why.
Because there is no answer.
Acceptance does not require our approval.
When I have acceptance in my heart, there is no
room for anger.
When I have acceptance in my heart, there is no
room for resentments,
which are just hardened chunks of anger waiting to
come out sideways.
Acceptance allows me to move through the universe
without chafing,
without bumping up against the hardships, the
ugliness, or the angst.
The act of acceptance is unconditional love.
Acceptance allows me to be at peace with me, at
peace with you,
at peace with decisions made by others,
and at peace with my place in the universe.

– Excerpt from Our Dad's Eulogy, Debi Tolbert Duggar

AFTER LEAVING HIGHLAND, ILLINOIS, PAUL AND I ARRIVED at my brother's house just before noon on Wednesday. We had left Denver on Monday; Dad's funeral was scheduled for Thursday. I was physically exhausted, emotionally numb, and tinged with a sensation akin to anger that I could not legitimately put a name or face to. My brother was his usual stoic self, my sister-in-law a flurry of efficiency. She ushered Paul and me into one of the guest bedrooms, knowing the first thing we wanted was a hot shower for which I was grateful. My brother and sister-in-law's house—impeccably decorated and immaculate— always looked as if it fell off the pages of *Better Homes and Gardens*. I felt like my very presence soiled the carpet I stood on, not to mention the weight of my tour pack wrinkling the expensive comforter topping the bed and our discarded riding gear crudely assaulting the pristine bedroom. All I could do was stand in the middle of the room, feeling bewildered and forlorn while Paul made his way to the shower.

Before I could figure out what to do next, my brother knocked on the door and entered as I stared at my tour pack, trying to will it to open and reveal instructions on how to behave. My brother started shoving envelopes stuffed with money in my hands with staccato-like bursts of explanation.

"This is your one third of the cash we found in Dad's wallet and stashed in various places in the house..."

"This is your one third of the money I got for the lawnmower I sold..." *You sold his lawnmower already?!*

"This is...blah, blah, blah." He couldn't stop talking, and I was too senseless to try and slow him down. I just nodded, pretending to understand while holding the envelopes of cash. Thought bubbles formed in my head in response to his actions and words:

"And you should go shopping to buy some funeral clothes..."

No, I thought we would just go as we are—biker people.

"The funeral is scheduled for..."

"Jodi and I took care of..."

"I need you to sign these papers, but you can wait until you've had a shower..."

Gee, thanks!

"We are all meeting at Dad's house to clear out the rest of his things..."

You mean you've already started?

The staccato bursts kept coming, each one like a blow to my aching head, and before I could find my voice to ask a question, protest, or scream, my brother stopped talking, turned, and walked out of the room just as abruptly as he had entered.

With a towel wrapped snuggly around his waist, Paul opened the bathroom door, a cloud of steam following his exit. He looked at me, started to ask a question but thought better of it and just pulled me close in a warm, soap-smell hug, the wads of cash and papers to sign crushed between us. It occurred to me at that moment that this was the first time Paul was meeting my family.

I showered, pulled on clean jeans and a T-shirt, and joined Paul in the kitchen. Caroline arrived from her cousin's house, and I gratefully acquiesced while she took charge of the pending shopping trip for "funeral clothes." My brother tossed the keys to one of their cars on the table, deeming our bikes unsuitable for the trip, and off we went to the Muncie Mall with the cash he had given me.

If the circumstances had been different, I could have taken great joy in an impromptu shopping spree with "found" money. But how can anyone enjoy buying funeral clothes?

Paul headed to the men's section of one of the better department stores we decided held the most promise for all three of us; Caroline and I sought out the women's section. We sifted through the fancy dresses, sliding over the bright colors and festive patterns, choosing instead the standard black funeral attire. Out of habit, I scoffed at the prices, and then remembered I had a bundle of cash I didn't have two hours ago and thought, *What the hell?*

I plucked the priciest black Ralph Lauren frock from the batch I brought to the dressing room and waited for my daughter to finish trying on her selections. Caroline couldn't decide. I told her, "Get the most expensive one," and that was that. We paid for our purchases and strolled over to the shoe department. Is there such a thing as funeral shoes? I chose a pair of Michael Kors' gladiator style, high-heeled, black patent leather sandals with gold zippers. My dad might be dead, but that shouldn't mean his girl had to wear ugly shoes.

As Caroline and I were leaving the shoe department, she announced emphatically,

"Mom, you have GOT to wear underwear to the funeral!"

"Why?" was my only reply. I'm not a fan of underwear, for a funeral or for any other day.

"Mom, it's a FUNERAL. You have to wear underwear," she pointed out indignantly, as if her twisted logic was carved in stone somewhere along with the other commandments such as "Thou Shalt Not Attend a Funeral Commando." Off we marched toward the lingerie section of this massive department store as I wondered if there were a special section for funeral underwear.

My daughter, still in charge, selected a pair of Spanx knee length panties in black, of course. Spanx underwear is simply a modern, lighter version of the girdles with garter snaps we used to wear to keep our nylon stockings up and our tummies in place. Thank God, the Women's Liberation Movement freed most of us from the bondage of such undergarments in the late sixties. Up to that point, women were not supposed to jiggle.

Before paying for the Spanx, I crossed over to the jewelry counter, and, in a fit of rebellion, I selected a gaudy gold chain choker and red garnet earrings trimmed in gold with a chunky matching bracelet. I *never* wear gold jewelry, but I felt obligated to sparkle, regardless of my grief, and the jewelry matched the gold zippers on my shoes. I tossed my Spanx on the glass counter along with the jewelry, looked at my daughter who was about to protest my flashy choices, and gave her a look that said, *Don't even go there,* while I plopped down what I considered an obscene amount of cash for my selections.

Caroline and I found Paul, wandering aimlessly in the men's shoe section, clutching a pair of khaki slacks and a white, long-sleeved, button-down shirt. I told him to choose a pair of black shoes, and when he started to protest, I snarled, "Just do it so we can get out of here."

Shopping for funeral clothes had lost its allure, and I was ready to stop. While he tried on a pair of shoes, I gathered up his clothes and waited for him at the cashier's register. He came over, placed his shoebox on the counter, and reached for his wallet to pay. I told him I had strict instructions from my brother to use the cash for funeral clothes and that's what I intended to do.

Caroline, Paul, and I left the department store, toting our respective purchases, elated we had procured the appropriate clothes to wear when we laid Dad to rest. The irony was that in a few days' time, Dad might roll over in his freshly dug grave if he could know how much money I spent to dress the three of us for his funeral.

I drove from the mall directly to Dad's house where my brother, sister, and our respective children were waiting outside. I got out of the car and gave my sister a perfunctory hug—no love lost between us. We had never been close. I affectionately hugged her sons—my nephews—who I don't see a lot for the reason I mentioned and embraced my nieces. I introduced Paul who was lingering in the background, unsure of his role in this afternoon's events.

"Why are you all standing outside?" I queried.

"I wanted us to go in together so everyone had an equal chance to look over the stuff and make their selections," my brother responded.

It felt as if clearing out our dad's house was a Black Friday sale, and we had to wait outside until the store opened before we rushed in and frantically started grabbing our desired items. I was getting a sense of drama vibe that was not welcome, but I had already vowed not to argue with anyone over "stuff." It was weird enough standing in front of my dad's house, knowing he had committed suicide not quite five days ago in his bedroom. I anticipated the worst.

All of us were all eerily quiet as we trooped single file through the front door, the house chilly despite the warm temperature outside. It smelled of fresh paint. My brother had hired someone to re-plaster and paint the walls and ceiling in the bedroom where Dad had committed the final, heinous act—erasing any evidence of the bullet that tore through my Dad's chin, out his skull, and into the ceiling above the bed where he lay. As if quickly erasing the evidence could reverse the act itself.

I looked around at bare walls, empty shelves, and flat surfaces void of all the "set-arounds" my mother was fond of. My brother and sister obviously had descended on the house before anyone else, cherry-picking the worldly possessions. It was exactly what I expected, but I found it impossible to generate any animosity toward them. When people succeed in meeting our expectations, it is difficult to become angry. My brother was the executor of the estate; he had every right to do whatever he deemed necessary. In the end, I was grateful to be relieved of all the tedious tasks left to take care of when the last parent dies.

Throughout the house, my sister (or someone) had strategically placed piles of framed pictures, table linens, dishes, Christmas ornaments in boxes, and all the accoutrements of a man's life in plain view where Dad's children and grandchildren could ascertain their "worth."

For the better part of the afternoon, we picked over the remnants of Dad's life like a flock of carrion birds, placing items in cardboard boxes, possessively grouped by family. The grandchildren were sadly tugging at the box of ornaments, taking turns choosing a memento by which to remember their grandpa. When the box was picked clean, we moved to the china and curio cabinets. I stood in front of the china cabinet with Caroline, examining not one but two sets of china. I never knew my mom had china. I urged my daughter to take one of the sets:

"Every girl should have a set of china," I claimed with a slightly less-than-convincing tone.

"I don't like it," she said in a gentle monotone.

"It's not about *liking* it, Doodle," I coaxed. "It's about memories and having a keepsake that you will pass along to your children one day."

"Then why don't you take it?" she asked.

"I already have my grandmother's china," I said, a little too defensively. This was becoming more of a verbal tug-o-war than choosing a set of china.

"I never had a meal here where we used the china. How can an object generate memories I don't have?"

I had to give her that one. I couldn't remember a meal served on this china either. I was already exhausted. I didn't want to have this conversation, I didn't want to stand in my dad's empty kitchen, and I didn't want to argue with my daughter over what she should and should not value of her grandparents' possessions. In the end, I boxed up one of the sets of china, and shipped it back to my house. Maybe someday, when I'm dead and gone, my daughters will stand in front of the china box and have this same conversation over who will take the china.

My cardboard box was noticeably empty. There were a few framed photographs that I gave to Dad as gifts over the years, and I placed those in my box. The only other item I wanted, sadly enough, was the .22 caliber pistol he used to shoot himself. I know. It sounds gruesome and hideous to want to possess such a thing. I walked into his bedroom where my brother was sorting through clothes and told him what I wanted. He looked at me in disbelief, then shrugged his shoulders. My sister walked into the room and asked, "What's going on?" When my brother told her, the drama started.

She looked at me with disgust, tears welling in her eyes, and with all the dramatic indignation of a third-rate stage actress, said, "I want the gun destroyed! Guns are evil, and I want this one destroyed!" She began to sob. I suppose by destroying the gun, she, too, thought it could reverse the odious act of suicide.

My dad, anticipating what might be the slightest tussle over his "stuff," made a provision in his will that if there were any item that two of us wanted, we were to draw straws—shortest one would win. Dad was a practical man who thought of everything. I looked at my brother, and said simply, "I guess we draw straws." My sister looked at me horrified and stormed out of the room.

My brother gave me a withering look and said, "Just a minute," and followed my sister out of the room. Within two minutes he returned, thrust the pistol in my hand and said, "Whatever."

Today, the pistol, along with a dried red rose from the flower arrangement on the casket, my dad's pocket knife, an old wooden fishing lure, and my favorite picture of us are arranged in a shadowbox with the inscription, "To Thine Own Self Be True." It hangs in my office where it reminds me to live life to its fullest, love unconditionally, take chances, travel often, dream big, and never take anything for granted.

By late afternoon, the personal remnants of my parents' life together were distributed between their children and grandchildren, creating a forlorn void in the home they shared. The items no one claimed, including Dad's clothes, would be donated to the Salvation Army or Goodwill. My brother planned to have the interior of the house painted and re-carpeted with the intention of fetching top dollar once it was placed on the market. Selling a home after the occupant committed suicide seemed like a gruesome endeavor, but I kept my concerns to myself, wondering what type of buyer could overlook that one chilling fact.

After my brother, sister, and our families had cleared the house of all its belongings, we went our separate ways to find a quiet space in which to process the afternoon's efforts. I asked my brother about a eulogy for tomorrow's service, but he implied he didn't want to do it himself—that would be too much like showing emotion. Since I was the oldest, I indicated it should be my responsibility, so I sequestered myself in my sister-in-law's den for the remainder of the evening to write Dad's eulogy. The words came easily, the tears flowed generously—like a cleansing.

THE GATHERING

Part 2

An abnormal reaction to an abnormal situation
is normal behavior.

– Viktor Emil Frankl, *Man's Search for Meaning*

ON THE MORNING OF DAD'S FUNERAL, MY BROTHER'S
house was a beehive of activity. Plans were made and a schedule of
events created. David arranged cars, assigned family members to a
specific car; Jacquie accepted food from neighbors and gave my brother
orders.

The funeral service—per my dad's last wishes—would be in
Marion with a lunch for the immediate family afterward at his church.
When my brother approached me with last- minute decisions, I quickly
acquiesced to his wishes. I felt like an extra sent from central casting to
play the part of a grieving daughter. None of us grasped the reality of
the day; we moved automatically, playing our roles the best we could.

My brother ushered each of us to the respective vehicles that
whisked us away to Needham-Story-Wampner Funeral Home, where
the service would be conducted. I admit we looked resplendent in our
funeral finery, albeit uncomfortable and out of character.

As scheduled, the family was the first to arrive so we could have private time with our father. Twenty or more immediate family members stood forlornly in the vestibule of the building, where we chatted quietly among ourselves. I was shocked to learn there would be an open casket. But my brother assured me that "the makeup person did a wonderful job making Dad look *normal.*"

The dimly lit outer foyer of the funeral home was thick with a cloying floral scent, and a soft dirge of music played through the ceiling tile speakers. The entire interior was decorated in varying shades of mauve, a decidedly "dead" color. A fresh-faced, youngish-looking attendant greeted us warmly, offered his sincerest condolences, and vowed to be "at our service" to make the occasion as comfortable as possible. He acted more like the concierge at a five-star hotel than a mortician. I believed him, regardless of his limp, clammy handshake.

Before entering the main parlor where Dad awaited our arrival, the attendant ushered us down a hallway where the family lounge was located. It was an inviting area with homemade cookies laid out on various trays and coffee and soft drinks available for us. I guessed that when the greeting and grieving became too much, we were expected to duck into the lounge for a quick snack.

My family was a mournful clutch of well-dressed children and grandchildren, moving in one tight group as if to ward off apprehension and heartache. We followed the attendant back through the foyer toward the main parlor. He stopped outside the ornate double doors and told us we would have thirty minutes alone with our dad before the other guests began arriving at 11:30 a.m. He then ushered us into the room. More mauve; I had no idea there were so many variations of mauve.

The large parlor was awash in a sea of floral arrangements; elaborate groupings surrounded the casket at the front of the room and lined the walls on either side. Smaller arrangements, but no less sumptuous, topped every flat surface—the scent of all those blossoms was over-whelming. All of us huddled near the doors. Paul's hand protectively clutched my elbow on one side, and I looped my other arm through Caroline's as we scanned the parlor, unsure of how to approach our dad.

My brother took the lead, and we followed warily down the carpeted path toward the casket. David, Jodi, and I formed a triumvirate and stepped forward, leaving our children and spouses behind. I peered into the casket. Dad looked peaceful and distinguished in his navy suit. I had no tears, although my brother and sister started to sob quietly. I stood stoically, looking for the bullet hole. It was there, but only if you knew it was there. I turned to my brother and said in a congratulatory tone, "You're right. The bullet hole is difficult to see."

As the remainder of the family stepped forward, David pulled my sister and me to the side. I noticed Paul retreating to the back to stand and chat with the other "outlaws," husbands of my cousin and nieces. "We have to agree on what we are going to tell everyone," he whispered, his hands stuffed awkwardly in his black suit pants as my sister nodded in agreement. They apparently had already discussed whatever it was we were discussing.

"What do you mean, 'tell everyone?'" I asked, more than a little perplexed.

"Well, we can't tell people Dad committed suicide," my brother said emphatically, lowering his voice for the word *suicide* as if it was a vulgar, illicit word. My sister, looking more than a little disgusted that this even had to be explained to me, was still nodding her agreement. *Oh, of course, I get it. Our dad's method of checking out doesn't fit with your sense of propriety.*

"But he *did* commit suicide," I reminded them.

My brother and sister exchanged knowing glances as if to say, "We knew she would do this," and my brother leaned in closer. "But what good will it do to tell everyone that?" he asked.

I reminded my siblings that I worked and lived in a program of honesty and that it would be difficult for me to stand there all afternoon, telling the biggest lie in the room. Not to mention that police reports had been filed and a handful of people, like Dad's neighbors, had heard the shot in the dark.

My brother proposed gently, as my sister moved away, giving him that I-told-you-so-look over her shoulder, "We are going to tell everyone he died suddenly."

"Yeah, real suddenly," I scoffed. I defiantly folded my arms across my chest and planted my Michael Kors a little more firmly into the plush carpet.

Exasperated with my attitude and visibly tired from his responsibilities of the past five days, he sighed heavily and uttered, "Do what you want," and moved toward Jacquie, who was understandably in collusion with both my brother and sister.

Now I was pissed; my face flushed with resentment. Not only did our dad commit suicide, but my siblings were embarrassed by his action. To them, it seemed his choice would tarnish our family name and violate some warped sense of social standing. I was expected to deny it happened and support my siblings' delusion.

All my life, the Tolbert clan had made a vocation out of sweeping any human failing, as well as all emotional unpleasantries, under the rug. Why should our dad's suicide be any different? *If we don't acknowledge it, then it didn't happen* was the family's preferred mantra. For too many years, I was bound and chastised by my mother's favorite plea, "But what will people think?" My own failings were a perpetual disappointment to my parents and most certainly to those people whose opinions Mom valued above her own child's struggles or pain. Now my brother was taking up the cause in her absence.

I wouldn't do it. I wouldn't let the elephant in the room take up residence. I turned away from the casket as I heard the first mourners approach the parlor. I straightened my spine in defiance, smoothed my Spanx—which was ruthlessly pinching at the waist—and moved over next to my brother in the receiving line. The unresolved issue of what to tell people hung heavy between us.

The first cluster of mourners was my dad's church ladies, an elderly group of gray-haired women who fawned over Dad from the moment Mom passed away to the present. His favorite, Evelyn, wheeled her walker, surprisingly fast, toward the casket as if she were a rock star's groupie, determined to snag a front row seat. She leaned over her walker, her soft pink and gray flowered dress blending nicely with the mauve in the room and wept openly into the casket while we stood uncomfortably at attention, ready to receive the onslaught of condolences. Evelyn blew her nose loudly into her linen handkerchief, navigated her walker away from the casket, and wheeled our way. David, Jodi, and I positioned ourselves—wholly unaware—in birth order to form the receiving line, putting me, the oldest, first. Evelyn took my hand and sobbed, "I had no idea he was even sick! How did it happen?"

And here was the moment of truth. I leaned over her walker, whispered in her ear, "He shot himself," and then stood back, waiting for the repercussion.

Evelyn's head snapped up, her expression blanching and eyes widening in disbelief. There was a sharp intake of breath as she clutched one hand to her perfumed bosom while the other gripped her walker. "What? No! Not John!" she exclaimed as she teetered backward, the front wheels of the walker tipping off the carpet with her considerable weight. My brother and I each grabbed a fleshy upper arm and pulled her upright, as he gave me a contemptuous look that said, *Are you satisfied now?*

I managed to settle Evelyn in the back of the parlor with the other mourners from dad's church and resumed my place in the receiving line next to my brother. I leaned over and said curtly, "Okay, I get it. He died suddenly." I knew full well that Evelyn would introduce everyone to the reality of the elephant in the room.

For the remainder of the viewing, I shook my head in solemn incomprehension when asked, "How did it happen?" I deferred demurely to my brother to provide details. When it came time for me to deliver the eulogy, my brother glanced at me, suddenly realizing he had not read—and therefore approved—the words I was about to say. I mouthed, "Don't worry," as I walked to the podium.

The parlor was packed—standing room only—with friends, relatives, business associates, and people who loved my dad as much as his family did. My dad's longtime friend and pastor, Tom, delivered the service. Tom is also a musician. My dad left instructions for Tom to play his guitar and sing "Nearer, My God, to Thee" and "Amazing Grace." I delivered the eulogy—my voice cracking with emotion only once—with every ounce of heartfelt appreciation I felt. I watched my brother and sister, tears welling in their eyes, wearing an expression of gratitude that I didn't mention the *S* word. Afterward, my brother hugged and congratulated me on a job well-done; my sister tossed me a sardonic, "Nice job, Debi."

Paul made his way from the back of the parlor where he had maintained an unobtrusive stance throughout my eulogy. He hugged me tightly and said, "Well done." Each time I looked up from the podium, I sought his face in the crowd as he smiled encouragement. My wingman, ever present and supportive.

After the service, a crush of mourners surrounded us again as my brother, sister, and I stood steadfastly near the casket. At some point, Paul steered me toward the exit and said, "It's time to go; the cars are waiting." I looked for Caroline, grabbed her hand, and tugged her out of the building with me.

My family and I managed to lay Dad to rest next to my mother in Grant Memorial Park that day with every bit of the dignity and respect befitting the man that he was, regardless of his demise. My daughter and I each took a rose from the blanket of blossoms atop the casket; we hugged each other. I saw Paul chatting with my brother; then, he headed over to Caroline and me to say once more, "It's time to go. Everyone is going to the church for lunch." Paul found purpose that day in making sure I didn't have to make too many decisions. He was diligent in being near when I needed him and fading into the crowd when my duties as a grieving daughter demanded my attention.

When the last parent dies, there is an interruption to the rhythm of your life. Your emotions scramble to identify your new place in the family order. As the oldest child, I moved up a notch in the familial hierarchy; now orphaned and lacking ballast, I tilted toward my brother.

Despite losing our patriarch, there was a celebratory cadence to the gathering that occurred a few days before and after the funeral. Cousins who hadn't seen each other in months chattered excitedly about their lives as we dished up the platters of food, delivered by generous neighbors, at my brother's house later that evening. I watched the next generation of our family take their rightful places around the dining room table. Though my sister and I had maintained an adversarial relationship at best, we broke bread together that day and talked guardedly; grief was the epoxy that cemented old wounds. Death has a solemn way of gathering families closer, regardless of differences.

FINAL THOUGHTS CARRY
ME HOME

All journeys eventually end in the same place, home.

– Chris Geiger, *Bad Cells*

I AWOKE THE MORNING AFTER THE FUNERAL WITH A FEEL-
ing of heaviness that went beyond fatigue. I felt as though a mighty
force with boxing gloves, gently—so as not to make visible marks—but
consistently had pummeled me from head to toe. In four short days,
I had traveled 1,500 miles on two wheels, buried my Dad, and settled
the estate with my siblings. Now it was time to go home. Indiana is the
place of my birth, but Florida will always be home.

As Paul and I tiptoed around the bedroom, gathering our belongings, I felt a sense of foreboding. It started last night at dinner as I glanced around the table at my family, diminished by one. What now? Our grandparents were gone, our mom was gone, and now our dad was no longer with us. Whom does the family gather around from this point forward? I was nobody's "child" anymore. There would be no Dad to come home to, no Dad to call for advice, no Dad to lend support. My siblings and I felt the emptiness, but no one gave voice to it.

Although Paul and I had said goodbye to my brother and sister-in-law the previous night, my brother was up, ready to see us off at 5:30 a.m. I checked the weather as I gulped my first cup of coffee. The ominous feeling intensified when I saw menacing slashes of red and yellow snaking across the radar, indicating severe weather along our route south.

As Paul and I packed our bikes, my brother bustled about the garage, avoiding the inevitable departure. For the past few days, I had tried to will him to break down and sob, show his emotion, show his anger. But, stoic as ever, he gave me the Tolbert "air" hug, not exactly a warm embrace, more like an "air kiss," only with hugging. Arms flapped, hands patted backs—plenty of air between our bodies. Over the years, I had become accustomed to the gesture; that day, however, the air between us was significant.

"Be safe. Give us a call when you arrive home," was my brother's farewell message. "Yes, of course. Thanks again for the hospitality," I stammered, unable to stifle the emotion clogging my throat.

Torn between not wanting to leave and not being able to leave fast enough, I straddled Bessie, and as two V-twin engines roared to life, the tranquil morning of my brother's well-ordered suburban neighborhood was shattered.

I chose a back road route as far south as possible before we would be forced to connect with I-75, the dreaded super slab. Farmland surrounded SR 3 to Russiaville, Indiana, everywhere I looked. The slightly damp morning air was cool and lush with the fecund smell of fresh earth and burgeoning crops. I surmised the young, green stalks of corn, poking robustly out of the fertile soil, would be knee-high by the Fourth of July. The familiar sights and smells of my home state made me sad all over again, and my tears flowed, blurring my vision. I felt sad to leave my dad, sad to leave Indiana, and sad for my family who must pick up the pieces. The wind scattered my tears, and I took comfort astride Bessie. The engine vibration soothed my shattered soul, and the miles slipped away, putting distance between the pain and me.

In the small town of Spiceland, Indiana, I saw a little restaurant with several pickup trucks parked out front—a good indication the food was tasty. I swung into the parking lot; Paul pulled up beside me and gave me a thumbs-up, which indicated he was ready for breakfast and another infusion of coffee. The morning air was heavy with a cold moisture that held the promise of rougher weather ahead of us.

As we entered the tiny restaurant, a bell attached above the door jingled softly, announcing our arrival. Eight older gentlemen assembled at a long table near the entrance, as if they are holding council, fell silent and turned their heads in our direction. Their tanned faces had been carved deeply by a livelihood in the elements. Most of them sported baseball caps with a John Deere logo or one from a local feed store; some wore denim bibbed overalls, softened by many washings. I stopped, looked directly at them, and quipped, "Are we in time for the meeting?"

They chuckled, gave us a collective, "Good morning," and returned to their conversation as Paul and I found a booth next to a window. One glance at the menu told me I was still in Indiana. Fried bologna was listed on the breakfast selections. I grew up on fried bologna sandwiches; they're a Hoosier delicacy. My dad would score the circle of pinkish mystery meat on four sides and fry it in oil until the circles were crispy around the edges. He then placed the bologna between two pieces of soft Wonder Bread, slathered with ketchup. The first bite was heaven; the warmth of the meat fused with the softness of the bread while the grease and ketchup dripped down your wrist. I had not had a fried bologna sandwich since I left home and didn't intend to order one for breakfast.

The eggs, home fries, and bacon were tasty. The service was friendly, and the generous flow of coffee boosted our spirits. Although I would have preferred to linger over our coffee in such a homey atmosphere and strike up a conversation with the "senior council," timing was everything today. Paul was scheduled to fly to his next project on Monday morning, and the weather in the South didn't look favorable for smooth travel.

Unlike the trip from Colorado to Indiana, where my thoughts ran rampant, I felt only a quiet melancholy as I saddled up for the next leg of our trip. I focused on keeping my thoughts in neutral as I shifted Bessie through the gears. Given the threatening weather on the radar, I needed all my concentration for Paul and me to arrive safely at our destination in Dalton, Georgia.

Fortified with coffee and a resolve to make it halfway home that day, we merged onto I-74 to Cincinnati and said goodbye to the last, two-lane road we would travel until we arrived in Lake County, Florida. There would be no sightseeing. We had to pass right by some of the best riding highways in the South—Cherohala Skyway, Tail of the Dragon, and US 441 through the Great Smoky Mountains—to stay on Paul's schedule.

Just outside of London, Kentucky, however, I made an exception. Wildcat Harley-Davidson, one of the best dealerships I have visited in my journeys, lies right off I-75. It has a gorgeous lounge for bikers who take the roads mentioned above. The merchandise manager is creative as well, and I always found items there that were unique: custom leather pieces, household items with the Harley-Davidson logo, and a clothing selection that goes beyond the usual destination T-shirts.

Paul and I meandered around the rustic, lodge-style store, choosing items to purchase for nearly an hour before I asked the girl at the front desk for a restaurant recommendation. She directed us to the Old Town Grille, just across the overpass. Paul and I crammed our purchases into already overstuffed saddlebags and made the short trip to the restaurant; a smattering of rain was beginning as darker clouds formed to the south.

The Old Town Grille was one of the best restaurants Paul and I had eaten in since we left home two weeks ago—which now felt like a lifetime ago. The menu offered fried green tomatoes with crunchy breading on the outside of tender, juicy slices; sweet, tangy barbeque; southern fried chicken along with a variety of steaks, burgers, and seafood. Even gator tail was listed, although I doubt it was none too fresh since Kentucky isn't known for its alligator population. Paul and I ordered the barbeque pork sandwich with a side of crunchy sweet coleslaw. They did not disappoint.

The service was prompt, and our waitress was downright personable. A spunky twentysomething with natural good looks who had an endearing southern drawl. I got the impression her waitressing gig was only a stopover for more lofty ambitions. For the second time that day, I was reluctant to leave the pleasant atmosphere of a restaurant; the foreboding that settled in at our departure from my brother's house that morning still lingered. Before we left our table, I checked the Weather Channel app only to find the same angry red and yellow slashes moving across the Southeast. It seemed like our entire route would be plagued by bad weather. We didn't have the luxury of time to wait it out or take a more circuitous course.

As Paul and I donned our rain suits in the parking lot of the restaurant, the ominous dark clouds to the south promised a wet ride directly into the belly of the stormy beast. Within minutes of leaving the restaurant and heading south on I-75, the temperature dropped, the wind howled, and the deluge hit. I flipped on my flashers, slowed to a safer fifty miles per hour speed in the right-hand lane and looked in my side mirror to make sure Paul was behind me. I couldn't see him because the rain was all-consuming. In fact, I couldn't see anything but the white line directly beneath me to my left. The peaceful, melancholy mood I cherished during the morning dissipated quickly as my neck and shoulders tensed from clenching the rain-slick handgrips and praying I wouldn't slam into the rear end of a vehicle I couldn't see until it was too late.

I kept scanning the shoulder to my right, seeking an exit; there was none. We rode in the blinding rain for thirty miles or so, the torrent refusing to subside, before I saw an exit for a rest area. I turned on my signal, hoping Paul could see it and make the exit.

The rest area was desolate with *no facilities for shelter.* We parked our bikes and ran to a clump of trees for cover. Paul and I huddled under the skimpy foliage for forty-five minutes while lightning and thunder crashed around us; chilly rain soaked us.

I shivered under the copse of trees and wondered aloud between clashes of thunder, "How much more do you think God will throw at me before I get back home?"

Paul chuckled. I looked at him, water droplets blurring both of our glasses, and asked, "How have you liked our first road trip together so far?"

We both burst out laughing hysterically; the bottled-up anxiety that had burdened us over the last week was finally unleashed. We laughed so hard I started to cry from relief, my salty tears indistinguishable from the stinging rain. I pulled my cell phone out of my soggy pocket—thankful for Otter Box protection—and snapped a rain-splattered selfie of Paul and me, all smiles under the trees, some-where off I-75 south in Kentucky.

We rode in a steady rain—sometimes blinding—all the way to Dalton, Georgia; the 223-mile distance seemed like 2,200 miles. Dalton was halfway between Indiana and our home in Florida. It was still sprin-kling rain when we pulled under the portico of the Hampton Inn in Dalton at 7:00 p.m., two hours later than we anticipated.

While Paul checked us in, I wearily climbed off Bessie, sat down on the curb beside my bike, and could not find the strength to move. Paul found me crumpled on the curb, my head in my hands, helmet still affixed, weeping softly. *I only want to be home. How many times in the past week has this kind man seen me at my absolute worst?*

I was beyond tired; I felt raw. My numb legs and limp arms were useless. Paul pulled me up off the curb and suggested we needed some-thing to eat. Why is it that food is usually the first go-to-fix for whatever tragedy or ailment comes our way? I tugged off my helmet, crammed my cap down over my matted hair, and followed Paul across the street to Cracker Barrel. I don't even remember what I had to eat; all I could think about was a hot shower and sleep.

A solid night's sleep was not in my future, however. Shortly after midnight, my cell phone blasted "Material Girl," my daughter's ring-tone. I bolted upright, and started hollering, "No, no, no! I can't. Not again. Not my daughter. No, no, no, no, no, no!" I shook uncontrollably.

Paul was awake too; the "Material Girl" ringtone was annoyingly persistent in the stillness of the room. Paul reached across me, grabbed the phone off the nightstand, and thrust it in my hands. I tapped *accept* and held my breath. Only when I heard my daughter's soft, "Mom?" did I exhale.

"Honey! Are you okay? What's wrong?"

"Mom, I'm okay. I'm locked out of the house. The keyless entry is dead, out of batteries."

"Oh, thank God," I exclaimed.

"Wait. What? Mom? It's after midnight, and I can't get into the house!" She had just returned to Florida from Indiana and driven home from the airport.

"No. I meant thank God, you are okay, and no one else is dead." Paul and I could not have gotten in the house either if we had arrived home before she did. We recently had installed the keyless entry and did not have actual keys in case the keypad didn't work, or it ran low on batteries. *What to do?* I wondered.

"Mom, I'm going to call Julie and see if I can spend the night." Julie was a friend who lived nearby.

"Good plan, honey." It seemed as though this kid, my oldest, has been the adult in our family since she was twelve. I reminded her where the spare key to the back door was hidden and that in daylight, she could get into the house. I didn't want her crawling over the garden wall after midnight.

"Mom loves you. Text me when you are safe at Julie's," I said. "Barring any unforeseen problems or the bad weather, we will be home by midafternoon."

"Okay, Mom. Be safe. I love you."

I set the phone on the nightstand, lay back down, still trembling, tossing and turning, until I received my daughter's *okay* text. By 4:00 a.m., I couldn't lie in bed any longer. I moved about the darkened room, dressed, and walked to the lobby to fetch coffee.

My movements were jerky, uncoordinated, unfamiliar like a marionette with strings attached to my limbs, a puppeteer manipulating my actions. I meandered through the lobby of the hotel as if I were dreaming. It took what seemed like hours to assemble four cups of coffee, add the creamer, affix the lids, and line them up on a tray. My arms were heavy, and my legs didn't cooperate as I moved erratically back across the lobby, trying to balance the coffee. I stumbled through the door to our room and nearly dropped the tray. Paul caught my elbow, grabbed the tray, and set it on the desk as I plopped down on the chair nearest the door.

"We are up awfully early," he stammered.

"Couldn't sleep, need to get home," I replied weakly.

"Are you okay?" he questioned.

"No. But I will be. I just want to be home."

Paul cast a wary eye in my direction as he turned to retrieve two hot, steaming cups of coffee, thrusting one in my direction. We sipped in silence, waiting on the caffeine to work its magic.

Traffic thickened just south of Dalton as we neared the northern suburbs of Atlanta. I've ridden through Atlanta several times on two wheels; that morning, I was hyperaware of the fast-moving vehicles *whooshing* past me. I felt as though I was standing still and Bessie could topple over any second, so I focused on the vehicle in front of me to ground myself in the present moment.

Attempting to connect tactilely with my bike, I gripped the handlebars, but I couldn't. The disconnected feeling I experienced in the hotel lobby had returned tenfold. I started to hyperventilate, fearing I will lose it right there on busy I-75. I neared an exit, managed to cross a lane of traffic, exited, and made an immediate right turn into a gas station.

I couldn't breathe, my chest was constricted, and tiny pinpoints of white light were stabbing at my peripheral vision. I barely got the kickstand down and off Bessie before my knees buckled, and I slumped to the greasy pavement. Paul pulled in a few seconds later to find me crumpled near my bike, trying to breathe. This poor man had been responsible for helping me keep it together for over a week now. Paul had never seen me NOT be able to handle my bike in adverse weather conditions or heavy traffic. He was just as alarmed and perplexed as I was. While I gasped for breath, he asked, "Should I call 911?"

"NO! I'll be fine," I lied. "Water. I need something cold."

Paul hurried into the convenience store to buy water while I tried to breathe evenly and bring my heart rate down. In hindsight, I believe I experienced a panic attack, which was made worse by a lack of sleep and very little food. My system was running on caffeine and nicotine. Sipping the cold water helped to calm me.

I looked up at Paul as I was still kneeling on the ground, fearful my legs wouldn't support me, and said, "You will have to take the lead through Atlanta. I'll follow you."

"Are you sure you're going to be okay? You nearly fell through the room with the coffee and now this. I think we need to call 911."

"No!" I said, emphatically. "Give me a few minutes; then you lead, I will follow. Don't make any quick lane changes and keep checking your side mirror," I instructed.

I figured if I passed out in the swift-moving swarm of Atlanta traffic, there wouldn't be enough left of Bessie and me to scrape off the pavement. I didn't confess to Paul that I had considered that possibility before I asked him to lead; if he were in the lead, he wouldn't be affected if I went down.

I stood up, praying the synapses would fire and send the correct messages to my legs, willing them to function properly. I took several more calming breaths, and my heart rate returned to normal as I straddled Bessie. Paul eased out of the gas station parking lot, I followed, keeping my eyes glued to his back, ignoring the rush of traffic. My wingman became my point-man through Atlanta and beyond.

We stopped only for fuel, eager to get home. During one of those stops, I felt confident enough to take the lead, relegating Paul to wingman status again; a look of relief flooded his face as he realized I might be all right after all.

The day was long, the heat kicked into high gear, and the threat of scattered thunderstorms plagued our journey again. As we exited the Florida Turnpike and turned south on US 27, thirty miles from home, the sky grew dark with roiled clouds. I pulled over, just past the toll booth, to cover my pack with the rain protector. I looked at Paul and said defiantly, "I refuse to put that rain gear on again." Rain mingled with sweat left us both damp; our clothes stuck to our bodies like Saran Wrap. Paul looked weary, certainly not a man refreshed from his would-be vacation.

"Okay. We're close to home."

I climbed back on Bessie, looked over at Paul and said, "I ain't skeered. Are you skeered?" Which is our favorite saying for when we face adverse weather conditions on the bikes.

He chuckled, and replied, "Nah, I ain't skeered either. After what we've been through this past week? Let's hit it!" And off we roared into the approaching storm.

The temperature dropped rapidly, the wind kicked across the road, and rain slammed into us. The black sky surrounded us with a quick, violent Florida storm that pops up unexpectedly and is over in thirty minutes. The chilly rain stung my unprotected skin, but it was refreshing in a morbid sense; a baptism of sorts, a renewal: *I am ALIVE!*

I returned to my ordinary world after venturing into the extraordinary world. I survived the trials and tribulations of an unforgettable week and came back, forever changed.

As Paul and I turned into our subdivision, the rain ceased, the sun appeared, and a dazzling, full-spectrum rainbow arched gracefully over the golf course. Its colors were strikingly vivid against a blue canvas sky. I was stunned. I stopped, just past the guard shack, to snap a picture. In Genesis, the rainbow became a sign of renewal, a covenant from God after the flooding of the Earth. I'm not sure what transpired between God and Noah on that day long ago, but I accepted the rainbow I saw as a message from my dad: "I'm glad you have made it home safely. I'm here, I will always be here, and I love you."

My daughter heard our bikes round the corner; she was standing in the garage, door up, ready to greet the weary travelers. I pulled the bike into the garage, climbed off, and dissolved into my daughter's arms, a teary mess, blabbing about the rainbow.

She patted my back and murmured, "Mom, you need some rest." I couldn't have agreed with her more.

AFTERMATH: STUCK IN NEUTRAL

Courage is not simply one of the virtues,
but the form of every virtue at the testing point.

– C.S. Lewis, *The Screwtape Letters*

I USUALLY EXPERIENCE A POST-ROAD TRIP DEPRESSION OF sorts. The anticipation of departure subsides, the thrill of the adventure is just a memory, and I must settle into my everyday life until I can begin to plan the next trip. During the days following my return from Indiana, more than usual, I felt a crush of gloominess after burying our dad in the middle of that summer's excursion. I recall those moments even now.

Bessie sits in the darkened garage, gleaming after her post-road-trip detailing and tune-up, awaiting my attention. But I am not inclined to ride anytime soon. Paul is on his way to the airport, headed for his usual two- or three-week stint on a project somewhere in Texas. I am alone for the first time in three weeks. The silence screams.

If I believe the words of the eulogy I wrote—and I do whole-heartedly—then I am in the throes of practicing acceptance. I remain bewildered by our dad's choice to take his life. I awake each morning of my life with gratitude in my heart. I am thankful for the simplicity of a strong cup of coffee sweetened with my favorite creamer and anticipate my day ahead, regardless of the responsibilities, or perhaps because of them. I cherish my children, my partner, my friends, and my students.

At the end of a day of teaching, I look forward to returning to a beautiful home, filled with treasured possessions, laughter, and love. I eagerly anticipate the next ride on Bessie, the next book I choose to get lost in, or the next blank page I will fill up with my writing. I cannot fathom the hopelessness required to check out of all of this by taking my own life. It saddens and bewilders me deeply to think Dad felt he had nothing to live for.

My life today is a direct result of the choices I have made along the way. In my early, drinking years, my judgments were often devastating, and the consequences far-reaching. But, in these last three decades of my life, I have become better at making decisions, and the results have given me a happy, productive life that feeds my soul.

Our dad lacked the courage to make the necessary decisions after Mom died to assure his happiness.

I saw my dad as a strong man when, in truth, he was weak in spirit. He sought answers from a God he could not honor. My desperation to unchain myself from addiction was not possible until I trusted in a God of my understanding and practiced absolute honesty.

I saw my dad as a brave man, willing to take on a woman he loved and another man's child all those years ago when, in truth, his soul had become spineless. How many times did I straighten my spine and walk tall regardless of my fears because my young daughters needed me? Taking my own life to relieve the pain of living was never an option. I saw Dad as a kind man when, in truth, he inflicted the cruelest kind of pain upon his children and grandchildren by taking his own life.

I saw my dad as an honest man when, in truth, his deceit had us all fooled. He was my hero, a hero who could not save himself. If only he could have shared his pain with us while he was alive, we would have understood and not thought less of him for it. I will never know what his truth was, but if I ground my bewilderment in the nuggets of truth I have experienced; they will appease my shattered heart.

Since coming home, I have been stuck in neutral. I find it difficult to gain momentum, to move forward. I sit, listen to music, and become sad. I read and become sad. Writing, however, gives me solace.

I will miss my dad's cards; he sent them almost weekly. Not just to me, but to everyone in his life. Greeting cards with their motivational and inspirational verses were small gifts that arrived in my mailbox. I am brokenhearted as I imagine my tall, strong dad standing at a display of greeting cards, carefully selecting each one for a specific person who required cheering up or a reminder to let them know he was thinking about them. But, ironically, he was a lonely man, weighted by hopelessness, selecting a card to send encouragement to another. Why didn't he reach out to my siblings or me? Three children and six beautiful grandchildren would have loved to comfort him, to lend support, to spend time with him.

It takes courage to say, "I need help;" this admission was key to my recovery.

My dad's cards always seemed to arrive at a time when I needed that extra *oomph* in my week. His uplifting words bolstered my spirit and told me I was loved. I realize now there will be no card or words to buoy me up when I feel the most depressed, and my spirit is lagging.

I will miss the weekly phone calls to Dad. He was my biggest fan. Although I had not seen him since last summer's road trip, we frequently talked—the last time right before I left for Colorado. I told him I would have the Go-Pro camera attached to the bike for the journey up Pikes Peak; he said he would be eager to see the video when Paul and I arrived in Indiana. He would never see it. I will never look at it, and I have tucked the GoPro into the bottom drawer of my camera cabinet.

Our frequent phone conversations centered around my work, his grandchildren, my travels, and the weather. He never talked about himself. I wish he had. We ended each conversation with *I love you*, and for that, I am grateful. I will always keep his phone number with our picture in my Favorites phone list.

Our dad exemplified the virtues of hard work, integrity, fortitude, self-control, encouragement, fairness, and truthfulness. It gives me comfort to think that at some point in our lives, every one of us children adopted these same virtues and, in turn, instilled them in our children—Dad's grandchildren.

During the difficult times in my life, Dad always reminded me that I was the resilient one—the one who met adversity and challenges head-on, refusing to let anything get me down.

How do you convince your adult self that you are resilient when you now feel you lack that virtue? If the testing of human virtues lies in one's courage, then I am at the testing point in my resiliency. Even while stuck in neutral, I hear Dad's voice, and I know I possess something he did not: the courage to go on living.

SOMEWHERE I'VE NEVER BEEN

Nothing is so painful to the human mind as a great and sudden change.

– Mary Wollstonecraft Shelley, *Frankenstein*

ON THE DAY PAUL AND I LEFT DENVER FOR OUR cross-country ride to attend my dad's funeral in Indiana, I accepted a phone call from the principal of the middle school in Central Florida who had interviewed me the previous week via Skype. Paul and I were sitting in Denny's restaurant just outside of Denver having breakfast, and I mouthed to Paul, *It's about the job,* as I walked outside to talk. The principal offered me the non-classroom, literacy coaching position that involved working with teachers. We had previously discussed the details, so I was ready to accept his offer.

In hindsight, it was the most unfortunate decision of my entire teaching career. At that moment, I considered the offer a positive turn of events in an otherwise dismal set of circumstances. I perceived the new position as a "challenge," although I was warned it might be an impossible challenge. I believed the task would also distract me from the loss I felt, but my hopes turned out to be the two most pernicious reasons to accept the new job.

I showed up for my fresh challenge a week ahead of my contract time to become familiar with the school, the administration, and my responsibilities. When the principal showed me to my office, my heart sank. Although it was spacious and took up an entire corner of the media center—it was a former photography classroom with a dark-room—every conceivable inch of floor and counter space was stacked with boxes of books. Even the former darkroom was packed to the ceiling with classroom sets of novels.

A narrow path wound through towering boxes of books that rose to the ceiling; dusty boxes were piled up on a desk as well. To my aston-ishment, the principal admitted the books "had not been used in quite a while," and that I could "do what I wanted with them."

Instead of preparing for my assigned responsibilities, I spent the entire week digging out from under the waste and sloth of my prede-cessor to have enough working space. It would take a full school year before I cleared the room of all the outdated textbooks and distributed the novels to classrooms. Hindsight being twenty-twenty, I realized much too late that the seemingly impossible condition of this office was a metaphor for the job itself.

Virtually the entire administration was not just new to the school, but new to the responsibilities of operating a school efficiently. They were hired to improve the school rankings which a previous admin-istration had allowed to sink to a failing status with the state. Like me, the other new staff members were optimistic about our ability to pull test scores up and elevate the school to a passing grade.

I was hired because of my track record of raising reading scores in my classroom as well as my credentials. I shared the administration's vision of cultivating a learning culture based on improved literacy skills.

Clearing space and moving out the boxes in my office proved to be the least arduous task those first few weeks. Faculty that had remained after the administrative shake-up was skeptical of the new leadership and downright hostile at times. Fifty percent of the freshly-hired faculty were inexperienced teachers, most lacking an actual degree in education. It would be my job to help them acclimate to the curriculum and train them "how to teach." By the time the three-day Labor Day weekend rolled around, I was ready for a break. I needed time in the saddle to gain a fresh perspective for a job that, by all accounts, would kick my ass. I looked forward to the *thump, thump, thump* of my Harley-Davidson and the wind in my face.

I planned a short trip for "somewhere I've never been," though my niece Kiley liked to say, "Aunt Debi, you've been everywhere!"

I reminded her, "No, I haven't been EVERYWHERE, but it's on my list!"

Paul had not cruised too many of my favorite Florida back roads, so any direction I led him in made him happy. That holiday weekend, I chose the interior of Florida; locals, as well as tourists, would be packing the beaches, grabbing the sunshine, surf, and sand of the last, long weekend of the summer.

I targeted Ocala and the surrounding area, which was an exit I had passed numerous times off I-75 but had never spent any time exploring. Paul and I didn't even discuss the details. At dinner on Friday, he asked, "Where are we going?"

"Ocala and Cedar Key."

He said, "Okay," and that was the extent of our planning.

Come Saturday morning, we tossed a few days' gear in our saddle-bags and headed north on SR 27. I didn't check the map; I intended to stay on back roads until we saw Ocala.

A few miles beyond Clermont, I veered onto CR 561 through scenic Lake County. I'm always amazed to see the gently rolling hills in this area where some of the state's best secondary roads are located. We connected with SR 19 outside of Tavares, looped around spring-fed Lake Eustis, where a natural canopy of oak trees sheltered us from the hot sun. We picked up SR 19 again to head north to the Ocala National Forest. Although it was the last weekend of summer, the Florida sun was broiling in a clear blue sky with little wind to relieve the oppressive humidity.

SR 19 ambled through sleepy little Florida towns like Eustis, Umatilla, and Altoona, where oaks grew thick near the highway, and Spanish moss dripped from their massive limbs that stretched over the road, offering cooling shade as we rode by. The landscape was void of fast-food restaurants and hotel chains. Miniature town squares were the source of social networking. I had never traveled these two-lane highways, and I was thrilled to discover another piece of the Sunshine State that was not thick with tourists. Paul and I encountered several other bikers, which told us we were on the right path.

The Ocala National Forest begins outside of Altoona, and SR 19 turns into Florida Black Bear Scenic Byway. The forest is thick with the Florida black bear; however, at the time of day we were traveling with temperatures in the nineties, I was confident the chances of encountering a bear were slim.

Our destination was the Don Garlits Museum of Drag Racing, right off Interstate 75. In his youth, Paul spent time on the drag racing circuit with his brother-in-law who raced alcohol funny cars. Both of us enjoy auto racing of any type; if it involves vehicles and goes fast, we're in! The Garlits' museum holds a history of the sport and the Garlits' classic car collection—a wonderful bonus for us.

Traveling SR 40 between Silver Springs and Ocala is like stepping back fifty years in time. Silver Springs State Park and its famous glass-bottom boats have attracted tourists since the 1870s when Florida was considered wild swampland. The park still advertises itself as Florida's First Tourist Attraction, where visitors still marvel at the underwater life of the crystal-clear springs as they peer through the boats' glass bottoms. Mom-and-pop hotels dot the roadside; neon signs softly beckon weary travelers as they have done for decades. There was a noticeable absence of fast-food restaurants and hotel chains here, too, as if the locals preferred to be linked with the past instead of catapulted into the current century.

Ramshackle barbeque joints—the scent of chargrilled goodness wafting from their outdoor grills—intermingled with weathered seafood shacks, all locally owned, and all seemed to have stood their ground for quite some time.

Our hotel was just off I-75, and I was reluctant to leave the area for the hustle and bustle of interstate commerce. However, one of the perks of Paul's job is his accumulation of "points" with several major hotel chains, which translates to free lodging. I was pleased to find the Hampton Inn nearly empty; Paul and I appeared to be the only travelers there. We stowed our gear, I plugged the address of the museum into my iPhone maps, and we were off to see the Drag Racing Wizard.

To say "Big Daddy" Don Garlits is a legend is like saying "Steve Jobs was good with technology," or "Bill Gates knows a thing or two about software," or "Leonardo da Vinci was a decent sculptor." We know those last three people were not just successful in their chosen field— they *defined* the field. And, Don Garlits defined the sport of drag racing.

He won his first major race in 1955, the year I was born. His swamp rat series of thirty-four hand-fabricated black race cars carried him to 144 national event wins and seventeen world championship titles. Big Daddy's living legacy and race car design innovations are so significant that his record-breaking Swamp Rat XXX is enshrined in the Smithsonian Museum of American History. Garlits was the first person to break the 200-miles-per-hour barrier in a gas-powered dragster in 1964 and later broke the 250-miles- per-hour barrier as well.

Born in 1932 in Tampa, Florida, Garlits still resides, as of 2018, in a modest home on the property where the museum sits. I experienced the thrill of watching Garlits race at an Indianapolis national drag racing competition when I was a teenager.

The museum is a cavernous treasure trove of drag-racing memorabilia; it's like the Louvre in Paris—impossible to absorb in one day. Paul and I did our best, however, moving with awe from one exhibit to another. We *oohed* and *aahed* at the photos, the cars, the gear, and the memories. Our conversation was limited to short, declarative sentences: "Remember this?" "Did you see him race?" "Wow, I remember...."

We spent an hour or two in the main museum, then stopped in the gift shop on our way out. I purchased a black and white signed photo of Shirley Muldowney, the first female to be licensed by the National Hot Rod Association (NHRA) in 1965 and the first to drive a top-fuel dragster. Muldowney, known as the First Lady of Drag Racing, won a total of eighteen NHRA national events. She paved the way for women, such as Brittany Force, who was the 2017 NHRA Drag Racing Series Top Fuel dragster champion, to dominate in a predominantly male sport. Clutching my prized souvenir—it hangs in my office today next to the signed lithograph by Willie G. Davidson—Paul and I walked next door to the Classic Car Collection, housed in a separate building adjacent to the museum.

The antique car collection literally represents the history of the American automobile. The immense building is stuffed to the rafters with every form of memorabilia a car buff could imagine. Display cases are filled with antique tools, oil cans, car parts, and accessories. Posters and garage signs document the history of the auto industry as did an incredible display of photography. I spent a good hour inspecting the photos while Paul ambled up and down the rows of classic cars, speechless in his admiration of the extensive collection. Although some of the vehicles had been donated, Garlits owned most of them. Satiated with our racing and classic car fix, Paul and I returned to the hotel for a relaxing evening in the spacious suite Hampton Inn put us in for the night.

A visit to Ocala, the Horse Capital of the World, is not complete without a tour of its famous horse country. It is a steel horse I ride; therefore, I'm not familiar with equine terms nor am I fascinated with the flesh and blood animals. I read an article in one of the hotel magazines that the Ocala's horse business, which includes breeding, training centers, and equine sporting events, is a seven-billion-dollar industry.

Ocala has served as the breeding and training ground for some of the best and strongest racehorses anywhere. (At the mention of "race" horses, Paul perked up). And Ocala has a legacy of winners. It boasts forty-seven national champions, six Kentucky Derby winners—we admit to being fans of the Derby and subsequent Triple Crown races— and twenty-three Breeders' Cup winners.

We thought about taking a customized tour of a breeding facility, visiting the museum, riding horseback, touring the Olympic Equestrian Training Facility, or experiencing the zip-line. We even anticipated rubbing elbows with a few horse-loving celebrities or the wealthy residents who lay claim to fortunes like Campbell's Soup and Firestone. But, we said no to all the above. Neither Paul nor I wanted to know that much about horses, and I prefer to enjoy the surrounding countryside with its natural order and beauty astride Bessie.

On Sunday morning, we backtracked to SR 40 to pick up CR 314, which took us through the western edge of the Ocala National Forest. Massive farms that cater to the equestrian set lined the edge of the forest; we noticed training centers for jumpers and racehorses. The farms were immaculate—impossibly green pastures enclosed by brilliant white fences and punctuated with an oval dirt track. The term *farm* is a bit of a misnomer; I suppose they "grow" horses. The horse "barns" resembled upscale hotels while opulent "estate" homes anchored the entire idyllic scene.

SR 315 was lined with stately oaks; the Spanish moss shielded us from the sun as we looked out over the pastures, where horses grazed lazily on the sweet Bahia grass. One or two lifted their heads in curiosity as we idled past. Except for a pickup truck or two hauling hay, we were the only vehicles on the back roads. I wondered what the crowd was like at the zip-line.

At random, deserted intersections, I made left turns, hoping to end up approximately where we started. I am never lost on two wheels, and if I am unsure of my whereabouts, my philosophy is to keep making left turns. Eventually, I connected with SR 24 and headed due west to Cedar Key and left the well-ordered equestrian landscape behind.

In Levy County, when you pass the outpost at Otter Creek, you know you are about twenty miles from Cedar Key and on the only road that goes into and out of the tiny island. The Cedar Keys are named for the red juniper tree and are primarily made up of several tiny islands that are migratory bird sanctuaries with hiking trails and a museum. The small fishing village of Cedar Key has under a thousand year-round residents, most of whom make their living from fishing and tourism.

I have visited Cedar Key on several occasions and not once have I encountered the clog of traffic and tourists that is characteristic of most Florida coastal villages. Nature lovers visit to hike the trails or kayak in the calm waters of the Gulf of Mexico. It seems to be a popular destination for bikers as the ride to this part of Florida is wide open countryside with very little traffic.

There were no large hotel chains, only mom-and-pops, and bed-and-breakfasts; my favorite is the quaint Cedar Key Bed and Breakfast, only a block from the waterfront. The oldest hotel, Island Hotel and Restaurant, was built in the mid-1800s and brags about their haunted rooms in their advertisements. It is one of the few restaurants in town where you will find cloth napkins—and a piano bar. Restaurants are locally owned, some funkier than others, all serving homemade food, and the fresh catch of the day; clams are harvested locally.

We rumbled into the heart of the village, angled into a parking space—it was hotter than Hades that day—and decided to eat lunch at Steamers Bar and Grill. The tiny waterfront smelled of salty, fresh seafood with the distinctive aroma of "something fried," wafting from the nearby restaurants. Our table by the window afforded us a stunning view of the Gulf of Mexico, and I was pleased to find the Rock and Roll Cowboy as the live entertainment. The Cowboy plays an eclectic set of rock and country, of course! He was amazingly good and made the hungry diners forget about the especially slow service. However, if a fast-paced environment is what you seek, you would be in the wrong place. Cedar Key is as laid-back as it gets: no hurry, no fuss, no worries. The fish tacos and grouper sandwich were worth the wait. Reluctantly, Paul and I climbed back on the bikes, did a quick tour of the island, and made for home.

As we journeyed south, I relished the new experiences Paul and I had enjoyed on the long Labor Day weekend. I calculated that I had discovered at least a dozen new roads. I also realized I did not look forward to returning to school on Tuesday. Each time I gave thought to my new job, my stomach churned, and a feeling of apprehension crept over me. I found myself "dismissing" the feelings and trying valiantly to pull the positive aspects of the job into the forefront. I had accepted a challenge, and I was determined to meet with success.

ALOHA TO YOU TOO!

A man who procrastinates in his choosing will inevitably have his choice
made for him by circumstance."

– Hunter S. Thompson, *The Proud Highway:*
Saga of a Desperate Southern Gentleman, 1955-1967

WHEN I REALIZED THAT TURNING SIXTY YEARS OLD WAS
not fatal, my only source of discontent that year was my job. It was killing me—literally. The stress of the daily two-hour commute coupled
with the school's toxic environment deposited a layer of flub on my
abdomen, and my blood pressure skyrocketed—I fight a genetic predis-
position for heart disease. Most days I arrived home after a nerve-jan-
gling trip in near tears, incapable of doing anything but plopping down
in front of the TV or reading a good book. The only thing that kept me
going to the end of the school year was our planned bike trip to Nova

Scotia to ride the Cabot Trail. It was a trip that had been seven years in the making after the ill-fated attempt with Butch.

Serendipity intervened in late May when Paul returned home from his usual two-week absence and announced his next assignment was in Pearl Harbor on the island of Oahu.

"I have to be there on June 16. Will you be finished with school?" he asked.

"Yes!"

"Do you want to go?"

"I can be packed in twenty minutes." About five seconds later, I realized the dates might interfere with our trip to Nova Scotia.

"Will we be back in time to go on our planned trip?"

"Yes. I am scheduled for fourteen days at Pearl Harbor."

I quickly did the math: in Oahu for fourteen days and then home for three days before we left again close to the Independence Day holiday. It was doable.

Although I didn't view a trip to Hawaii as "peculiar" as Vonnegut's character Bokonon described unexpected travel, I saw it as an opportunity to soothe my ravaged soul. Paul would be working each day, and I would be ensconced at the Marriott Resort on Waikiki Beach in Honolulu, left to my own devices. Not a bad start to my summer break. The only hitch was that I wouldn't be available for a data-training event my administration suggested I attend, but their schedule was outside my contract time and for me to go was entirely voluntary. Hmm. Waikiki Beach for two weeks *or* three days of looking at data? It was a no-brainer, and I informed my principal the following Monday. In hindsight, it was the beginning of the end of our working relationship and my allegiance to his administration.

As this book is about my travel on two wheels, I relay my Hawaiian trip story only because Paul and I had every intention of renting motorcycles on the island. But as my Grandma used to say, "The road to hell is paved with good intentions." And our decision *not* to rent bikes is my one real regret that summer.

Traveling with a frequent-business-flyer like Paul has its perks; we were bumped to first class for the long flight from Orlando to Los Angeles, then again for the equally long flight from Los Angeles to Honolulu. The ride from the airport to Waikiki Beach—west of downtown Honolulu—gave us a glimpse of the island and the densely-populated city of Honolulu. It reminded me of Miami, only with an Asian influence. The Marriott Resort sat directly across the street from the world-famous Waikiki Beach, and our balcony room offered a sweeping view of the beach and Diamond Head in the distance. Not a bad place to hang out for two weeks.

I planned a trip to the Big Island, Hawaii's largest island, for the only weekend Paul had off from work. We planned to rent bikes for a day before taking a guided "circle tour" of the island, which included Volcano National Park. During my first week on Oahu, I kissed Paul goodbye in the morning and embarked on my solo sightseeing tour of Honolulu.

I started each morning by walking four or five miles in various directions from the hotel; Honolulu is a busy city that seems never to sleep. My walks gave me a glimpse of the uglier side of what is otherwise an island paradise: a plentiful homeless population who had set up living quarters on the beach and lots of copious drug users right out in the open.

I bought a map and a city bus pass, and, armed with a list of must-see attractions, busied myself with sightseeing until early afternoon. Paul returned to the hotel around 3:00 p.m. to find me poolside, where he joined me, and we relaxed and soaked up the tropical sun until dinnertime. On my forays into the neighborhood, I scoped out where the locals ate, so we could avoid the obscenely priced restaurants along the main tourist drag.

It didn't take long to establish a routine, and we quickly fell under the spell of the constant ocean breeze and a balmy seventy-five-degree temperature. The hotel staff pampered us, and Kona coffee with delicious confections called malasadas—a donut-like pastry filled with tropical tasting creams, deep-fried, and dusted with cinnamon and sugar—seduced our palates. For the first time in a long time, I honestly felt relaxed.

Paul and I flew to the Kona International Airport on the Big Island on Friday and settled into a gorgeous hotel perched on a rocky cliff overlooking the azure waters of the Pacific. The Harley-Davidson dealership was within walking distance of our hotel. We planned to rent bikes for the afternoon as our guided tour of the island on Saturday would take up the entire day. As Paul and I trudged up the hill toward the dealership, ominous dark clouds formed in the distance; it produced the only rain or inclement weather we experienced in the two weeks we were in Hawaii.

I had refrained from reserving bikes in advance because Paul's work schedule sometimes included weekends. We inquired at the rental counter whether two bikes were available for the afternoon as thunder clapped in the distance. They told us yes, they could put us on two bikes—no problem. Then the guy behind the counter gave the cost. Over $2,300 for four hours! A significant chunk of that cost was "insurance" that would be credited back to us but not for two weeks or more.

Paul and I looked at each other, considered the cash outlay, and decided it wasn't worth the cost to ride ninety miles across the island and about one hundred and twenty-five miles around it—with an imminent storm on the horizon.

As I write this, I am still kicking myself for that decision for the following summer, I would click off riding a motorcycle in all forty-nine states instead of fifty. Except for Hawaii. But, hindsight is always twenty-twenty. Paul and I bought T-shirts at the dealership and walked back down the hill to enjoy dinner while we watched a tropical downpour from the verandah of the restaurant.

The tour of the island the next day was fabulous. Our tour guide, a young teacher who made extra cash in the summer introducing tourists to her adopted state, was not only knowledgeable but also personable as well. I wish I had a two-wheeled version of the sights we saw, but alas, we were escorted around the island on four wheels with eight other tourists.

Sunday afternoon came, and we flew back to Honolulu; Paul returned to work on Monday. I spent the second week of our stay alternating between the beach and the pool. I took hula lessons, learned how to make a traditional Hawaiian lei, and finished reading two books while lounging by the pool with lunch served poolside—along with a steady flow of sweet tea.

What are my final thoughts on our impromptu Hawaiian vacation? Been there, done that. The only reason I will return is to check off that fiftieth state from my Bike-It! list! The islands are breathtakingly beautiful, and the people we met were warm, friendly, and welcoming. It is a costly place to vacation, however, and probably an expensive place to live.

Paul and I started our day to return home beachside with Kona coffee and malasadas just as the sun was beginning to rise. We hopped on a plane at noon to head west and saw the sunset from first class as we approached Catalina Island and Los Angeles International Airport. We boarded another flight a few hours later and saw the sun peek above the horizon as we flew into Orlando—all within twenty hours.

My toughest choice during our flight home was whether I wanted stir-fry beef or potato gnocchi for dinner and which of three toppings I preferred on my ice cream sundae. All this while hurtling six hundred miles per hour through the stratosphere! When people complain about the "inconveniences" of air travel, I want to look at them and say, "Relax. And try to grasp how amazing all of this is!" I hope I never lose the child-like fascination and excitement of wonders like air travel, space shuttles, my iPhone—and of course, Bessie.

NEVER HESITATE TO RUN THE BREAK-DOWN LANE

Confidence comes not from always being right
but from not fearing to be wrong.

– Peter T. McIntyre, artist

BEFORE A ROAD TRIP, ANTICIPATION ALWAYS KEEPS ME from a sound sleep. That and two cats piled on the bed! Nevertheless, on Wednesday, July 1, Paul and I were up at 4:30 a.m., and our bikes were packed and ready to go. Our goal was to reach Portland, Maine, by Friday—1,500 miles on a Fourth of July weekend. It was the only weekend Paul could see both of his boys; one resided in Maine, the other in Massachusetts. I understood how special it was to have both of your children in the same zip code at the same time.

Paul was also "road captain" on this trip, meaning he mapped out the way we would go. It was the first time I had agreed to allow anyone to choose my route, and the decision wasn't without its rough patches between us. It takes me about a hundred miles to shake the knot of anxiety that accompanies the anticipation of a road trip. Paul chose all interstates since we needed to click off 500 miles each day to reach Portland by Friday afternoon; this was my least favorite kind of road trip. After our visit in Portland with his sons, we were going to head up to Nova Scotia at a much more leisurely pace on secondary roads.

The weather was hot and muggy, but the overcast skies made the heat bearable. Traffic was thick, but that is what you expect when you embark on a road trip over a holiday weekend. The best bumper sticker I saw—yes, I read bumper stickers, mud flaps, billboards, semi-trailer advertisements, graffiti, or anything to keep me occupied on interstate travel—was on a Sebring convertible: "Tofu Slut!" Was that a vegan with a sense of humor? Halfway through the first 501 miles we had covered, I was thinking that the three short days we had at home following our return from Hawaii were not quite enough to repair my jet lag and find my center. Embarking on a grueling road trip with very little sleep was not always the best choice. Coupled with my angst over starting another school year at a job I have come to abhor weighed heavily on my mind.

We stopped for the night somewhere in South Carolina.

My alarm the next morning was like fingernails on a chalkboard at 5:30 a.m.; Paul and I were sleeping like the dead when it went off, signaling it was time to hit the road. I loathe this kind of two-wheel riding, which is reminiscent of the hauling-ass travel from sunup to sundown with Butch.

Over breakfast in the hotel lobby, I pulled out the atlas and took another look at the route Paul had marked. When I first saw that it took us up through Pennsylvania, I told Paul it was a bad idea (See previous chapters for my experience on Pennsylvania roads). We had discussed other options before we left home, but they added time to the trip, which would have prevented us from reaching Portland on the designated date to meet Paul's boys.

As I slugged back my third cup of coffee, I looked at the map again, hoping a quicker route around Pennsylvania would magically appear. It didn't. I grabbed a coffee to go, and we secured our bags on the bikes. Following Paul out of the hotel parking lot, I reluctantly segued into the thick stream of vehicles on the Interstate 81.

No more than fifty miles into Pennsylvania, traffic came to a complete standstill on I-81. As Paul and I inched our way forward, unaware of two separate accidents involving tractor trailers within the next eighty miles that had caused the traffic snarl, my I-told-you-so attitude kicked into high gear. We were baking in the heavy leather we had donned at 6:00 a.m. to ward off the chill. The morning sun had ramped up the heat.

I signaled to Paul to pull over into the break-down lane so we could shed the leather at least; it didn't look like we were going anywhere, anytime soon.

We parked the bikes, flashers on, and peeled off our leather coats and stuffed them in our saddlebags. I refrained from mumbling my I-told-you-so speech but announced to Paul that we would ride in the break-down lane to the next exit, which, according to my iPhone GPS, was a half-mile from where we had stopped. From there, we could take a back road around the interstate until we found an opening to get back on. He looked at me warily and shrugged; Paul is a rule-follower; I'm not. Riding the break-down lane is against the law, and he was going to follow the law. Within minutes, a state trooper pulled up behind us and stepped out of his car.

"Is everything okay here?" asked the officer.

"Yes, officer, we just needed to shed the heavy leather. Any idea how far this traffic is backed up?" Paul replied.

"There has been a fatal accident about six miles up the road; you will be here for some time before it's cleared."

I stood silent with the thought bubble popping out of my head: *Like hell we will!*

As the officer started to walk back to his car, Paul asked, "Sir, let me ask you something."

I'm thinking, *No, no, no, don't ask him anything!*

"Would it be okay to ride the break-down lane to the next exit?"

Are you kidding me, Paul? You don't ask a state trooper for permission to break the law; you beg forgiveness afterward!

The trooper looked at us through his mirrored aviators and said, "No, I can't give you permission to do that."

"Okay, thank you, sir," Paul, the Boy Scout, replied as I smacked my forehead and did a serious eye-roll behind my own mirrored aviators. The trooper inched his vehicle across three lanes of clogged interstate, made a U-turn in the median and headed in the opposite direction.

I looked at Paul and said, "Why did you do that? There is an exit about a half mile up, and we can ride in this lane to get off this damn interstate."

"You heard the officer. We can't do that."

"I can! And I intend to. I'm not sitting here in the broiling sun indefinitely when we have two wheels that can get us off this clogged highway."

I strapped on my helmet and saddled Bessie. I looked at Paul and said, "Let's go! Either follow me or sit here. I'll let you know where I stop tonight." I fired up Bessie.

Riding in the break-down lane is never a good option; road junk can puncture a tire and, of course, it is illegal, so the prospect of a ticket is possible. I was willing to take both risks to expedite my travel. I cautiously moved Bessie forward, gazing down at the pavement to avoid any tire-puncturing debris. Paul remained by his bike.

Several stranded motorists rolled down their windows and yelled encouragement in my direction; fists pumped out of windows to show support for my daring to escape the tangle of traffic. Paul still stood by his bike. It wouldn't be the first time I had taken off on my own because of a difference of opinion with him; no doubt it wouldn't be the last either.

Bessie and I inched our way to the next exit, only to find it completely blocked with a tractor trailer, which was crossways on the off-ramp. How the driver got in that precarious position, I will never know. I stopped, kept Bessie idling, and surveyed my options. The truck driver got out, pointed to a strip off the pavement between his truck and the grass and said, "Come on! You can make it!" And, I did.

The exit had one lone gas station that was swamped with people needing fuel and a bathroom. I pulled into a parking space, joined the queue for the restroom, and waited. Nearly thirty minutes later, I walked out of the sweltering and smelly bathroom to see Paul's bike parked next to mine. He tromped out of the station with two bottles of water and a menacing look on his face.

"I see you decided to join me," I quipped, taking the bottle of water from him.

Before he could respond, I said, "This was the only choice if you intend to see your boys at the appointed time."

He couldn't argue with that, and I knew he didn't want a full-blown repeat of "Kansas" right here in the parking lot, surrounded by at least a hundred weary travelers. "I've checked the route, and this highway here"—gesturing to the secondary road in front of the gas station— "will take us at least twenty miles north along the interstate and around the congestion," I added. "As it is, we are not going to make it to Maine today, so you need to call Jay and let him know we have hit traffic and that we will be there tomorrow."

Paul still seemed to want to start an argument, but I wasn't in the mood. While he made a phone call, I finished drinking my water and strapped on my helmet.

Leaving the interstate snarl gave us the most fun we had that day. The secondary road that ran parallel with I-81 north was nirvana; rolling, twisty rural asphalt took us through lush farmland. We stayed on it for over an hour before I stopped and asked a farmer how to get back to the interstate. Not that I wanted to go, but we did have someplace to be. He directed us to SR 61 north that eventually hooked us back up with I-80. And, yes, we had skated around the traffic snafu. At least one of us had a smile on our face.

If I had been standing, not riding, I would have jumped for joy at the New York state line when we pulled into the welcome center; I was so happy to be out of Pennsylvania! Paul and I climbed wearily off the bikes, established an unspoken peace, and walked to the welcome center for refreshments. A veterans' group was selling drinks and fresh baked goods as a fundraiser. Paul handed them twenty dollars, and we scooped up the much-needed snacks with gusto—I didn't remember us eating lunch. We settled under an I- (heart)-NY sign to regroup. While devouring brownies and peanut butter cookies, we discussed our options and decided that when we ran out the three-fourths tank of gas we had, we would stop for the night.

Our tanks hit empty at a Best Western, three miles off I-88 in Cobleskill, New York. We had ridden well past our usual stopping time; the air cooled as the sun started to set.

As I stiffly climbed off Bessie while Paul checked us in, I glanced at my phone. It had taken us nine hours to travel 360 miles on bone-jarring, bladder-busting, frame-twisting, rim-bending, traffic-snarled Pennsylvania roads. I so badly wanted to have that I-told-you-so argument, but I took one look at Paul's weary face as he walked toward me and realized I would rather be happy than right. My wingman was as exhausted as I was. We were five hours from Paul's son's house in Maine. We should have been there that afternoon, but we would make it safely to his home before noon the next day.

EXTREME GEOGRAPHY

The real moment of success is not the moment
apparent to the crowd.

– George Bernard Shaw,

THE THREE DAYS WE SPENT WITH PAUL'S BOYS OUTSIDE OF
Old Orchard Beach, Maine, were all too short. I kept wondering why
Paul and I both chose to separate ourselves geographically from our
loved ones. It is a mysterious bond he and I share. Seeing him interact
with his youngest son, Jay, made me long for my younger child whom
I haven't seen in several years now. It's funny—both of our youngest
children are mini-versions of ourselves.

On Monday morning, June 7, 2015, after a leisurely breakfast, Paul
and I packed our bikes and headed to "down east" Maine. Our destination was West Quoddy Head, Maine, specifically the West Quoddy
Head Lighthouse, which is the easternmost point on the US mainland.

I am a self-professed "extreme geography" nut. I like seeking out the roadside oddities, the out-of-the-way places, and the unique travel locations on my journeys. Anyone can visit Arcadia National Park, but would you venture out to West Quoddy Head? The farthest point east in the United States? No. Most people don't. The effort adds another dimension to the travel itinerary.

When I started traveling extensively on two wheels a few years back, I came across a list of extreme points of the United States that fascinated me. After studying it, I realized I could check off a few of those points and vowed to pursue some of the other places on the list in my travels. The "points" on the list are designations for extreme places, elevations, and distances in the United States. North, south, east, and west extremes are determined by latitude and longitude—the prime meridian is the dividing line between east and west. Experts calculate the points on the extreme list three ways, most of which baffle but fascinate me nonetheless. While on the Big Island of Hawaii a week ago, I realized we were on the westernmost geographic center of the United States, and while in Hilo, we were at the southernmost place with a population over 25,000 in the fifty states. Not to worry, Key West, Florida. You are the southernmost incorporated place in the contiguous forty-eight states! On the long flight back from Hawaii, I perused the list to determine how many Paul and I could check off on our trip to Nova Scotia. Imagine my excitement when I saw West Quoddy Head in Maine!

From Old Orchard Beach, Paul and I planned to travel along Maine's coastal US 1 to Calais, Maine, where we would cross the border into Canada. Travel along the coastal road is picturesque but slow. Quaint little New England towns like Camden, Bucksport, and Freeport, the Yuppie Capital of the US and home of L. L. Bean retail store, dotted the highway.

Small fishing enclaves along the route suggested a serene but rugged coastal life; the salty smell of the ocean, sometimes frigid wind, rough seas, and the threat of violent storms told us much about the life there.

We stopped for lunch at a roadside lobster shack, which was painted a dazzling red with multi-colored buoys hung like garlands around the exterior. The scarlet crustaceans were cooked in large metal drums over an open fire and served whole or as po'boys: chunky, meaty lobster salad with similar ingredients you would find in tuna salad on a crusty, submarine-type roll. The po'boys' recipe varies with the region. I chose the sandwich, as I'm not fond of pulling my food apart (shellfish, chicken-on-the-bone, ribs, etc.) and fell in love with the sweetness of the lobster meat mingled with tangy relish and sauce on crusty bread. Paul and I chose one of the brightly painted picnic tables adjacent to the shack to sit and enjoy our lunch. The air was crisp, the sun warm, the breeze tinged with the salty smell of the ocean.

Somewhere near Whiting Maine, we exited US 1 to SR 189 to go out to South Lubec and West Quoddy Point. The area was remote, and the road fraught with frost heaves: after a winter freeze, the pavement buckles, creating speed-bump-like hazards. We had to slow the bikes to thirty miles per hour or risk severe damage to life and limb—not to mention motorcycle frames.

The temperature dramatically dropped as we neared the ocean; I consider any temp below seventy degrees *cold*, meaning this dip in temperature was frigid! I signaled to Paul that we needed to pull over; there were no commercial establishments and no other traffic, so the side of the road would have to do. Paul questioned my determination to reach the West Quoddy Head Lighthouse as we pulled our leather jackets and gloves out of the saddlebags; it was the first week in July! I kept thinking that *never* will I visit Maine in the dead of winter. We encountered one grocery-store-type wide spot in the road in a 200-mile ride; the landscape suggested a beautiful but rugged existence.

The route from Lubec became narrower, winding around low marshland—called bogs in this part of the country—and the salty, fecund smell tickled my nostrils. I didn't see any houses as we left the outskirts of Lubec. The last patch of the road leading down to the lighthouse was gravel! Holy crap! Bikes don't do well in gravel. It was one of those no-turning-back-now moments; we were committed. We slipped and slid into a parking area; two cars were in the tiny gravel lot with an honor system paybox. While Paul dropped six bucks—how he calculated our visit was worth that amount I will never know—into the slot, I was already halfway down the hill to the lighthouse. I didn't see any other visitors milling about, although the two cars in the parking area suggested otherwise.

The pristine white main house sat atop a rocky cliff several hundred feet above the water on the greenest patch of grass I had ever seen. A white picket fence etched a perfect square around the grass. It was like an oasis among the rocks. The lighthouse itself was initially commissioned by President Thomas Jefferson in 1808; the tower I stood in front of was built in 1858. Brilliant red and white candy stripes circled the tower's circumference with a solid black turret that housed the beacon.

The lighthouse, which guides ships through the fog and the Quoddy Narrows, was fully automated in 1988; therefore, no lighthouse keeper lives in the home, which now serves as the visitor center and museum. It stands on a patch of ground surrounded by a rocky, jagged coastline where the cold, gray Atlantic crashes relentlessly onto the shoreline even on a calm day. I can only imagine how brutal it is to live there when Mother Nature unleashes a genuine nor'easter that slams into Quoddy Point.

This easternmost point in the United States is a stark contrast to the warm, sparkling turquoise waters of the Pacific that slam the lava rock shoreline in Hilo, Hawaii. I stand amazed at the vast diversity of our country's landscapes and am grateful that I can experience the "extreme geography" it offers.

Unfortunately, the visitor center and museum were closed when Paul and I arrived. We walked around the perimeter of the compound, craning our necks to look up at the candy-striped lighthouse while waves thrashed on the rocks below.

It was late in the day; the sun was setting, and the cloudy sky was darkening to a leaden gray. With the waning sun, the temperature dropped even lower, and the brackish wind off the water added to the chill.

We didn't dawdle—mission had been accomplished. Paul and I paused halfway up the hill to our bikes, the picturesque lighthouse in the distance, and snapped a selfie. We had stood on the easternmost point of the United States just one week after standing on the westernmost point in the United States. I could check those two items off the Extreme Geography list!

I gave the map a quick check, looked warily at the *uphill* gravel road, and gave Paul a let's-do-this look. I decided the best approach was to get a decent running start and not let up on the throttle. It worked, albeit slippery, and we made it back to SR 189, the narrow road through the bogs.

Very shortly, though, we were stopped by construction—no, it was a BLASTING area right in the middle of a Maine woods. An odd, metallic-gun-powdery-woodsy smell permeated the area, along with enormous dust clouds from the stripped road. Times like these, you wish you had an off-road BMW instead of a big cruiser. We waited our turn with the few other vehicles on the narrow road to drive down the stripped-to-the-gravel roadbed, while crews dynamited out sections of the woods.

Paul and I cruised into Calais, Maine, in the nippy waning twilight. Our arms and shoulders ached from maneuvering the rugged roads, and we were hungry. My previous research indicated that the "best" hotel in Calais was the Calais Motor Inn. Several other bikes and a variety of work trucks were parked in the lot. We checked in—only seventy-nine dollars for a room—and the receptionist handed us actual room *keys*, not a plastic credit card thing, but a room key! I had not seen a room key since the seventies.

The downstairs pub was the best option for dinner, which was fine by us, as we were too tired to climb back on our bikes or walk into the small downtown area. Located on a lower, sub-level of the building, the pub's interior was dark, illuminated softly by the warm glow of neon beer signs festooning the walls. The crack of billiard balls and the tunes floating from the jukebox mingled with the muffled conversations of a few other diners created a welcome respite for dinner.

Paul and I ordered meatloaf with mashed potatoes, and while we relished the warm, comfort-food goodness of the meal, our conversation lulled. We focused our attention on the two men playing pool while we ate. One of the many things I love about being with Paul is our ability to say nothing and still be intimate. I could only guess he was thinking about his boys and his granddaughter. I didn't ask. I allowed him the space to savor the memories while they were still fresh.

A full tummy, a hot shower, and sleep refreshed us. The next day we crossed the Canadian-US border into St. Stephens, New Brunswick, Canada, just across the St. Croix River from Calais. It was a trip I had waited six years to finish.

CABOT TRAIL-PART I

I have travelled the globe. I have seen the Canadian and American
Rockies, the Andes and the Alps, the highlands of Scotland, but for
simple beauty, Cape Breton outrivals them all.

– Alexander Graham Bell

MORNING CAME TOO QUICKLY FOR OUR WEARY BODIES,
but the coffee was strong, and I couldn't deny my excitement of crossing a border I had attempted to do six years ago.

The overcast morning was chilly, the streets damp and slick from
an overnight drizzle. Paul and I wiped down our bikes, secured the
packs, and readied our passports. St. Stephen, New Brunswick, Canada,
lay directly across the St. Croix River from Calais, Maine. I pulled Bessie
up to the border guard's station, handed over my passport, and chirped,
"Good Morning!"

The border agent gave me a curt nod—no smile. After directing me to "take off your sunglasses, please," I got the third degree. It was my mirrored aviators; they unnerve some people.

"What brings you to Canada?"

Do you really want the dirty details of my last attempt to cross a border here?

"Where are you traveling from? Why were you in Maine for so long?" he queried.

I had extreme geography to see, and I kinda have to come this way to get to where I want to go in Canada.

"How long will you be in Canada? Where do you plan to stay?" Paul and I had no reservations for a hotel, so the guard was suspicious. With any border between countries, agents are on the alert for possible contraband.

By the time the agent stamped and handed my passport back to me, I felt as though I could do any sort of bad things, and, apparently, my appearance suggested the same. Paul followed behind me and handed over his passport; the agent stamped it, nodded, and Paul, the Boy Scout, was finished in two minutes.

Our first stop was to eat breakfast at Tim Hortons. I had become fond of their vanilla lattes—they have their own brand of coffee—while motoring through western Canada three years ago. Tim Hortons chain is an upscale Dunkin' Donuts—except they are efficient and friendly. In fact, everyone I've ever met while traveling in Canada was friendly! Over a latte and a blueberry muffin for breakfast, I made it a point to tell Paul how grateful I was that we could make this trip. He had ridden the Cabot Trail before but barely remembered anything about it. He also knew about my struggle to make the trip with Butch and how badly that attempt ended.

My first goal, as we continued riding on New Brunswick Route 1, was to gaze out over the Bay of Fundy. We had barely glimpsed it when we visited Quoddy Point. Several years ago, I read a hauntingly beautiful book *The Birth House* by Ami McKay, which was set in a remote area of the Bay of Fundy. I have yearned to see it ever since.

I exited the highway at the first sign I saw for the Fundy Coastal Drive and headed toward the bay. The air was downright frosty, the road filled with twists and turns, and thick fingers of fog reached out over the landscape, making visibility minimal. I cautiously slowed our pace. Through the mist, I discerned a few clapboard houses, sitting just off the road in weathered shades of pastel. Their presence indicated we were approaching a small village.

One last turn and there it was—the Bay of Fundy, shrouded in dense fog as its dark water gently lapped at the rock-strewn shoreline; the breeze off the water carried a briny, fishy smell. I turned again and went down a narrow asphalt strip toward the water—and soon realized our bikes were extremely loud in that tiny, quiet fishing village. Out of respect for the tranquil setting, I pulled to a stop near the edge of the road and water and switched off the engine. I climbed off Bessie, faced the dark water, and peered out over the bay, where a thick wall of white blocked the horizon line. It looked exactly how I pictured it while reading McKay's book: cold, foggy, gloomy, and hauntingly beautiful. I felt a deep sense of isolation—what Dora, the book's main character, must have felt—in the stillness of the remote, sleepy village as the water lapped quietly at the shoreline. The thick fog shrouded it all, softening the edges, lending a dream-like quality to the scene.

The moment was lost on Paul, but that was okay. I pulled out the map in my saddlebag for inspection—no sense riding on a murky road, so I looked for an alternate route.

A man in his late sixties or perhaps early seventies appeared out of the mist on his morning walk about town. When he encountered us near our bikes, he gave a friendly wave and approached us. "Are you lost? he asked. Apparently, the village didn't see many visitors. He was short, thick in the middle, and reminded me of an aging high school football coach. He wore athletic-type shorts, a light windbreaker over a T-shirt, and white sneakers. I thought he looked cold, but I guess if this weather is what you're accustomed to in the summer, his attire was appropriate.

"We are not exactly lost. I just wanted to see the Bay of Fundy," I replied.

Paul and I introduced ourselves to "Erick." He was born and raised where we were standing—he mentioned we were in Beaver Harbour, New Brunswick, an unincorporated fishing village—but he had left in the 1960s. He wintered in Arizona and spent summers in Beaver Harbour.

I asked about the structure that stretched out over the water at the end of a short wooden pier. It was Connor Brothers Limited, a sardine and fish-processing plant. The odd floating raft anchored adjacent to it was a sardine catcher of sorts; trawlers dragged it out into the bay to "catch" the sardines. Erick went on to tell us a brief history of the area, which was settled by Quakers in the late 1700s, and then he asked about our travels on two wheels.

If there had been a coffee shop in sight, I would have asked Erick to join us for a *cuppa*. I thrive on talking to locals when I travel. While we chatted, I started to shake because of the damp chill coming off the water even though I had a heavy leather jacket and gloves on. We said goodbye to Erick, thanked him for his brief history of the village, and climbed back on our bikes.

The Canadian Maritimes, consisting of New Brunswick, Nova Scotia, and Prince Edward Island, are mostly farmland and forest with fishing businesses along the coast. My next must-see at the Bay of Fundy was the Hopewell Rocks, which are forty to seventy feet high rock formations created by tidal erosion along the coast.

I exited off New Brunswick Highway 2 to yet another back road—the worst one we had encountered thus far. The first sign I noticed read "Forty-one Miles to the Bay of Fundy." There was no way we could be on that road for forty-one miles without dumping the bikes. Large, gaping potholes had been recently filled with fresh tar gravel, haphazardly strewn everywhere, making two-wheel travel treacherous. A large, orange sign, just a mile off the exit, read "Motorcycles Take Caution." Paul and I slipped, slid, and banged for a few miles; I naively refused to believe all the warnings in pursuit of my love of rocks. After nearly dumping the bike twice, I decided we shouldn't risk life and machine for forty miles "just to see a bunch of rocks," so I negotiated a tricky U-turn on a hill in gravel.

It was back to Trans-Canada Highway 1, which was unlike our busy United States' interstates. Traffic was sparse, and we rode many miles without encountering another vehicle on well-maintained, pothole-free asphalt. I reluctantly passed the exit to the bridge that connected Prince Edward Island to the *Anne of Green Gables* house, a literary landmark. There was so much to see up here, but Paul's schedule for returning to work dictated our timeline. Our primary goal was to ride the Cabot Trail in Nova Scotia.

Paul and I, along with a busload of Chinese tourists, stopped at the welcome center as we crossed into Nova Scotia. The enthusiastic lady at the information desk put a map in my hand. She pointed us in the direction along the coast and recommended a hotel at about the point we would stop for the night.

With maps in hand, we set out for the Sunrise Trail, the scenic route along Nova Scotia's northeastern coast, referred to as the Northumberland Shore. The coastal road was rough—frost heaves again—but fair winds blew through sweet-smelling farmland and picturesque villages. We had been eight hours on the road since leaving Calais, Maine, that morning. It was fewer than 300 miles, but factoring in the side trips, the wind, the cold air, and it added up to a long day. I scanned the road ahead of me for a mileage sign for Tatamagouche, our stopping point for the day.

Tatamagouche, first settled by the French Acadians, is a coastal village with exactly four hotels and a handful of restaurants, all closed by the time Paul and I rolled in. The Balmoral Motel is a low slung, sixties-era establishment, situated atop a rise with a sweeping view of the Gulf of Saint Lawrence beyond its Northumberland Strait. It was quiet; few vehicles were in the gravel parking lot. Once again, a proprietor handed us a *real* room key and explained that we could park the bikes directly in front of the room, always a plus!.

Our room overlooked a meadow, filled with clusters of wildflowers, that led to the Northumberland Strait and an endless horizon. The prospects for dinner were slim since most of the restaurants were closed, which was unfortunate because the area is known for fresh oysters and quahog clams.

As I wearily unpacked my bike, I noticed a Foodliner grocery store across the street and suggested to Paul that we walk over and see what was available for "dinner." When you ride all day, battle the elements and road hazards, it is exhausting. After a shower, I just wanted to lie down and sleep. The prospect of climbing back on a motorcycle and looking for a restaurant in an unfamiliar town was too daunting.

The Foodliner had good food possibilities for us, so we bought freshly fried chicken, a fruit bowl, and cookies for dessert. We spread our "picnic" out on the small, side table outside our motel door and settled into the two chairs; the air cooled to the mid-fifties, and, while we ate, the setting sun painted the sky a warm palette of orange, pink, and yellow.

I awoke the next morning, not only with a chill in the room from the window we left open, but also with the pink and gold light of a spectacular sunrise streaming through the window. I jumped out of bed, pulled on my leather jacket, grabbed my camera, and walked around the back of the motel to watch the dawning of a new day. My bare feet hit the wet grass, crunchy with frost, jolting me awake. But what I saw was God's light show; every hue of pink, brushed with yellow and outlined in gold, exploded over the horizon, spilling over the sleepy, frost-tinged meadow. The frost sparkled; the water danced in the distance. If I had seen nothing else on this trip, watching this unforgettable sunrise was worth the journey.

Paul and I discovered the Balmoral didn't provide coffee until 7:00 a.m.—not good. Moving like zombies, we packed the bikes, layered up, because not only was it chilly, there was a storm front chasing us; the air was heavy with the scent of rain.

We bid adieu to sleepy, little Tatamagouche hamlet, fired up the hogs—late sleepers hate us—and headed east. We passed two more villages and saw nothing open for coffee; Paul and I were desperate for caffeine by this time.

About fifteen kilometers from Tatamagouche, somewhere around Marshville, I spied a wide spot in the road with gas pumps. Coffee? We hoped so. It was a rundown, dilapidated gas station, privately-owned that served as a feedstore, hardware store, DVD rental place, coffee bar, and auto parts place. I swung into the dirt lot with Paul behind me and parked on the side of the building out of the wind. The occupants of two pickup trucks stared as we stripped off helmets and one outer layer of clothes.

A very fat, viciously barking wiener dog, who sensed that we were not locals, greeted us at the door. The Asian lady behind the counter called off the wiener dog so we could step inside; its stomach dragged the cement floor as it waddled away.

I looked at her and said, "Thank you. Coffee?" Three words. She jerked her head toward the back. We made our way through the myriad of sundries—densely stacked on metal shelves that seemed to buckle under the weight—that towered above my head. The "coffee bar" was basic: coffee pot, white sugar, powdered creamer. It would do.

As I noisily sipped the hot liquid, I glanced back at the Asian lady who also operated the Noodle Emporium attached to the gas station. I sensed she had a fascinating story about how she ended up on the Northumberland shore of Nova Scotia, but I was too self- absorbed with my caffeine need to strike up a conversation.

Paul had discovered a bottle of vanilla syrup tucked behind the coffee maker and waived it in my direction. My eyes lit up, and I poured a slug into my cup, feeling quite cosmopolitan.

Feeling chattier after two sips of coffee, I introduced myself to the proprietress, Meh, who perched behind the untidy counter—as if her very name was a lack of opinion, an afterthought. But, before we could exchange more information, the fat wiener dog went nuts again, barking and wobbling around our feet in a frenzy. Meh removed her house slipper, hefted herself off the stool, screamed something at the dog in her native tongue (was it Chinese? Korean?) and threw her house shoe at it. The dog retreated slowly to a darkened corner near the coffee bar, out of the reach of Meh's other house shoe. Meh seemed angry and unapproachable. I thought better of striking up a conversation. Paul paid for our coffee, and Meh grunted a "thank you," and, like the fat, wiener dog, we retreated.

Paul and I sat outside at the weathered picnic table, not talking, just getting our fix. A cold wind blew off the coastline; a fine mist settled over us as we sipped our coffee. We watched the clouds grow thicker and knew rain was imminent. I had worn two shirts since we crossed north of the Mason-Dixon line over a week ago. I had begun the day wearing a long-sleeved shirt, a cold-gear underlayer, a long-sleeved T-shirt over that. A Gore-Tex pullover, rain pants over my jeans, a heavy leather jacket, and then my rain jacket completed my outfit. I felt like the wiener dog looked: so fat I could hardly leg up over the bike!

Pictou Harbour and a Tim Hortons were another sixty miles down the road, which meant breakfast and more strong coffee were not that far away. I thought about Meh as we rode those sixty miles. Was she all alone with her fat wiener dog in this isolated area of the country? Did she have a lover? A husband? Was she a widow? Had she been jilted? People's stories fascinate me.

In drizzling rain, we pulled into the parking lot of Tim Horton's. I gave Paul my order after we arrived and made my way to the restroom. I had to shed two layers of clothes just to go to the bathroom!

At that point in our journey, Paul and I moved away from the coastal route and took Nova Scotia Highway 104 to Cape Breton Island. As we finished breakfast, the weather changed from it feeling like rain was coming to a real misty shower. Paul suited up in his rain gear; I had had mine on all morning, attempting to stay warm. The beautiful ride took us through forests, farmland, and seaside villages. Regardless of the drizzle, I was in awe of the lupine that grew in abundance along the roadways and open fields. Deep purple to white, with every conceivable shade deviation in between, the tall flowers seemed to bend their heads in greeting as we passed by.

The Cabot Trail is named in honor of John Cabot, an Italian explorer who sailed to Cape Breton Island, located at the northern tip of Nova Scotia (New Scotland) in 1497. The 185-mile trail, which loops around the northern tip of Cape Breton Island, is considered one of the most spectacular scenic drives in all North America; some would say it is the most spectacular drive on the entire planet. Travelers are selling themselves short if they plan to spend fewer than three days—preferably five—to ride the trail. The mainland of Nova Scotia is connected to Cape Breton Island by Canso Causeway, the deepest causeway in the world. A sign just before we reached it read, "Caution! Blowing snow ahead." If the temperature had dropped any lower, the fine mist might quickly have become snow flurries.

Traffic stopped both ways at the causeway for the swing bridge to allow large freighters through the channel. The wind picked up, pelting us with rain as we waited nearly thirty minutes for the bridge to descend so we could cross. We headed north to the Cabot Trail on Highway 104 and stopped for lunch at the Dancing Goat, a tiny, urban café in the middle of nowhere. Freshly baked bread, homemade soups, and desserts—my goat was dancing! I had an avocado bacon sandwich on multigrain bread with black bean potato soup. Paul tried the roast beef sandwich and tomato soup. I topped it off with a rhubarb apple crisp that reminded me of my grandma Fisher's rhubarb pie. Yum!

I had made reservations at a Chéticamp hotel that the owners of Balmoral Motel in Tatamagouche had recommended and planned to stop early so Paul and I could do some sightseeing.

From the Canso Causeway, we connected with the Cabot Trail on Nova Scotia Highway 19 shortly after lunch; I was nearly giddy! I pulled off the road near the "official" sign indicating we were on the Trail to snap a selfie of two rain-soaked travelers, wet but smiling from ear to ear. Our route would take us clockwise around the island.

The Cabot Trail winds toward the coast rather quickly as the elevation rises, and the first glimpse of the water from the top of a soaring cliff took my breath away. The Trail itself is a mostly maintained paved road—narrow, but wide enough for two large size vehicles. I stopped at the first pull over on the highway to take photos and soak in the magnificent view.

Chéticamp, Nova Scotia, is an Acadian fishing village situated on a rocky cliff; its stunning coastline overlooks the water. It was early afternoon when we checked into our hotel, and we soon discovered that the friendly proprietors spent their winters in St. Petersburg, Florida.

Paul and I settled into our small but comfortable room and then walked out onto the deck. We took a seat on the deck chairs, propped our boots on the deck railing, and watched the fishing boats come into the harbor. We chatted about the ride a few minutes, then fell into a companionable silence as we watched the boats.

I realized at that moment that the trip six years ago with Butch was never meant to be. Butch was not a prop-your-feet-on-the-deck-railing kind of guy who found comfort in silence. I said a silent prayer of gratitude as I took Paul's hand in mine and smiled. We strolled down the Main Street and on down to the boardwalk along the water, where we checked out a few shops.

Anna Casnos was hooking rugs in a small, cluttered shop above the harbor. She was a comfortable-looking woman, about my age, with a ready smile and deft fingers that worked the punch needle quickly in and out of the webbed backing. The rugs, so lovely—more like wall hangings because you would not want to walk on these works of art. The ladies who made the rugs called themselves the Hookers of Chéticamp . I chatted with Anna for a little while about her craft. She eagerly explained that life in Chéticamp was dependent on the sea, and, in hard times throughout the town's history, the hooked rugs the women made brought in extra money or were exchanged for other goods. In today's world, the intricate tapestries are sought after as works of art. I bought two small pieces: One had a colorful Christmas design about a foot square; the other, a tiny harbor scene the size of a coaster.

Across the street in front of Le Gabriel restaurant, I spotted a sign that touted "Live Music." We checked out the posted menu—primarily seafood—and learned the music started at 7:00 p.m.

Paul and I went back to our hotel, showered, and returned to the restaurant for a leisurely dinner and live music. As we approached it, we commented on the packed parking lot for a weeknight and figured the Celtic fiddle player was the draw.

What looked like an army of rustic tables filled the vast bar area where the performer would play his music on a small stage in one corner. Large, framed black and white photos on the walls depicted the history of the harbor town of Chéticamp .

Nearly every item on the menu included seafood. The waitress, in a conspiratorial tone, the back of her hand to her mouth as she leaned into us, said, "The chef has halibut cheeks on the menu as tonight's special." I'm intrigued by the emphasis she gives to the words *tonight's special*. I discovered that halibut cheeks are a delicacy, rarely appearing on the menu, generally reserved for the fisherman's dinner. The small chunks of fish come from the halibut's head.

"I'll have the halibut cheeks," I told her with gusto. Paul ordered the scalloped lobster.

A little later, our waitress plunked down a large platter of delicately breaded, tender strips of fish that melted in my mouth. I don't even remember the sides. The fish was heaven on my tongue. In all my travels, I've not heard of this delicacy served anywhere else.

Satiated by the rich seafood, Paul and I waited for the music. The bar area grew to standing-room-only capacity for Colin Grant, a popular regional and award-winning Celtic music artist. And wow! That guy could play a fiddle! The crowd went wild the second he seated himself on the lone chair near a microphone. His energetic fiddle playing had us all clapping, stomping, and cheering. A piano player (whose name I have forgotten) joined him, and the two of them were mesmerizing. For two hours, Paul and I hooted and hollered with the locals, thoroughly enjoying the Celtic music. As soon as I returned to the hotel, I friended Colin on Facebook and downloaded some of his music!

Paul and I strolled back through the sleepy little village, hand in hand, congratulating ourselves for stopping early to enjoy the local culture of this gracious town of Chéticamp. Moored to docks, the boats bobbed gently on the water, and the moon shone brightly over the harbor as Paul and I made our way slowly up the hill to our hotel. The town of Chéticamp and our evening of Celtic music ranks as one of my favorite experiences, and one I am eager to visit again.

CABOT TRAIL-PART 2

I left the light on in my heart in case you ever want to come back home.

– Lennon Hodson, poet, writer

AS PAUL AND I LEFT THE CHARMING SEASIDE TOWN OF Chéticamp at daybreak, I let the arctic wind take my tears as we cruised north on the western shore of the Trail. It was my youngest daughter Mallory's birthday. She turned twenty-three years old on that day. She was sixteen the last time I celebrated her birthday with her. The chambers of my heart are scraped dry from grief over her absence. An absence I am powerless to change.

After honoring her special day with recollections of past birthday celebrations, I locked the memories back in that tiny chamber of my heart reserved only for her. I do anything I can to keep my thoughts of her at bay; allowing them free rein over my consciousness would destroy me. She chose to disengage herself from our family; it was her journey, and I remained on mine, always hoping to see her one day. I reminded myself of that as I had done many times.

Just outside of Chéticamp, Paul and I entered Cape Breton Highlands National Park, known for its sweeping ocean vistas. A heart-stopping view materialized around every curve: forested plateaus topped rugged cliffs that dropped sharply toward the vast Atlantic Ocean below. Every turn could inspire an unforgettable photograph. The Cabot Trail, chiseled into the side of the mountains, curves sharply, yielding with the landscape. I had to remind myself to focus on where I was going; otherwise, if I gazed too long at the magnificent wonders, I could easily have missed a curve.

It was the height of the tourist summer season, yet we encountered few vehicles. The park is extensive—366 square miles—and offered camping, lodging, hiking trails, and fishing.

Paul and I stopped for breakfast at the MidTrail Motel, located in Pleasant Bay. It was a funky, rambling, faded pink building, sitting on top of a cliff, where anyone could peer out at the Gulf of Saint Lawrence, described as a semi-enclosed sea. There were few diners, and the service was slow, but I reminded myself that we were in no hurry. The waitress was liberal with the coffee refills; the hot, strong liquid warmed our core after a chilly ride. By the end of the day, we would go full circle on the Cabot Trail, a journey I was reluctant to complete. Our breakfast was worth the wait: fluffy scrambled eggs, crispy bacon, and a mound of home fries. The server brought us a tub of Cheez Whiz along with the assorted little tubs of jelly; we had never been served Cheez Whiz in a restaurant, so we treated ourselves to cheese toast!

Paul and I practically had the highway to ourselves that morning: just us, leisurely negotiating the curves and elevations, often stopping to absorb the panoramic seascapes and coastlines. My eyes could not get enough of the visual feast spread out before us. Miles of uninhabited, unspoiled coastline; rocky cliffs at the end of lush forests dropped dramatically to the ocean below; an endless blue horizon with the sun dancing across the water filled us with its beauty.

At White Hill, the northern point of the Trail and its highest elevation (1,755 feet), we came over a rise, and right in front of us was—a female moose! I gradually came to a stop. Paul had seen it ahead of me. Not wanting to make any sudden movements, I slowly retrieved my phone from my windshield bag to get a picture. She stared directly at us as I brought my phone up over the windshield, careful to move slowly so not to disturb her, to click a photo. Snap! It was as if she posed for us before she sauntered to the opposite side of the road and disappeared into the thick yellow birch and balsam fir woods.

As Paul and I began the "downhill run" from the northern tip of the island, we stopped at Neil's Harbor, situated between Ingonish and Dingwall. If I were going to buy a postcard depicting quaint little fishing villages that mark the Cabot Trail coastline, it would have to be one of Neil's Harbor. Weathered clapboard houses, painted in once bright colors, ringed the harbor and jagged coastline. Worn fishing boats, tied to bright orange buoys, bobbed in the waves, and a wooden lighthouse—its white paint fresh and glowing—jutted out over the far edge of the harbor.

I had become accustomed to the ocean's clean, pungent scent, tinged with the odor of abundant aquatic life that lived beneath the surface. A different aroma floating on the salt air enticed my taste buds that afternoon: fresh lobster chowder. The Chowder House restaurant, which sits at the tip of a spit of land overlooking the harbor, is a non-descript, cinder block building from which an aroma of rich, creamy chowder beckoned two chilly bikers.

We parked the bikes in the hard-packed dirt parking area and followed our noses inside. The interior was as basic as the exterior; a serve-yourself order window, picnic tables inside and out, a generous roll of paper towels on each. Although the menu was extensive with fresh seafood items, we chose the chowder. We carried steaming bowls of velvety smooth bisque, bursting with reddish-pink chunks of lobster meat, to a table to eat. The rich, peppery, buttery taste danced on my tongue as the heat warmed my core.

The Scottish heritage seemed more pronounced on this side of Cape Breton Island, and both English and Gaelic road signs greeted us. According to the literature I had read at various hotels, Canadian or Cape Breton Gaelic has been spoken here for 241 years and is their community language. The Scottish Gaels settled in Nova Scotia in 1773.

Outside the pristine, rural community of Ingonish, which reminded me of villages in Switzerland, was an expansive boardwalk and Ingonish Beach. White clapboard houses with bright red or green roofs were visible from the Trail. Small wooden boats, their hulls painted in dazzling hues of yellow, blue, and red, dipped and swayed in the small harbor. Paul and I strolled on the wooden walkway while we scanned the horizon for whales. I noticed more tourists—or perhaps they were locals—on the boardwalk than I had seen anywhere else we had been along the Trail. Maybe it was the warm sun that drew them to the beach.

According to the informational signs along the walk, twelve different species of whales visit the waters off Cape Breton. Unfortunately, we did not see any from the beach. A couple of whale-watching tourist boats operated out of Ingonish and offered tourists better sightseeing opportunities.

The weather was spectacular: warm sun, cool air, cloudless sky. Paul and I declined the opportunity to swim, however; I had worn a layer of Under Armour cold gear under a long-sleeved shirt since we left upstate New York! I could only imagine how cold the North Atlantic water must have been!

Just outside of Ingonish, the Trail became one daring downhill switchback after another. The road bent to the left toward a staggering drop off to the ocean, and then made an immediate 180-degree turn to the right; we maneuvered the twisting bends for about five miles to just outside of Cape Smokey. It sported a 320-meter ski mountain and hiking trails.

At this point on the Cabot Trail, the road became dangerous, which we had been warned about. Since our trip on the Cabot Trail in 2015, I had read that the Canadian government had made significant road repairs in the Cape Breton area. Other than this specific section, we had ridden on well-maintained and navigable highways in Nova Scotia. However, at this juncture, we bumped and banged down to North Shore on the pothole-plagued highway.

The eighteen-mile section of road from Indian Brook to St. Ann's was so bad that Paul and I idled along at ten miles per hour over the broken and torn-up asphalt. It was worse than a gravel road: Massive chunks of asphalt lay helter-skelter next to deep, potholes with loose pieces scattered everywhere. Roads that are bombed or blasted by dynamite would likely resemble what we endured. While trying to dodge the fragments, we risked falling into a hole or sliding on the smaller ones. My white knuckles gripped the handlebars, and I prayed for the nightmare to end.

Finally, just outside of St. Ann's, the road smoothed out a little as we approached Baddeck, signaling the end of the Cabot Trail. I was sad to see that our journey was almost over; it had been a spectacular ride and worth the six years I had waited to experience it.

Paul and I stopped at a gas station to shake off the anxiety generated by the dangerous road. Adjacent to the station was a field of lupine—a stunning display of dense purple blossoms on stalks, swaying in the breeze. I climbed up the small hill and basked in the color surrounding me while Paul snapped a photo to commemorate the end of our Cabot Trail ride. From here, we began our journey home.

NOVA SCOTIA, *TÌORAIDH!*

A person is the product of their dreams. So make sure to dream great
dreams. And then try to live your dream.

– Maya Angelou, *Wouldn't Take Nothing for My Journey Now*

PAUL AND I SPENT OUR LAST NIGHT ON CAPE BRETON
Island in Sydney, another harbor town on the island's east coast. We
booked passage on the *Nova Star* ferry from the world's largest lobster
fishing grounds, Yarmouth, Nova Scotia, to Portland, Maine. Taking
the *Nova Star* would cut at least two days off travel time in places where
we had already travelled.

At breakfast that morning, I realized there was no longer a Harley-
Davidson shop at Yarmouth. *Where will we buy T-shirts?* No convenient Harley-Davidson store is a dilemma for anyone who cherishes
destination T-shirts or other such clothing. Paul and I had already left

Sydney behind us, so we changed course and headed to Halifax to hit up the huge Privateers Harley-Davidson dealership to buy our shirts.

We were on Nova Scotia Highway 102 for about an hour when I spotted a sign near Stewiacke. My extreme geography nerve started to tingle, for we had crossed the 45th parallel north, the dividing line between the equator and the north pole! The large green rectangular sign was incongruous, stuck alongside the road. A non-observant rider would have missed it; an extreme geography buff homed in on it. Unfortunately, there was no safe place to stop for a photo.

Though Halifax is one of the larger cities in Nova Scotia, it is not too congested, which made navigating easy for the forty-two miles from Stewiacke to Harley-Davidson. We discovered a big HOG rally taking place at the dealership. Motorcycles were everywhere! I snagged two shirts, Paul got his, we purchased them, and then headed outside to chat with some of the locals. And, for the one-hundredth time since leaving home, we heard, "*Florida?* Did you ride *all* the way up here or did you trailer?"

"No, we don't trailer. We ride."

Out of Halifax, we took Nova Scotia Highway 333, which winds for about forty miles along the Atlantic coast. It's good asphalt with tight curves along a shoreline that looked as if Norman Rockwell himself wielded his brush to paint the idyllic scene.

Before Paul and I went to Yarmouth to catch the ferry, we rode over to Peggy's Cove, a small fishing community located on the eastern shore of St. Margaret's Bay. Virtually all the chamber-of-commerce tourism photos you see of this maritime province feature this picturesque village. Its scenery is indicative of many eastern seaboard coastal towns in Nova Scotia.

Still operational, Peggy's Point Lighthouse sits on an outcropping of wave-washed boulders that anchors the little town next to the sea. It is said to be the most photographed lighthouse in all of Canada;

considering there are 161 lighthouses in Nova Scotia alone, it is one popular lighthouse!

As I rounded the curve and made a slight descent toward the village, I saw cars, buses, bikes jammed every which way on the main street and parked haphazardly on tiny side streets. From large tour buses, idling in a sandy parking lot, sightseers emptied out into groups throughout the village. In ten days of travel, it was the largest concentration of tourists Paul and I had encountered in Nova Scotia. We wedged our bikes in the sandy berm between two cars, hoping no one would back into them or that they would sink into the sand.

With camera in hand, we set off toward the lighthouse to take the compulsory photo. The place teemed with people of many different nationalities; I felt like I was in a Disney World version of Peggy's Cove, or at the fictional Amity Island at Universal Studios. Massive stone boulders, bleached a blondish color and washed smooth by the waves and wind, anchored the lighthouse. The cylindrical lighthouse is constructed of whitewashed brick, and the light at the top is encased in a bright red housing. A lone bagpiper stood atop a boulder overlooking the lighthouse, his Kelly-green plaid kilt and starched white shirt in sharp contrast to the muted tones of the boulders. He hugged the wind instrument close to his body as his fingers worked the chanter; the winsome sound of the bagpipe wafted over the rocks, lending a solemn tone to the experience.

The strong sun warmed me, and my first thought was, *Oh to be a salamander and rest my belly on the warm, smooth stones!* But so many people were out on the rocks that a salamander would have had a tough time finding a quiet place to rest.

I handed my phone to a fellow tourist and asked him to take our photo with the lighthouse in the background. I would have preferred a solitary afternoon to bask among the boulders with the distinctive sound of the bagpipes mixing with the hypnotic sound of the waves to soothe me instead of the quick trip.

Alas, our travel schedule precluded lingering at the cove. Paul and I hiked back up the hill to the Sou'Wester restaurant and gift shop overlooking the lighthouse. A few trinkets from the gift shop, a tasty lunch of lobster chowder, and we bid adieu to Peggy's Cove.

Paul and I intended to ride the coastal road, Route 3, all the way to Yarmouth, approximately 142 miles, to avoid Nova Scotia Highway 103. However, after an hour of maneuvering through so many twists, turns, and small villages, I figured out we had covered only thirty miles! To make our ferry departure from Yarmouth, we would have to relinquish the coastal road in favor of the highway.

Outside of Peggy's Cove sits the memorial for Swissair Flight 111 that crashed into the Atlantic Ocean on its descent into Halifax Stanfield International Airport in September 1998, killing all 229 people on board. We bypassed the sober reminder and cut over to Highway 103 as it was already midafternoon, and we had to catch the ferry out of Yarmouth the next morning.

Yarmouth, founded in 1761, is a quiet, historic port town on the Bay of Fundy. Fewer than 7,000 residents live there, and even at the height of the tourist season, it is not crowded.

We checked into the "best" hotel in town, the Best Western Mermaid and walked downtown for dinner. Rudder's Seafood Restaurant-Brew on the harbor was booming with diners—the best recommendation for an eating establishment. Paul and I sat at a table on the patio overlooking the harbor where the warm sun began its descent into the west, casting a golden glow on boats bobbing in the water.

I perused the menu out of habit, but I already knew I wanted the regional specialty, Digby scallops. They are harvested from scallop beds at Digby, a small fishing village about 100 miles north of Yarmouth on the Bay of Fundy. Their fleet of trawlers is world famous for harvesting the plump, juicy sea mollusks.

I ordered mine pan-seared; Paul decided on the heartier Coquilles St. Jacques, a classic French preparation of scallops in a rich cream sauce, topped with cheese and bread crumbs, and baked. The waitress plunked the platters of food—enough for two more people—in front of us, and I was astounded at their size. Fat, succulent, tender bites about two inches in diameter sat plump and seared to perfection on my plate. These are not to be confused with the tiny, cylindrical, freshwater scallops. The sides that came with the entrée were similar to a traditional Low Country boil: potatoes and onions with corn on the cob. The food was superb—a perfect ending to our Nova Scotia travels.

The Best Western Mermaid Inn was only a few miles from the *Nova Star* ferry terminal. I awoke the next morning feeling as though I had spent the night on a medieval torture rack. I seriously doubted mermaids slept in such uncomfortable accommodations. The advertised "continental breakfast" consisted of a neglected package of powdered sugar donuts next to a pot of hot water and a jar of instant coffee. I suspected mermaids never ate powdered donuts or drank instant coffee either. I stared at the pitiful presentation in horror; instant coffee is acceptable only during hurricane season when the power is out, leaving the gas grill the only device for coffee making and cooking. Thankfully, we had seen a Tim Hortons on our walk back from the restaurant the previous night.

Paul and I made a sharp pivot away from the "breakfast" bar in the motel lobby, packed the bikes, and headed straight for Tim Hortons just a block away. After a hefty amount of caffeine, a decent breakfast, and some ibuprofen for good measure, we headed to the terminal.

When I traveled throughout British Columbia, I traversed its many waterways on ferries—some small, some very small, and a few rather large—so I was not expecting to see a mini cruise ship as we pulled into the departure area of the terminal. The *Nova Star* had three decks for vehicles as well as sleeping cabins if a passenger was on an overnight trip from Portland to Yarmouth. It was a ten-hour passage; Paul and I have trouble sitting still for an hour, but, it was a forced relaxation after several days of a throttle-twisting journey—3,000 miles to date.

Paul and I lined our motorcycles up with the other bikes, showed our passports at security, and pulled them into the gaping jaws of the giant ship. Paul, as well as all the other men, watched the crew like a hawk while they tied the bikes down on four points—must be a guy thing.

I was the only female rider; all the other women were passengers, and we heard the same question: "Did you ride all the way from *Florida*?"

I would have been happy if we could have taken this luxurious boat all the way to Port Canaveral, Florida, avoiding Pennsylvania *and* the megalopolises on the Eastern seaboard. Paul and I spread out in the aft section where we had six business class seats and a table to ourselves. Once the boat was underway, we explored the different areas of the ship; there was even a casino where I lost two dollars in the penny slots in a matter of minutes. I'm not a gambler with my money; the sport holds no allure for me.

Settling back into our seats, I pulled out the Nova Scotia travel guide, and Paul and I relived our trip over the past ten days. We also marveled at all the things we didn't have a chance to explore, vowing we would make this trip again in a heartbeat. Each Canadian town had two or three museums, and I was especially sorry we missed the Sardine Museum. Thumbing through pages and pages of attractions, cultural events, and music festivals, we realized we could have spent a month in Nova Scotia and not experienced a fraction of its appeal. We loved our days of riding on two wheels through Canada's second-smallest province as well as the food, the music, the weather, but most of all, we enjoyed the friendly Nova Scotians.

Part of our passage on the boat included a buffet—for lunch *and* dinner. Paul and I had traveled for four weeks, eating scrumptious food and feeling our jeans get a little tighter after each meal. I had the fresh haddock and lobster mac 'n cheese; topped it off with apple crisp pie and coffee, and then we waddled back to our seats and promptly fell asleep for an hour or so.

Afterward, Paul and I settled into the lounge at the front of the *Nova Star* to watch its approach into Cape Elizabeth Harbor, Portland. The coastline is beautiful—full of big ships, sailboats, small craft, and windsurfers. For the first time in days, I felt comfortable and relaxed. I had waited six years to make this journey. I reflected on the ill-fated morning and the showdown with Butch in the ferry terminal at Bar Harbor. It was a showdown that liberated me from the crippling relationship and started me on the healing road for my wounded soul. I looked over at Paul as the ferry approached the Portland harbor, grabbed his hand, and said, "Thank you."

He was somewhat perplexed, but squeezed my hand and said, "For What?"

"For being my wingman on this trip." He just smiled and gave me a quick hug. We congratulated ourselves for taking the boat and enjoying the time to relax and reflect on our journey.

The call came for those of us with vehicles to go below, where workers had detached the straps from the bikes. We rearranged our packs and waited for the boat to dock. After Paul and I disembarked, we sat idling in line with the other vehicles, waiting to go through customs. I passed the time reading all the stickers on the BMW bike in front of me. Its boxy exterior was plastered with an embarrassing array of bumper stickers that no self-respecting Harley owner would dare mar their paint job with. To each his own.

One of the stickers read: *Paved roads are just another example of a waste of taxpayers' money.* After some of the treacherous roads we had recently navigated, I tended to disagree. If I were to affix a bumper sticker to Bessie—which I would not—it would say, "The proper wingman makes the journey more enjoyable."

NON-NEGOTIABLE

Excitement is found along the road, not at the end, and likewise, peace is not a fixed point—except perhaps in the unwanted "rest in peace" sense. PEACE is the breathing space between destinations, between excitements, an occasional part of the journey, if you're lucky. PEACE is a space you move through very rarely, and very briefly—but you're not allowed to stay there. You have to keep moving, and go do what you do, because you can.

– Neil Peart, *Far and Away: A Prize Every Time*

AS I BASKED IN THE PEACE THAT FOLLOWED THE WELL-planned, well-traveled trip to Nova Scotia, the "breathing space between destinations" didn't last very long. I began a new school year, teaching in a situation that proved more toxic than the previous year. The stress, which I vehemently dismissed and denied, was taking a toll. Instead of anticipating each school day that was filled with promise, I awoke with dread.

I always enjoyed my years in education, feeling at day's end that I had made a difference, no matter how small, in the life of a student or my field. Not true with my current position. My dissatisfying days ended with a long, frustrating commute in which tears of frustration flowed all too frequently as I drove home.

I cried easily. I snapped quickly at the slightest inconvenience or provocation, and I was physically drained. Shortly after the school year began, Paul was assigned another job in France for a minimum of five months; it was a difficult assignment, an impossible commute, and a strain on even the best relationships. By the last quarter of the school year, my soul pleaded with me, as Peart wrote, "to keep moving."

When I bought my first bike in January of 2008, I jotted down all the places I wanted to see on two wheels. Not a bucket list, but a Bike-It list. I pulled it out of my desk drawer in March of 2016 on a particularly "down" day and crossed off several places that Paul and I had visited on our recent road trip. Since I am a habitual list-maker, I have a great feeling of accomplishment when I can draw a line through a destination or item or task. Right then, I realized I was only five states short of reaching my goal of traveling on a motorcycle in all fifty states—astride Bessie!

I had to forget traveling in Hawaii for the time being. I had the chance and missed it, but I had faith that another opportunity would come. That left only four states remaining: Idaho, Oregon, Washington, and Alaska. I studied the worn, tattered, and taped atlas that resides on the shelf in my nightstand, and plans for my next road trip started to percolate. Paul and I had discussed visiting Alaska, but I intended to *ride* on Bessie to our fiftieth state, clicking off Idaho, Oregon, and Washington on the way.

Paul flew home from France for a long weekend in April, and I broached the subject over dinner during his first night home in four weeks. We were seated at our favorite steak house; the din of talkative diners, the too-loud music, and silverware tinkling on platters of food forced me to practically shout. Paul looked weary from his long flight with bags under his bloodshot eyes. I almost felt guilty for laying out my plans for an epic ride to a man who was so drained.

"I want to ride to Alaska," I said. Subtlety is not my forte. Here was a man who had been commuting from Europe for the last several months, and the last thing he wanted to consider was a blockbuster road trip!

"You want to do *what?*" was his weary reply.

"I only have five states to click off to meet my goal of riding in all fifty states. We already missed our chance in Hawaii, so that leaves only four—Idaho, Oregon, Washington, and Alaska," I explained. To Paul's credit as my wingman, he knew I was dead serious, and he didn't waiver in his reply.

"How long will it take, how much will it cost, and when do you want to do it?" he answered. He directed his attention toward his steak that the waitress had just plunked down in front of him, not toward meeting my intense gaze.

"I just started planning," I replied. "The next time you come home, I'll have it mapped out."

"Okay," was his only response as he slowly cut into his steak. I shifted my attention to my charbroiled salmon, letting him enjoy his meal in peace. I kept the conversation light for the remainder of our dinner.

Scrutinizing the atlas each evening after a brutal day at school revitalized me. I can endure anything if I know I'm going on a new adventure as soon as I possibly can, and that attitude helped me slog through the last days of the school year. I was fortunate to have several weeks off in the summer, so I had no time constraints on my travels—only financial limitations.

Paul, however, had only three official weeks of vacation but appreciated several long holiday weekends and a week between Christmas and New Year's. He spent one of those weeks in Massachusetts at a hunting camp, something he had done for over thirty years. It was one of the "negotiating points" Paul and I discussed when we considered cohabiting. His commitment to doing the things that fed his soul was something I admired so much about Paul. I, too, had my "negotiating points," such as taking an annual trip with my daughter around Christmas to see *The Nutcracker* as well as making at least one solo trip on Bessie each year. During that fateful lunch at the Olive Garden in 2013, Paul and I laid our souls bare and deeply discussed what was important to us and which aspects of our single life we wanted to preserve. We agreed wholeheartedly to each other's desires.

However, if I wanted Paul to cross the United States with me to get to Alaska and back, I would have to convince him to forego his hunting trip and use the full three weeks to go with me—which I knew was a long shot. Additionally, while riding on two wheels from Florida to Alaska in three weeks was doable, it would mean sticking to a brutal travel schedule. Possible, but not enjoyable.

But, I had developed a plan B, and since life is all about how one carefully handles plan Bs, I knew I could meet my goal one way or the other.

Paul returned home the following month; it was an arduous commute from France to Florida every four weeks for a total of four days at home. As we enjoyed the setting sun over Lake Shipp at Harborside Restaurant, I raised the subject a little more carefully this time over dinner.

"Making the trip to Alaska from here will require a minimum of three weeks," I explained, as I took a deep breath and slowly exhaled, hoping my insistence on talking about this topic wasn't wearing Paul down even more than his commute from France.

"I don't have three weeks," he flatly replied.

"You do if you forego the hunting camp this *year*," I offered brightly. (Maybe my words weren't as subtle or cautious as I had hoped.)

Paul looked up from his plate, steak knife poised in midair over his sirloin, and responded, 'No!" He sliced a chunk of medium rare meat and stuffed it into his mouth as he smiled ruefully at me. His words hit me like a punch in the gut, but I refused to react negatively. I took a deep breath, a bite of my grouper, and smiled at him.

"Okay. Fair enough. I knew it was a longshot to ask, but I had to try," I offered apologetically.

"How far is it anyway," he asked, intent on keeping the possibility alive for me.

"Forty-seven hundred miles—one way," I answered as I cut another piece of my broiled grouper steak.

"Even if I wanted to give up my week at the hunting camp, which I don't, that's nearly nine thousand miles in three weeks! Not enough time to enjoy the trip. Not enough time to factor in bad weather, sightseeing, or potential mechanical problems," he offered. Paul was a rational guy. I knew he would counter with logic.

"You're right," I conceded. "Which is why I have a plan B," I said, triumphantly.

A slow smile crept across his face, and he said, "You always do."

"So, this will be my yearly solo trip. I will ride to Anchorage, you fly to Anchorage; we rent a bike for you, and we click off a few hundred miles in Alaska. You fly back, I ride back," I said, as I smiled at Paul. No way he was going to scoff at my plan since it was my turn to hold fast with a "non-negotiable." Paul wasn't surprised by my suggestion; he just looked confounded.

"You want to ride all the way to Alaska...*by yourself*?" he asked softly. By then, we had finished with our meal, and the waitress was hovering, intent on taking our plates and asking if we wanted dessert.

"Yes!" I stated, emphatically, while looking at Paul. He waited silently while the waitress cleared our table before he spoke.

"Okay. You make the plans, tell me what my part involves, when you want to go, and how much it will cost," Paul said. He looked at me with a big grin on his face.

I looked at the waitress and said, "We will split a piece of carrot cake!" I was almost ready to shout.

Paul returned to Europe the following week, and I immersed myself in researching a route to Alaska.

CHASING A DREAM

Talk is cheap and easy; making dreams real takes hard, humble work.
Dreams in the Midwest are acceptable, just keep them to yourself. Maybe
tell your family, but don't just talk—do something about it.

– Peter Jenkins, *Looking for Alaska*

DURING 2016, I LOOKED FORWARD TO THE END OF THE DAY
when I arrived home from work. As usual, I settled at my desk to research
the Alaskan portion of my trip that would follow my cross-country
excursion. Traversing the geography between my home state of Florida
and the Pacific Northwest would be easy. But, finding the pieces of
the puzzle map to take me through Idaho, Oregon, and Washington
and connect me with the Alaska Highway in Dawson Creek, British
Columbia, Canada, was what I needed to discover. I planned to ride
at least 4,700 miles in one direction; the final leg of the journey would
be "the last frontier" of known civilization. I fully comprehended the

number of miles I intended to ride; however, I had little perception of the *scope* of such a journey—*solo.*

I am a devotee of Neil Peart's travel writing, specifically his bold and heartwarming book *Ghost Rider*. Most people know Peart as the lyricist and Hall of Fame drummer for the legendary rock band Rush. Peart is an intrepid pilgrim on two wheels; his choice is a BMW motorcycle. My adventures pale in comparison to Peart's, but I live vicariously through his writings.

Soon after I decided to ride alone to wild and scenic Alaska, I reread the chapters "North to Inuvik" and "West to Alaska" from *Ghost Rider*, hoping to glean a few travel tips from a professional rider who had journeyed in our forty-ninth state. I also perused various websites devoted to Alaskan travel, the official tourism website of Alaska, TripAdvisor, and a variety of others. They presented glossy, sanitized versions of how to tour the Alaska Highway; I knew Peart would provide the nitty-gritty reality of traveling on two wheels.

I am the first to admit that BMW explorers are far more capable of "adventure" riding than those of us on large, Harley-Davidson touring bikes. BMW bikes are designed with high clearance for easier navigability over gravel, dirt, mud, and partially paved roads. By contrast, my Harley sits low to the road. BMWs have a long travel suspension, which translates to easier handling over the terrain. As I related in a previous chapter about my recent travels on the treacherous pavement in Nova Scotia, handling a bigger, heavier bike with low ground clearance can be problematic. I wanted Peart to assure me it could be done on the 1,387-mile Alaska Highway.

In his chapter, "North to Inuvik," Peart relates his trials on the 457-mile Dempster Highway, outside a hamlet named Ft. McPherson:

> …a long stretch of the road had been graded bare of
> gravel and soaked by water trucks, presumably to hold

down the dust. An older "flag lady" with a walkie-talkie was controlling the traffic on the one open lane, and when she waved me forward, my wheels sank into the greasy clay ruts. I rode as slowly as I could, gently fighting for control, but with zero traction available, my rear tire slipped sideways, and in an instant, I was down and sliding in the mud, the bike bearing down on me from behind in a slow circle.

Okay, fine. I knew I would not attempt the Dempster Highway on my route to Anchorage.

My hopes soared as I read the chapter, "West to Alaska," and Peart's description of the Top of the World Highway between Dawson City, British Columbia, and Chicken, Alaska:

> The narrow, paved road twisted along the top of a high ridge with sweeping views on either side, looking down steep green mountain slopes and far off to the distant ranges of purple and gray. It truly felt like the top of the world, and I decided it was one of the most spectacular roads I had ever traveled.

Yes! Peart's description called to my gypsy soul to ride that road! Then I read a report on *The Milepost* website:

> The remote Top of the World Highway connects Klondike Loop from Dawson City and the Taylor Highway linking Chicken, Eagle and the Alaska Highway. The 65-mile Top of the World Highway is a winding, sometimes narrow road with frequent surface breaks, potholes, washboard and little to no shoulder. Wet weather can make the surface slippery and you must be mindful of

soft shoulders, the absence of guardrails and the necessity of traveling slowly.

I wasn't exactly intimidated by the "absence of guardrails," but the road conditions, combined with the overall remoteness of the region, started to give me pause about traveling alone to Alaska.

If my bike broke down, could I call AAA? Cell service was doubtful or non-existent in remote regions. If I managed to be rescued because of a mechanical problem, where would the nearest mechanic in the Arctic wilderness be located? Even Neil Peart had to travel all the way to Fairbanks to find a mechanic! What if I dropped the bike in loose gravel or muck? My Road King is a beast to pick up, although I've been taught "how," but doing it under stressful circumstances or mired in the muck is another story.

As I scanned the photos of the Northwest Territory, its vast remoteness displayed in vivid color, I thought about the accident I had already survived on my bike. It took a year to recover from my injuries. If I was injured far away from immediate help, I could be attacked by a grizzly bear sensing road kill before someone from Life Flight rescued me.

Undaunted, I searched blogs for other two-wheel travelers—were there any *women?* —who had made the trip to Alaska from the lower forty-eight states.

Motorcycle Cruiser, an online magazine, featured a humorous, informative blog about three men who traveled the Alaska Highway and described it as

> … a very long two-lane back road that skirts modern reality. It's perhaps the only way to absolutely experience what it must have been like to set out 60 years ago when our mainland routes were lonely, meandering affairs.

Their description sounded civilized enough until they related the fact that the locals along the highway refer to motorcyclists as "Meals on Wheels." The writer said that "grizzlies can accelerate as fast as a quarter horse and carry an 800-pound moose in their jaws without letting it touch the ground." Those words lent credence to my earlier concern about a motorcycle accident in this wilderness. No Life Flight needed— the brown grizzlies would have their Meals on Wheels.

I learned from other riders that fuel is "mostly" available; the key was to top off at each fuel stop—my Road King can travel approximately 280 miles on a tank of gas. All the blogs I read agreed on one thing: the Alaska Highway was a pretty good paved road—until it wasn't. Paul and I had experienced the frost heaves—deep wrinkles in the pavement caused by freezing temperatures in northern Maine—so I could imagine the pavement damage after an Arctic winter. Travelers related horror stories of the pavement dropping away unexpectedly, leaving gravel roads that turned to slick muck after a rain. Bottom line? Be prepared to ride some gravel or clay mud if you're on the Alaska Highway, and be aware that many areas don't have proper signs to tell you of a hazard.

I read several comments on TripAdvisor about the unavailability of cell phone service along the road. In the event of a breakdown, with no cell service in the area, a stranded motorist's only choice was to flag down a truck driver who had a CB radio. It could take hours before a tow truck reached your location, not to mention the high cost of the tow.

My confidence was starting to wane with each blog I read. Don't misunderstand. Plenty of bikers have covered the miles without incident. I talked with two acquaintances that had made the trip successfully—and would do it again in a heartbeat. Both were men who were riding in groups. The only niggling fear for me was the *solo* part. My irrational self, screamed, *No, don't hold back! You can do it!* The rational self said, *Now, hold up. Let's think this through.* With age comes reservation.

My other option, which theoretically moved me to Plan C, was to consider the Alaska Marine Highway System (AMHS). Founded in 1949 and headquartered out of Ketchikan, Alaska, the AMHS is a series of ferries that transport people and vehicles from Bellingham, Washington, to several different ports on the Alaska Inside Passage. The ferry ships provide overnight accommodations for a nominal fee; you can even camp on the deck if you wish to pitch a tent. This option sounded adventuresome and reasonably safe, plus, if I chose this alternative, I could enjoy the Alaskan Inside Passage route that weaves in and out of its waterways.

I scrutinized their route map and determined Bessie and I could bike to Whittier, Alaska, the port town sixty-one miles south of Anchorage, from Bellingham, Washington, on a series of four different ferries. We would be on and off in four different ports along the Inside Passage in six to eight days. The fare was unbelievably cost-effective; the sailing schedule was erratic, however, and the probability of being held over in one of the ports while waiting on the next ferry was very likely.

Paul's schedule was another challenge in coordinating my portion of the trip. Once he flew to Anchorage from France, I didn't want him cooling his heels, waiting on me to arrive.

After mapping out the ferry routes, I called AMHS reservations to obtain a better understanding of their schedule, get a quote, and make my reservation. I outlined my plans to the online agent who calmly responded to my request: "I'm sorry, all of our reservations are booked for the summer of 2016. Would you like to make your reservations for 2017?" I deflated like a helium balloon pierced with a giant pin. Plan C was in ruins.

Paul returned home again in May, eager to hear about my proposal for our summer road trip. The look of sheer relief on his face was unmistakable when I admitted I scrapped my notion of riding to Alaska. He countered, "Okay, we can make that trip together when I retire." His words softened the blow to my ego and left the option open for future consideration. I told him about my intentions to travel on the Alaska Marine Highway until I found out that reservations had to be made a year in advance. Paul was intrigued by the possibility of this mode of transportation as well; we filed the idea for future reference.

"So, are we traveling to Alaska or not this summer?" Paul asked, hopefully.

"Of course, and I've mapped out Plan D," I replied, optimistically. "Here's what we can do. I want to ride to Seattle, Washington, thus meeting my goal of riding in all the lower forty-eight states. I have contacted the Harley-Davidson dealership in Tacoma, Washington, and they are happy to service my bike and store it for two weeks while you and I tour Alaska.

"You can fly to Seattle to meet me, and from there, we will fly to Anchorage. Once in Anchorage, we can rent bikes and travel the Seward Peninsula, which allows me to click off my forty-ninth state.

"After touring Alaska for two weeks, we will fly back to Seattle. I pick up Bessie and ride to Florida via the Pacific Coast Highway and through the Southwest; you get to fly home in first-class, climate-controlled comfort."

Paul laughed. He said, "I'm exhausted just listening to you. Write down the dates so I can make the arrangements at work. I'll need a couple of days at home to acclimate since I'm still working in France before meeting you in Seattle."

We settled on a date for my departure and a date for my arrival in Seattle, so Paul could book his flight to get there the same day. This schedule gave Bessie and me ten days to travel from our home in Central Florida to Seattle, Washington.

Paul booked our flights to Anchorage. I contacted the only motorcycle rental company in Anchorage to reserve two bikes for the first week we would be in Alaska. Unfortunately, their inventory was small, their riding season short, and all their bikes were scheduled for guided tours on the dates we planned to visit there. Was Plan D doomed to crumble as well?

"All I can do is rent you two bikes for two days," said the online agent. "However, the models of bikes and dates you want are not available."

"I'll take what you have," I snapped, unwilling to let my goal of riding in my forty-ninth state drift away.

"All I have available is a Heritage Softail Deluxe and an Indian Chief," she clarified.

"Hey, two wheels are two wheels. Please reserve those two bikes for the dates we discussed," I replied. I completed the reservation, paid the fee, and disconnected.

I immediately jumped for joy and danced around my office; it appeared my dream of riding all in forty-nine states would become a reality after all.

STRAINING AT THE HARNESS

Old longings nomadic leap,
Chafing at custom's chain;
Again from its brumal sleep
Wakens the ferine strain.

– John Myers O'Hara, "Atavism"

ON JUNE 22, 2016, I WOULD SET OUT ON THE NEXT LEG OF
my journey that would take me to the last four states on my Bike-It
List: Idaho, Montana, Washington, and Alaska—over 4,000 miles on
two wheels. My wingman would meet me in Seattle ten days later, and
from there, we planned to travel to Anchorage for two weeks. Bessie

would stay at the Eastside Harley-Davidson in Bellevue, Washington, about ten minutes east of Seattle, until I returned.

Only a handful of people *did not* think me crazy at that point. It was not my first solo trip, so I was a little bewildered by the comments and concerns. Paul and my daughter were relieved I was going "only as far as Seattle" and not attempting the ride on to Alaska. I knew who my good friends were because when I outlined my travel plans on faithful Bessie, their only comments went something like this: "Cool! Post photos and be sure you blog."

But the nay-sayers who didn't know me were quick to make remarks:

"You're doing WHAT?"

I said, "I am going to travel solo across America on my bike."

"And you are doing this by *yourself?*"

"Yes, a penis is not required," I replied.

"Aren't you afraid?" another queried.

"I'm more afraid of *not* following my bliss."

"But you're sixty-one years old!"

"Well, darn! Maybe I should trade my motorcycle for a rocking chair! Don't let a number define your dreams."

"You are either very brave or just plain crazy," several told me.

"A little of both, thank you."

"Are you riding all that way, or will you trailer most of the way?"

"I plan to ride, God willing."

"What will you do if it rains?"

"Put on my rain gear."

"What will you do if the bike breaks down?"

"Call AAA. They help motorcyclists as well as automobile drivers."

"I would be afraid for my safety—a woman alone on a motorcycle."

"Bessie and I never go anywhere without protection," I replied. I keep the Scout motto in mind: Be prepared.

"What do you pack for a trip like that?"

"I pack three pairs of jeans, three short-sleeved T-shirts, three long-sleeved T-shirts, Under Armour Heat Gear and Cold Gear, two pairs of Columbia pants with three Columbia T-shirts, two camisoles with drawstring pants for sleeping, socks, heavy leather, gloves, face-mask, rain gear, and a light jacket. And yes, it all fits nicely in my tour pack and saddlebags. I also carry a camera, iPad, and selfie stick in my backpack on the luggage rack."

A considerable part of my love for traveling on two wheels is stripping down to the essentials for a road trip; my only jewelry is my ring, thin silver hoops; my only makeup is mascara, lipstick, sunblock, and a lot of moisturizers!

I embraced the aloneness of the next ten days; it had been a difficult year, and my time astride Bessie helped me make sense of my place in the universe. Although I had agreed contractually to return to my position at the end of August, my time in the wind lent perspective to whether I would or should return. I felt unappreciated and undervalued with the current administration. I had hung on tenaciously in this school district for nine years; I networked, gained experience, and planned to move into an administrative position one day.

The toxic environment in which I had operated for the past two years, however, had taken its toll. The experience caused me to doubt my plans. I missed the daily contact with students, the ability to exercise my creativity in the classroom, and the relative calm of managing a class versus directing adults.

My wingman had spent the better part of the year working in Europe—a grueling separation for both of us; we missed being geographically close when we needed each other to lean on. I looked forward to the two weeks of uninterrupted time we would have together. For the past several months, I had also watched my older child struggle, and I had endured another year of my younger daughter's absence.

But no matter how difficult the days had been, I remained grateful, especially for the opportunity I had to ride Bessie—unaccompanied—on the cross-country adventure.

For a whole year, I had strained at the harness that attached me to a normal way of life. Like Buck, part St. Bernard, part Scotch Shepherd dog in *The Call of the Wild*, who leaves civilization and becomes a part of the wilderness, I was ready to cut loose, test myself, permit my thoughts to unfurl behind me like the many white lines on black asphalt. I wanted to rediscover whatever lay dormant inside me. I longed to meet those challenges the open road hurled in my path: *Please, God, don't let them be insurmountable.* My soul screamed to be fed and nourished by the open road because I knew when I returned home, I would be forever changed.

The familiar *resfeber* kept me awake most of the night, so much so that I posted a version of this chapter on my blog at 2:38 a.m. that morning. Energy surged through me like an electrical current. My daughter was asleep on the other side of the house, so I moved about quietly as I dressed, splashed cold water on my face, and applied sunblock.

Bessie was packed and waited patiently in the garage; I will strap my backpack, the last item to secure, onto the luggage rack after I close the door.

I walked softly into the kitchen and hit the brew button on the coffee maker, hoping the smell would not rouse my daughter as it was 4:00 a.m. I sat on the sunporch, listening to the morning sounds and sipping my coffee. I asked God for safe travel.

Paul sent a text message; it was 9:00 a.m. in France: "Please be safe on the road today. Text me when you stop this evening. I love you."

I replied, "Of course. I love you too."

I said an additional prayer of gratitude for this man in my life. Our relationship is home base for us; we give each other the latitude to "go out and come back" without restraint.

It was time—that magic hour when the sun peered over the horizon, awakened a new day and urged me to move on down the road. I tiptoed into my daughter's room, stood just inside her door, and gazed at her sleeping figure lying peacefully in the rumpled bed. Etching the memory in my heart would sustain me.

The light from the kitchen awoke her. "Are you leaving now?'" she asked sleepily.

I walked to the bed and sat down, "Yes, I am, honey. I will call you this evening when I stop. Mom loves you, and I don't want you to worry."

"Be careful, Mom. I love you too."

I bent down and kissed the top of her head and deeply inhaled my daughter's scent, just as I did when she was a baby. No matter how old she becomes, I will always savor the sweet smell of her nearness. I softly closed the door and sent a prayer to my younger child to say, "Mom loves you, wherever you are."

As I secured the backpack to the luggage rack, fastened my helmet, and swung my leg over Bessie and into the saddle, I realized that it had taken me eight years from the time I began this quest to meet my goal of riding in all forty-nine states. For ten months, I did not ride after I was in a terrible accident. It was time to unleash the harness and cast my soul to the wind for healing.

I fired Bessie up, shattering the silence of the morning and reminded myself of Neil Peart's favorite mantra when embarking on a road trip: "Whatever happens cannot be my fault" ("Travels on the Healing Road," *Ghost Rider*).

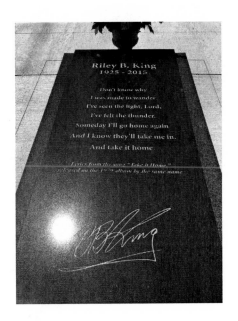

CROSS-COUNTRY: THE SOUTH

"She's got so many azalea bushes, her yard's going to look like *Gone with the Wind* come spring. I don't like azaleas and I sure didn't like that movie, the way they made slavery look like a big happy tea party. If I'd played Mammy, I'd of told Scarlett to stick those green draperies up her white little pooper. Make her own damn man-catching dress," said Minnie.

– *The Help* by Kathryn Stockett

TRAVELING NORTH ON SR 19 THROUGH FLORIDA, BESSIE and I had the road pretty much to ourselves. The weather gods were smiling: sunny, hot, and not a cloud in the sky. My aim on this trip was to visit landmarks I had not seen before and tackle a few of the top one hundred motorcycle roads I wanted to check off my list. And, I could click off the last four states in working toward my goal of riding in all forty-nine states.

I love rural Florida, and I'm always amazed that it takes me five hours or more to leave the state when I travel north and then west. I stopped in Perry for a spectacularly plain breakfast of watery grits, runny eggs, and limp bacon at a Huddle House, served up with a slice of sarcasm by a disgruntled waitress. A travel breakfast is the highlight of my morning; there's just nothing better than starting the day at a local diner with high octane coffee, biscuits so fluffy they could float to the table themselves, and a server who is damn glad you stopped in. Rather than yank this woman's already tight chain, I smiled, marveled at her skills, and left a generous tip in the hopes that she would stop whining about life in general.

Leaving the back roads of rural Florida, I reluctantly merged on to I-10 long enough to bypass Tallahassee. Interstate 10 begins in Jacksonville, Florida, and ends in Los Angeles, California. I've traveled every section of it on two wheels or four, and it ranks near the top for being one of the most monotonous rides in the whole United States. I planned to travel secondary roads and use the interstates to skirt the larger cities.

I connected to US 231 north and headed to Alabama, right into the deep, live oak South. Although I've lived over half my life in the South—some would argue Florida is not *really* part of the South, but I say that it *is* because it lies *below* the Mason-Dixon line—I was and still am considered an interloper in many places. My fast-talking, Yankee speech has never slowed enough to resemble a southern drawl, but when I visit my home state of Indiana, I'm accused of having acquired a slight drawl. Go figure. I accept the fact that as a transplanted Yankee, I lack the gentility and pedigree to qualify as a true southerner and confess my fondness for grits with my eggs or shrimp is an acquired taste, not inherent in my DNA. Despite my ancestral lack of qualifications to be a charming belle of the South, I adore the region that lies below the Mason-Dixon line. I love the food and sweet tea, the people, the geography, the literature, the music, and even the weather. There's an unhurried, poignant, and lyrical rhythm here that's like a raw, emotive, twelve-bar blues song, a tonic for what ails you.

When Bessie and I got to south Alabama, we were in the land of tupelo honey, moonshine jelly, and gator jerky country. We rode along fields of cotton, peanuts, and vegetables, and I could easily have sung "Dixie" as I passed them. In 2016, Alabama ranked sixth among cotton-producing states according to the *World Atlas* website.

Small, one-room shotgun shacks dotted the outer edges of a few fields. The small towns I passed through reminded me of a poor relative who doesn't have much in the way of material things, but they make up for it in appearances: tidy yards, clean streets, and houses that are old but maintained. The gentle ride to Montgomery, my destination for the first day, stretched along on smooth back roads through rolling farmland.

By late afternoon, I approached the outskirts of Montgomery and looked for a hotel. I saw only decaying, abandoned hotels with very little commerce other than the brisk, street-corner business conducted by hustlers. I was apparently on the "wrong" side of town. That's one of the risks of staying on back roads in some areas of the US; the mom-and-pop places have been left to decay, or the owners have resorted to renting their rooms hourly to survive.

I passed up the Relax Inn for $37.99—not sure if that was hourly or nightly. I merged onto I-65, hoping to find a better section of town to spend the night. We couldn't, so Bessie and I traveled fifty miles back south to find a Hampton Inn. That was okay; it was almost new, safe, and available. All I needed was a hot shower, a salad from the nearby Wendy's, and access to the internet. I called my daughter to tell her I was safely ensconced for the night, cleaned the bugs off Bessie, and looked at the map for tomorrow's ride.

On March 7, 1965, I was ten years old. I remember watching the tragic evening news with my grandparents; wide-eyed, we viewed the violent images of National Guard troops inflicting brutal harm to peaceful, black civil rights activists marching for voting rights. My grandma put her hands to her face and exclaimed, "It's awful, just awful!" I believe that moment shaped my sense of social justice.

At ten years of age, I knew the deep division between the races in our country was wrong. The cruel policies of the Jim Crow South were wrong. Beating black citizens with billy clubs and spraying tear gas and high-powered water hoses to quell the demonstrators who were peacefully marching for their right to vote was wrong, totally wrong.

The event my grandmother and I watched was labeled Bloody Sunday, and it took place on the Edmund Pettus Bridge as marchers tried to cross it on a journey from Selma, Alabama, to Montgomery Alabama, the state capital. Although state and local law enforcement officers drove the marchers back across the bridge to Selma, Federal District Court Judge Frank M. Johnson, Jr., a white Republican, issued a ruling. The *National Park Service* website says that he

> weighed the right of mobility against the right to march and ruled in favor of the demonstrators. Judge Johnson said, "The law is clear that the right to petition one's government for the redress of grievances may be exercised in large groups, and these rights may be exercised by marching, even along public highways."

On Sunday, March 21, 1965, Dr. Martin Luther King led 3,200 demonstrators on the fifty-one-mile march from Selma to Montgomery. They walked twelve miles each day, slept in fields, and depended on the kindness of people along the route for food and water. By the time the group reached Montgomery, after peacefully crossing the Edmund Pettus Bridge where a few weeks before they had been viciously attacked, they were 25,000 strong. Less than five months later on May 26, President Lyndon B. Johnson signed the Voting Rights Act of 1965. Today, the section of US 80 where people marched for African-Americans to have equal rights is known as the Selma to Montgomery National Historic Trail.

Bessie and I rode US 80 from Montgomery toward Selma and stopped at the Edmund Pettus Bridge in Selma. Rural Alabama was lush and fecund; the thick, perfumed air hung low, undisturbed by any wind. I inhaled a mixture of swamp foliage, magnolia and honeysuckle blooms as Bessie and I cruised leisurely along the historic route. Shotgun houses surrounded by azaleas, hydrangeas, and bougainvillea—brilliant blossoms in sharp contrast to the weathered exterior of the structures—sat along the highways.

An older black man, bent over an ancient push mower, looked up as I approached and waved gently in my direction. I returned the wave and did the same several times as other residents along the route beckoned hello from their front porch or garden patch, welcoming me on my journey. I passed through small towns seemingly trapped in the 1950s, especially Selma. Old wood boarded up the windows of deserted buildings.

I parked Bessie on Water Avenue, which runs along the Alabama River, in front of Rexall Drugs. Next door was Tulips, a women's clothing shop that specialized in church clothes—literally. Extravagant, generously embellished dresses or two-piece suits clothed the mannequins in the store windows. Lavish hats, festooned with flowers or feathers, adorned their heads.

The area near the Edmund Pettus Bridge has been fashioned into a memorial boardwalk of sorts with benches that faced the river and bridge. I sat quietly on one of the benches, recalling the evening news and the vivid images I witnessed so long ago in 1965. I can still hear the shouts, the screams, horses' hooves stomping on the bricks as state troopers charged the peaceful protestors, preventing them from crossing the bridge. As I sat there on that quiet weekday, watching the gently flowing river, the bridge rising majestically above it, it would have been difficult to imagine the racially violent scenes if I had not seen it on television for myself.

In my contemplation, I felt disheartened to realize that in 2016, violence in America was still present; some profiles had changed: Muslim, gay, and female faces had joined black and brown faces who had experienced ugly discrimination. I said a short prayer for peace among the diversity of people who occupy this planet.

I walked over to see the St. James Hotel, which offered views of the Alabama River. The hotel, built in 1837, is said to be one of the most haunted places in Alabama. After the Civil War, Benjamin Sterling Turner, who was the first black man ever elected to the United States Congress, bought the hotel.

In 1881, Turner's guests supposedly included the legendary outlaws Frank and Jesse James. It is Jesse James' and his girlfriend Lucinda's ghosts who populate the hotel most regularly, according to guests who "ghost hunt." Many have also felt the presence of ghosts in the hotel's courtyard.

I sat in the courtyard, sipped a cup of coffee, and gazed out over the river, thrilled with the possibility of seeing a ghost. I'm sad to report that I had no paranormal experience, nor did I see apparitions dressed in 1890's garb. I simply enjoyed the scenery, the pre-Civil War architecture, and the building's place in local history.

I walked back to the bike, climbed astride Bessie, and cruised through Selma to I-20 west, which took me around Meridian and Jackson, Mississippi. As far as interstates go, I-20 wasn't so bad that day: very little traffic and clean rest areas. Magnolia trees in full bloom lined portions of the interstate. Their fragrance was intoxicating.

Twenty miles on both side of Jackson, however, the interstate was in horrible shape, and I had to slow down to dodge bad pavement and construction crews. I rode over 300 miles across Alabama and Mississippi and did not see one state or county cop until I got to Greenville, Mississippi, where one was leading a funeral procession! Amazing.

Just northwest of Jackson, Mississippi, I connected with US 49 north, part of the Delta Blues Trail. I've traveled US 61 from Vicksburg to Clarksdale, Mississippi—ground zero for the blues—and part of the Mississippi Blues Trail, but in keeping with my desire to "do and see things I had not done and seen," I chose Route 49 to Indianola, Mississippi, to pay homage to the great blues man himself, B. B. King.

US 49 runs through rural towns like Floral, Pocahontas, and Yazoo City, and for long stretches of highway, I was the only traveler on the road. More shotgun houses were scattered among the fields where decrepit front porches still supported the fine art of porch sitting.

Heat and humidity hovered over the fields. If you ride in the South at the height of summer, you give up comfort and accept a suffocating, drenched feeling.

About twenty miles south of my destination, which was the B. B. King Museum in Indianola, I saw something fly off the back of my bike in my right rearview mirror. I quickly realized it was my backpack, holding an expensive camera, lenses, and iPad, that was tumbling down the road behind me! The shoulder of the highway was gravel, so I couldn't stop. I kept moving until I saw a crossover and pulled into the middle of the two-lane divided highway. After kicking Bessie into neutral, I left her idling with the kickstand down and took off back down the road at a full jog toward my backpack.

The temperature was one hundred degrees—the humidity close to that. I was jogging in knee-high boots, a long-sleeved shirt, and a helmet strapped to my head for about an eighth of a mile, back to where my tattered pack lay bereft on the pavement.

Fortunately, there were no other vehicles on the highway, so neither my pack nor I were run over. Then, I remembered Bessie was idling; I snatched the pack and ran back to the bike, saturated in sweat and about ready to collapse from heat exhaustion. I strapped the back-pack on the rack a little more securely and decided to wait to investigate whether it and its contents had been damaged.

The B.B. King Museum and Delta Interpretive Center is a funky, rusted-out industrial complex just off US 49 in Indianola, where the King of Delta Blues grew up. The second I pulled into the parking lot and switched off Bessie, I could hear B.B. Loudspeakers blasted his music all day long at the museum, inside and out.

I unleashed my pack, opened the zippered top, expecting to find the contents destroyed. Fortunately, I had lined the inside with a thick piece of foam rubber and snuggled my 5-D Canon camera down into the foam to protect it from the constant vibration of a Harley-Davidson. The vibrations alone could have disrupted the calibrations I had set, but I had not dreamed of it flying off the back and bouncing on the pavement. My iPad took the brunt of the impact; the corner was dented, and the screen cracked, but it was still functional. The camera lens was scratched but still intact. I slung it over my shoulder and decided that taking photos was the only way to determine if it still worked. (Frankly, it takes pictures, but it has not been the same since bouncing on the pavement).

I spent a leisurely hour or so, an air-conditioned respite from the heat, engrossed in the history of the Delta Blues and Riley B. King's rise to stardom. He is buried on the museum grounds in a beautiful memorial courtyard. His tour bus sits in the lot next to the gravesite, relegated to a museum piece instead of a working musician's mode of transportation. All of B.B.'s Grammys and several versions of "Lucille," the affectionate name he gave to whatever guitar he played, are on display.

I was reluctant to leave, not only because I loved the rich history of the Delta Blues and the life of one of the original Delta Blues Men, but also because the icy air conditioning had cooled me off. This was my second trip to Mississippi to absorb the history of a genre of music I love; I knew it would not be my last.

In search of a hotel before the day ended, I took US 80 west to Greenville, Mississippi, where I spied a Holiday Inn sign just twenty miles up the road and decided that was the one for me. I was drenched with sweat and looked forward to a shower.

Oddly enough, when I went into the hotel to register, I noticed it was swarming with women tennis players. I guessed that there was a tournament in little ole Greenville, Mississippi.

I dropped my bag near the bed, stepped into the bathroom, and peeled the sweaty clothes off my clammy body. As I slowly pulled down my jeans, I felt a piercing sting on the inside calf of my right leg. Looking down, I saw four nickel-sized blisters along the calf. A combination of highway heat and the heat pumping out of my catalytic converter had fried my leg.

Before I searched for a nearby restaurant, I looked for a drugstore where I could buy supplies to treat my burn. Not wanting to climb back on Bessie, I limped six blocks to a drugstore, no restaurant in sight, and loaded up on bandages and Neosporin. Stopping at a convenience store on my painful way back to the hotel, I bought fruit, yogurt, chips, and water for "dinner." A fabulous day of riding and sightseeing in my beloved South did not have a glamorous ending.

CROSS-COUNTRY:
ARKANSAS AND THE MIDWEST

The explanation requiring the fewest assumptions is
most likely to be correct.

– William of Ockham (also Occam), c. 1287-1347, Franciscan friar

LEAVING GREENVILLE, MISSISSIPPI, ON A SWELTERING JULY
morning was uneventful as I turned north toward Arkansas; it had been
a hot, humid ride across the fertile Mississippi Delta. I had awakened
to an emotion I had not known in months. My baby soul felt light,
refreshed, and free from the constraints my job at school had placed

on me during the past year. The knots in my stomach had relaxed—and gone away; three days of wind therapy had cleared my head.

As I crossed the mighty Mississippi River bridge, I connected with the possibilities of the future. I've crossed the Mississippi River numerous times on my travel over the years, and I am never disappointed when I see the longest river in America. Its significance in the history of our country is boundless as is its inspiration for writers such as Mark Twain and Tennessee Williams. Similarly, the mighty river—its fertile banks juxtaposed with the poverty of the inhabitants of the Delta—has influenced many of my favorite musicians such as Muddy Waters, Howlin' Wolf, John Lee Hooker, and Sonny Boy Williamson and others.

I felt a little sad to leave the Delta as I relate deeply on a spiritual level with the musical legacy of the region. "The blues are the roots, and the other musics are the fruits," claimed Willie Dixon, a prolific songwriter who did much to influence the Chicago blues sound after migrating north following World War II. The Delta Blues genre is a descendent of songs known as "field hollers," which were chanted by slaves as they toiled in the South's cotton fields. Their blues, with themes about hardship, heartbreak, rambling, and life on the road, was a clandestine way of rebelling against the injustices of slavery and Jim Crow laws. It was the music of damnation and salvation.

The Pig Trail is right off Interstate 40 in northwest Arkansas and runs north from Ozark to Eureka Springs for about eighty miles on SR 23 through the Boston mountains in the Ozarks.

The heat continued to plague me into Arkansas. Still considered the "South," although many argue that Arkansas is in that nether region of the United States between what is labeled "West," and "Midwest." Nevertheless, it sports the same hot, sultry weather as the "deep South."

My blistered leg throbbed all day as the air temperature, combined with the heat of the asphalt and the catalytic converter, continued to scorch my lower right calf. The heat shields attached to the front of the bike and side of the motor did little to deflect the scorching temperature.

I planned to spend two days in Hot Springs to ride the twisting and turning back roads through the Ozarks. However, when I arrived in Hot Springs, I found it akin to International Drive in Orlando, which is a mecca for tourists visiting Disney World. A throng of traffic sat bumper-to-bumper at major intersections; the brain-boiling temperature made me lightheaded. It didn't take me long to determine I didn't want to stay in Hot Springs, so I navigated over to SR 7 north, known as the Scenic 7 Byway, featured in one of my travel bibles as one of the most picturesque drives in North America. I rode it to Interstate 40, and it didn't disappoint. It reminded me of the Gauntlet in North Georgia, which is a gently rolling, twisty highway, not too challenging. The Ozarks were beautiful; I want to return in autumn or spring when the weather is not so oppressive.

Before the Scenic 7 Byway connected with I-40, I stopped to get my bearings and choose a place to spend the night. While riding every day on my cross-country journey, I was careful to keep my rendezvous date with Paul in Seattle in mind.

I stopped at a tiny, remote gas station, no more than a graveled wide-spot in the road, somewhere in the Ozark hills. The reek of greasy fried food hung heavy in the air, but the air conditioning was icy cold. After visiting the ladies' room, I was grateful I would not be eating any of the prepared food as cleanliness was not a priority for this establishment. I grabbed a bottle of water from the cooler, paid the cashier, and chose one of the red plastic tables in the small eating area. After brushing crumbs off the tabletop, I spread out the atlas and slugged down my water.

Each day I calculated the mileage I needed to cover so I could meet Paul in Seattle, careful not to meander too much. If I rode the entire Pig Trail, it would mean staying another night in Arkansas as the day was already at an end for riding. It was time to pick a landing spot and nurse my blistered calf. I decided to forego the back roads and ride the interstate north to find a hotel.

Bessie and I rolled into Springdale, Arkansas, which was only a hop, skip, and jump to the Pig Trail. We were hot, weary, and way past our usual stopping time as it was nearly dark. Happy hour was in full swing in the lobby of the DoubleTree, which suited me just fine. I perused the vegetable tray with dip, cubed cheese, and wings—standard hotel happy hour fare. I was too tired to venture out to a restaurant, so, before I checked into my room, I indulged in the buffet offerings while most of my fellow travelers imbibed the free wine and beer.

As I peeled my damp clothes off to take a shower, I realized my burned calf looked like an undercooked piece of meat. The heat had raised more blisters, and I contemplated whether I should go to an urgent care facility for treatment. Instead, I called my friend Ann, who is a nurse, and she said the best remedy was to keep the dressing off and the calf dry. I told her I would sacrifice the bandage tomorrow and see how it felt; unfortunately, my jeans and boots put friction on the raw skin.

No coffee in the room, no coffee in the lobby—how could I get going without a cup of joe? It was early morning, and all I needed was one cup to kick-start my brain. While standing in the lobby looking for the coffee bar, I smelled a pot brewing behind the reception desk. I begged coffee from the front desk guy, packed the bike, and headed out before daylight.

It was blissfully cool! I planned to connect with the northern portion of the Pig Trail as I rode north to Missouri. With very little traffic, Bessie and I cruised along, relishing the refreshing air, when boom! Bessie's engine light came on, and she went into "limp mode," a safety feature that cuts the engine to about twenty miles per hour and no throttle, so you literally limp to safety. *Whatever happened cannot be my fault*, I said to myself.

Thankfully, I was a half mile from an exit, and at that early hour on a Saturday, I wasn't in jeopardy of a car hitting me or my having to dodge traffic. I'm not a panicky, whining broad in these situations; I couldn't do what I do on a motorcycle solo if I were. I exited the interstate safely.

Now what? I knew if I stopped, that was it. I probably couldn't start the engine again, I surmised, as I had not experienced limp mode before. I slowed on the exit ramp and quickly pulled over in the ample break-down lane. Bessie died halfway up the slight incline of the exit.

When I meet adversity, I quickly run through a gratitude list in my head. My list grew rapidly as I got off Bessie: *I am not in the middle of Bumfuck, Arkansas, like yesterday; it is not hot yet; I have AAA; I have money and a credit card with a zero balance just for emergencies; I have cell phone service; I'm safe—no body parts have scraped the pavement,* and on and on.

I left Bessie on the side of the exit road and hopped a drainage ditch to find a patch of grass to plop down on while I called AAA. I related my dilemma with the agent, Amnesia—not her real name—but her real name rhymed with *amnesia*.

"Thank you for calling Triple A roadside assistance! My name is Amnesia. How can I help you today?"

I gave Amnesia my name, address, phone number, and account information and told her what my predicament was.

"I'm so sorry this has happened to you! Are you safe?"

"Yes, Amnesia, I'm sorry it has happened as well, and yes, I'm as safe as I can be sitting on the side of an exit ramp."

"Well, let me see what I can do to help as quickly as possible!"

Then Amnesia embarked on a series of questions, which I assume is standard operating procedure but seem mundane and frustrating when you are the person stranded at the side of the road.

"What kind of motorcycle is it?"

"Harley-Davidson Road King."

"What's wrong with it?"

"If I knew, Amnesia, I probably wouldn't need you or a tow truck. I'm not a mechanic."

"Of course. I have to ask."

"When can I expect a tow truck?"

"First, I have to determine your location so I can give the driver exact directions. "

"I am just off I-49 in Springdale, Arkansas, at exit 82. My motorcycle is in the break-down lane halfway up the exit ramp."

"To avoid confusion, I need a distinguishing feature of your motorcycle, so the driver doesn't have a problem identifying you. What color is your motorcycle? Is it pink?"

And here is where I lost my shit with Amnesia.

"PINK? I would die before I rode a pink bike, Amnesia. (No offense to my Wind Sisters who ride pink motorcycles; it's just not me!) What difference does it make? My BLACK motorcycle is the ONLY motorcycle broke down on Exit 82 off I-49 in Springdale, Arkansas, at 6:00 a.m. today! I don't think the tow truck driver will have any trouble finding me."

I immediately felt bad. Amnesia was just trying to do her job, and it was probably not a good idea to piss off the one person standing between me and roadside assistance.

As I paced the grassy patch near the exit like a caged lioness, Amnesia put me on hold while she located a tow service. Once she returned to the line, I apologized for my outburst and thanked her for her thoroughness. Amnesia never wavered in her perky demeanor and helpful approach to my dilemma.

The emergency road service came to my rescue in forty minutes. The driver was a nice, twentysomething biker dude named Ryan who was excited because a few months before, he had convinced his boss to install an electric wench device on the truck to load disabled motorcycles. I guess the company's proximity to the Pig Trail kept them busy towing bikes. I was excited that he was excited. *So, let's see this new wench do its job and get Bessie off the side of the road!*

After Ryan expertly got Bessie onto the truck, he explained that the Pig Trail Harley-Davidson dealership was just five miles up the road in Eureka Springs, but they didn't open until 8:30 a.m.

"If you'll go to a coffee shop, I'll treat both of us to coffee and breakfast," I suggested. Ryan was reluctant. "I hate to leave my wife all morning. She wasn't happy I had to come out on a Saturday." But, he agreed to stop at a nearby Starbuck's for coffee.

Ryan deposited Bessie and me safely outside the service department of the dealership. I gave Ryan a generous tip, thanked him for his care, and said goodbye. Just about the time I finished my venti caramel macchiato, the service department opened. Bessie and I were finished in under an hour—long enough for me to sip the last drop of my coffee and drop $125 on new apparel. I snagged a destination T-shirt and a gorgeous sweater-type wrap with a blingy Harley-Davidson logo on the back.

The fix was simple—it was a malfunctioning throttle sensor—and under $200. I was almost giddy paying the bill! Back on the road by 10:30 a.m., I was still bothered by my calf-searing heat issue.

I had had the Road King for three years. Its catalytic converter pumps out lots of heat—which is just the nature of the beast I ride. But it had never blistered my leg. I had ridden to Nova Scotia last summer, out to Colorado (west Texas is hot in July) two summers ago, and the heat was not a problem.

I propped my feet on my highway pegs to keep my leg away from the heat while I cruised down the highway. *What variable had*

I introduced to the equation on this trip that wasn't present on previous trips? That thought kept crossing my mind.

My undergraduate degree was in psychology where I learned several principles that I use almost daily. Jean Piaget's theory of child development was a useful tool after my first child was born. I tacked his elaborate chart of milestones inside one of my kitchen cabinets, and as each milestone age for her approached, I looked for signs that she was "developing." The one thing Piaget forgot to mention was that children would grow just fine on their own schedule, oblivious to any chart tacked to the inside of the cabinet.

I practice B. F. Skinners Classical and Operant Conditioning Theories for behavior management every day in my classroom. Abraham Maslow's hierarchy of needs has taught me much about myself. I admit to wallowing way too long at the bottom of Maslow's triangle, but I can confidently say that I am now closer to that pinnacle of self-actualization. I learned about Occam's Razor, or to use my two years of Latin, *lex parsimoniae*, the law of parsimony. It is a line of reasoning that says the simplest answer to a dilemma is often correct.

As I biked along the interstate, keeping my feet propped up on the highway pegs, I looked down and saw that the most recent variable I had added was the new thigh bag I had bought at Bike Week and had not used until this trip. It was a military-style bag that clipped around my waist and thigh; it kept everything I needed at my fingertips. I wore it on my right leg because I'm right handed—and it was also on the side where all the heat from the engine was pumped out. I realized that THE BAG WAS TRAPPING THE HEAT! I took the first exit I came to, stopped, jumped off Bessie, and switched the bag to my left thigh. Problem solved! I didn't get that expensive formal education for it to go to waste.

My ride through the Midwest was brief. I went north on US 71 through Missouri, steered clear of Kansas, then skipped over to the southeast corner of Nebraska.

Bessie and I meandered along the unhurried secondary highway through plain vanilla Midwest farmland, not unlike my home state of Indiana. I inhaled the fragrance of freshly tilled earth and crops nearly ripe for harvesting. After skirting Kansas City, Missouri, I stopped early for the night just north of Kansas City in St. Joseph, hoping to talk with Paul in France before he went to sleep.

As I traveled further west, the time difference between mine and Paul's locations became greater, making communication tricky. Before leaving home, Paul, my daughter, and I downloaded the mobile phone tracker app on our iPhones. Both tracked my route as I moved across the United States, but I told them only to worry if the blue dot didn't move. Paul awoke each morning in the south of France, eager to check the blue dot's journey; only then did he know I was okay. I missed my wingman on this trip.

I nestled Bessie into place under the hotel portico and before checking in, I called Paul. It was good to hear his voice and reassure him that my trip was going well.

Regrettably, I was not able to stick around in St Joseph, Missouri, and tour the Glore Psychiatric Museum, formerly the State Lunatic Asylum No. 2—another time perhaps. It is precisely the type of oddity that I enjoy seeing on my travels.

A glorious, sunny morning dawned the next day as Bessie and I set our sights on the Great Plains as we journeyed west.

CROSS-COUNTRY:
THE GREAT PLAINS

I salute the light within your eyes where the whole universe dwells. For
when you are at that center within you and I am at that place within me,
we shall as be one.

– Chief Crazy Horse, Oglala Lakota Sioux, 1877

THE RIDE NORTH TO SIOUX FALLS FROM FLORIDA FELT
interminable. I needed to feel like my goal of clicking off my last three
states was in sight, so that meant I had to turn west. After I stopped for
lunch at a desolate truck stop off US 77, I discovered my driver's license
was missing. I always travel with my passport, too, and the two pieces
of plastic have my picture on them, so I didn't stress too much. I would
deal with the problem when I settled for the evening. It didn't occur to

me as I stood in a dusty, dirt parking lot in western Iowa, that my missing license would prove problematic a week later in Anchorage, Alaska.

I had dodged the glut of construction around Sioux Falls, South Dakota, by early afternoon. After whizzing along the posted eighty-mile-per-hour speed limit—a mere suggestion for most of my fellow travelers—from Sioux City to Sioux Falls, seeing fifty-five miles per hour was a welcomed respite. Once I hit Interstate 90 west, I felt as though I was finally "on my way," despite the fact I had been on the road for six days!

I have traveled every quadrant of our nation on two wheels or four, and I had never grasped the scope or vastness of the United States until I visited the Great Plains; even grander and more expansive are the prairies of South-Central Canada. Immense ranches and farmlands in the Upper Midwest appear to stretch toward infinity; the scrumptious smell of freshly cut hay sweeten the hot, dusty air. The sky, an immeasurable cobalt dome, converges with the horizon in all directions, uninterrupted by glass and steel structures or mountain peaks.

Lack of concern and understanding, however, have marred the stark splendor of the Great Plains. An estimated twenty million bison once roamed the territory, but at the beginning of the twenty-first century, authorities say the count is a mere 500,000. Only through conservation efforts is the number that large.

Great tribes of Sioux and Cherokee Native Americans populated the region, following the bison and living off the land they cherished. The same sadness and shame I felt in Selma, Alabama as I gazed at the Edmund Pettus Bridge overwhelmed me as I thought of how Native Americans have been callously relegated to impoverished reservations.

Once I turned west on I-90, I decided to travel as far as Mitchell, South Dakota, which was less than 350 miles. On my list of "Things I Have Not Seen Before," was Mitchell's Corn Palace. Before iBooks, my grandma Fisher painstakingly glued photos from her trips into large, bulky photograph albums, securing each one with tiny, black mounting corners that she pasted on the pages. One of those photos was of the Corn Palace from the mid-seventies. Grandma marveled at the murals on the exterior of the building made entirely from corn. I owed it to her to visit the folk-art icon.

Bessie and I parked a block away from the Palace and strolled over to see what impressed my grandmother so many years ago. According to the Chamber of Commerce literature, the Palace was originally built in 1892 as a gathering place for farmers, ranchers, and townsfolk when the prairie was beginning to boom. Artists change the murals on the exterior of the building each year to reflect a different theme; the theme for 2016 was Rock of Ages. I gazed up with my camera in one hand and shaded my eyes from the sun with the other and stared unbelievably at the intricate artwork. I must admit that seeing an eight-foot-tall Willie Nelson and Elvis Presley likeness, made entirely from corn, was riveting.

The Palace itself is more like a convention center. The cavernous main hall showcased a plethora of arts and crafts, most of them featuring some design made from corn. I scored a bag of caramel corn and snapped a few pictures. Perhaps my grandchildren will someday wonder about the Corn Palace after seeing my photo and set off on their own journey of discovery.

My riding gear desperately needed washing; therefore, I spent the evening writing and doing laundry while savoring the sweet, crunchy caramel corn directly from the Palace.

Bessie and I started early the following morning to travel west to Rapid City, South Dakota, the gateway to the Badlands and the Black Hills. I confess that my must-see list featured mostly sites in the Plains and Pacific Northwest. I had traveled through this area with my grandparents decades ago, but I remembered very little.

The air was blissfully cool, so I donned two jackets, full gloves, and my face mask, a stark contrast to the weather I had encountered so far. SR 240 cut off I-90 before Wall, South Dakota, and looped through the Badlands. After two days of riding through the wide-open spaces of the prairie, I was startled when I entered the Badlands—the Lakota Sioux call it *Makȟóšiča* or *Mako Sica*. It looked as if an ancient being used the "J" hook can opener on a Swiss Army knife to randomly pry open the smooth, grassy prairie with ragged tears to reveal prehistoric rock formations.

A Sioux legend tells of the Great Spirit who, weary of the various tribes warring with each other on the peaceful prairie,

> sent dark clouds to hide the sun from the face of the world. Lightning streaked across the blackness, and thunder rumbled high over the hills. From the ground flamed forth fire, and earth shuddered and rocked. A wide gulf opened, and into it sank the mountain tribe, all their people, and all they possessed. With them sank all life, the waving grass and clear spring and animals (badlandsmythology.www.nps.gov).

The Great Spirit left the Badlands, which became vast remnants of both his power and his punishment. Deep, striated gorges slice through the formations where "all the earth colors of the painter's palette are out there in the many miles of bad lands," wrote Georgia O'Keeffe, an American artist renowned for her paintings of enlarged flowers and barren landscapes. The landscape colors are determined by the position of the sun; bright sun reflects a world of muted browns. As the sun moves to the west, the rocks and ravines turn to rich tones of mossy green, autumn-leaf red, Georgia-clay orange, and slight hints of heather or rosewood. It is a kaleidoscope of colors found only in nature.

I felt at peace among the sedimentary rocks, where energy radiates from the prehistoric formations that crop up out of the South Dakota plains. The Native Americans of this region considered the

Black Hills their point of creation. Their reverence for the land was part of a spiritual component; the rock structures were their cathedrals for worship. I have visited the Canadian Badlands with their oddly-shaped rock formations in southern Alberta as well; the spellbinding, twenty-feet-tall Hoodoos of Drumheller Valley emitted a spirit, formed from earth and sky.

Bessie and I cruised into Badlands National Park late morning. Except for a few titanic RVs, notorious for taking up their narrow lane of pavement AND my lane, the park was quiet and sparsely populated with tourists. I put Bessie next to a BMW bike—New Jersey license plate—at one of the overlook vistas and walked up to the small, concrete pavilion. The other biker and I nodded silently at each other out of respect for the solitude of the moment. He didn't come up here to converse, and neither did I. I moved out toward the edge of the patio-like foundation, its knee-high wall a deterrent for anyone who might be apt to ignore safety precautions and tumble down the steep ravine.

The sun, not yet on broil, had heated the colors of the landscape to multiple shades of brown, brushed with strokes of khaki and avoca-do-green vegetation. A thick morning fog hung over the horizon as if it was reluctant to leave, choosing instead to hang heavy, absorbing the heat. It was quiet—the kind of quiet found only in nature, disturbed by minimal rustlings of vegetation, the hushed scurrying of creatures who inhabited the rocks, an occasional screech from a winged predator, and the softly moving wind that felt like an air kiss on my cheek.

The stillness soothed me; my baby soul lifted its face toward the sun, soaking in its warm rays, inhaling the clean air, and exhaling gratitude for the moment of calm. Several minutes later, I heard the footsteps of the other biker behind me as he left the pavilion and descended to his bike.

I cherished my solitude while overlooking the extravagant landscape. I forgot the turmoil of my job, the stress-induced physical ailments, and concentrated on healing mentally and spiritually.

All too soon, my quiet contemplation came to an end when I heard a car door slam at the bottom of the overlook; children's voices shouted excitedly as they scampered up the steps to the pavilion.

I was hit with a pang of envy, a longing for my own two children at that age, as the parents shouted, "Be careful!" My frequent desire for aloneness was a double-edged sword. I shook off the melancholy, waved to the family who had joined me on the overlook, and ambled back to Bessie. I looped the park trail several times, spending most of the morning among the silent rocks. By noon, Bessie and I left to visit the next stop on my list.

Over two million visitors a year visit Wall, South Dakota, unofficially known as "the geographical center of nowhere." Since 1931, weary travelers have sought a respite from the heat or desolate geography by stopping at Wall Drug, for "free ice water." Wall, populated by 800 or so full-time residents, occupies no more than a dusty, wide spot just off Interstate 90. The town swells during the tourist months, especially during Sturgis Bike Week when motorcyclists from all over the country converge on the Black Hills.

It was a steel horse I rode down the dusty Main Street; it was easy to imagine cowboys in leather chaps, their faces grimy from long hours in the saddle, on flesh and blood steeds, riding into town the same way. I parked my steed in an expansive parking lot behind the main drag and headed over to Wall Drug to see what all the fuss was about and take part in a long draw on some of the free ice water.

Wall Drug is an assault on the senses. The second I stepped through the narrow door, my vision somersaulted; every shelf, every inch of wall space, every angle, every nook and cranny from floor to ceiling was crammed with stuff. At some point in its history, Wall Drug stopped being a drugstore and became a tourist mecca with every conceivable trinket tourists would ever want to purchase. I wandered the aisles as the worn, wooden floorboards dipped and creaked under my boots for several minutes before realizing there was very little I wanted to buy.

The mouth-watering scents wafting from the cafeteria, which was haphazardly attached to the main building, intrigued my nose and beckoned me toward the aroma. The original dwelling had morphed over the years until it consumed an entire block of interconnecting specialty shops. I ordered lunch, tapped my portion of free ice water, and enjoyed a delicious burger while I tried to read every caption on the plethora of old-timey photos that plastered the wall. They were mostly photos of the early years of the region's development. I bought a magnet to add to my collection, checked Wall Drug off my list, and headed down the road.

In the southwest corner of South Dakota in the Black Hills, you will find some of the most breathtaking scenery in all North America. Needles Highway is thirty-seven miles of road through giant, needle-like rock formations, pointing toward the heavens. It runs through Custer State Park, where buffalo roam. Bessie and I could have spent a few days meandering among the rocks.

I followed the signs for Mount Rushmore and the Crazy Horse Monument located in the Black Hills. Outside the little town of Keystone, the road wound up into the Black Hills, then boom! I rounded a curve, and there it was—Mount Rushmore, its four carved faces in stone peering over the highway. There was a place to pull over to take pictures, and I regret not stopping to snap my selfie, but instead, I forked over $11.00 at the official Mount Rushmore monument plaza and circled the lot for twenty minutes before finding a parking spot. I dismounted Bessie and trucked up several flights of stairs in boots, jeans, Under Armour heat gear, and jostled elbow to elbow with other onlookers to get an unencumbered view of the mountain.

I stood on the observation deck and stared face-to-face with the stoic stone expressions of Washington, Jefferson, Roosevelt, and Lincoln. I wondered about Gutzon Borglum, the sculptor, and how he arrived at such an undertaking. Was he sitting around playing cards one night and said to himself, *I think I'll carve four American presidents' faces in relief on the side of that mountain?* The answer is no. Borglum, originally from France, was well-known in the early 1900s for his American sculptures and was approached by the South Dakota Historical Society to create what became Mount Rushmore. He died before the project was completed, leaving his son, Lincoln Borglum, to complete the sculpture.

By midafternoon the sun had ramped up to blast-furnace hot; the festively decorated plaza area below the mountain was crawling with sightseers, and the line for ice cream was intolerable. I'm not a fan of crowded, touristy areas. I took off on Bessie for my next stop, the Crazy Horse Memorial, the world's largest mountain carving still in progress.

I first read about the memorial to Lakota Sioux Chief Crazy Horse several years ago in a now-forgotten publication. The sculptor, Korczak Ziolkowski, initially traveled to the Black Hills in 1939 to work on Mount Rushmore with Gutzon Borglum. Henry Standing Bear, an Oglala Lakota Sioux Chief, heard of Ziolkowski's achievements in other endeavors, and in 1947, invited the sculptor to consider carving the memorial to Crazy Horse.

The first blast of the mountain occurred on May 3, 1947. Five survivors of the Battle of Little Big Horn joined others in the audience who watched it. What interested me the most when I first read about the project was that the Memorial does not accept federal or state funding. It is financed entirely by contributions and admission fees to the property and museum. The mission of the Crazy Horse Memorial Foundation "is to protect and preserve the culture, tradition and living heritage of the North American Indians."

The trip up to the mountain was another spectacular ride through the Black Hills. At the base of the mountain, where the carving is in progress—once finished, it will stand broader in scope and size to Mount Rushmore—was a sprawling complex housing the Indian Museum of North America. Plan to stay awhile if you visit. The Native American artifacts are remarkable and provide a rich, visual history. An extensive display of maps and photos tell the history of the carving of the mountain. The sculpting thus far featured the chiseled face of Crazy Horse with his fierce warrior face glaring out over the Black Hills. The sheer size of the leviathan stone outcropping where the sculpting is taking place was more than amazing.

The museum was packed with memorabilia, original manuscripts, beautiful beaded authentic clothing, jewelry, hand-crafted tools, teepees, dugout canoes, and pictures of what life on the plains was like for Native Americans. Not uncharacteristically, I spent a good deal of time in the museum bookstore. I had never encountered such an extensive collection of books on Native American history. By the time I heard the first earsplitting clap of thunder in the distance—the Sioux called it *Wakinyan* or Thunder Birds—I was clutching an armful of books.

I glanced outside and saw angry black clouds advancing toward the mountain. I made my way to the cashier, giving little thought to where I was going to store five paperback books in my already-crowded saddlebags. I hurried back through the museum to the exit as the thunder crashed closer, and the lights flickered briefly.

As I approached Bessie, the temperature dropped dramatically, and the heavens opened; cold, heavy rain hurled pea-size hail upon me. Quickly, I unlocked my saddlebag and fished out my rain jacket. The winds raged, blowing rain sideways. I pulled my leather jacket out and threw it over the camera pack since I didn't have time to put the rain covers on them. My helmet, hanging upside down on my handlebars, caught the hail like a bucket. I ran back to the museum and stood huddled under the entrance portico with several others to wait out the storm.

Once the deluge was over, I walked back to my bike—my thighs chafing noisily in wet jeans—dumped ice pellets out of my helmet, packed the soggy jacket, and sat on a very wet seat. As luck would have it, Bessie and I traveled about five miles down the road and came right back into the hailstorm again! Thankfully, there wasn't a lot of traffic on US 16, because there was nowhere to pull over, and I was blinded by rain.

I flicked the flashers on, slowed to twenty or thirty miles per hour, and prayed a fast-moving vehicle didn't come up behind me. Ten miles down the road, just outside of Rapid City, the sun shone—fiercely.

The desk clerk handed me the key to my hotel room in Rapid City and a map of the complex. I wasn't crazy about my hotel choice, but the options in this part of South Dakota were limited. It had seen better days; the crumbly, one-story buildings sprawled out over a parking lot of several acres. I had rarely felt unsafe in any of my solo travels—until now.

My room was in the very last building, which looked like an afterthought; it faced a chain-link fence with a few abandoned vehicles in the parking lot. My first thought was, *If I scream for help, no one will hear me.*

I backed Bessie into the space facing the room, thinking, *If I back in, I can make a quick getaway if I have to,* and tugged my pack off the luggage rack. The ceilings in the hallway were so low that I could reach up and touch them; the smell of mildew and stale bodies hit me like a sledgehammer. For this, I paid $130.00?

The carpet in the room looked like it might have been clean once, maybe when Nixon was still president. The décor was a feeble attempt at funky, faux western, but it totally missed the mark. The bed visibly sagged toward the middle underneath the paper-thin bedspread, and I shuddered to think of the activity that poor mattress had experienced.

Sadly, during Sturgis Bike Week, the room fetched upward of $250 per night.

I was tired and sweaty, and I had been pelted by hail, plus my jeans were still soggy. I was hungry, and I didn't feel inclined to look for another hotel. I resigned myself to staying and getting revenge the next day by leaving a scathing review on TripAdvisor, that is if I managed to avoid getting raped and beaten during the night. Yes, it was that bad. I dared not mention the horrible conditions to my daughter or Paul when I checked in with them a few hours later.

I was not sorry to pack the bike and leave earlier than usual the following morning. I had managed to escape any harm to life or limb—unless you count my twisted spine after a night on the torture rack of a bed in the "Hotel of Horrors."

I stopped off in Sturgis; it's a quiet little town except when 700,000-plus bikers, which was the estimated number of attendees during the 2015 Sturgis Bike Week, are in its city limits. As I snapped a photo of Bessie in front of Sturgis' Harley-Davidson dealership, I was a little dismayed that I was there too early to buy a T-shirt, so I headed west. I wanted to make it to the northwest corner of Wyoming and then on into Montana.

The Black Hills appeared to be on fire outside of Gillette, Wyoming; dense clouds of smoke blurred the distant landscape, and its acrid smell tingled my nose and veiled the surrounding interstate. I filled my tank in Sturgis, calculated the miles to Sheridan, Wyoming, and decided I would have plenty of gas to make it. At least, I thought I did.

It's a remote route along Interstate 90 in the northwest corner of Wyoming; services are few and far between. I wanted to take a picture of the Big Horn Mountains in the distance, so I exited at a spot where road crews were working on the bridge and the exit area. What I didn't realize was there was no way to get back on the exit going west, only east. Apparently, the road crew removed the sign warning travelers of "No Reentry Westbound" while they were working. After stopping to snap a picture, I was dismayed to realize I was headed back to where I came from with very little gas—not enough to return to Gillette, not enough to make it to Sheridan, if I found a spot to turn back west. As if worrying about not having enough gas was bad enough, I had to pee.

I remembered seeing a deserted-looking rest stop, void of any vehicles or people, that serviced both sides of the interstate going westward several miles ago. I had to risk stopping. If I had to push my bike or wait for AAA, I didn't want to have a full bladder!

As I exited the interstate and idled toward the tumbled-down dwelling housing the restrooms, I noticed two motorcycles were the only other vehicles in the lot. I pulled Bessie into a slot a few feet away from them. A shirtless guy with long, braided, jet-black pigtails hanging over his shoulders, a colorful bandana around his head, and heavy gauge hoops through pierced nipples, looked over and said, "Which way you headed?"

I mentioned I was headed west but got turned around at the exit with the construction. I added, "Now I'm concerned I don't have enough gas to make it back to Gillette, where I saw a station."

A tall, dark-skinned girl with the same braided pigtails, same colorful bandana as her partner, walked up to the bikes and declared, "We have gas!" She pointed to the little plastic jug on the back of her motorcycle that held a gallon of gas.

The girl rode a much smaller bike than her partner, was originally from Canada, and understood the need to carry her own gas! I had a similar experience on the north shore of Lake Superior in Ontario, and out in West Texas. Richard, her shirtless partner, emptied the gas from the can into my tank, I tried to pay them, but they refused. Instead, Denise said, "Just pay it forward."

I'm forever amazed at the kindness I experience while traveling, especially from fellow bikers. I wished them safe travels, thanked them again, and got back on I-90 to head west. I thought of Richard and Denise often over the next few days. People cross our paths so briefly, yet they often leave a lasting impression. I would like to have spent some time getting to know them as a couple.

The northeast corner of Wyoming was vast, wide-open with gently rolling hills but very few services or turnouts. The weather remained cool, and I rode most of the morning with my heavy leather jacket on. I bypassed the junction for the scenic byway to the Grand Tetons and Yellowstone National Park. I had visited both many years ago, and alas, they were not on my list for that trip. I will save those two places when my wingman can join me; he has not been to either place on two wheels.

My time was running short, however, for when I was scheduled to meet Paul in Seattle; he had limited vacation time, and our flights were booked for Alaska. There was no wiggle room for my dawdling.

I crossed the Little Bighorn River and saw signs pointing to the battlefield where General George Custer made his last stand against the combined forces of the Lakota, Northern Cheyenne, and Arapaho tribes, led by Sitting Bull. The stop was not on my list, but I had not seen the infamous battleground where the U. S. Army 7th Cavalry fought the Native Americans, resulting in the defeat of US forces.

The park was packed; you would think it was summer and the continental anniversary of the national parks or something. I paid my fee but declined to go to the visitors' center where busloads of tourists milled about. Instead, I chose to cruise the uncongested, one-way asphalt path through the battlefield. Small, white tombstones, no bigger than the size of my desktop computer screen at home, graced the hillside, indicating where a 7th Cavalry soldier died (approximately 260 soldiers died that day). A few brown tombstones marked the spot where a Native American Indian died.

The fierce battle was fought on June 25, 1876, along the grassy ridge (known to the natives as Greasy Grass) on the banks of the Little Bighorn River. In an act of defiance, several tribes refused to report to their assigned reservation in the Montana Territory, which resulted in General Custer and his troops being directed to restore order. It would be Custer's "last stand." He got his ass kicked by the likes of Sitting Bull and Crazy Horse. I parked Bessie at the top of a rise with a panoramic view of the battlefield.

Closing my eyes, I tried to imagine the fierceness with which the natives defended their land—a land that was slowly being stolen by the white man. It makes me angry, and I feel compelled to apologize to someone, anyone, for the way "my people" have treated Native Americans.

The sun beat down from directly overhead and told me it was time to continue moving. I stowed my leather jacket, snapped a few pictures, and slowly wound my way back to the park exit.

Interstate 90 cut through the eastern quadrant of the 3,600-square miles in the Crow Indian Reservation in Montana. The tiny towns of Wyola, Lodge Grass, and Crow are rife with dilapidated buildings and decrepit mobile homes littering the hillside. Forlorn casinos sit in the hot sun, their neon lights flashing garishly—like so many other reservations across the country.

I stopped at a combination gas station and convenience store at the edge of the reservation for something to drink. It was not the glitzy, fresh-faced, well-ordered 7-Eleven type store in an urban area. The floor was greasy, and the merchandise was carelessly displayed on dirty shelves. The smell of stale cooking grease mingled with sweat permeated the tepid air in the cramped interior. Beer, cigarettes, rolling papers, and lottery tickets were the primary commodities.

As I walked into the store, all activity stopped; the several male customers turned, looked at me with—what? A leering look of disgust?

Mistrust? Vehemence? I didn't feel as though they wanted to harm me; they appeared to prefer I make my purchase and move on.

I walked to the large cooler at the back of the store, grabbed two bottles of water, and placed them near the cash register. The man, who was about the size of a refrigerator, nodded, took my five-dollar-bill with a pudgy hand, and plunked the few coins of change down on the counter. I went out the grungy door.

I stood near my bike, not wanting to make myself at home on the grimy bench outside the store, to rehydrate and glance at my atlas. I decided to call it a day somewhere near Bozeman, Montana, the foot-hills to the Rocky Mountains.

The Yellowstone River meanders along I-90 for most of the ride to Bozeman. The elevation gradually changed as I left the Great Plains behind and cruised toward the mountains of the west. I glanced at my odometer and realized I had logged nearly 600 miles in one day's travel. The temperature has vacillated from cold to blistering hot and back to cool. I was road weary.

I didn't have a hotel reservation, and for reasons I never fathomed other than the summer is the height of the season, tourists had packed Bozeman. I exited where I saw several hotel billboard signs reaching up over the exit. I have a nifty app on my iPhone called Hotel Tonight. I simply activate the app, my phone's GPS determines my location, then the app shows the hotels in the immediate vicinity with their rates. No more stopping at multiple hotels to check cost or availability. The rates that pop up are usually lower than the quoted price since these are rooms the hotel needs to sell before the end of the day. One of two choices from where I stood was Days Inn, which had only one room left according to my app. I clicked "reserve," and since my credit card information was already stored within the app, I was on my way to a hot shower and rest. I would begin the end of my journey the next day.

CROSS-COUNTRY: THE PACIFIC NORTHWEST

Embrace your capabilities and honor your limitations.

– Debi Tolbert Duggar

THE COLD, SHARP WIND SHOCKED ME AWAKE AS I STEPPED outside the Days Inn in Bozeman, Montana; an intricate pattern of tiny ice crystals randomly covered my windshield. The temperature had dropped to the low thirties overnight. Shivering in the early morning chill, I secured my pack to the bike and dug my heavy leather, stiff with cold, from the saddlebag. I dashed back to my room, laid my leather pants and jacket out on the bed so they could warm up, and pulled my heavy gloves and ear-warmers out of the pocket of my coat. It would be a nippy ride west.

However, the chill did little to dampen my excitement; the day would mark the beginning of the end of my solo journey across the United States. I was to rendezvous with Paul in Seattle in two days, so I had only forty-eight hours to cover my last three states on Bessie and make several stops at places on my Bike-It List. It was a grueling schedule.

I stood in the hotel room, surveyed my riding gear, and suited up for the ride like a warrior preparing for battle. A thin layer of Under Armour cold gear went on first, and then my leather jeans, wool socks, knee-high leather boots, and a long-sleeved thermal T-shirt. After pulling a balaclava over my head to cover my neck and face, I slipped into a light jacket and a heavy leather jacket. The ear-warmers, insulated full-finger gloves, and finally my helmet completed my defense against the cold and wind. I flashbacked to how my grandmother dressed my younger self to "go outside and play in the snow;" she wrapped me in layers of wool and a bulky snowsuit. I felt the same way as I dressed on that cold, cold morning. The weather throughout the journey from Florida had been one of extremes: extremely hot or extremely cold and very little comfort in between.

The hot coffee I downed at breakfast to ward off the raw cold had not lasted very long; as I rolled west out of Bozeman, the sharp wind stung my eyes, sending watery rivulets down my cheeks.

The traffic on I-90 at this early hour consisted mostly of pickups and delivery trucks. The sun, coming up behind me, awakened the majestic mountains in the distance; its warm glow outlined snowcapped peaks with their juts and ridges emerging from the shadows. The highest peak near Bozeman is Sacajawea Peak (9,839 ft.) in the Bridger Mountains, which is part of the Rocky Mountains in southern Montana. The beauty of the moment did nothing to soften the biting cold permeating every cell in my body. I rode west for an hour. Unable to tolerate the frigid temperatures another minute, I exited when I saw a small outpost advertising freshly baked muffins and hot coffee. The building appeared to be a converted gas station, turned into a rustic watering hole.

I stiffly climbed off Bessie and peeled the heavy gloves off my frozen hands. The interior was warm, homey, and inviting. I strolled up to the order counter, placed my order for a giant cup of coffee, and glanced over at the baked goods on full display. I chose an oversized cinnamon roll about the diameter of my helmet to accompany the coffee. The warmth of the small restaurant, infused with the sweet aroma of baked goodness, began to thaw my body while I alternated sipping strong coffee with the gooey goodness of the cinnamon roll.

My body slowly warmed from the inside, and I remember thinking, *I could sit here all morning rather than face the cold again.* I felt cozy and safe.

A glance at my GPS revealed my location was only thirty miles from the Idaho state line; my goal was in sight, yet my emotions were tangled. To travel on Bessie in forty-eight states had been my focus for the last several years, but what would happen after I had achieved my objective?

I'm a Type A personality—always needing goals and lists to keep my momentum, to maintain perspective, and to feel I have accomplished a purpose. It's as if I don't exist unless I am chasing a plan or checking a completed item off my list. Perhaps I've exaggerated the effort, but so what? I had set out to ride my motorcycle in every state.

At that point near Idaho, however, fear tempered my excitement. Fear of the letdown associated with finally completing a goal; fear of not quite ending the quest successfully; fear of disappointment or fear that nobody but me cared about my success. It was the kind of mental masturbation that often plagued me. Intellectually, I knew what I felt was cognitive dissonance, conflicting attitudes. However, there was a better word for what I felt: *numinous,* from the Latin word *numen,* meaning "divine will," which, for me, was a feeling of both fear *and* awe for what lay before me in the next twenty-four hours.

I also knew I was physically tired; I missed home and the people I loved—thoughts which played on my nagging self-doubt. It didn't matter "who cared," but it was important that "I cared." I had chased my dream for the better part of eight years, and it mattered to only me that I succeeded in my mission.

I downed the remaining coffee, leaving over half of the cinnamon roll, its doughy goodness already heavy in my stomach, and as I walked out to where Bessie was parked, my attitude was, *Hell yes! Last three states? Bring them on!*

The Lewis and Clark National Historic Trail begins in Pennsylvania, extends from Illinois, and goes to the mouth of the Columbia River near Astoria, Oregon. It commemorates the significant contributions of thirty-one men, one woman, and a baby in their quest to discover a water route to the Pacific Ocean between May 1804 and September 1806. Bessie and I planned to follow the Lewis and Clark Trail through Idaho, Washington, and Oregon. Four years ago, I made the same journey on four wheels through Washington.

When I was a young girl in elementary school, perhaps in the fourth or fifth grade, I paid rapt attention to the history lessons about Merriweather Lewis and Captain William Clark as they explored and mapped what was known to them as the Louisiana Territory. More importantly, I was fascinated with the young Shoshone Indian girl Sacagawea (1788-1812) who accompanied the Army Corps of Discovery in their exploration of the West.

Sacagawea was one of several wives (by "wife," I mean she was captured by a warring tribe and "sold" at the age of thirteen) of French-Canadian trapper Toussaint Charbonneau who spoke both French and

English. The expedition recruited Charbonneau in Idaho because of his knowledge of the West and his ability to translate. His young wife, pregnant with her first child, was brought along as a symbol of peace to any Native Americans they would encounter on their journey.

I've read many accounts of Sacagawea's life over the years. Hers was a biography of hardship and abuse, tempered by her courageous spirit and character strength. Her son, Jean Baptiste "Pomp" Charbonneau, was born in 1805 during their journey to the West, and Merriweather Lewis assisted in the birth. By all accounts, Sacagawea saved the lives of the more than forty men many times over through her knowledge of survival skills in the wilderness and her ability to converse with potentially dangerous tribes.

Six years after the expedition ended successfully near the Pacific Ocean, and they had returned home, William Clark, who had developed a strong affinity for "Pomp," convinced Charbonneau to move his family near St. Louis, Missouri, so that Clark could educate the boy. Tragically, Charbonneau, tired of "civilization," returned with Sacagawea to the Indian village in Idaho, leaving her son to be raised by Clark. She never saw him again. Much later in life, I came to understand the heartbreak she must have felt losing her child to someone else to rear and never seeing him again.

As the day heated up—thankfully—Bessie and I turned southwest outside of Missoula, Montana. Unfortunately, my venture into Oregon was brief; a short "dip" of Bessie's two wheels in the northeast corner of the state had to suffice. Time didn't allow me to ride through Hells Canyon as I had hoped, but I noted the place as a future must-see.

US 12, the Lochsa River Scenic Byway, part of the Lewis and Clark Trail in Idaho, stretches from Missoula to Lewiston and cuts through the Bitterroot National Forest and the Nez Perce National Forest. The remote road was in good shape. Giant pines lined the highway, their tops lost in the fog that shrouded the upper reaches of the forest. Leaving the emerging sunshine behind in Missoula, Bessie and I enjoyed a meandering ride; the heavy moisture and the pungent smell of the pine forest enveloped us. I clocked nearly ninety miles before reaching a town with a gas station at the small outpost of Syringa, Idaho, where the road turned back northwest, away from the deep forest.

Somewhere outside of Orofino, Idaho, I stopped for a break at a small rest area. The weather had warmed to the point I felt comfortable shedding my heavy leather jacket. I tucked it, my balaclava, ear-warmers, and heavy gloves back in the saddlebag, and walked over to a bench near the small restroom pavilion. I plopped down and took a mental inventory.

Ten days on the road, over 3,000 miles, and I was fatigued; I felt as though I had pushed my capabilities to the limit and then some. As the saying goes, "Life begins where your comfort zone ends." I knew Paul would arrive in Florida from France and stay just long enough to repack and fly to Seattle in two days to meet me. I thought about my plan to store Bessie in Seattle while we toured Alaska, and after returning to Seattle, ride back to Florida. It would take another ten or twelve days, but I didn't want to follow the route I had already taken. I had decided to go south along the Oregon-California coast, cut across the Southwest, which was a route I had already made on two wheels, and from there, ride on back to Florida.

My thoughts swirled, and I retrieved a Tatiana to help me think; I fired up one of the sweet-tasting chocolate minis, inhaled deeply, and exhaled with my decision. Once I dipped into Oregon and rode across Washington, I had met my goal. From that point forward, any direction I pointed Bessie was one where I had already been.

I dug my phone out of my thigh bag; there was one phone call I had to make before I touched base with Paul.

"Air Van Moving, how can I help you?" answered the husky male voice.

"I need to ship a motorcycle from Seattle, Washington, to Orlando, Florida," I stated.

"Not a problem. What kind of bike is it, and what dates are you talking about?" he replied.

My rational-self and my adventurous-self argued briefly over the decision to ship Bessie back to Florida rather than ride. My adventurous-self considered it an act of defeat somehow, perhaps not a full realization of my dream. My rational-self maintained that once we crossed Washington, I would have met my goal to ride on two wheels in all the lower forty-eight states. Then my rational-self whispered, *Honor your limitations.*

My rational-self declared victory; for a fraction of the cost of traveling back home for ten days, I could ship the bike. Bessie would be waiting for me in Orlando, and I could fly home with my wingman in climate-controlled comfort.

I talked with the nice man at Air Van Moving for several minutes, gave him my credit card number, and agreed to print out the shipping papers once I settled at a hotel for the night. It was done. I had one more phone call to make.

"Hi, honey! How was your flight from France?" I chirped into Paul's ear when he answered my call.

"Long. Where are you?" he replied. His voice sounded very tired. The monthly commute between Florida and France over the last five months had begun to wear on him.

"I'm somewhere in Idaho, and I need you to do me a favor," I said.

"Oh? Is everything okay? What do you need?" He seemed a tad bit alarmed.

"I'm fine. I want you to get me a plane ticket on the same flight you're on from Seattle to Orlando," I explained, rushing into the next bit of information before he had time to panic. "I've just made arrangements to ship Bessie back to Florida once we get back to Seattle."

"You did *what*?" he said incredulously. I repeated what I had just told him.

"Really? Are you sure?" he asked. My wingman knew how important this ride was for me, and his question touched me deeply.

"Yes. I'm sure. We can talk about it when I see you on Saturday. Can you do that for me?"

"Of course," he replied. His voice told me he was all too happy to make the arrangements for me to fly home with him. I gave him my current location, where I was headed next, and that I would talk with him later in the evening. The time difference between Paul in Florida and me in the Northwest was three hours, not six as it was when he was in France. I planned to stop somewhere mid-Washington state for the evening.

"Okay. Be careful; I love you."

"Love you too."

And the flight arrangements were just that simple. I climbed back on Bessie with a different attitude, eager to travel. I knew intimately how to embrace my capabilities, and I had turned another corner in my journey by knowing when to honor my limitations.

At Lewiston, Idaho, I headed south on Washington SR129, a short ride to the Oregon border. I crossed into Washington briefly but refused to count it a valid ride in the state just yet. A fist pump heavenward signified my dip into Oregon, but I regretted that I couldn't travel through Hells Canyon on this trip. Then, I literally turned around and pointed Bessie back north toward Interstate 90, the longest interstate highway in the United States, and Spokane, Washington. As I cruised along 1-90, I searched for a road sign or anything that declared, "Welcome to Washington," so I could stop, claim victory, and take a selfie to celebrate the occasion. I saw none.

The terrain in eastern Washington is significantly different from the western portion of the state. Rolling farm and pasture land, broken only by a random copse of trees, reminded me of Kansas—without the wind.

I stopped in Spokane for refreshments and a break to check the map. I didn't want to travel the 300-plus miles to Seattle in one day; there were a few mountains I wanted to climb before giving up Bessie.

It was early Thursday afternoon, and Paul was to arrive in Seattle on Saturday evening, and I had arranged to deliver Bessie at the port in Tacoma on Saturday morning. I picked a spot on the map—Ellensburg, Washington—to stop for the night. That would put me in the southern Cascade Mountain range near Mount Rainier and Mount St. Helens.

The sun had cranked up to full broil as I turned west out of Spokane. Still no "Welcome to Washington" sign along I-90 for my celebratory selfie; I resisted the urge to pull into a gas station and shout to random people, "Hey! I just crossed into Washington and completed my journey to my forty-eighth state on two wheels!" Instead, I marveled at the plethora of crops in eastern Washington. Someone had posted signs along the fences, indicating the type of crops such as hops, potatoes, cabbage, green beans, kale, carrots pumpkins, and peas. The farmland featured a cornucopia of vegetables and fruits—apples, blueberries, cherries, pears—and vineyards along the hillsides. I thought, *Should I stop and take a selfie next to the potato field or the grape arbors?*

Vast expanses of fertile fields hugged the never-ending interstate on both sides. My due west route put me in direct alignment with the sun's westward movement; its glare blinded me, and the arid temperature felt oppressive. My sunblock had stopped blocking the blistering sun. Spotting a directional sign for Wild Horse Canyon as I neared the Columbia River, I wondered, *Maybe this is the location for my selfie?*

I steered Bessie to the asphalt pull-off and cautiously surveyed the scene before I switched off the ignition. The remote area had a stunning overlook nestled between a deep gorge overlooking the Columbia River. One thing I don't do while riding alone is to stop in desolate places, even if they are paved and right off the interstate. I saw a semi-tractor trailer parked at the far end and a seemingly abandoned RV near it. Circling the pavement, I parked Bessie with her front end headed out toward the interstate, an easy get-away if necessary, and I didn't take off my helmet and gloves. Grabbing my phone, I walked toward the informational signs that told the story of Wild Horse Canyon. Standing at the edge of the cliff, I looked up and down the river, the heat creating a thick haze, shimmering and dancing through the canyon.

Suddenly, my legs wanted to buckle, and vertigo crept in, making my head swim. I felt as though my legs were melting out from under me; I stumbled backward, away from the edge of the cliff, and shook off my weakness, chalking it up to the heat exhaustion and weariness.

I turned my back to the sweeping vista and snapped a bad selfie to celebrate my goal with this final crossing into Washington state. Then, quite unexpectedly, I just stood there and sobbed. I threw my helmeted head back and let out a low moan that swelled to an out-and-out sobbing. With my hands on my knees, I bent over, trying to gulp the thick, humid air, each gulp catching in my throat, releasing a choking sob.

There was no victory dance, no congratulatory high five, no fireworks. It was just me, alone on the edge of achievement. I felt as though I had come full circle and reached the end—simultaneously.

My dark clothing absorbed the brutal heat from the sun. As I lifted my head to gaze once more down into the deep gorge, I took slow, deep breaths to quell the sobs that kept welling up from my gut. Tears and snot mingled with sweat as I ran my sleeve along my sunburned face.

I snapped a panoramic picture of the canyon and prepared to walk back up the incline to the parking area. As I turned, I noticed two Asian tourists, perhaps mother and daughter, who had also stopped to admire the view. They were staring at me, which led me to believe they had been there all along—or at least long enough to witness my meltdown on the edge of Wild Horse Canyon. Once I started walking in their direction, they diverted their attention to the informational sign. Out of respect for my distress, they ignored my slow climb back to where my bike was parked.

I climbed astride Bessie, tears still mingling with the sweat trickling down my face and pooling around my neck. It took several miles of wind therapy to make sense of the meltdown.

Twenty miles on the outskirts of Ellensburg, the highway on the westbound side of the interstate ended, leaving an exposed roadbed of grated rock and dirt. Shortly after hitting the roadbed, I saw the caution signs that signaled road construction. Perhaps placing the road signs *before* it ended would have been a better idea? The asphalt had been stripped away, leaving what was essentially rumble strips with gravel.

Traffic slowed to a crawl for the next ten miles as I struggled to keep Bessie upright on the rocky, rutted road. I took the first exit for Ellensburg and pulled into the closest hotel parking lot, an old Howard Johnson's that had seen its heyday in the seventies. I glanced at my odometer: 658 miles since leaving Bozeman at dawn; it was past time for a hot shower, sustenance, and rest.

The hotel lobby was as dreary as the exterior, although the middle-aged woman behind the check-in desk was cheerful. She handed me the room key, and I schlepped my bags down an endless hallway that twisted and turned with what appeared to be each renovation in the building's history. The room was functional; that is the kindest thing I can say about it. At least, I didn't feel for my safety as I did back in Rapid City. I dropped the bags and went back out to scan the horizon for a restaurant. Unfortunately, it looked like another convenience store dinner for me.

An early start the following morning was the only way I would have enough time to climb a couple of mountains before arriving in Tacoma. The weather was cold and drizzling rain in the quiet, early morning darkness as I packed Bessie for the day's travel. After a quick fill-up at a gas station, I turned south out of Ellensburg on I-82 towards Yakima.

I again picked up US 12, the White Pass Scenic Byway, to go to the southern portion of Mount Rainier National Park and then ride south to Mount St. Helens; the area is referred to as Washington's Volcanic Playground.

The fog was dense. Leaving the flat farmland behind, the wilderness of old-growth temperate rainforests enveloped me in an eerie, fog-shrouded chill; condensation formed on my windshield. This was the weather and landscape more typically associated with the Pacific Northwest.

Mount Rainier, elevation 14,410 feet, is the highest mountain in the Cascades and the highest mountain peak in Washington. It is also considered one of the most dangerous, active volcanoes in the world—although it has not erupted in modern history as has its neighbor to the south Mount St. Helens—because of the massive amounts of glacial ice covering the top of the mountain. If an eruption occurred, the glacial ice would produce massive mudflows, not to mention molten hot lava. I planned to ride through the area without worry of any such natural disaster.

The White Pass Scenic Byway begins just outside of Naches from the east and Mary's Corner from the west. A dizzying array of scenic-driving loops run through the Washington Volcanic Playground, some of which stay closed because of snowfall until May or June. The downloadable PDF maps and current road openings from the White Pass Scenic Byway were very useful in planning this trip.

The road began as a meandering ride through the Wenatchee National Forest. The deep green of the towering coniferous trees shaded the way, locking in the chill of the crisp morning air. With every other curve or so, the forest opened to reveal a mountain meadow scattered with alpine wildflowers in bloom. Their vibrant hues of purple, yellow, and pink were like deftly placed brushstrokes on the canvas of the landscape; the mist lent an impressionistic quality to the meadow. Monet would have been pleased.

I pulled over at the lookout on Rimrock Lake, which sits along the course of the Tieton River; the snowcapped peak of Mount Rainier was still mostly obscured by the fog, and the sun was having a difficult time breaking through the almost constant curtain of mist.

I was alone at the lookout surrounded by woodsy quiet; the condensation in the air was so close to rain that I heard tiny droplets dripping in the forest and splatting on Bessie. I had seen a handful of cars since leaving the interstate a few hours ago and only one or two since traveling the Byway. Unlike my meltdown at Wild Horse Canyon, I possessed a keener sense of awareness and a sense of peace with my surroundings this time.

The climb in elevation was gradual as the road ascended to the White Pass. The temperature dropped to the low forties to the point that I thought all the condensation around me might turn to snow. At the 4,500-foot peak was the White Pass ski area; barren dirt paths etched a pattern on the mountain that was void of skiers at that time of the year. The main lodge stays open to welcome summer travelers seeking respite from the cold.

I stopped for a hot cup of coffee to warm my core and thaw my fingers. I was the sole occupant in the small, cozy snack bar with a good selection of seventies' rock and roll playing softly on the stereo system. Snow-ski memorabilia and historical photos of the construction of the road going up the mountain covered the walls. I sipped my coffee and ambled around the room, reading captions and old newspaper clippings.

A "newer" poster caught my eye; it was an elaborate, multi-colored chart of the different varieties of marijuana available at a nearby dispensary. It identified the name, type, origin, effects, and medicinal benefits of each strain of marijuana, which is legal in Washington state. Oh, the times; they are a-changin'!

As I finished my coffee and grabbed my leather jacket off the back of the chair, the young man behind the counter said, "The road up ahead is partially washed out, so be careful." He was in his early twenties, tall and thin with longish hair. I pictured him as a snowboarder, not a skier. Since I first walked into the restaurant, he was friendly and outgoing, probably just whiling away the summer hours until he could get back on the slopes.

"Wait. What?" I asked.

"Yeah, the runoff from the winter snow has washed out a portion of the road and sent it right down the mountain. If you are going that way (and he pointed in the direction I was headed), you will have to wait in one-lane traffic. It is the other side of the road that's washed out."

"Thanks."

Sure enough, just around the bend from the lodge, the few cars on the road had stopped to allow the oncoming vehicles to detour around a sizeable section of the pavement that had washed down the mountain. The rapidly flowing stream of water was falling over the remaining lane, and, apparently, we would drive right under it. I waited. Bessie idled steadily beneath me, the engine warming as maybe a half-dozen cars passed us before it was our turn to traverse the gaping section of highway and dodge the stream of water.

A road crew directed the minimal traffic, and we inched forward. Spray from the waterfall misted my windshield, impairing visibility. I glanced to my left and realized I was no more than four feet from the jagged pavement and a tumble down the side of the mountain. The water cascaded with a loud splash as it continued its erosion.

I slowly moved closer to the solid rock on my right to avoid the water; the road crew waved and gave me a thumbs-up. As I made my way back down the mountain on the other side, it occurred to me that I had not seen another two-wheeled traveler all day.

The condensation on the forest road was heavy as clouds engulfed the treetops and droplets of water collected on my windshield. I felt as though I was riding through a medieval forest on my trusty steed.

Shortly before noon, I stopped outside of Randle, Washington, where I planned to pick up National Forest Road 99 to St. Helens. The shroud of wet weather still hovered heavy in the thick forest, blocking any effort by the sun to penetrate it; the damp chill had found a home in my core despite the heavy leather.

Approaching the Forest Road, I spotted an orange road sign that had settled haphazardly on the side of the road, almost undetectable; it warned, "Closed for Repairs." I was dismayed that I would not see Mount St. Helens on this trip. The area was remote, and I had not passed another vehicle since leaving Randle. I pulled Bessie onto the cracked and aging asphalt of an abandoned 1950's-style gas station, put the kickstand down and left her idling while I checked my map.

The low clouds, tired of holding their moisture, loosed with a steady drizzle of rain. I pulled rainwear from the saddlebag, stowed the map, and ducked for cover under a dilapidated awning near the ruins of the main building. As I donned my waterproof suit, the rain segued from a drizzle to a full-on downpour. I fished for my cell phone in my thigh bag, hoping for a signal so I could check the radar. Menacing green and yellow covered the entire southwest region of Washington state, and future weather radar indicated rain into the late afternoon. The Mount Rainier website's weather advisory warned, "Not good. Low visibility on the mountain roads."

As I stood under the little awning while the rain pelted Bessie, still idling strongly in the desolate, abandoned lot, I tried to decide how to proceed. I remembered something my friend Karen A. once told me: "You can make all the plans you want, just don't plan the outcome." She believed that a power greater than ourselves was ultimately in charge of the consequences; therefore, we shouldn't waste time or energy trying to manipulate or control how a situation would end. Sometimes plans work, and sometimes, like that day, plans must be amended.

The weather gods were not with me in my desire to see Mount Rainier. The app made it clear that the rain would not let up anytime soon, and that the weather was better in the direction of Tacoma, my destination. If I had had a nice comfy lawn chair, I would have sat under the awning for a spell to listen to the rain, surrounded by the wet, fragrant smell of the forest.

I continued riding on US 12 west to Interstate 5 north; I was nearly out of the Cascade Mountain range, and it was a short ride to Tacoma. Air Van Moving expected Bessie first thing the next morning, and I could not leave any gear on the bike, which meant I had to ship a few items home by parcel and condense the gear I needed for Alaska into my one small tour pack.

Not for the first time on this trip, I cursed the tight time frame I had set for myself. Our country is so vast that ten days of traveling from coast-to-coast is not nearly enough time to see even a decent portion that lies between.

I left the relative safety and dryness of the dilapidated building, straddled a wet seat, and pulled Bessie cautiously onto the road. I clicked on my flashers so any vehicle coming up behind me in the fog and rain would see a motorcycle in front of them. I was not worried about traffic since Bessie and I seemed to be the only vehicle on the road. Reluctantly, I traveled in the opposite direction of two mountains I had hoped to conquer on this trip.

ALASKA

The Great Perhaps was upon us, and we were invincible.
The plan may have faults, but we did not.

– John Green, *Looking for Alaska*

I PACED BACK AND FORTH IN THE SMALL, CLUTTERED
office of Moto Quest, the motorcycle rental company in Anchorage,
Alaska, trying to clamp down my frustration while Paul attempted to
reason with Al, the beefy, cantankerous manager. Losing my driver's
license was a major roadblock to renting a motorcycle in this, my forty-
ninth state. I had reserved the last two available bikes in the state a few
months ago, and now I was faced with proving to the rental manager
that I could legally ride a motorcycle. Oh, the irony.

Paul's approach to adversity or obstinate people is to be gentle
and compromising—a sharp contrast to how I handle unfavorable
situations. I knew my bulldozer approach to the manager's legitimate

518

and legal position of requiring I present a valid driver's license with a motorcycle endorsement would not end well. My anger was fueled by his condescending attitude and apparent disbelief that the fuming woman in front of him could ride a motorcycle. A copy of our valid driver's licenses, faxed to Moto Quest upon confirmation and payment of the rental, had been required. Although Al was looking at a photocopy of my license, he was sticking to his guns by requiring I actually produce the license.

Paul, bless his heart, said to the manager, "Look, she just rode her Harley-Davidson Road King all the way from Florida to Tacoma, Washington. Do you think she did that without a license?"

"People do it all the time, mister," replied Al, as he shrugged indifferently. He busied himself behind the counter, not even making eye contact with Paul or me. We were being dismissed.

"She lost her license somewhere in Missouri and contacted the Department of Motor Vehicles for a replacement, but it didn't arrive before I left home."

"Too bad," said Al, his button-down shirt with the Moto Quest logo pulled taut across his barrel chest as he spread his hands wide in a who-cares gesture. "I have no idea who she is and no idea if she can safely operate a motorcycle."

"What if we contact the dealership where she completed the safety class. They will have a record of her endorsement. Will you accept that?"

"And have someone I don't know vouch for someone else I don't know? Sorry, Pal," said Al with a mocking chuckle. I wanted to smack the smirk off his jowly face. From my position behind Paul, I reminded the man that he held photocopies of both our driver's licenses, which was required at the time I booked the rental and paid a deposit. I waved three additional pieces of identification, including my passport with my picture, in front of him that proved the photocopied license was mine. Al was not swayed.

"Doesn't matter. The law requires you to present your valid driver's license before I let these bikes go outta here," the beefy man sputtered, looking over Paul's shoulder and directly at me.

"If you allow me to use your computer, I will access my license online with the Florida Department of Motor Vehicles," I said through clenched teeth.

The other employee with the Moto Quest logo shirt was a stocky, eager young guy, who appeared to be in his mid-twenties, and was hovering just inside the door. He said, "Yeah, that should do it, right Al?"

He was apparently on my side and already had the two bikes sitting outside in the parking lot, gassed up and looking shiny for our ride.

I stepped in front of Paul and positioned myself defiantly in front of Al who was seated at his desk where the computer sat, half-buried by papers, discarded fast-food bags, and a couple of motorcycle parts. He tossed the rental documentation papers onto his littered desk like a petulant child, pushed back his chair, got up, and stomped out to the garage as if he was disgusted with the whole process.

I sat down in the squeaky chair, pushed a stack of papers off the greasy keyboard, and accessed the Florida DMV website. I had not gone that far in my journey to let irascible Al stand in my way of traveling in Alaska. I accessed my DMV information that clearly showed I was a valid driver—on two wheels as well as four.

Meanwhile, the young kid followed Al out to the garage, where he evidently convinced him that I could sign a waiver of responsibility that would hold me liable if my "reckless inexperience" resulted in damage to their motorcycle. They walked back into the office, and before I could show Al the computer screen, the young kid presented his solution. Al marched back outside, not wanting to admit defeat.

The kid hastily drew up a handwritten, two-sentence "waiver of liability" that loosely said I assumed all financial responsibility, regardless of fault, if something happened to damage their motorcycle. Plus, Paul and I were required to sign waivers that stated we would *not* take the rental bikes on the Dalton Highway as part of the original rental agreement for all customers. The Dalton Highway, or the North Slope Haul Road as it is also known, is the gravel road used to transport oil and supplies from just north of Fairbanks to Prudhoe Bay, Alaska, near the Arctic Ocean. I looked at Paul; he shrugged as if to say, "Why not?"

After Paul and I signed the papers, the kid handed us the keys to the bikes. I thanked him for his problem-solving savvy—I don't remember his name—and apologized for the inconvenience. Al disappeared, which was just as well, because the young man's gracious attitude was not enough to prompt an apology from Al for his behavior on this Saturday morning. I made a note to call the booking agent in California and relay my experience.

We had arrived in Anchorage late Thursday night as the midnight sun cast a warm, purple glow on the Alaska Mountain Range to the north. All of us passengers craned our necks near the windows, attempting to get a glimpse of Denali, America's tallest mountain, as the plane circled its descent into Ted Stevens Anchorage International Airport. Alas, the great mountain was shrouded in thick clouds, veiling her majesty.

Paul and I spent most of Friday ambling around Anchorage and shaking off the jet-lag. The weather was "cold" by my standards—in the fifties with misty rain. We picked up the bikes Saturday morning and had only a short, twenty-four hours to scout the extraordinary terrain. That didn't seem like much time to explore in such a vast wilderness as Alaska but considering the availability of passable roads and at least twenty-two hours of sunlight, we felt we could go for a pleasant tour of a portion of the 9,000-square-mile Kenai Peninsula.

Saturday morning was cold and damp; the same eerie gray sunlight from last night created a pewter-colored dawn. We packed our rain suits on the rental bikes—mine a Harley-Davidson Softail, Paul on an Indian Chief—and wore heavy leather, hoping at some point during the morning that the sun would burn off the gray dampness.

Our destination was Seward, Alaska, on the southeast side of the Kenai Peninsula, and about 120 miles from Anchorage. Paul and I picked up the Seward Highway, a designated National Scenic Byway, just south of Anchorage. The cold wind bit through my leather jacket and stung my face. We cruised along the spectacular coastline of Turnagain Arm; the four-mile-wide flats in Cook Inlet stretch to the high, sloping Chugach Mountains on the opposite side. The arm of the inlet was named for British explorer James Cook who was forced to "turn again" when the waterway didn't hold the fabled Northwest Passage during his 1778 voyage.

Paul and I stopped at Beluga Point Lookout to gaze out over the turbulent brown water, thrashing through the inlet. Signs cautioned of the bore tide that rushes into the flats, topping speeds of twenty miles per hour; it fills the muddy landscape and sloshes against either side of the inlet. We scanned the water for Beluga whales and thought perhaps they preferred the inlet during the calmer hours of midafternoon once the incoming tide settled.

We saw Dall sheep, however, making their way precariously up the mountain on the opposite side of the highway. I counted a dozen white, furry bodies zig-zagging their way up the steep slope on spindly legs. While we were stopped, I dug my face mask and heavier gloves out of the pack. Thick, voluminous clouds blocked any attempt by the sun to warm or brighten the morning.

The Seward Highway turned away from Cook Inlet, just past the Potter Marsh Bird Sanctuary, and went toward Prince William Sound. A sign for Portage Glacier caught my eye. and I signaled to Paul we were going off the planned route to investigate the glacier. Off the main high-way, we quickly noticed the road became more than a little potholed and rough. We rocked along, dodging gravel-filled holes for six or seven miles; the rugged Chugach Mountains towered skyward on either side of us. My favorite scent of frosty pine forest rose heavy in the air.

The last stretch of road that led into the paved parking area of the visitor center was pure gravel. I slid the rental bike into the deserted parking lot, grateful for solid asphalt. The visitor's center was not open, so Paul and I wandered around the rocky perimeter of the lake, snap-ping photos. The sun was finally burning off a layer of gray clouds, lend-ing the mountains in the distance an indigo tint and scattering sparkles over the glistening, mirror surface of the lake. The snow-capped peaks, part of the Chugach National Forest, one of them being Portage Glacier, is the source of the crystal-clear water of Portage Lake. We wrestled the bikes back over the graveled entrance and down the rugged access road to the Seward Highway which would take us toward Hope Junction.

The off-the-beaten-path town of Hope is one of Alaska's original gold-mining camps, nestled in the northern tip of the Kenai Mountains. Many original buildings still stand with hitching posts for "parking" your trusty steed while shopping. The ride from Portage Lake to Hope Junction, with only one outhouse-type rest stop, was on a good high-way with little traffic to impede our adventure.

Thirty miles outside of Seward was the charming, rustic town of Moose Pass, no more than a moment's hesitation on either side of the highway. It appeared to be a base camp for hikers, fishermen, and bush pilots as well as home to Alaska Float Ratings, a world-renown bush pilot flight school. We stopped long enough to layer on another jacket to ward off the chilly "summer" weather.

An enterprising local had built a giant waterwheel, and his welcome sign encouraged visitors to stop: *Moose Pass is a peaceful little town. If you have an ax to grind, do it here.* I rounded a curve just outside of Moose Pass and had to screech to a stop for a mama moose and her calf ambling across the road. Paul and I sat in the middle of the road, engines idling, while she took her time crossing to the woods on the other side.

The elevation from Moose Pass dropped toward Seward, situated on the water between the Gulf of Alaska to the south and Prince William Sound to the north. As we neared Seward, the traffic became surprisingly heavy for such a small city. Paul and I jockeyed the rental bikes into one parking space on a downhill side street, shed our heavy leather, and set off on foot to explore this bustling little place. The main road was blocked off, and runners with numbers pinned to their singlets mingled in the street. I asked someone, "What's going on?"

He pointed to the mountain that towered over the coastal city of Seward and said, "It's the Mount Marathon 5K. Look up there. See the little dots moving up and down the mountain? Those are runners."

Our eyes followed the arc of his pointing arm. Holy crap! There were people "running" up 3,020 feet and then back down the mountain, on into town, and over the finish line! A carnival atmosphere filled the city with street vendors, music, and townspeople mingling in the streets to celebrate the Mountain Marathon 5K.

Paul and I wandered over to the Seward Boat Harbor and watched the fishing boats come in with the morning's catch. Large halibut hung as trophies at one end of the dock while a brawny, wader-clad fisherman expertly filleted the daily catch, the tip of his scruffy white beard nearly touching the wet, scaly filleting board. Huge, screeching seagulls bobbed in the water just under the filet station, waiting for the fish scraps. I noticed a couple of large vessels that advertised whale-watching tours of the Kenai Fjords National Park and Prince William Sound. I urged Paul in the direction of the ticket kiosk to ask about a tour. We had two weeks in Alaska and planned to return to Seward by car, so we made arrangements for the boat tour the following weekend.

Hoben Park lay at the southern-most point of Seward on the Gulf of Alaska. The Alaska Sealife Center, which is a "cold-water research center that promotes valuable scientific understand of marine mammals, birds, and fish," and the historic Alaska Railroad Historic Depot are the focal points in the park. The National Historic Iditarod Trail, which begins on a paved bike path, starts in Hoben Park—Mile 0 to 2,300 miles of winter trails. The famous Iditarod Trail Sled Dog Race begins in Anchorage, not here.

I walked down to Resurrection Bay, a fjord, near the water's edge and started picking up rocks. Paul stood on the path above, watching, knowing I intended to build an inukshuk and say a silent prayer for my dad. He patiently watched as I assembled the rocks, the biggest and flattest on the bottom, then stacked the increasingly smaller stones, one on top of the other. By now, he was accustomed to watching me build these stone structures when we traveled. I managed to balance a rock tower about a foot high on the shore of the Gulf of Alaska. As I knelt on the stony shore, I whispered to the wind, "Take care, Dad. I trust you are on the right path."

I climbed back up the small embankment. Paul reached out his hand to help me up the last few feet. He hugged me and said, "We missed lunch. Let's find a place to eat before we ride back to Anchorage."

Hand in hand, we walked back toward the edge of town; his warmth gave me solace as the tinges of grief made their insidious way into the corners of my consciousness that afternoon.

As we strolled back into town, I waved to a couple sitting on their front porch with a prime view of the runners going up Mount Marathon. I stopped and asked if they could suggest the best place to eat in Seward. Without hesitating, they said, "Thorns! About five blocks up on Fourth Avenue."

I searched the name on my iPhone, got the walking directions, and said "Thank you" to the couple on the porch. The blue dot on my phone led us to Thorn's Showcase Lounge. We stepped into the dimly lit, funky, fifties hole-in-the-wall, and found it packed in the middle of the afternoon. A server showed us to the only table available in the back of the small dining room. The booths, chairs, barstools, the front of the bar, and even portions of the wall behind the bar were covered in deep red, brass-tufted leather that reminded me of old Las Vegas nightclub decor. What fascinated me the most was the floor-to-ceiling shelves of varying height and width on every wall with dramatic back lighting behind the wall of shelves. Each shelf held what appeared to be a collector's bottle or decanter. Bottles shaped like animals, cars, sports figures, movie stars, royalty, US states, and even an entire chess set.

When our waitress arrived, I asked her about the bottles. Dressed in jeans and sneakers with a black apron tied tight around her waist, she was one of those women whose age could have been twenty or forty: hair piled haphazardly on her head, a harried crease across her forehead, and no makeup.

"Oh, those are all Jim Beam collector decanters. The owner has accumulated them for years," she explained, gesturing nonchalantly around the room. Since the place was packed, she was more focused on taking our order, but she patiently answered my questions.

"Wow, that's some collection. Are they still full of Jim Beam?" I asked.

"Some of them are, and some of them hold the cremated remains of long-time patrons of the bar," she said matter-of-factly, pencil poised over her order pad. "Have you decided on your order?" She was all business, but I had more questions about the bottles.

"Wait. What? You mean those shelves hold a Jim Beam graveyard of sorts?" I said incredulously.

She laughed. "Yeah, I guess you could say that. The same owner has had the bar since the 1950s, and regular customers over the years have requested their remains be kept in their favorite decanter from his collection. Pretty cool, huh?" I agreed it *was* pretty cool.

The beer-battered halibut was beyond cool as well—it was out-of-this-world delicious. Paul and I dove into the generous basket of delicately fried fish nuggets, sweet coleslaw, and, of course, a mountain of fries. Except for the reindeer sausage we tasted from an Anchorage street vendor, we ate halibut or salmon the entire two weeks we toured Alaska. As I enjoyed the late-lunch-early-dinner, I couldn't take my eyes off the Jim Beam decanters. I spied a replica of a sparkly white jumpsuit Elvis decanter and looked over at Paul and asked, "Which one would you like to be stored in after you're cremated, honey?"

"Hmm," he said as he looked around the room. "I see a 1964 Mustang over there." He gestured over my head with his fork. "That would be cool."

By early evening, Paul and I had returned to Anchorage. With twenty hours of sunlight, we didn't worry about "darkness" descending before we made it back. My years of traveling on two wheels were nearing the end of my goal of riding in forty-nine states. My heart soared to the mountain peaks surrounding us, full of the adventure that day's ride in my forty-ninth state delivered. My soul was satiated, and I embraced a level of accomplishment no words could describe. As we parked the bikes in front of the Hampton Inn and climbed off, Paul gave me a high five, affirming the significance of that moment in my life.

Paul and I spent the next two weeks touring Alaska by train, plane, car, and boat. We traveled to Denali National Park—where I built another inukshuk—traversed the rugged Dalton Highway, and reached the Arctic Circle where we soaked in the warm, healing water of Chena Hot Springs. We marveled at the beauty of Homer in the Kenai Peninsula and watched orca whales, sea lions, and bald eagles during the boat tour of Prince William Sound.

The wilderness wonder of Alaska's rugged terrain is magical. Nothing I have ever seen—the Rocky Mountains, the Oregon coastline, the sweeping vistas of the Cabot Trail, the frigid shores of Lake Superior, the Grand Canyon, or the Swiss Alps—can compare with the grandeur that is the Land of the Midnight Sun. Paul and I were enchanted with our experience and vowed to return.

As I closed the blackout drapes in our hotel room, shutting out the perpetual daylight, I said a prayer of thanksgiving.

JOURNEY'S END

The privilege of a lifetime is being who you are.

– Joseph Campbell, *A Joseph Campbell Companion: Reflections
on the Art of Living*

AFTER A RESTLESS NINE HOURS IN THE SEATTLE-TACOMA
International Airport on our return flight from Anchorage, I gratefully
settled into the plush leather comfort of a first-class seat. Paul and I
had spent a good portion of the nine-hour layover touring downtown
Seattle, and we were exhausted.

It was after 9:00 p.m. when we boarded, and Paul was asleep beside
me before the plane pushed back from the gate. If there is anything I

dislike about this man, it is the ease with which he can slip into dreamland anywhere. I have never been able to sleep on a plane, but a sleepless night of cross-country flight seemed far easier than the ten days of two-wheeled travel back to Florida that I originally had planned. Bessie was comfortably tucked into the transport carrier on her way back to Florida, both of us content with my decision to ship her back instead of riding her to our home.

The last streaks of the sunset's oranges and reds were fading across the horizon as the plane took off down the runway, hurtling us into the encroaching night. I turned toward the window to watch the last vestiges of the colorful sunset before the deep, rich hues gave way to darkness.

I said a silent prayer of gratitude for my opportunity over the past month to achieve my goal to ride a motorcycle in forty-nine states and tour the stunningly beautiful state of Alaska with my wingman.

As the airplane gained altitude and broke through the cloud layers, there it was—the last remnants of crimson glow from the setting sun on Mount Rainier! The snow-capped peak jutted majestically through the clouds as the altitude of the plane afforded me a bird's-eye view of the mountain.

I turned to jostle Paul awake so he could share in the sight but decided the scene was all mine and left him to his slumber. I turned back to the window to soak up as much of the scene the aircraft's increasing speed and altitude afforded me. For days, the summits of Mount Rainier, Mount St. Helens, and Denali had eluded me.

At that moment, I could almost hear the mountain speak to me as I was carried away on silver wings: "I'm here. I've always been here." And, in the ancient whisperings, I heard Robert Pirsig's voice telling me, "The only Zen you find at the top of the mountain is the Zen you bring up there."

While my fellow passengers settled quietly for the cross-country flight, my thoughts drifted to the day over two weeks ago that Bessie and I arrived at Wild Horse Canyon overlooking the 1,243-mile Columbia River in Washington. I stood at the edge of the cliff—the proverbial abyss—and sobbed. At that point, my transformation was complete. I had traversed over 500,000 miles of asphalt since purchasing my first bike in January of 2008, seeking a balm for my battered soul, trying to connect with the Zen and its meditative calmness. Until that day at Wild Horse Canyon, I never fully understood that I already possessed everything I needed inside of me.

My journey on Bessie through the adversities in my life had come full circle. I crossed the threshold of a new life when I purchased my motorcycle a decade ago. My soul was screaming for healing when I unshackled myself from a detrimental relationship that day in the ferry terminal in Bar Harbor, Maine. I answered the siren call to live my own life by embarking on the remainder of the journey, *Soul-O*. Astride Bessie, I learned new skills along life's highways, meeting with success and transforming my life with two wheels. Bessie and I encountered many trials over the following years; each one offered a new revelation, and new insight on my journey of the soul. The "loss" of my daughter and the loss of my dad left me standing at the edge of the abyss. But, I refused to go over. In the process, I acquired a new self that is confident, fearless, and capable.

I was returning to my old world, my natural environment with a transformed soul intact. There are pieces of my life puzzle still missing, and perhaps, they always will be. And, perhaps those missing pieces will require another journey along the healing road.

I will not hesitate to answer the call to travel again as I am stronger, more capable, and the miles have legitimized my intrepid spirit. They have sanctioned the nurturing of my spiritual self, the connection with the God of my understanding, and my trust in the adage, "The Universe will provide."

I stood more times than I can count at a chasm, trying to decide if I needed to fill it, bridge it, or jump into it. What my soul knew to be truth as I stood at the edge of Wild Horse Canyon that day is that my life is already full, and that there is nothing more beautiful or stronger than a woman who is unapologetically herself.

As the plane started its descent into the Orlando International Airport, I arrived full circle to the place I started…home.

AUTHOR BIO

From the time she was 16-years-old, Debi Tolbert Duggar was hopping on the back of a boy's motorcycle for the thrill of two wheeled travel. After years of being someone's' 'backrest,' she bought her own motorcycle at the age of 52 and preceded to click off 49 states and 7 Canadian Provinces over an eight-year period. Somewhere along the open road, the author recognized her motorcycle was not just another mode of travel, but the vehicle for her spiritual quest. She realized she could navigate life's bumps and slippery gravel patches astride her beloved Bessie and reach the end of the road stronger in spirit, her soul in-tact. Riding Soul-O is a compilation of her travel blog and her gut-wrenching honesty about love, loss, challenges, and triumph over adversity.

Debi Tolbert Duggar is an avid motorcycle enthusiast, educator, and writer who lives and works in Central Florida. *Riding Soul-O* is her first book, inspired by her love of two-wheeled travel.